The Death Census of Black '47
Eyewitness Accounts of Ireland's Great Famine

By
Liam Kennedy
Donald M. MacRaild
Lewis Darwen
Brian Gurrin

ANTHEM PRESS

Anthem Press
An imprint of Wimbledon Publishing Company
www.anthempress.com

This edition first published in UK and USA 2026
by ANTHEM PRESS
75–76 Blackfriars Road, London SE1 8HA, UK
or PO Box 9779, London SW19 7ZG, UK
and
244 Madison Ave #116, New York, NY 10016, USA

First published in the UK and USA by Anthem Press in 2023

British Library Cataloguing-in-Publication Data
A catalogue record for this book is available from the British Library.

Library of Congress Control Number: 2026942623

ISBN-13: 978-1-80136-054-8 (Pbk)
ISBN-10: 1-80136-054-5 (Pbk)

This title is also available as an eBook.

For Cormac Ó Gráda
Historian of Famine

CONTENTS

LIST OF FIGURES, TABLES, AND MAPS

Figures

Tables

Maps

ACKNOWLEDGEMENTS

Any large historical project accumulates debts that are in proportion to the work itself. Numerous people and institutions have supported us over the years. We have scoured libraries and archives, both online and on the ground, too many to mention. Archivists and librarians are crucial to the work we historians do and we are highly appreciative of their support. Our first and most significant debt is to the Leverhulme Trust whose committee and referees decided to support us with a three-year project grant (RPG-2015-404) to undertake the research for this book and the associated articles. To the Trust, we express our deepest gratitude.

Academic support has been given by many. Enda Delaney read the manuscript and made many helpful suggestions. Eamon Healy, PhD student at NUI Maynooth, shared thoughts on several parishes included here. Don Akenson not only helped us along the way but was a source of inspiration. We have benefited also from conversations with Vincent Comerford, Peter Solar, Christine Kinealy and David A. Wilson.

Our preliminary findings were presented at a number of conferences where participants shared freely their expertise with us in the best traditions of academic collaboration. These occasions included the European Social Science History Conference, Belfast 2018, the annual Irish Famine Commemoration, Strokestown, Ireland, 2018, and the annual Canadian Association for Irish Studies, Magee University College, Northern Ireland. The Cambridge Group for the History of Population and Social Structure hosted our paper on pre-Famine Irish famines. Other presentations included Ulster University, Queen's University Belfast and Roehampton University, London. In North America, we benefited from helpful comment in seminars at Quinnipiac University and the University of Toronto.

The readers for Anthem Press challenged us to think further on issues addressed in this work and we thank them for their careful attention to our arguments. We also wish to record our sincere gratitude to the reviewers who improved the initial proposal and those who provided deep insights in their assessments of the final manuscript of this book. None of the above is in any way responsible for errors or omissions.

Finally, and above all, we would like to thank our friend, fellow historian and famine specialist, Cormac Ó Gráda. As always, he has been a model of generosity with his time, encouraging us, sharing his own research and suggesting new lines of enquiry. He has done this for decades for many scholars. For them, as well as on our own behalf, we dedicate this work to Cormac.

Finally, we all wish to thank our families. Many long hours have been taken from them. As ever, we are endlessly grateful for their patience, forbearance and love.

INTRODUCTION

A million dead. A million fled. That is how one distinguished writer summarised the devastating consequences of the Great Famine in Ireland.[1] In season after season in the later 1840s, a mysterious plant disease destroyed the potato crop which was the main source of food of the labouring classes. Hunger stalked the land, followed in quick succession by killer diseases. notably typhus, which preyed upon those weakened by famine. Malnutrition, disease, suffering, and, finally, death, sealed the fate of a million or so souls. As in famines elsewhere, those most affected were the poorest. In Ireland, these were the cottiers and the rural labourers, as well as a sprinkling of town labourers, who even in the best of times struggled to make a living. But these were the worst of times. When a population census was taken in 1851 at the end of the famine, a quarter of the population had vanished through death or emigration. This collapse was brutally compressed within the space of a few years.

In the context of Irish history, it was the greatest disaster since the other great famine of 1740–41. Taking a wider view, relative to population size, the catastrophe ranks among the most severe famines of the modern world.[2] It retains an important place in the psyche of the Irish people and the Irish diaspora to this day. In recent decades, its history has become the focus of considerable scholarly and popular attention. In particular, a tremendous amount of work has been completed on mortality, emigration, relief efforts and the wider political, social and psychological consequences of the calamity, though highly politicised accounts such as genocidal interpretations of the Famine no longer enjoy wide currency.[3] Our understanding of the Great Famine is now much more comprehensive and nuanced, as well as being firmly located in a comparative context.

Yet much remains to be retrieved and understood, particularly at the level of the rural poor. The 'holy grail' in terms of grasping the *experience* of the crisis surely must be a set of famine diaries produced by those most badly affected, small farmers, cottiers and labourers. Such personal accounts have never materialised, though at least one fake

1. Michael Nicholson, *Irish Times*, 14 December 2015.
2. Cormac Ó Gráda, *The Great Irish Famine*, Dublin: Gill & Macmillan, 9.
3. The political uses to which the genocide thesis has been put are discussed in Liam Kennedy, *Unhappy the Land: The Most Oppressed People Ever, The Irish?* Dublin: Merrion Press, 2016, 99–104. Perhaps the best-known example in modern times of a genocidal interpretation is Tim Pat Coogan's *The Famine Plot: England's Role in Ireland's Greatest Tragedy*, New York: St. Martin's Press, 2012.

diary captured the public imagination in the 1990s.[4] The absence of such testaments to human suffering is understandable as many of those who managed to survive lacked the rudiments of learning, many were Gaelic speakers and no doubt they had much else on their minds. Thus, by default, the historiography of the Famine has been constructed from 'above' or from oblique angles in the social structure. This is fine in many respects for studies ranging from the weakness of the pre-Famine economy to the actions of policymakers and politicians. The accounts of travellers and visitors to Ireland, and even government officials, bring us a bit closer to the bitter realities of the Famine itself. But can we manage to get closer still?

Astonishingly, there is a large volume of reports on social conditions in the Irish localities that has never been used systematically by historians; indeed, is rarely used at all. The collective title for these reports is the *Death Census*. This survey into the progress of the famine was conducted during the late spring of 1847 as hunger and disease became commonplace across Ireland. The compilers, who were more participant observers than commentators, were parochial clergymen from the Roman Catholic Church. Most historians and writers are simply unaware of the existence of this documentation of extreme distress. Donal Kerr's fine study of the Catholic Church during the Famine, for instance, passes these sources by, while they also fail to gain a mention in the much earlier famine history published by Revd John O'Rourke.[5] A handful of local historians have cited one or other of the individual reports for their particular locality, while Ó Muchadha in his recent book on the Great Famine has drawn on some of these commentaries.[6] But the overarching and interconnected nature of the Death Census as a corpus of work remains to be appreciated. We have to admit in our own case that we came across these reports purely by chance.

It is not as if the reports had never seen the light of day. They found ephemeral expression in a range of local and national newspapers during the worst year of the crisis, or Black '47 as it is known in oral tradition. The Death Census, it appears, was quickly overshadowed by other events and simply disappeared from view. Intended as a national survey, it was organised by Daniel O'Connell's association for Repeal of the Union. Those compiling the local reports were the clergy of the Catholic Church, which of course was the major religious denomination in Ireland. While hunger and famine-related disease wreaked havoc across all religious denominations, Catholics were the worst affected by virtue of their generally lower socio-economic status.

---

4. Mark McGowan, 'Famine, Facts and Fabrication: An Examination of Diaries from the Irish Famine Migration to Canada', *Canadian Journal of Irish Studies*, 33, no.2 (2007): 48–55.
5. Donal A. Kerr, *The Catholic Church and the Famine*, Blackrock: Columba Press, 1996; Rev. J. O'Rourke, *The History of the Great Irish Famine of 1847, with Notices of Earlier Irish Famines*, Dublin: James Duffy and Co., 1875. One of the exceptions is Bryan MacMahon who makes use of returns from north Kerry in his *The Great Famine in Tralee and North Kerry*, Cork: Mercier Press 2017, 135–36.
6. Ciarán Ó Murchadha, *The Great Famine: Ireland's Agony, 1845–52*, London: Continuum Press, 2011, ch. 4.

The outstanding feature of this collective survey is that the authors of the individual reports were men who were intimately engaged with the lives of their parishioners and thus were well placed to comment on the unfolding tragedy. Catholic clergymen officiated at vital moments in the life cycle of the people, most notably at birth (baptism), marriage and death (burial). They observed the daily toil of their parishioners. Some supervised local schools. Some engaged in part-time farming. Though not of the same social class as the cottiers and labourers – priests tended to be drawn from the ranks of the better-off farmers and shopkeepers – they were still much closer to these social strata than landlords, land agents and state functionaries.[7] The economic nexus also mattered. Priests were dependent on and were voluntarily supported by the donations of their flocks. The unity of priests and people, though sometimes exaggerated, is not to be gainsaid and least of all during the course of a prolonged and terrible crisis.

How did the priests become involved? To answer this question, we need to take a step backwards in time. The date is Monday, 19 April 1847. The place is Conciliation Hall, a venue capable of holding 5,000 people, located at Burgh Quay on the Liffey, in the heart of Dublin.[8] A large crowd is being addressed by John O'Connell (son of the 'Liberator', Daniel O'Connell). His listeners were there to attend the weekly rally in favour of Repeal of the Union of Britain and Ireland. 'A fortnight ago I felt it my duty [...] to take steps to procure a proper census of the deaths caused by the present starvation, and the inadequate relief measures of the parliament and government of England'.[9] With those words, O'Connell introduced the first of a series of reports from Catholic clergymen describing the ravages of hunger and disease in their respective parishes.

The existence of the Death Census was not only a surprise to us (and to most historians of Ireland we venture to add), but there were other surprises in store. Further research turned up the awkward fact that John O'Connell was not the originator of the idea. More than that, he had initially opposed the concept of a 'death census' conducted by the Catholic clergy of Ireland. So, where did the project come from and why did O'Connell change his mind, all within a matter of weeks? We traced the germ of the idea back to Westminster and the famine debates of the time. It turns out that complex political manoeuvrings and motivations were involved, both inside and outside of parliament.

The Death Census was anything but a set of disinterested documents. It was designed to influence policy. As the Repeal Association put it, they aimed to show the outside world the extent of misery and suffering unfolding in Ireland, with the ultimate objective of convincing the British Government that more active and better-resourced relief policies were necessary. Thus, we pay particular attention to the reception of the reports by Whig, Tory, Radical, Repeal and Young Ireland politicians. This helps shed light on the attitudes and reactions of policymakers and opinion formers. We explore

---

7. On classic accounts of the social origins of the priesthood, see K. H. Connell, *Irish Peasant Society: Four Historical Essays*, Oxford: Clarendon Press, 1968 and S. J. Connolly, *Priests and People in Pre-Famine Ireland, 1780–1845*, Dublin: Gill & Macmillan, 1982.
8. Kinealy, *Repeal and Revolution*, 32.
9. *The Pilot*, 21 April 1847.

these different facets in some detail in what is a novel angle on the politics of famine within the polity of the United Kingdom.

The Death Census is composed of 100 eyewitness statements from different parts of Ireland and amounts to almost 50,000 words of testimony. These are among the richest surviving historical materials on the early impact of the Famine at local level. The reports were published originally in a rather haphazard fashion, were never re-published and have never been pulled together in composite form. Yet here is a storehouse of testimonies from within local communities that awaits the attention of students of famine in Ireland and beyond. Most of these documents are coloured by politics, which in itself is revealing, but the descriptions of the horror facing a famishing people within the 'little society' of the parish, accompanied by appeals, explicit or implicit, to the humanitarian instincts of the wider society, have the ring of authenticity. Taken as a body of work, these locally generated accounts of destitution, suffering and death bring us close, or at least closer, to the heart of the Famine experience. In short, the Death Census is one of the major 'lost' texts of modern Irish history.

The structure of this volume is as follows. There are two parts. The opening chapter of Part I offers an overview of the famine period that is the essential context for later discussions of the Death Census. In Chapter Two, we engage directly with the Death Census, its form and structure, bearing in mind that the investigation was conducted under conditions of severe social dislocation. It is helpful to understand also that the Death Census fitted into a pre-existing tradition of informal census taking by clergymen that extends back into the eighteenth century. Thus, the priests were not confronted with a task that might have seemed wholly alien to their calling. Chapter Three explores the politics of this Repeal initiative which so far has not attracted the attention of historians. Chapter Four engages with methodological problems thrown up by the Census, including issues of reliability, uncertainties as to parish boundaries and proportions of the local population that were Catholic. Crucially, this chapter analyses pre-crisis and crisis mortality in the localities which lies at the heart of any reconstruction of the Famine episode. In the fifth chapter, the more visceral qualitative information presented by the priest-respondents is analysed. These textured narratives bring us deep into the world of the rural poor. The concluding chapter of Part I explores the relationship between priests and people and offers an assessment of the competence and reliability of the priests as witnesses to famine conditions in their respective localities. It also documents the political sentiments of these Catholic clergymen, not all of whom were of one mind. Part II occupies the greater part of the book. It includes full transcriptions of the parish reports that make up the Death Census. These original texts should prove rewarding for historians, historical geographers and the interested public. By way of context, background information on local social conditions and the political leanings of the priest-respondent have been added for the parishes covered by the Census. These commentaries, when allied to the original text for a particular parish, furnish evidential building blocks for local historians, genealogists, teachers and students. Viewed overall, the volume offers a unique resource for students of the Irish Famine whether working at the local, regional or the national level.

Part I

Chapter One

THE GREAT FAMINE

> The population of this parish at the commencement of last year was nearly 12,000; it is now reduced to 9,860 persons – 478 died of famine and its immediate consequences since 1 October 1846. There are at present 138 families suffering from fever. The great bulk of the people hold very little land, which is of inferior quality; it barely supplied potatoes in past years, and now that the potato crop is gone the poor are in the greatest distress. I find that 129 families were obliged to desert their little holdings and cabins. There are at present 470 families, consisting of 2,246 persons, in extreme want, living on turnips and a little Indian meal; no language can describe the miserable condition of most of them …
>
> No private charities can meet the crisis. If the government do not give immediate and extensive employment the people will be lost.
>
> Denis Tighe, Parish Priest, Ballaghaderrin, 1847[1]

Prelude

It was the summer of 1845, the weather not very different from the usual pattern of intermittent rain, sunshine and seasonal temperatures. Thoughts were turning naturally enough towards prospects for the harvest, the vital bounty of grain and potatoes that sustained the Irish people. The signs were good and expectations high after some poor harvests earlier in the decade. Beyond the horizon but unknown to the eight and a half million inhabitants of the island, invading forces, this time in the biosphere, were gathering strength. Two years earlier, a mysterious disease had ravaged potato crops in North America. From there, transatlantic traffic carried the disease to Europe. Geography was no barrier. By the early summer of 1845, the infection had reached Belgium and some other parts of continental Europe. With remarkable rapidity, the disease crossed the Channel. By August 1845, it was debilitating potato crops in the south of England. The following month, it had reached several parts of eastern Ireland. From Waterford and Wexford, there were alarming newspaper reports of a pestilence, as yet unnamed, attacking the potato fields. The nauseous stench of decay marked the progress of the disease. The leaves on potato stalks were turning black and the infection was spreading in all directions.

---

1. *Death Census*, return by Revd Denis Tighe, P. P. of Ballaghaderrin (Ballaghaderreen), published 17 November 1847. This parish is in the west of Ireland, on the Mayo–Roscommon border.

By mid-October, there were authoritative voices expressing alarm from as far away as the western parts of Ireland, though the correspondent of the *Freeman's Journal* feared that the threat of 'the plague' was not yet fully appreciated by the poorer people there.

> In fact, the labourers will dig out tubers affected by the rot in its incipient stages and not be aware of the presence of the disease. Yet in a short space of time – perhaps not over four-and-twenty hours – those potatoes, so recently healthy looking, will be found rotten to their very centre.[2]

He was right. When the tubers were dug from the ground, they were indeed found to be worthless. The people's food was putrefying before their despairing eyes. The Prime Minister, Sir Robert Peel, was 'advised of an imminent crisis'.[3] A scientific commission set up by the government failed to isolate the cause. It was many more years before the terrifying affliction was identified as an air-borne fungal disease, *Phytophthora infestans*. Disease-carrying spores were carried by the prevailing winds across the countryside. Not until the 1880s was an effective antidote discovered.

Because the potato blight struck late in the growing season of 1845, the shortfall in the yield was of the order of a quarter to one-third. This was still a large loss but was manageable because potatoes were also fed to pigs and poultry and so could be diverted to human consumption. Moreover, the geography of spread meant that eastern rather than the poorer western regions of the island were most affected. Few died during the succeeding nine months. In the following summer of 1846, blight struck again with fearsome consequences. The bulk of the potato crop, perhaps 80–90 per cent, was destroyed. Signs of distress that were soon to become familiar followed in quick succession. By the autumn of that year, the workhouses were filling, a panic-stricken exodus out of Ireland was underway, while famine fevers were exacting a heavy toll on the Irish poor. Blight was absent in Black '47, but the produce was miserably small. In desperation, many of the rural poor had already consumed their seed potatoes, so the acreage sown was well below the 2.5 million acres normally sown.[4] Moreover, typhus fever, long endemic in Ireland, struck Ireland harder than the neighbouring island. Hordes of hungry and infected people roamed the countryside in search of alms, some heading for the towns and ports. Others too weak to move huddled in their one-roomed cabins, debilitated and demoralised, standards of cleanliness abandoned, living and sleeping in filthy clothing. Overcrowding, poor hygiene and weakened

2. *Freeman's Journal*, 18 October 1845.
3. The dramatic, unfolding events are described in detail by Helen E. Hatton, *The Largest Amount of Good: Quaker Relief in Ireland, 1654–1921*, Montreal and Kingston: McGill-Queen's University Press, 1993, *passim* (quotation at 79).
4. P. M. A. Bourke, 'The Use of the Potato Crop in Pre-Famine Ireland', *Journal of the Statistical and Social Inquiry Society of Ireland*, 21, no. 6 (1967–68): 72–96.

constitutions proved ideal for the spread of typhus and other diseases. The death toll soared, as was the case also in overcrowded and poorly managed workhouses.[5] Emigration, which had been an increasingly important component of pre-Famine demography, now assumed exodus proportions.[6] The *Great* Famine gave rise to a *great* emigration.

Not all social groups suffered equally. In the Famine literature, the tradition has been to emphasise the classic conflict between landlords and their agents on the one hand and tenant farmers on the other, rather than considering inequality and class differences more generally.[7] This simple dichotomy tends to neglect the many gradations of status within the farming class and to obscure also the conflict of interest between labour-employing farmers and the cottiers and labourers working on their farms. How out of touch, or how indifferent some of the propertied and professional sections of society were, can be glimpsed through the window of the general election of July–August 1847. One might have expected the crisis facing the rural poor in a largely agrarian society to dominate that election campaign, if not in Britain at least in Ireland. With a few exceptions, this was not the case.[8] Irish politicians, in the main, adopted the class-bound assumption that the worst was past and gave prominence to other issues. This turned out to be a false hope, and a cruel one at that. Though blight was absent, the produce of potatoes was small. The blight returned the following year, and there were further, though more localised failures in 1849 and 1850.

Abnormally also, the economic and demographic consequences rolled on for a century or more (Figure 1.1). Unlike pre-industrial famines or famines generally, there was no bounce back in population in the aftermath of the crisis. Some have conferred the title of the 'last great subsistence crisis in the western world' on the Irish Famine, perhaps overlooking the Finnish famines of the 1860s.[9] Famines in twentieth-century Europe were largely the product of warfare, though harvest shortfalls as in the Ukraine in the 1930s might also shape the death toll. No doubt, it was a help that the Irish Famine took place in times of peace. Strikingly, this did not itself prevent an extraordinary loss of life, a fact that serves to point up the failure of famine relief policies.

5. Lewis Darwen, Donald M. MacRaild, Brian Gurrin and Liam Kennedy, '"Irish fever" in Britain during the Great Famine: immigration, disease and the legacy of Black '47', *Irish Historical Studies* 44, 166 (2020): 270–94.
6. Roughly a million Irish emigrated between 1846 and 1851. See W. E. Vaughan, *Irish Historical Statistics: Population, 1821–1971*, Dublin: Royal Irish Academy, 1978, 260–61.
7. Marguérite Corporaal and Peter Gray eds., *The Great Irish Famine and Social Class: Conflicts, Responsibilities, Representations*, Oxford: Peter Lang, 2019, 7.
8. Brian Walker, 'Politicians, Elections and Catastrophe: The General Election of 1847', *Irish Political Studies*, 42, no. 1 (2007): 1–34.
9. Declan Curran, Lubomyr Luciuk and Andrew G. Newby, eds. *Famines in European Economic History: The Last Great European Famines Reconsidered*, London: Routledge, 2015.

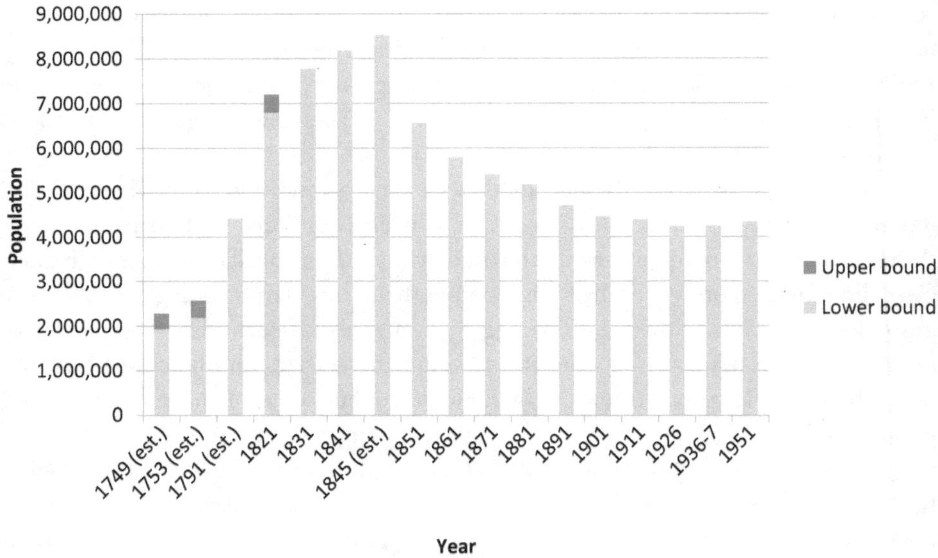

Figure 1.1 Population of Ireland, 1749–1951

Source: Estimates for 1749–1791 from D. Dickson, C. Ó. Gráda and S. Daultrey, 'Hearth tax, household size and Irish population change, 1672–1821', *Proceedings of Royal Irish Academy*, 82, C, 156 (upper and lower bound estimates given); census figures for 1821–1951 from W. E. Vaughan and A. J. Fitzpatrick, *Irish Historical Statistics: Population, 1821–1971* (Dublin, 1978), 3; 1821 upper bound estimate from J. Lee, 'On the accuracy of pre-Famine Irish censuses' in J. M. Goldstrom and L. A. Clarkson eds., *Irish population, Economy, and Society* (Oxford, 1981), 46.

Population Explosion

It is difficult to understand Ireland's vulnerability to repeated harvest failure without considering population growth during the century before the Famine. The multiplication of mouths was the fastest in Europe. Between the 1740s and the end of that century, the population of the country doubled, and it had nearly doubled again by the eve of the Famine.[10] How extraordinary this was becomes clearer when viewed in comparative perspective. The rate of population growth in the century before the Famine was 1.3 per cent per year in Ireland, 1.0 per cent in England, 0.7 per cent in Sweden and 0.8 per cent in Scotland.[11] France was remarkably low at 0.4 per cent per annum (though even a low rate of growth operating over a hundred years builds cumulatively to a substantial growth in population).[12] Those reproducing most rapidly were the poorer social groups. Consequently, the social structure became more unbalanced as the poor

10. David Dickson, Cormac Ó Gráda and Stuart Daultrey, 'Hearth Tax, Household Size and Irish Population Change, 1672–1821', *Proceedings of Royal Irish Academy*, 82, C (1982): 125–60, 162–81, table 6b, 156.
11. To give a sense of proportion, a growth rate of 1.3 per cent per annum would produce a doubling of population every half century (or to be precise every 54 years).
12. Joel Mokyr and Cormac Ó Gráda, 'New Developments in Irish Population History, 1700–1850', *Economic History Review*, 37, no. 4 (1984): 476.

expanded relatively to the middling and better-off sections of society. Population pushed out onto the bogs and up the sides of mountains. In sheltered coastal districts along the Atlantic seaboard, including the offshore islands, families reproduced seemingly without restraint or constraint.

Hand in hand with population expansion went profoundly negative dietary changes. The food of the rural poor narrowed until it was largely potatoes three times a day, with a sup of buttermilk at times. In the better-off regions of Leinster and in east Ulster, bread, oatmeal and milk supplemented the ubiquitous tuber. When the potato failed, widespread destitution was inevitable. The workhouse, the emigrant ship and, in extremis, the graveyard beckoned.

It is true that potato-based dietary cultures could support very high population densities. Whether the widespread adoption of the potato, in place of cereals and dairy produce as in earlier centuries in Ireland, was the cause or consequence of the rapid population increase is still an open question. It may make more sense to see the answer as a two-way simultaneous relationship, the one reinforcing the other in an ultimately unsustainable population spiral. Modern research suggests that the prolific tuber, like rice, was a more efficient source of carbohydrates than costly alternatives such as cereals, not to mention high-protein livestock products that required large acreages of land.[13] The distinguishing property of the potato was that it was an almost complete food. Taken in sufficient quantities with some skimmed milk, it satisfied virtually all of the protein, carbohydrate, vitamin and mineral needs of human life.[14] Little wonder that Irish labourers were noted for their height and physical strength. Maize is deficient by comparison, something that became apparent following massive importations and consumption of that foodstuff during the Famine itself.[15]

For all its miracle properties, the potato had its drawbacks. While the potato was a nutritious food, its keeping quality was limited to eight or nine months of the year. Unlike cereals, it was not possible to carry over stocks from one year to the next, thereby evening out consumption or insuring against a bad harvest. Even in good years, the rural poor suffered several hungry months between the rotting of the old potatoes and the arrival of the new crop. Oatmeal, milk, fish (in coastal and riverside locations) and large-scale begging helped fill the 'hungry gap' between late spring and early summer. Potatoes were the cheapest food available, hence their widespread adoption. It did mean, however, that people could not trade down to a cheaper foodstuff should

---

13. P. M. A. Bourke et al., *'The Visitation of God': The Potato and the Great Irish Famine*, Dublin: Lilliput Press 1993; M. O. Cooper and W. J. Spillman, 'Human Food from an Acre of Staple Farm Products', *Farmers' Bulletin*, Washington, DC: US Department of Agriculture, Office of the Secretary, 1917, 4.
14. K. H. Connell, *The Population of Ireland, 1750–1845*, Oxford: Oxford University Press, 1950; Mokyr, *Why Ireland Starved: A Quantitative and Analytical History of the Irish Economy, 1800–1850*, London: Allen & Unwin, 1985, 7–8.
15. E. Margaret Crawford, 'Subsistence Crises and Famines in Ireland: A Nutritionist's View', in E. Margaret Crawford ed., *Famine: The Irish Experience, 900–1900*, Edinburgh: John Donald, 1989, 211–14.

the potato fail. Also reflecting poverty, the type of potato that was gaining ground in the decades before the Famine was the high-yielding but less nutritious and disease-prone lumper variety. Finally, though hidden from view until disaster struck, the physio-chemical make-up of the potato plant made it susceptible to almost total wipeout from fungal attack, at least of the type represented by *P. infestans.*

The Paradox of Poverty and Potatoes

Average income on the eve of the Famine was less than half the British level.[16] Poverty rather than potatoes was the Irish problem, though of course poverty was intimately associated with dependence on the potato crop. It strains credulity to believe that country people would submit willingly to the monotony of so narrow a diet, and a vegetarian one at that, *unless* under the pressure of want. As we know, those farther up the social scale from the rural poor commanded a more diversified diet that included tea, sugar, bread, dairy produce and, depending on circumstances, sometimes meat.[17] Thus, it is hard to accept the judgement of one historian of Ireland who suggests that 'the peculiar basket of consumer goods consumed in Ireland' may have arisen simply because the Irish preferred a different consumption pattern to people in other societies.[18] If so, it would be hard to explain why, when labourers' incomes rose in the post-Famine period, they chose to spend their wage gains on a more diversified diet.[19] The obvious conclusion is that a consumption bundle dominated by a single foodstuff arose, not from some remarkable Irish preference for potatoes, but from poverty. The degree of reliance on a diet consisting almost exclusively of the cheapest foodstuff of the time is both the definition of and the principal measure of poverty in pre-Famine Irish society.[20]

The fragile eco-system of pre-Famine Ireland was the product of a distinctive social system that had been in the making for a century or more. By the eve of the Famine, about a quarter of the rural population out of a population of 8.5 million was landless and potato-dependent.[21] Another quarter – cottiers, very small farmers, trades people, fishermen – were not far removed above the margin of subsistence set by the landless proletariat. This was a bottom-heavy, highly unequal social structure. Completing the social pyramid, there were the middling-sized farmers employing labour, then

16. Joel Mokyr, *Why Ireland Starved*, 24–29, 274.
17. L. M. Cullen, *An Economic History of Ireland since 1660*, London: Batsford, 1972, 116–17. Note also the richly varied diet of Franciscan clergy in the 'hungry' 1840s as documented in Liam Kennedy and Clare Murphy, eds., *The Franciscan Community at Cork, and Its Account Books*, Dublin: Irish Manuscripts Commission, 2012.
18. Mokyr, *Why Ireland Starved*, 8.
19. L. A. Clarkson and Margaret Crawford, *Feast and Famine: A History of Food in Ireland*, 1500–1920, Oxford: Oxford University Press, 2001: 89–110.
20. Some historians, particularly econometric historians, use more conventional measures such as income per capita, acreage of potatoes per capita, housing quality or literacy, presumably because these are more readily quantifiable. While useful in some respects, this runs the danger of missing the big story.
21. Bourke, 'Use of the Potato Crop in Pre-Famine Ireland', 72–96.

the even less numerous large farmers, merchants and professionals, and at the apex the landlord class. The landowning elite was composed of about 10,000 families, thinly spread and rich in land, though frequently mired in debt. This landed gentry accounted for less than one per cent of the population. In summary, this was a highly unequal, largely agrarian society in which at least 40 per cent of the people were heavily dependent on the potato for sustenance.

An escape from mass poverty required a higher productivity agriculture, modern industrialisation and in all likelihood broader emigration in terms of social class and region. All that would take time and, as it turned out, the hour glass was almost empty by 1845. Outside of east Ulster, modern industry had made little progress. Worse still, rural industry, particularly in hand-crafted woollen and linen textiles, was in retreat under intense competitive pressure from cheaper, factory-produced goods. The age of the industrial revolution was transforming production and distribution and, in the process, destroying traditional methods of production. This was not just in Ireland but in rural Europe more generally. With some exaggeration, the doyen of Irish economic historians, L. M. Cullen, has written: 'The background to the Famine, through the crisis in domestic industry, is as much an industrial as an agrarian one'.[22]

Not all was gloomy in terms of longer-term forces for change. The gradual modernisation and commercialisation of Irish society, particularly in the hinterland of large towns and port cities, as well as on the larger farms, was noticeable. Markets, communications, transport links and even literacy were improving. Rising food and textile exports signified an increasingly open, market-oriented society. Modern industry was putting down roots in the Lagan Valley, though at the cost of displacing the hand-spinning of linen yarn in outer Ulster and north Connacht. Of fundamental importance, this was a society struggling through emigration, and reduced fertility in some regions of eastern Ireland, to achieve a more sustainable relationship between population and its resource base. And as previous subsistence crises had shown, this was also a society capable of absorbing a 'normal' or more traditional harvest failure without heavy casualties. This argues against a simple Malthusian interpretation of a positive check to Irish population in the 1840s. It does not, however, dispose of the hypothesis that regions of Ireland were prospectively Malthusian at the time.

Shaping the Crisis

The conjuncture of short-run forces and contingent events, acting and reacting on the structural weaknesses of pre-Famine society, combined to produce a tragedy of almost unimaginable proportions. This is not the place to sketch these forces in detail, but they may be summarised as follows: In the economic sphere, there were simultaneous harvest failures in other European countries in the late summer of 1846[23] (thereby pushing up prices and reducing flows of grain between countries),

22. Cullen, *Economic History of Ireland*, 121.
23. Peter M. Solar, 'The Potato Famine in Europe', in *Famine 150*, Cormac Ó Gráda ed., Dublin: Teagasc, 1997, 113–27.

financial panics in Britain in April and October 1847, which adversely influenced Famine policy, and a recession in the British economy with rising unemployment and misery afflicting the British working classes in 1846–47. The cumulative effect was to limit financial transfers to Ireland and to reduce sympathy on the part of the British public. In the political sphere, a Whig administration, under the weak leadership of Lord John Russell, came to power at Westminster after the repeal of the Corn Laws in June 1846 and was responsible for Famine policy for the duration of the crisis. This was a minority government that found itself under pressure to reduce public expenditure on Ireland and unable to force through reforms that might alleviate the worst effects of the crisis.[24]

The ideological climate of the time was anything but helpful. For some, the 'laws' of political economy were reflections of divine law and should not be interfered with, even in the face of a rapidly escalating crisis.[25] Providentialist notions of this kind, allied to economic doctrines that extolled the virtues of limiting the role of the state in society and relying on the market to meet people's needs, militated against more ambitious interventions by the central state.[26] Such belief systems, which might be loosely placed under the heading of laissez-faire, served for some as a useful cloak for economic and political interests. In retrospect, one can say that problems in the real economy of the UK, the delicate balance of power at Westminster, and ideological forces all helped in shaping the evolution of the crisis.

Unhelpfully also, the Irish members of parliament failed to unite round a set of proposals that might have influenced government thinking in more constructive directions. The largest faction, the Repeal party of Irish MPs led by the aged and ailing Daniel O'Connell clouded the problem of the moment – a famine of Biblical proportions – by its insistence, not only on relief but on the panacea of repeal of the Act of Union and the return of an Irish parliament in College Green, Dublin. The Repealers' opposition to the extension of income tax to Ireland confirmed for many in Britain the selfishness of the propertied classes in Ireland (though they might counter that property rates in Ireland were exceptionally high because of the financial burdens of the Irish poor-law system).[27]

In the administrative sphere, there were limitations from the past. In dealing with prospective famine, employment on public works was an established part of the repertoire of state intervention but never on the scale forced into operation in 1846.[28] Additional misfortune dogged the relief efforts. The winter of 1846–47 in north-west

24. Peter Gray, *Famine, Land and Politics: British Government and Irish Society 1843–50*, Dublin: Irish Academic Press, 1999, 194–6.
25. Ibid., 15–16.
26. Enda Delaney, *The Curse of Reason: A Survey of the Great Irish Famine*, 1845–52, Dublin: Gill & Macmillan, 2012, 227–35.
27. Charles Read, *The Great Famine in Ireland and British Financial Crisis*, Martlesham: Boydell Press, 2022, chapter four.
28. Timothy P. O'Neill, 'The State, Poverty and Distress in Ireland, 1815–45', PhD dissertation, University College Dublin, 1971.

Europe was one of the most severe on record, with reports of blocks of ice floating on the river Thames.[29] In Ireland, winter gales and snow blizzards lashed the hordes of ill-clad, malnourished workers labouring outdoors on famine relief works. These pitiful scenes opened the way to the ravages of infectious diseases, principally typhus, typhoid and dysentery. These rather than outright starvation were the major killers during the Famine, but the prior cycle of hunger, filth and demoralisation laid waste resistance to their lethal effects.

Government Policy during the Crisis: The First Phase, 1845–46

Many aspects of government policy on famine relief came in for severe criticism in the reports furnished to the Death Census, so it is important to understand these policies and their context. The initial response of the British government to the crisis was remarkably swift. On hearing of the extent of the potato failure in the autumn of 1845, Prime Minister Robert Peel made secret provision to buy maize to the value of £100,000 from North America.[30] The intention was to release this grain onto the market when local supplies of food ran low and prices rose during the following spring and summer. Government grain stores were concentrated in the poor western regions of Ireland, with some serviced by coastal steamers.

Another standard policy measure to deal with harvest failure was rolling out public work schemes to employ hungry small farmers and labourers. The body responsible, the Board of Works, approved 318 different famine projects before the end of 1845 and many were in operation by the summer of 1846. The poor and the destitute were offered employment working on roads, bridges, drainage schemes and other infrastructural projects. The thinking behind this was that the poor would have to work to gain an entitlement to a wage payment, this in turn would be a test of their need for state support, and money received might then be used to purchase food for themselves and their dependents.

The most radical policy departure, however, was Peel's decision to repeal the Corn Laws. These were tariffs that protected British and indeed Irish cereal growers from imported foreign grain. In the teeth of fierce opposition from landed interests, Peel succeeded in forcing the repeal bill through the House of Commons in May 1846. This controversial move was in part a response to fear of famine in Ireland and Scotland. This reform, in principle, favoured the Irish urban and rural poor at the expense of landlords and tenant farmers by allowing cheaper grain imports to Ireland. However, poor grain harvests across Europe in the autumn of 1845, and poorer still the following autumn, meant that grain as well as potato prices soared in 1846 and 1847.[31] The most immediate impact of the repeal of the Corn Laws was in the political sphere.

29. *The Atlas*, 13 February 1847; *Dublin Evening Mail*, 12 February 1847.
30. Robin Haines, *Charles Trevelyan and the Great Irish Famine*, Dublin: Four Courts Press, 2004, viii–x.
31. J. C. Zadoks, 'The Potato Murrain on the European Continent and the Revolutions of 1848', *Potato Research*, 51, no. 1 (2008): 5–45.

The Conservative Party split, and Peel's government fell in June 1846. It was succeeded by a minority Whig administration, led by Lord John Russell. It largely maintained the Peelite policies already in place.

It was apparent by early 1847 that the main policy to combat hunger – employment on public work schemes – was failing to hold back the rising tide of mortality. Unlike earlier subsistence crises, as in 1817, 1822, 1831, 1835 and 1842, this was a national rather than a regional crisis. The difference in scale was enormous and needs to be borne in mind. Worse still, the failure of the potato for the second season in a row meant that the public works had to be extended into the harsh winter of 1846–47. The congregating together of hordes of famished and ill-clad labourers, small farmers, paupers and others made for ideal conditions for the transmission of disease.

The scheme was also proving to be much more expensive than anticipated. Officials worried about interfering with 'the ordinary operations of private business', feared the 'encouragement of idleness' and above all were concerned about the 'lavish expenditure' on the relief operations.[32] The wages paid by the Board of Works were set at local wage levels. In March 1846, the Office of Public Works (OPW) published general guidelines, recommending rates ranging from 10*d.* to 12*d.* per day. This took only partial account of rising food prices. Ever concerned to effect economies, the OPW cautioned 'where infirm persons are employed they will, of course, not be paid at the same rate as the able-bodied'. The Board itself recognised that the non-able-bodied 'poor cannot live on the wages'.[33] Other than reliance on charity, for these unfortunates, the workhouse attached to each poor-law union was the final refuge. Wages on the public works made no allowance for family size. As against that, families were not restricted to a single representative. The Death Census and indeed other sources are silent on the matter, but women and children were also given employment. The partial figures that survive point to women and children forming a small but significant fraction of the labour force. Moreover, their numbers increased disproportionately as the crisis took hold. In the first week in October 1846, for example, women accounted for about one per cent and 'boys' for about five per cent of the Board's 20,000-strong work force. Four weeks later, the numbers had expanded exponentially to 150,000, in itself a remarkable achievement. Women and boys now accounted for almost 1 in 10 of those employed. By the close of 1846, 9,000 women and 28,000 boys were working, and the numbers and proportions continued to increase into the following year (Table 1.1).[34]

The standard policy template, dating from Robert Peel's handling of subsistence crises in 1816–18, had a strong seasonal character. Public works were concentrated in the late spring and early summer during slack periods in the farming cycle, and then wound down or discontinued. The Board of Works did in fact cut back on the schemes

32. Treasury minute, 3 April 1846, *Accounts and Papers, House of Commons* (28 vols), xiii (session: 22 January–28 August 1846), 291.

33. Instructions for the guidance of engineers, 9 March 1846, *Accounts and Papers, House of Commons* (28 vols), xiii (session: 22 January–28 August 1846), 298. Reduction in wages for the infirm, ibid., 299.

34. Late returns and employment on drainage schemes are not included.

Table 1.1 Average numbers employed on Public Works by gender and age, October 1846–January 1847

Week ending	Numbers employed (daily)				Proportion of all employed		
	Men	Women	Boys	Total	Men (per cent)	Women (per cent)	Boys (per cent)
3 Oct. 1846	18,864	211	1,060	20,135	93.7	1.0	5.3
17 Oct. 1846	45,929	514	3,466	49,909	92.0	1.0	6.9
7 Nov. 1846	135,700	2,660	11,908	150,268	90.3	1.8	7.9
26 Dec. 1846	329,744	9,129	28,450	367,323	89.8	2.5	7.7
2 Jan. 1847	400,907	11,914	34,450	447,271	89.6	2.7	7.7
9 Jan. 1847	423,643	14,819	37,428	475,890	89.0	3.1	7.9
16 Jan. 1847	451,309	17,651	43,720	512,680	88.0	3.4	8.5
23 Jan. 1847	496,604	22,666	49,879	569,149	87.3	4.0	8.8
30 Jan. 1847	487,730	27,507	56,428	571,665	85.3	4.8	9.9

Source: *Correspondence, July 1846 to January 1847, relating to measures adopted for relief of distress in Ireland. Board of Works Series,* (British Parliamentary Papers) BPP, Command Paper (1847), 764, vol. 50, l.1, 116, 143, 212, 475, 481; 1847 (797) *Correspondence, January to March 1847 relating to measures adopted for relief of distress in Ireland. Board of Works Series,* BPP, Command Papers, vol. 52, lii.1, 48.

in the late summer and early autumn of 1846. However, the second successive failure of the potato crop forced its hand. In the face of widespread destitution, and in the absence of other policies, public work schemes had to be ramped up again. More than a third of a million were back on the payroll in the bad weather at the end of 1846. By the first week of March 1847, a record three-quarters of a million people were employed daily on hundreds of state-sponsored schemes across the island. This is a staggering figure, unprecedented in nineteenth-century Ireland. If we take dependents into account, these schemes were aiding more than three million people at the height of the public works (Figure 1.2).[35]

The kinds of criticisms that emerge in the Death Census include the slow start to the schemes in some localities, their hasty termination before alternative relief was made available, wage rates that did not take into account the surge in food prices, late payments of wages and allegations of favouritism and corruption in the allocation of employment. Exceptionally bad weather in the winter of 1846–47 meant exposure to biting winds, sleet and snow. Framed against bleak landscapes, malnourished and poorly clad gangs of workers struggled to perform manual labour. Many were on piece rates that increased the hardship and discriminated against the weak. Burning up calories

35. The 1841 census indicates a mean household size of 5.5. Thus, with five or six persons per household, on average, unless there was widespread employment of two persons per household, support for at least three million seems plausible.

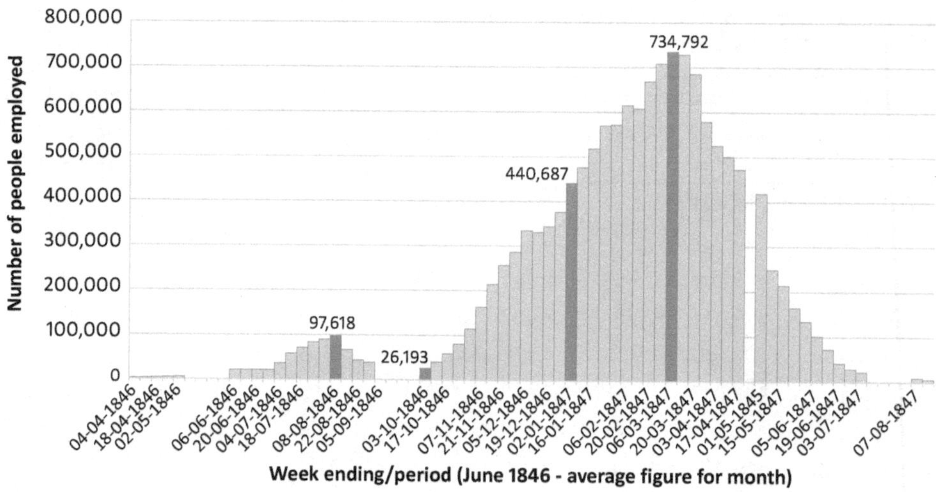

Figure 1.2 Average daily employment on Public Works, Ireland, April 1846–August 1847

Source: *Correspondence explanatory of the measures adopted by Her Majesty's government for the relief of distress arising from the failure of the potato crop in Ireland*, BPP, Command Papers (1846), 735, vol. 37, xxxvii.41, 317, 336, 351 (average daily figures, average figure for June 1846); *Correspondence from July 1846 to January 1847 relating to the measures adopted for the relief of distress in Ireland. Board of Works Series*, BPP, Command Papers (1847), 764, vol. 50, L.1, 80, 195, 344, 486; *Correspondence from January to March 1847, relating to the measures adopted for the relief of the distress in Ireland. Board of Works Series. [Second part]*, BPP, Command Papers (1847), 797, vol. 52, lii.1, 34, 189; 1847 (834, 860) *Public works – Ireland. Report of the Board of Public Works in Ireland, relating to measures adopted for the relief of distress in June, 1847*, BPP, Command Papers, vol. 17, 603, xvii, 591, 595, 598 603; *Public works, Ireland. Final report from the Board of Public Works, Ireland, relating to measures adopted for the relief of distress in July and August 1847, with appendices*, BPP, Command Papers (1849), 1047, vol. 23, xxiii.725, 732.

through hard labour led to weakened constitutions, leaving workers and indirectly their dependents more vulnerable to infectious diseases.[36]

The easy option for historians and others is to denounce the organisers and the organisation of the public work schemes, bell, book and candle. However, to expect a quick and timely retreat from tried-and-trusted relief measures during the first year of severe famine (1846–47) is to assume a degree of responsiveness in political and bureaucratic mindsets not obviously evident in the case of public health calamities in later historical time periods.[37] (Famine years are best viewed in terms of farming or harvest years, so we are speaking of roughly October 1846 to the summer of 1847.) We might also recall that there was popular support for these schemes. Indeed, proposals to replace them with free soup rations (discussed in the next section) gave rise to protest

36. An extreme illustration from two decades later is furnished by public works schemes in parts of Finland during the famines of the 1860s where starving men, women and children worked at temperatures of –25 degrees. Antti Hakkinen and Henrik Forsberg, 'Finland's Famine Years of the 1860s', in Curran et al., ed., *Famines in European Economic History*, 111.
37. Cases in point might be the flu epidemic following World War I, the AIDS crisis of the 1980s and for some countries the Coronavirus (Covid-19) pandemic of 2020–21. (The famine year in question above is the harvest year, roughly October 1846 to September 1847.)

and rioting *in favour of* work for wages.[38] Still, it was evident by the beginning of 1847 that the government had lost control of the crisis and that new famine relief measures were desperately needed. It is to the discredit of British policymakers, the Prime Minister Lord John Russell, Charles Wood at the Treasury and Charles Trevelyan as the civil servant primarily responsible for overseeing famine relief, that implementing the switch in policy was delayed until well after the winter of 1846–47.

The Second Phase, Temporary Soup Kitchens, 1847

The public work schemes proved to be not only of limited value in containing the crisis, they were also costly. Rising food prices, domestically and internationally, inflated the famine relief bill. The people of Ireland accounted for almost 30 per cent of the population of the UK at this time, so the potential drag on the public finances and the British economy more generally was no small matter. In fact, of the £9–£10 million spent by central government on famine relief (worth about a billion sterling in current value), most of this spending was concentrated in the first half of the famine, the year 1846 and the first two-thirds of 1847. Concerns about cost and the state of the economy sparked the change in policy.[39]

In February 1847, a Temporary Relief (Soup Kitchen) Act was passed to provide emergency food at hundreds of feeding stations across Ireland. The aim was to phase out work schemes that were failing to arrest famine deaths and replace them with soup kitchens and the free distribution of soup and grain rations. [40] In making this policy shift, the government was emulating the approach of the Quakers (Society of Friends) who were voluntarily providing soup rations in some of the worst affected areas in the west of Ireland. However, in response to a financial panic in April 1847, the government cut back sharply on anticipated public expenditure. For Ireland, this meant the precipitate winding down of the massive public works schemes, sometimes before the new feeding stations had come on stream.

The gigantic scale of direct feeding is all the more remarkable when one considers that certain ideological reservations had to be overcome. The previous October Trevelyan had warned an official at the OPW in Dublin of the dangers of gratuitous relief, offering the almost surreal piece of advice that the official should read particular pages in Edmund Burke's *Thoughts on Scarcity* (1800).[41] Fortunately, such scruples

38. Andrés Eriksson, 'Food Supply and Food Riots', *Famine 150*, 67–93; James S. Donnelly, jr., *The Great Irish Potato Famine*, Stroud: The History Press, 2010, 85–89.
39. Read, *The Great Famine in Ireland*, chapters four and five. Expenditure by the central government on famine relief, according to Read, was close to £10 million. He also presents the figure of £8.1 million for famine expenditure by local authorities, while philanthropic aid was on the much lower plane of £1–£2 million.
40. J. S. Donnelly, jr., 'The Soup kitchens', *New History of Ireland, V: Ireland under the Union, 1801–70*, ed. W. E. Vaughan, Oxford: Oxford University Press, 1989, 272–331.
41. Mr Trevelyan to Lieutenant-Colonel Jones, 14 October 1846; *Correspondence from July 1846 to January 1847 relating to the measures adopted for the relief of distress in Ireland. Board of Works Series*, BPP, Command Papers (1847), 764, vol. 50, L.1, 140; Edmund Burke, *Thoughts and Details*

Table 1.2 Numbers in receipt of relief under the Temporary Relief Act, 1847 (various periods)

Date	Electoral divisions			Rations			
	Providing relief	Returns deficient	Not under Act	Free	Sold	Total	Cost per ration
15 May 1847	1,248	NA	NA	NA	NA	NA	
5 June 1847	1,677	312	60	1,923,361	92,326	2,015,687	2½ *d.*
3 July 1847	1,823	166	60	2,342,900	79,636	2,422,536	2 *d.*
31 July 1847	1,707	283	59	1,845,868	45,839	1,891,707	2 *d.*
28 Aug. 1847	888	210	951	772,725	9,795	782,520	
11 Sept. 1847	563	60	1,426	400,100	42,639	442,739	

Note: There were 2,049 electoral divisions in Ireland in 1847 and, following review, this number was increased to 3,438 by 1850.

Source: *Distress (Ireland). Second report of the Relief Commissioners*, BPP, Command Papers (1847), 819, vol. 17, xvii.75, 3; *Distress (Ireland). Third report of the Relief Commissioners*, BPP, Command Papers (1847), 836, vol.17, xvii.103, 9; 1847 (859) *Distress (Ireland). Fourth report of the of Relief Commissioners*, BPP, Command Papers, vol. 17, xvii.143, 3; *Distress (Ireland). Fifth, sixth and seventh reports of the Relief Commissioners, and correspondence connected therewith*, BPP, Command Papers (1847–48), 876, vol.29, xxix.27, 3–7.

buckled in the face of mounting evidence as to the reality of the crisis. Table 1.2 gives the numbers of those in receipt of relief under the Temporary Relief Act, although for all periods the totals are underestimates as some electoral divisions failed to make returns to the Commission. By the beginning of June 1847, more than two million full rations were being distributed daily, but even relief on such a scale was insufficient to stem the rising tide of famine mortality.

The decentralised nature of food relief is worth highlighting. In 1838, less than a decade before the Famine, a poor-law system based on the English model was introduced to Ireland. The country was divided into 130 spatial and administrative units or unions,[42] each with a workhouse and some medical facilities. The workhouse provided care, under the most austere conditions, for the destitute, the aged and the infirm, and was funded by rates paid by local landlords, tenant farmers and other

on Scarcity, London: F & C. Rivingston, 1800, 31, 40–41, 47–48. Equally curiously, at least to modern ears, at the annual meeting of the Catholic Prelates of Ireland in October 1847, the assembled bishops came out against 'gratuitous relief from the government for the numbers of able-bodied men who are without food' on the grounds that 'such gratuitous relief has a demoralising tendency [...]'. See *Battersby's Registry for the Whole World, or the Complete Catholic Directory* [...] *for 1848*, Dublin: Battersby, 1848, 240.

42. During the Famine, some large poor-law unions were subdivided, for example, the Dingle peninsula was hived off from Tralee, to create a more manageable administrative unit. By 1851, there were 163 poor-law unions.

propertied households. The new system had taken shape, just about, by the eve of the Famine, but it was never designed to deal with subsistence crises, still less famine. Each poor-law union was subdivided into electoral divisions, of which there were 2,049, and these furnished the geographical frame for the deployment of soup kitchens. So, by early July 1847, at least 1,823 of the 2,049 electoral divisions were supplying provisions to 2,343,000 people for free and another 80,000 were catered for at a subsidised charge. Making allowance for some missing returns, it seems a staggering total of 2.6 million full rations were being provided each day, the equivalent of free or subsidised food for 755,00 children and 2,266,000 adults – more than three million people in all, 'exceeding one-third of the entire population of the country'.[43] By this time, only four Poor Law Unions, all in the neighbourhood of Belfast and reflecting local pride as well as superior economic circumstance, remained aloof from the Temporary Relief Act.

The soup kitchens were always intended to be temporary. Indeed, legislation limited the life of the scheme.[44] In line with laissez-faire ideology but responding also to a deterioration in the public finances, Russell's minority government resolved to shift the balance of responsibility for the crisis from the national to the local level. A long-standing antipathy towards the Irish landlord class on the part of Whig and radical politicians, rather than towards the common people, made the policy shift even more attractive at Westminster.[45] So, in a radical but disastrous move, Lord John Russell's government threw the burden of famine relief back on Ireland and its rate payers. With ill-founded optimism, the cabinet chose to believe that a 'very abundant' harvest was in the offing in the autumn of 1847.[46] Henceforth, Irish property rather than central government would be responsible for Irish poverty.[47]

Inevitably with a country-wide scheme, there were difficulties and delays. The Death Census and other sources record the dismay in different parts of Ireland at the rapid winding down of the public works schemes from their peak in the first week of March 1847 when an army of 735,000 workers was on the pay roll. Moreover, as mentioned,

43. *Distress (Ireland). Third report of the Relief Commissioners*, BPP, Command Papers (1847), 836, vol. 17, xvii.103, 3; 1847–48 (876) *Distress (Ireland.) Fifth, sixth, and seventh reports of the Relief Commissioners, and correspondence connected therewith*, BPP, Command Papers, vol. 29, xxix.27, 3.
44. The Act would remain in operation only until the 1847 harvest, and 'no warrant shall be issued under this Act, nor shall any grant or loan be made by the Commissioners of Her Majesty's Treasury in aid of any rate to be levied under this Act, after the First Day of October in this year [1847]' *Bill got Temporary Relief of Destitute Persons in Ireland*, BPP (1847), 19, Bills & Acts, I, I.243, 8.
45. This point is often misunderstood by writers who view the tussles over relief policies as mainly expressions of anti-Irish racism or colonial domination. Relatedly, they tend to downplay the variety of contemporary understandings of the role of the state in society, and the constraints these implied, as well as the real-world dilemmas facing policymakers.
46. *Distress (Ireland). Fourth report of the of Relief Commissioners*, BPP (1847), 859, Command Papers, vol. 17, xvii.143, 3.
47. Daly, *Famine in Ireland*, 92–93.

in some localities, the work schemes were dismantled before the alternative of the direct feeding of the poor was phased in, adding a new twist to the older notion of a hungry gap. There were also complaints about the nutritional quality of the soup, and this seems to have varied between localities. The lack of fresh vegetables in the diet led to a further infliction, that of scurvy, arising from vitamin C deficiency.

The achievements of this short-lived famine relief measure should not be gainsaid. A vast network of soup kitchens was created across the country and at its peak in July 1847 some three million rations were being distributed daily. There is no doubt that many lives were saved. Broadly speaking, this distinctive episode in famine relief took centre stage from April 1847 to August of that year. It was a temporary measure and always intended to be so. That is the key criticism. After less than six months in operation, most of the soup stations were phased out in August and September 1847.

Russell's minority government, heavily influenced by the apprehensions of Charles Wood, Chancellor of the Exchequer (1846–52) regarding the state of public finances, had come to the conclusion that Irish property, rather than central government, should pay for Irish poverty. The new master plan, which was consistent with Whig ideology and the interests of British taxpayers, was to phase out from mid-August onwards the direct provision of food and to throw the burden of Famine relief back on the 130 poor-law unions into which Ireland had been divided, using the workhouse in each union as the coordinating centre for indoor and outdoor relief. Executed with haste, this meant the property owners of Ireland, landlords, merchants and tenant farmers with a property valuation greater than £4 became responsible for shouldering the huge burden of famine poverty. With this momentous shift in policy, famine relief entered its third phase.

The Third Phase: October 1847 Onwards

In the autumn of 1847, the Irish poor faced into their third year of hunger. The principal safety net for the destitute was now the poor law, funded by local property holders. Philanthropic donations continued but on a reduced scale as donor fatigue set in. Entering the bleak world of the workhouse was the test of destitution, in effect a rationing device. Families were broken up and the sexes rigidly segregated. Institutional discipline was strict. Meals were barely sufficient. Worst of all, the crowded workhouses were centres for the dissemination of disease. Mortality soared, especially in the winter months. The workhouse was the refuge of last resort and a dangerous one at that. Some entered, or were sent by relatives in a heavily diseased and emaciated state, simply to get a coffin and a decent burial. At times, some could not even gain admission due to overcrowding. The disastrous consequences were soon evident, not only in high death rates but also in the fact that many of the poor-law administrations in the west of Ireland went bankrupt. Nonetheless, the British government persisted with the policy that Irish property should pay for Irish poverty.

The policies pursued by the poor-law guardians evolved over time. Resistance to giving relief outside the workhouse had to be relaxed during the second half of the Famine. Initially, the 'impotent poor', defined as the aged, the sick and widows with more than two children, were allowed to be relieved outside of the workhouse (known as 'outdoor relief'). By early 1848 in the south and west where the workhouses were overflowing, it proved necessary to give outdoor relief to the able-bodied poor as well. The destitution test had to be set aside, at least temporarily.

Disease was of course the big killer and the poor-law system struggled to provide infirmaries and fever sheds to contain infection. Fermoy workhouse in County Cork furnishes a dire example of the kinds of problems that might be encountered: the mixing of sick and healthy led to a 24 per cent death rate in its workhouse in the first three months of 1847.[48] As if the challenges were not forbidding enough, in 1849, a cholera epidemic, largely unrelated to hunger, swept through the country and carried off more than 40,000 souls.

The effectiveness of the poor-law system has been much debated. While the system undoubtedly saved lives, it put others at risk because of the way diseases spread in confined spaces. The major problem, to take a very different economic context, was similar to that faced by poor-law unions in northern England.[49] Just as workhouses were not built to deal with mass unemployment in factory towns, where thousands could be turned out of work at a moment's notice, the Irish system was not designed to cope with the mass destitution caused by famine conditions. Poor-law provision in Ireland was for 100,000, not the millions that were forced by want onto public assistance. It has been largely forgotten that George Nicholls, the architect of the Irish poor-law system, had in fact anticipated this point: 'The occurrence of a famine, however, if general, seems to be a contingency altogether above the powers of a Poor Law to provide for'.[50]

Perspectives on the Great Famine

It is no easy task to grasp the complexity as well as the horror of the Great Famine. It was a catastrophe that unhinged the lower strata of society, yet left many of the better-off little affected materially.[51] We know little of the psychological coping mechanisms at different levels of society, though it is a sobering thought that in the Franciscan convent of Broad Lane, on the edge of a slum in the centre of Cork city, the members of this male religious community enjoyed bread, meat, vegetables, wine and whiskey all through the crisis.[52] Living like lords, we might say, and they were not alone. None of the temporal lords of the land were reported to have suffered from hunger, still less starvation.

48. Donnelly, 'Administration of poor relief', 318.
49. On issues relating to the new English poor law, see Nicholas C. Edsall, *The Anti-Poor Law Movement, 1834–44*, Manchester: Manchester University Press, 1971; Felix Driver, *Power and Pauperism: The Workhouse System, 1834–1884*, Cambridge: Cambridge University Press, 1993, 147–63; Lewis Darwen, *Implementing and Administering the New Poor Law in the Industrial North: A Case Study of Preston Union in Regional Context, 1837–1861*, PhD dissertation, Nottingham Trent University, 2016, 163–65.
50. *Poor Laws – Ireland: Three Reports by George Nicholls Esq*, London: Her Majesty's Stationery Office [H.M.S.O.] 1838, 37.
51. Enda Delaney, 'There but for the Grace of God Go I': Middle-Class Catholic Responses to Ireland's Great Famine', *English Historical Review*, 135, 577 (December 2020), 1433–60.
52. Kennedy and Murphy eds., *Franciscan Community at Cork*, *passim*.

This inequality is but one of many paradoxes. Another is that the Irish Famine took place less than two centuries ago when serious subsistence crises had vanished from most parts of Europe. There is not only its lateness in historical time to consider, it took place within the context of one of the most economically and politically advanced countries in the world. By the same token, we should not ignore the existence at that time of great swathes of poverty, economic insecurity and slum housing across industrialising Britain. Still, in UK terms, the Irish famine was a regional rather than a national disaster. In Ireland, no such geographical distancing was possible, although the severity was much more pronounced in the western areas of the country.

Little wonder that we encounter angry voices in the Death Census that prefigure the more politicised interpretations of later commentators. So how might we conceptualise, interpret and judge? The ecological is a natural starting point. The potato blight originated in the world of nature. It was an unanticipated, tuber-destroying fungal disease that spread with alarming speed and thoroughness. Its power of destruction was almost total, in a way that had no parallel among harvest failures affecting cereals and other foodstuffs. It was unstoppable at the time; worse still, it kept coming back.

Irrespective of origins, the impact of a natural disaster is greatly influenced by the nature of the society it lashes and that society's international support networks. The ramshackle character of Irish economy and society in the middle of the nineteenth century is hardly in doubt, particularly in its lower reaches. Its vulnerability had much to do with the pressure of decades of runaway population growth in a largely agrarian economy, a bottom-heavy social structure and the consequent retreat to a risky, low-cost, if nutritious mono diet. The effect of harvest failure is also influenced by the scale of the food deficit. Deaths were inevitable, as they would have been in most European societies at the time under conditions of repeated destruction of the principal foodstuff. Irish society, in this and other respects, was unlucky to have to undergo an ordeal reserved for it alone. Perhaps the closest in terms of exposure were the Highlands and Islands of Scotland but even there famine mortality was on a much lower plane due in part to the paternalism of Scottish landlords and the charitable exertions of Presbyterian churches.[53]

Ireland was also unlucky in terms of the timing of the scourge. Rigid versions of political economy were in the ascendant, which would not have been the case a few decades later. More immediately, a financial panic in April 1847 and an economic recession (short-lived as it turned out) in Britain caused the Chancellor of the Exchequer to rein in public expenditure, including spending on famine relief. There is still controversy as to the relative importance of economic ideology as against overreaction to shorter-term economic disturbances in determining policy shifts. In a recent revisionist intervention, Charles Read argues that the financial panic of April 1847, and the fears it engendered as to the stability of the public finances, led directly to less

53. T. M. Devine, *The Great Highland Famine: Hunger, Emigration and the Scottish Highlands in the Nineteenth Century*, Edinburgh: Birlinn 1988.

generous provision for famine relief than originally envisaged.[54] Read places particular stress on confused macroeconomic policy thinking, operating largely independently of the prevailing ideologies of laissez-faire and providentialism. Enda Delaney, by contrast, places the main emphasis on ideological dogma limiting state intervention.[55]

There is an important aspect of political economy that has received insufficient attention. The idea of local responsibility (and indeed individual responsibility) was deeply ingrained in conventional thinking and came to play the dominant part in the later years of the Irish Famine. The transfer of responsibility from the Treasury to the poor-law unions in Ireland in the autumn of 1847, while certainly self-serving, was not as peculiar as might appear to later eyes. The experience of Liverpool, on the neighbouring island, illuminates the point. The poor-law institutions in Liverpool were almost overwhelmed by the tens of thousands of destitute, fever-carrying Irish disembarking in the city in 1846–47.[56] The city fathers and local politicians lobbied vigorously for financial support, arguing this was a national emergency. However, Westminster rebuffed these demands and insisted that the relief of poverty and destitution was a *local* and not a national responsibility.[57] Local authorities in Liverpool, Glasgow and other places in Britain in turn saw these destitute migrants as the responsibility of Irish landowners and sent many back to Ireland. In mitigation, they might well argue that Irish landowners were in receipt of a substantial rental income of £10–£12 million annually. Not only that, and unlike their British counterparts, they did not pay income tax. It followed that Irish landowners should be held responsible for the poverty arising on their estates.

Perhaps there is another sense in which Ireland was unlucky in terms of timing. For all its dark associations, the Irish poor-law system was a reforming institution that furnished a safety net for the destitute in normal times. An intriguing counterfactual is that, on balance, it might have been better if Ireland had not had a poor-law system in the 1840s. Had its introduction been delayed by a decade or so, this set of institutions would not have been available to the Whig government in 1847 when responsibility was thrown back on the Irish poor law and Irish property holders. In that case, presumably the Government would have been obliged to continue with more *ad hoc* measures such as the soup kitchens, support for emigration schemes and perhaps a renewed public works programme. Food prices were falling from their inflated famine levels as early as the summer of 1847. Between June and July alone, the cost of supporting an applicant at a feeding station fell by 20 per cent (Table 1.2), and the trend in the prices of basic

54. Charles Read, 'Laissez-Faire, the Irish Famine, and British Financial Crisis', *Economic History Review*, 69 (2016), 425–29.
55. Delaney, *Curse of Reason*, 166–84.
56. Frank Neal, *Black '47: Britain and the Famine Irish*, Basingstoke: Macmillan 1997, *passim*. Revealingly, James Joyce, in *Finnegans Wake*, made a point of referring to the city as 'Liver*poor*'.
57. Lewis Darwen, Donald MacRaild, Brian Gurrin, Liam Kennedy, '"Unhappy and Wretched Creatures": Charity, Poor Relief and Pauper Removal in Britain and Ireland during the Great Famine', *English Historical Review*, 134, no. 568 (June 2019): 589–619.

foodstuffs was downwards.[58] Had the state persisted with the policy of directly feeding the impoverished millions, it would have benefited from progressively reducing costs.

So, to summarise: when the luck of the Irish ran out, it ran out with a vengeance. The Famine was precipitated by an 'ecological accident' (the potato blight)[59]; its impact was shaped by long-run economic and demographic forces (rapid population growth, declining living standards and declining food security); it was both ameliorated and aggravated by political stances at Westminster (on the part of Tories, Whigs and O'Connell's ineffectual Repeal party); and it was shaped locally by the behaviour of landlords, labour-employing farmers and poor-law guardians. The role of many Irish landlords in dispossessing or evicting tens of thousands of cottiers and smallholders played out at local level and was a potent force in producing destitution and death.[60] Some Irish tenant farmers were equally ruthless in dispensing with the services of their agricultural labourers or gobbling up the holdings of destitute cottiers.

Harvest failure across northern Europe in 1846 made accessing cereals from neighbouring countries both difficult and costly. But in important other respects the international environment of the 1840s was broadly favourable to those at risk of starvation. The plight of the Irish attracted worldwide attention. The British Association was especially effective in coordinating fundraising in the neighbouring island and channelling charitable relief to Ireland. Queen Victoria personally donated £2,000 (in present-day values, roughly £200,000) and the Pope less than half that, at 800 crowns. British, American and Irish Quakers were trailblazers in developing relief initiatives. American charity and grain shipments helped, and the UK's shift towards free trade in foodstuffs after 1846 was a positive development. The emigrant remittances sent to families back home in Ireland were vital and helped pull hundreds of thousands of kin across the Atlantic, in many cases, to a better life in the New World. In effect, emigration turned out to be an important form of famine relief.[61] Helpfully, fares to North America had fallen heavily during the 1830s and 1840s.[62] The implication is that state support for emigration could have been an effective means of famine relief but Treasury funding was pared back in 1847. The tragedy of contemporary refugees from Africa, Asia and Latin America denied entry to Europe or North America reminds us that the labour markets of Britain and North America

58. Liam Kennedy and Peter M. Solar, *Irish Agriculture: A Price History*, Dublin: Royal Irish Academy 2007, 140–52.

59. Cormac Ó Gráda, *The Great Irish Famine*, Cambridge: Cambridge University Press, 1995, 68.

60. James S. Donnelly, Jr., *Irish Potato Famine*, Stroud: Sutton, 2010, 138–40.

61. Cormac Ó Gráda and Kevin H. O'Rourke, 'Migration as Disaster Relief: Lessons from the Great Irish Famine', *European Review of Economic History*, 1, no. 1 (1997): 3–25.

62. John Killick, 'Transatlantic steerage fares, British and Irish migration, and return migration, 1815–60', *Economic History Review*, 67, no. 1 (2014): 170–91. The average steerage fare on transatlantic shipping from Liverpool to Philadelphia, USA, was £5 in 1831, £3.6 in 1840 and £3.2 in 1846 (around a quarter of a wage labourer's annual earnings). Fares rose marginally during the later famine years but were as low as £3.2 in 1851, by which time emigration had fallen from the exalted levels of more than 200,000 per year to 150,000 for that year.

were open to Irish migrants in the nineteenth century. These employment lifelines saved many lives. Though it is unfashionable to say so, the relief measures promoted by the British government, for all their inadequacies, saved multitudes of lives that otherwise would have been lost.

Explaining Famine: Two Approaches

A distinction is drawn in the academic literature between famines caused by an absolute shortage of food and famines where the supply of food overall was adequate but for various reasons was not available to the poorer sections of society. Examples of the first are harvest shortfalls or the destruction of food stocks through warfare. The pioneering work of the Indian economist, Amartya Sen, shifted the emphasis from these traditional explanations of famine to an alternative possibility: the poor might starve, not because of an absolute shortage of food ('food availability decline') but because the poor no longer had the resources to acquire food.[63] In the jargon, this is referred to as a 'failure of entitlements'. Thus, hunger might ensue because wages or incomes were no longer capable of purchasing a sufficiency of food in the context of rising food prices and a constant or falling money income. An increase in unemployment or underemployment could give rise to a similar effect. Other entitlements that might ensure survival such as welfare provision by local or national authorities might or might not exist.

Does Sen's perspective cast much light on the Irish experience? Contrary to Sen's hypothesis, we can say without hesitation that there was an absolute shortage of food in the autumn, winter and early spring of 1846–47, such was the extent of self-provisioning, dependence on the potato crop and the scale of its destruction.[64] The country could just about cope with the failure of the preceding harvest year from its own resources. Later, from mid-1847, given the volume of American grain imports, it is more difficult to speak of an absolute shortage of foodstuffs (Table 1.1). In 1847, for instance, grain imports dwarfed grain exports. As is well known, ships were leaving Irish ports laden with food and other produce, destined mainly for the neighbouring island. But coming in the opposite direction into Irish ports were much larger volumes of shipping and cargoes of grain. So, the likelihood is there was no absolute shortage of food during the later years of the Famine, nor in the opening year either. Sen's insights enter the picture but with a time lag. After 1847, the problem was twofold: unequal access to food and raging disease epidemics, with the latter delivering the fatal blow to malnourished and debilitated victims.

Clearly there is something to be said for Sen's framework, but it does require *international* grain supplies to be brought into the picture (Table 1.3). If speaking of *domestic* food production, however, there is no doubt that there was a deficit in food availability

63. Amartya K. Sen, *Poverty and Famine: An Essay on Entitlement and Deprivation*, Oxford: Oxford University Press, 1981.
64. Cormac Ó Gráda, *Black '47 and Beyond: The Great Irish Famine in History, Economy, and Memory*, Princeton: Stamford University Press, 1999, 83.

Table 1.3 Irish grain exports and imports, 1844–48 (000 tons of grain equivalent)

	Exports	Imports	Surplus/deficit	Maize imports
1844	424	30	+394	1
1845	513	28	+485	7
1846	284	197	+87	122
1847	146	889	–743	632
1848	314	439	–125	306

Source: P. M. A. Bourke, 'The Irish Grain Trade, 1839–48', *Irish Historical Studies*, 20, no. 78 (September 1976): 168.

during most of the famine years.[65] In view of the fact that the rural poor were normally self-provisioning – growing food for their own consumption and relying heavily on the devastated potato crop – that is what really counts. Viewing the calamity through the prism of social class or geographical region brings the harsh realities more clearly into focus. Food availability, or rather its opposite, afflicted the rural poor more acutely and for longer periods than society as a whole. In other words, an aggregate approach that focuses on national per capita figures on food stocks, and includes imports, fails to tell the relevant story. It might be added, the poorer, less accessible western and southern districts of the island, where self-provisioning had long been the norm, suffered longer intervals of absolute food shortage than other regions.

To compound the problem, there was no legal entitlement to support under the Irish poor-law system. Once the workhouses were full or over-full, the doors could be shut and relief refused.[66] Depending on the resources of the union and the sentiments of the poor-law guardians who administered the system, there might be recourse to giving relief outside the workhouse, as indeed happened in some unions. However, rate payers tended to resist this, as some priest-respondents to the Death Census noticed. The poorer unions in the west and south struggled and many went bankrupt. The consequences were calamitous for those lacking either food or the money necessary to purchase food. At the level of the destitute household, typically a nuclear family, the two explanatory sketches introduced earlier prove to be salient. But in the end, in terms of understanding the Irish famine of the 1840s, it is the food availability deficit that proves the more illuminating of the two approaches.

65. Solar, 'No Ordinary Subsistence Crisis', 123. Solar finds a deficiency in calories for the whole period 1846–50, even allowing for grain imports. The case is a tight one. If population decline and animal foodstuffs are taken into account, the gap or deficit would likely disappear. But placing all farm animals into any food availability calculus is an abstract exercise as there was little chance of this happening in real life.

66. Michelle O'Mahony, *Famine in Cork City: Famine Life at Cork Union Workhouse*, Cork: Mercier Press, 2005, 47–58; William J. Smyth, 'Classify, Confine, Discipline and Punish – the Roscrea Union: A Microgeography of the Workhouse System during the Famine' in *Atlas of the Great Irish Famine, 1845–52*, John Crowley, William J. Smyth, Mike Murphy, Charlie Roche and Tomás Kelly, eds. Cork: Cork University Press, 2012, 135–39.

Finally, there are the age and gender dimensions. As might be expected, the very young and the very old were especially vulnerable.[67] It is not obvious at first sight whether males or females might suffer disproportionately. The outcome depended on conditions of work, intra-household bargaining and physiology. Exposure to hard work and the elements on public works schemes, for instance, disadvantaged men (see Table 1.1). On the other hand, breadwinners might be expected to receive larger portions of food. In any case, the differences in outcomes turn out to be slight. Excess mortality was marginally lower for Irish women, which is in line with findings from other famines.[68]

Failures

Hallowed as are the rights of property, those of life are still more sacred [...]

Catholic Prelates of Ireland, October 1847[69]

There were different levels of failure during the Great Famine, though these are clearer in retrospect. The Whig administration persisted with the energy-sapping public works schemes for too long. Direct feeding of the poor and the destitute might have been initiated earlier and maintained for longer. State-assisted emigration might have been implemented on a large scale, though limits to shipping space need to be borne in mind. A short-lived prohibition on cereal exports between the harvest of 1846 and the spring of 1847 (by which time massive American grain imports were reaching Ireland) probably would have helped.[70] An outright ban on grain and other food exports from Ireland, however, would have been counterproductive.

This is a much-misunderstood point. A ban would have damaged the livelihoods of hundreds of thousands of tenant farmers who produced marketable surpluses; it would have reduced their ability to pay rates to finance the poor-law system; and it would have aggravated social tensions between the landless and those with some stake in the land. Still, the sight of carts laden with grain leaving famine districts, sometimes under military or police escort, or of ships departing the Irish ports with grain, butter and livestock on board, naturally excited popular anger. And such images would later be fashioned into potent ideological weapons in the cause of Irish separatism.[71] But in welfare terms and viewed nationally, there was net benefit in exporting high-value foods and importing a low-cost American substitute food.

There was failure at the level of politics. The Tory government led by Sir Robert Peel performed well during the first year of scarcity, using well-established measures to

67. 'Introduction' in *Children and the Great Hunger in Ireland*, by Christine Kinealy, Jason King and Gerard Moran, eds. Hamden, CT: Qunnipac University Press, 2018, xxi–xxx.
68. Jonathan Healey, 'Famine and the Female Mortality Advantage: Sex, Gender and Mortality in Northwest England, c. 1590–1630', *Continuity and Change*, 30, no. 2 (2015): 153–92, and the studies cited therein.
69. *Battersby's Registry*, 239.
70. As argued by Bourke, 'Irish Grain Trade', 165–66.
71. John Mitchel, *The Last Conquest of Ireland (Perhaps)*, New York: Lynch, Cole and Meehan, 1873.

handle the usual type of Irish subsistence crisis. The trouble, as Peter Solar emphasises, was that this was 'no ordinary subsistence crisis'. The second and subsequent years of famine were presided over by Lord John Russell and the Whigs, generally with the support of the Peelites in parliament. There was government failure through bureaucratic rigidities, inappropriate relief measures, and an abdication of central-government responsibility when it transferred the burden of famine relief onto local authorities. Its failure to curb evictions, though it made some efforts to do so, was also destructive of lives and livelihoods.[72] Evictions and emigration reassured some moralising government officials that here was an opportunity to reconstruct a backward and unsustainable agrarian economy along modern lines.[73] This made sense in the longer term but not in the midst of a crisis. Most of all, there was little learning. Policies were if anything worse during the second half of the Famine. An indication is the large (excess) mortality still being recorded as late as 1849.

Ireland's political representatives, including the O'Connellite Repeal party, didn't have a 'good famine' either.[74] Beating the drum of repeal in the face of an existential threat was of doubtful value to a starving Mayo peasant and served to weaken British sympathy both inside and outside of parliament. The Repeal party contained 34 of the 105 Irish MPs at Westminster in 1847 and thus could have been a significant force in a deeply divided parliament.[75] It supported, albeit reluctantly, the switch in policy to reliance on the poor law. It was an Irish MP, William Gregory, with the support of most Irish MPs at Westminster, who introduced the infamous Gregory clause, that is, anyone with more than a quarter acre of land had to surrender land above that limit in order to qualify for relief from the local poor-law guardians. In this way, hundreds of thousands were separated from their cabins and potato patches, some voluntarily, others under pressure or forcibly evicted. The gesture of rebellion by Young Irelanders in 1848 – little more than a skirmish at the Widow McCormack's cottage in Ballingarry, County Tipperary – was ill-judged and only served to alienate British public opinion.

The most difficult question of all is whether Irish society failed. Some landlords actively helped, others remained indifferent and some took advantage of the crisis to rid themselves of unwanted tenants. We do not know the proportions in each category. The role of the Irish middle classes, Catholic and Protestant, is even more opaque, though the current understanding is not particularly favourable.[76] We might remember, though, that the middle-class strata of society were especially thin in the worst affected, western districts of the country. Often it might only be the priest or parson, hence the importance of their personal testimonies.

72. Gray, *Famine, Land and Politics*, 191–94.
73. See the discussion in Delaney, *The Curse of Reason*, 227–33.
74. Mary E. Daly, *The Famine in Ireland*, Dundalk: Dundalgan Press, 1994, 115.
75. The complete Irish representation after the 1847 general election was 34 Repealers (up from 18 in 1841), 2 Confederates, 29 Liberals and 40 Conservatives. See Brian Walker, 'Politicians, Elections and Catastrophe: The General Election of 1847, *Irish Political Studies*, 22, no. 1 (2007): 31.
76. Enda Delaney, '"There but the for the Grace of God go I"', 1433–60.

Pre-Famine peasant society had a strong ethic of sharing which was congruent with survival strategies, religious values and superstitious beliefs.[77] But prolonged hunger ripped apart traditional norms. Irish folklore speaks of instances of exemplary charity during the Famine, but these accounts are often wrapped in miraculous clothing, thereby raising the suspicion that they were less common than supposed.[78] The social divide between farmers and labourers almost certainly widened. Some tenant farmers shot, assaulted or prosecuted food-stealing labourers. The land holdings of cottiers and labourers were amalgamated into larger farms, their occupiers driven to the workhouse, the grave or beyond the seas. Corpses lay by the roadside or in cabins, as neighbours passed by. Even within families, there were individual acts of savagery and abandonment. Famine conditions gave rise to abnormal times and, unsurprisingly, abnormal behaviour. Unlike famines in some other countries or in earlier Irish history, reports of cannibalism were rare.[79] As the threat of starvation drew closer, feelings of empathy narrowed to the family and kindred, and *in extremis* to the individual person. Instances of family cruelty notwithstanding, the norm was shared suffering and kin solidarity. One of the astonishing achievements of the Famine generation was financing mass emigration. In the region of one million were helped overseas by family and extended family in Ireland, Britain and North America. Though not recorded in any systematic way, it is clear that family and kin networks undertook large sacrifices to save lives. Unlike so many other agencies, the Irish family, by and large, did not fail.

The historical record indicates that in the region of one million died. It is an appalling death toll. Another million looked for refuge outside of Ireland. Against a backdrop of absolute food shortages, as emphasised here, famine mortality could have been much higher. That it was not owes much to the relief measures, however inadequate relative to need, implemented by the British government and local authorities in Ireland, and supplemented by charitable and private initiative. Many of the respondents to the Death Census might well not agree. Overwhelmed by the misery before their eyes, as repeated day in and day out, and traumatised by scenes of sickness and death, it is not hard to see why the tone of their testimonies is generally sombre. More surprisingly, as is apparent in Part II of this volume, a small number of priests reported little or no famine among their congregations. It is a reminder that, even with a calamity as devastating as the Irish Famine, the degree of destitution varied, socially, geographically and by religious congregation and denomination.

---

77. Niall Ó Ciosáin, *Ireland in Official Print Culture, 1800–1850: A New Reading of the Poor Inquiry*, Oxford: Oxford University Press, 2014, 82–90.
78. Cathal Póirtéir, 'Folk Memory and the Famine' in *The Irish Famine*, ed. Póirtéir, Cork: Mercier Press, 1995, 219–31.
79. Cormac Ó Gráda, *Eating People Is Wrong, and Other Essays on Famine, Its Past, and Its Future*, Princeton: Princeton University Press, 2015, 30–37. But, as he warns, these silences may not necessarily reflect the actuality.

Chapter Two

THE DEATH CENSUS OF 1847: STRUCTURE AND CONTENT

> [...] the death census of 1846 and 1847 will form a new and astounding era in Irish history, and will be transmitted through generations yet unborn with increasing execrations of the present period and its policy, until the dead are summoned to rise again, and come to judgement.[1]

During the depths of the harshest year of the Famine, 'Black '47', it may seem a little curious that leading Irish members of parliament were occupying themselves with matters of population and population counts. Such interests were not of recent vintage. The Irish were a much-counted people. Censuses and census-type surveys dated back to the seventeenth century and continued into the eighteenth century in large part driven by the insecurities of the British state and the Established Church in Ireland.[2] Unlike Britain, the great majority of the inhabitants was Roman Catholic, of Gaelic and Old English stock, and hence suspect on grounds of religion and loyalty. The penal laws against Catholics and Protestant dissenters were progressively relaxed during the eighteenth century. By the end of that century, individuals within the Catholic community were expressing an interest in ascertaining the size and relative strength of the Catholic population. The first initiative of this kind was formulated by Edward Hay, scion of a prosperous landed family and later a leading advocate of Catholic rights, who in 1795 proposed a national religious census.[3] The outbreak of regional rebellions in Ireland in 1798 put paid to this idea.

But the spirit of the age favoured such empirical inquiries, in part stimulated by the contributions of Thomas Malthus and his critics on the progress of population. Early in the new century, the political economist Thomas Newenham arranged with southern Catholic clergymen the collection of population estimates for their parishes. These partial

1. Sentiments of Revd John Sheehan, parish priest, Ennistymon, County Clare, as quoted in the Repeal newspaper, *The Pilot*, 23 June 1847, 3.
2. For more details, see Brian Gurrin, K. A. Miller and Liam Kennedy, *Irish Religious Censuses of the 1760s: Catholics and Protestants in Eighteenth-Century Ireland*, Dublin: Irish Manuscripts Commission, 2022. See also Oliver Rafferty, ed., *Irish Catholic Identities*, Manchester: Manchester University Press, 2013, and the chapters therein.
3. Edward Hay, *History of the Irish Insurrection of 1798*, New York: John Kennedy, 1847, 12–14; Edward Hay, *History of Insurrection of the County of Wexford*, Dublin: J. Stockdale, 1803, vi–vii, Appendix, xxxvii–xxxx; Alvin Jackson, *The Oxford Handbook of Modern History*, Oxford: Oxford University Press, 2014, 522.

surveys were published in his *Population of Ireland* and *View of Ireland*.[4] A series of other informal surveys followed.[5] There was even a suggestion that the Catholic clergy were especially well placed to conduct population counts.[6] A prefiguration of later, Famine-time initiatives was the attempt by Daniel O'Connell's 'Popish Parliament' to organise a national religious census in Ireland in the 1820s. O'Connell was a strong critic of the 1821 statutory census which had reported a national population of 6.8 million. Not long after the publication of these results he was suggesting the hugely inflated estimate that the national population might be 'far above eight millions', with 'seven of those eight millions as Catholics'.[7] By March 1824, the Association had taken initial steps to organise its own census, a move that attracted strong criticism in the House of Commons. 'Can any man doubt what their bullying, contemptible, and vapourising leader means, when he moves for a census to be taken of the Roman Catholic population'.[8] The Whig MP, one of two representatives for Armagh, Charles Brownlow, also expressed strong disapproval: 'not only had they their Board, upon which Petitions were laid, not only had they their Committees and their Reports, and done other acts of Parliamentary power and usage, but they had even directed a census of the People to be taken.'[9]

In June 1824, as anticipated by these comments, the Catholic Association 'directed a census of the people to be taken'.[10] It is unclear how far this project had been advanced by March 1825 when the Catholic Association was suppressed. One Mayo parish withheld £4 10s payment to the Association at the time to cover 'advertising and making an accurate census' of its parishioners.[11] The suppression of the Catholic Association

4. Thomas Newenham, *A View of the Natural, Political, and Commercial Circumstances of Ireland*, London: T. Cadell and W. Davies, 1809, Appendix, 22–33; Thomas Newenham, *A Statistical and Historical Inquiry into the Progress and Magnitude of the Population of Ireland*, London: C. and R. Baldwin, 1805.
5. See, for example, the population figures for Kildare and Leighlin, organised by Bishop James Doyle, *The Life of the Rt. Rev. Dr Doyle, Compiled from Authentic Documents: By the Author of "The Priesthood Vindicated"*, Dublin: Coldwell, 1835, 25–27.
6. Commenting on Shaw Mason's *Statistical Account of Ireland*, Ch[arles] Dupin, Member of the Royal Institute of France, noted that 'we cannot help remarking that in a country where the Roman Catholics are four times more numerous than the Protestants, by confining himself to the clergy of the latter persuasion, he has, perhaps, exposed himself to the risk of obtaining incomplete and doubtful information on more subjects than one'. *Dublin Weekly Register*, 5 August 1820, 1. Shaw Mason had attempted to determine the religious breakdown in Ireland in 1814, but by limiting his inquiries to the clergy of the Established Church, he skewed the sample in favour of Protestant numbers. William Shaw Mason, *A Statistical Account or Parochial Survey of Ireland*, 3 vols, Dublin: J Cumming, 1814–19, vol. 3, xlix.
7. O'Connell proposed this at a meeting of the Catholic Association, 4 February 1824. *Dublin Evening Post*, 5 February 1824.
8. *Dublin Correspondent*, 13 March 1824.
9. Speaking in the House of Commons, 31 May 1824, and reported in the *Dublin Evening Post*, 3 June 1824.
10. *Public Ledger and Daily Advertiser*, 1 June 1824; *Evening Mail*, 31 May–2 June 1824.
11. Catholic Rent accounts note £19-10-0 collected from Kilmoremoy parish, County Mayo (Killala diocese), but £4-10-0 was retained for 'advertising and making an accurate census of the parish'. *Dublin Morning Register*, 10 March 1825.

in 1825 did not bring the project to an end, and following the Lords rejection of the 1825 Emancipation Bill, an 'aggregate meeting of the Catholics of Ireland' was convened, at which Richard Sheil, a founder of the Catholic Association, called for a religious census to prove the strength of the Catholic population in Ireland:

> The Catholic question has been thrown out by a majority of 48 in the House of Lords – 48 non-contents have produced seven millions of malcontents. That we are mal-contents they admit; that we are seven millions they deny. What, then, is to be done? Let there be a census of the Catholics of Ireland. [...] An enumeration of the Catholic people may be easily effected through the instrumentality of the Catholic Clergy. For this purpose a [new] Catholic Association shall be established.[12]

O'Connell, at the same meeting, made clear that the taking of an ambitious, detailed national religious census would be a principal aim of the new Association. He went so far as to announce to or threaten 'England' with a new Catholic Association and the collection of a campaigning rent:

> The people shall be enumerated – the census from the parishes are already coming in. I have this day got a census from the parish of Ardcastle [Ardcath] in the diocese of Meath, the return of the Catholic population is as follows:- males, 682, females, 561 [...] males and females, they make a total of 1,243 Catholics. And then as to the Protestants – there is but one Protestant inhabitant in the parish.
>
> We shall have a list of the inhabitants of every parish, Catholics, Protestants, and Dissenters. There shall be no more random calculations like Mr Foster's, who allows 3 Catholics and two-thirds for every Protestant. Now we will make him a present of the fraction, and we will give him whole numbers.[13]

At the inaugural meeting of the new Catholic Association, O'Connell reiterated his belief that the Irish population 'exceeded eight millions' and committed his new organisation to take a national census which would 'as far as possible, distinguish the Protestants from the Catholics [and] the Dissenters from the Protestants'.[14] The strategy was to request the Catholic bishops 'to allow the clergy under their charge to commence, with as much expedition as might be practicable, the great work of a "national census"'.[15] At the second meeting of the new Association, the taking of a census was approved, and prioritised, though it was promptly suspended until later in 1825. Census taking was the preserve of government, so a survey of religious affiliation, as actually happened in the following decade, had to be disguised as an inquiry providing statistics for the introduction of a new system of education.[16] Not wholly surprisingly,

12. *Dublin Morning Register*, 9 June 1825.
13. *Dublin Morning Register*, 9 June 1825. For additional details, see Part II.
14. *Saunders' News-Letter*, 18 July 1825.
15. Thomas Wyse, *Historical Sketch of the Late Catholic Association of Ireland*, 2 vols, London: Henry Colburn, 1829, vol. I, 247–49.
16. *Dublin Morning Register*, 26 July 1825; *Dublin Evening Post*, 6 August 1825, 13 December 1825.

the Association's initiative fell short of its goals, but it was part of an apprenticeship in people counting that also found expression in the estimates supplied to the Public Instruction Commission in 1834 and 1835 by Catholic clergy (as well as by the ministers of other denominations).[17] In Chapter Four, we draw on the massively detailed report of the Public Instruction Commission to derive estimates of Catholic parish populations at the time of the Death Census.

There was relevant experience also in the regular recording of baptisms and marriages, and in some parishes, of burials as well. How extensive the recording of burials was it is hard to say, but it seems the practice was not widespread. In terms of the survival of Catholic parish records, it is clear that far fewer death registers have come down to us as compared to marriage and baptism registers. In any case, we are speaking of a clergy with some experience in the handling and recording of vital events. During the Famine, a willingness to commit estimates of destitution and death to paper is apparent. In November 1847, Henry Grattan, MP for County Meath, declared to the House of Commons that he had with him 'copies of 515 letters from Roman Catholic clergymen, in answer to letters sent them by the relief committee of this country, stating the numbers of persons in distress in each of those parishes, the length of time which the distress had lasted, and the means which had been adopted to remove its pressure.'[18] Grattan went on to explain that of the 515 parishes, 244 parishes had food for nine months, 6 for eight months, 1 for seven months, 4 for six months, 21 for five months, 50 for four months, 80 for three months, 30 for two months, 13 for one month, and in 25 parishes where there was not food for four weeks, the population exceeded 160,000 souls.[19]

There are clear similarities between Grattan's evidence and the findings of the Death Census. The correspondence drawn on by Grattan seems not to have survived, as indeed is the case also for the original handwritten reports that constitute the Death Census. Other local surveys, albeit on a small scale, were taking place. An informal census was conducted in Skibbereen, County Cork, in May 1847, with the intention of gaining some idea 'of the amount of mortality which has occurred here for the last four months'.[20] In Carrigaline, also in County Cork, the relief committee 'had a person employed taking the census of 21 ploughlands in the electoral district'.[21] Further east, counts in the electoral divisions of East Courceys and West Courceys, near Kinsale, were taken in November 1847, reporting 507 deaths and 498 emigrants from a population of 7,500 between 1 November 1846 and 1 November 1847. Mortality, it was claimed, was less extreme here than elsewhere because a grant from Pennsylvania had permitted the local relief committee to provide food aid between the termination of Public Works and the commencement of the Temporary Relief Act (soup kitchens). A second grant from the same source made it possible to provide aid to '800 helpless poor'

17. *First Report of the Commissioners of Public Instruction* (1835), 45–46, 47, vol. 33, 829, 34, xxxiii.1, 829, 1, xxxiv.
18. *Freeman's Journal*, 25 November 1847.
19. *Hansard*, 23 November 1847, vol. 95 cc 64–148.
20. *Freeman's Journal*, 20 May 1847.
21. *Dublin Evening Mail*, 21 May 1847.

after the closing of the soup kitchens in September 1847.[22] A census of Carrickbeg, on the Tipperary–Waterford border, in 1846 found the remarkable ratio of 2,373 destitute individuals in a population of 3,500.[23] Ennistymon Union organised a census to see who might be eligible for relief under the 1847 Gregory Clause.[24] A census at the close of 1847 in Oranmore and Ballynacourty, County Galway, found the destitute numbering 'very many, amounting to full three thousand at present, and in two months' time there will be five thousand in the same condition in these two parishes'.[25] In the Tuosist electoral division (Kenmare Poor Law Union), established under the Temporary Relief Act, the guardians undertook a count of the entire population ('including the rich as well as the poor'[26]), giving the name, age, condition, and other circumstances of each individual as a 'check on the return of members of a family, made by each claimant for relief'. This survey found the resident population in 1847 to be 6,766, which was well below the level of 7,485 in 1841.[27] It assumed a 12 per cent increase in population over the period, on which basis the Guardians projected a much larger population, of the order of 8,383 by 1847. This was not allowing for outmigration, however, and interestingly the Guardians report that more than 700 former inhabitants had been forced back to the area having been refused outdoor relief elsewhere. These migrants are not included in the population figure of 6,766 mentioned above, so the Guardians exaggeratedly estimated excess mortality at 1,617, which would imply that roughly 20 per cent of the population had been wiped out by famine. Still, mortality appears to have been high as we find Tuosist described in the *Tralee Chronicle* as 'a second Skibbereen'.[28]

This survey of widely scattered local investigations is by no means comprehensive. Suffice it to say that the Death Census emerged against the backdrop of widespread population counting in Ireland during 'Black '47', as local officials and clergymen sought to determine the number and conditions of their parishioners, presumably with a view to influencing government officials, locally and nationally, and spurring philanthropic giving.

Organisation of the Death Census

The Repeal Association sent out its circulars in mid-April 1847, and most of the completed returns had been received by mid-June of that year. In a few cases, the priest respondent furnished more than one report: the Revd Michael Gill, curate of Kilmaine, County Mayo, contributed three such reports. This was exceptional. We do not know how many circulars were *actually* distributed. What we do know is that the census was originally conceived as a national survey, but it fell far short of that lofty ambition. In total, the 100 returns received by the Repeal Association account for 10 per cent of Ireland's 1,020 Catholic parishes. Whether the partial nature of the survey was primarily a result of

22. *Southern Reporter and Cork Commercial Courier*, 27 November 1847.
23. *Tipperary Free Press*, 27 November 1847.
24. *Clare Journal and Ennis Advertiser*, 4 November 1847.
25. *Galway Mercury and Connaught Weekly Advertiser*, 18 December 1847.
26. *Dublin Evening Post*, 14 September 1847.
27. *Dublin Evening Post*, 27 September 1847.
28. *Tralee Chronicle*, 16 January 1847.

clergymen failing to respond to the circulars (because they did not have either the time or inclination to do so), or because the Repeal Association only distributed the circulars to selected parishes, we cannot know for sure. The evidence suggests that the answer lies somewhere between the two, and likely closer to the latter. Parish priests were certainly overworked because of the Famine and would have struggled to find time to complete the questionnaire. Many of them, as we shall see, stated this as the reason they had delayed sending in their return. The Repeal Association was also constrained by tight finances at this time, and it is possible that financial limitations prevented circulars being sent to every parish; although, at a penny a piece, sending out 1,000 circulars would only have cost around £4. In any case, the parishes for which Death Census returns survive are shown in Map 2.1, and the diocesan coverage is presented in Table 2.1.

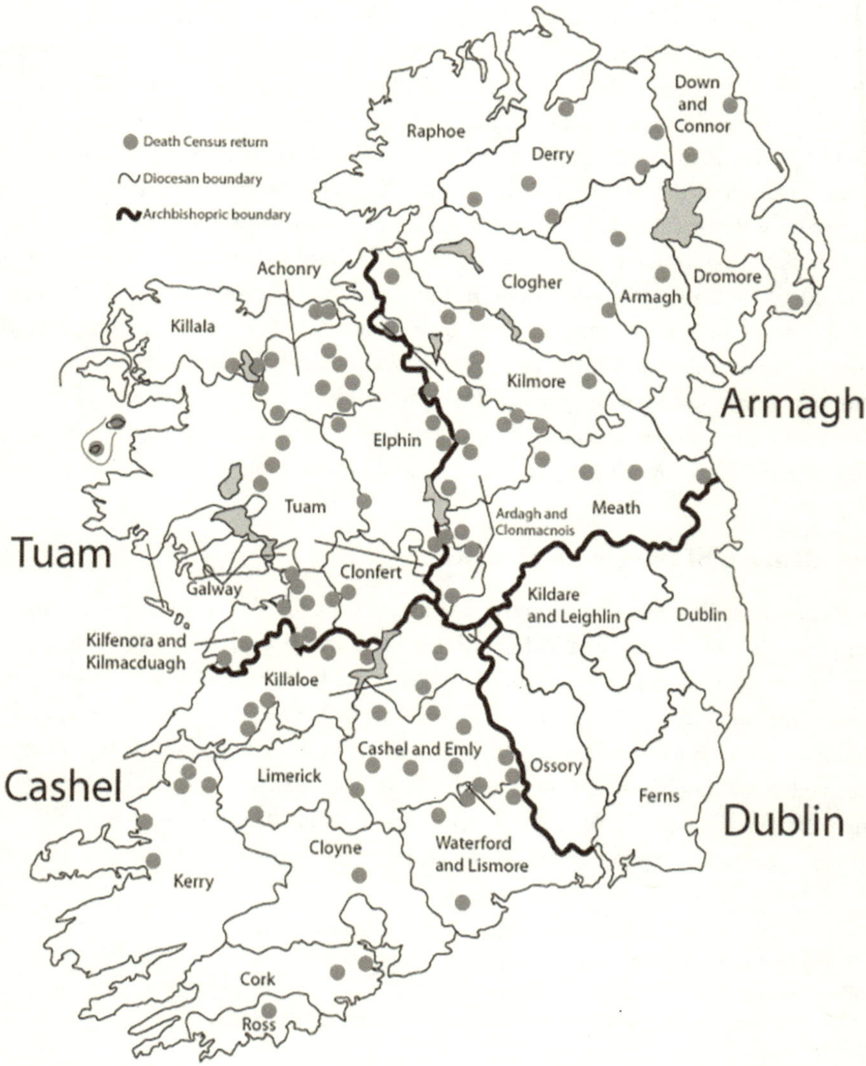

Map 2.1 Parishes with surviving Death Census returns (by Diocese)

Table 2.1 Diocesan participation in the Death Census

Diocese	**Parishes**	**Death Census returns**
Armagh	51	2
Derry	36	6
Clogher	37	2
Raphoe	32	None
Down and Connor	39	3
Kilmore	43	6
Ardagh	42	13
Meath	64	4
Dromore	17	None
Total, Armagh Archdiocese	**361**	**36**
Dublin	48	None
Kildare and Leighlin	47	None
Ossory	31	None
Ferns	36	None
Total, Dublin Archdiocese	**162**	**None**
Cashel and Emly	47	11
Cork	33	1
Killaloe	49	8
Kerry	43	5
Limerick	40	1
Waterford and Lismore	37	3
Cloyne and Ross	53	2
Total, Cashel and Emly Archdiocese	**302**	**31**
Tuam	50	5
Clonfert	23	None
Achonry	25	9
Elphin	43	5
Kilmacduagh and Kilfenora	19 (11 and 8)	8 (6 and 2)
Galway	12	1
Killala	23	4
Total, Tuam	**195**	**32**
Uncertain		1
Total, Ireland	**1,020**	**100**

Source: Information on dioceses and numbers of parishes is taken from the *Catholic Directory and Annual Register, 1839*, 111–48.

The expectation might be that the coverage of eastern Ireland would have been particularly good, as the Catholic Church was better organised there as compared to the western half of the country. Arguably also, the crisis-time demands on priests would have been less onerous, at least relatively speaking. In fact, the opposite turns out to be the case. The absence of returns from the more prosperous south-east – the Archbishopric of Dublin – is especially noticeable. It is possible that the Repeal Association targeted the hardest hit parishes, as these were more likely to provide the kind of evidence that might be politically useful. Yet, this assumption does not explain the handful of returns from the north of Ireland, where the Famine was much less severe. The role of ecclesiastical politics may be a more fruitful line of enquiry. The lack of a single return from the Dublin Archbishopric, for example, may have reflected Archbishop Murray's less than enthusiastic interest in the Repeal project.[29] The contrast with the 1820s is instructive. Back then, Murray was firmly behind the drive for Catholic Emancipation, and about a quarter of Dublin's parishes had responded favourably to the O'Connell initiative in census taking (as mentioned earlier). The liberal-minded Murray, who played a pivotal role in channelling charitable aid to parishes badly affected by Famine, was his own man.

In responding to the circular issued by the Repeal Association, a number of Catholic clergy were apologetic about delays, understandably putting this down to their increased workloads. Revd Thomas Carmody of Castlemaine, County Kerry, explained that he was unable to provide mortality figures for his parish because all his time had been taken 'preparing the unfortunate people for death'.[30] In Castletownroche, County Cork, Revd James Fitzpatrick told a similar story. He only provided a partial report as his curate had 'so much to do in attending sick calls [...] that he cannot spare time to make out the mortality census'.[31] Elsewhere, Revd McConochy of Drumreilly Lower, County Leitrim, regretted his delayed response, explaining that the 'absence of the parish priest, and heavy duty on my part, rendered it almost impossible to be attended to sooner', while Revd Michael O'Flynn of Attymass, County Mayo, blamed his delay on 'the extraordinary duties I have both day and night to perform, in consequence of dysentery brought on by starvation'.[32] In most cases, the clergymen did provide full returns, some of them in considerable detail. In two cases (Castletownroche, County Cork, and Kilmaine, County Mayo), the clergymen went as far as to provide a list of the names of the dead, one of whom (Kilmaine) provided the names of more than 200 of his parishioners who had died during the previous six months.[33]

29. Thomas O'Connor, 'Murray, Daniel', in *Dictionary of Irish Biography*, James McGuire and James Quinn, eds., Cambridge: Cambridge University Press, 2009, available online: http://dib.cambridge.org/viewReadPage.do?articleId=a6110 [accessed 3 June 2022].
30. Revd Thomas Carmody, see Part II, p. [X].
31. *The Pilot*, 19 May 1847.
32. *The Pilot*, 11 June, 28 May 1847.
33. See Part II, p. [X].

In our count of 100 parishes, we have only included reports that conform closely to the instructions set out by the Repeal Association. There are partial accounts or fragments to be found in the newspapers of the time that look as if they were influenced by the Death Census. The following, a letter from the Revd Edmund Waldron to the editor of the *Freeman's Journal*, may be a case in point.[34]

> MY DEAR SIR, I regret to say that we are in a deplorable state here at present. The public works almost suspended – a few only of the people employed, but all the stewards, check clerks, &c. retained, and paid as well as when they had work to do.
>
> Fever and dysentery, brought on by bad and insufficient food, are mowing down the people. We had 150 deaths in these parishes these five months past, and I fear that our population will shortly be reduced to one-half.
>
> Although nine persons have property in these two parishes, only two of these, *viz.*, Lord Kilmaine and R. Cooper, Esq., of Bundoran, County Meath, came to the aid of their starving tenants – these two have been always attentive to the wants of their tenants.

Fragments such as these are valuable, but we consider it helpful to draw a firm boundary around the reports from priests that are unambiguously in response to the Catholic Association and the Death Census initiative. These add up to the conveniently round figure of 100. It is conceivable that a few further reports may turn up at some stage in the future but very few, if any, is our expectation.

Let us now turn our attention to the questions asked in the Death Census. The circulars made three interlinked inquiries, all of which were related to the issue of mortality. They were as follows:

> What has been the number of deaths in the parish between 1 October 1846 and 1 April 1847?
>
> What is the number of such deaths known to be occasioned by famine?
>
> What was the number of deaths in the same period last?

In effect, what was being sought was a comparison of pre-Famine and Famine mortality at parish level, with the added attempt to identify excess mortality due to famine conditions. To their credit, and to our benefit, the priests usually included detailed descriptions of the local impact of the Famine, in addition to their mortality estimates (see Chapters Four and Five). The reports from the localities cannot of course be read in isolation from the political context of the times, nor can the documents themselves be viewed as apolitical creations. To these and related issues, we turn in Chapter Three.

34. *Freeman's Journal*, 26 May 1847.

Chapter Three

THE POLITICS OF FAMINE MORTALITY

On 5 April 1847 John O'Connell announced at a regular meeting of the Repeal Association that steps were being taken to 'procure a census of deaths which have occurred and are occurring in Ireland from starvation'. He continued:

> The secretary has received instructions [...] to address the Catholic clergy, and other influential individuals, who have local knowledge, requesting that, as far as is consistent with the discharge of their most onerous duties, which have been greatly increased by the famine, they will furnish us with the means of presenting to the world the appalling loss of human life in our unfortunate country, which has occurred in consequence of the misgovernment of England in former times, and which her present legislation falls far short of remedying.[1]

O'Connell had recently assumed the role of *de facto* leader of the Repeal Association. The organisation had been formed in 1840 by his father, Daniel, and enjoyed widespread support at both national and local level. Shopkeepers, priests, and other professionals filled the local leadership roles.[2] While the elderly O'Connell remained the unchallenged figurehead of the Repeal movement, declining health impaired his effectiveness and in early 1847, sick and weary, he embarked on a pilgrimage to Rome. The 'Liberator', as he was known to his faithful followers, died *en route* at Genoa, Italy, in May 1847, aged 71. True to the principle of dynastic succession – a deeply ingrained feature of Irish life – his son John took control of the Association.

The case for a Death Census, as John O'Connell's pronouncement makes clear, locates it within both the immediate crisis of the Great Famine and the longer-term demand for repeal of the Act of Union of 1800. Its genesis was, therefore, deeply political, and drenched in criticism of the British parliament. John's stated intention was to reveal to the world the terrible events unfolding in Ireland, and reflected his view that many people in Britain, including most MPs, were failing to recognise the severity of the crisis. This was despite the fact that the O'Connells and other Irish MPs had been

1. *The Pilot*, 7 April 1847.
2. Oliver MacDonagh, 'Ideas and institutions, 1830–45', in W. E. Vaughan, ed., *New History of Ireland*, V (Oxford, 1989), 202; Kyle Hughes and Donald M. MacRaild, *Ribbon Societies in Nineteenth Century Ireland and its Diaspora: The Persistence of Tradition*, Liverpool: Liverpool University Press, 2018, passim.

informing parliament about the Irish situation for the best part of a year.[3] 'There were still in that House many hon. Members', John stated in the Commons in February 1847, 'who even yet were not fully cognizant of the fearful extent of the calamity which afflicted Ireland'.[4] O'Connell was concerned that unless MPs recognised the extent of the crisis, and quickly, the consequences would be tragic. 'I am under the deep conviction', he warned during another February 1847 speech in the Commons, 'that the Government, and the House, and the English public generally, greatly underestimated the expenditure that would be necessary [...] to prevent one-fourth, and even one-third, of the Irish population from perishing'.[5] His hope was that the Death Census would provide the firm evidence needed to drive home the point about the severity of the crisis and so compel the Government to widen its relief efforts and save the famishing masses.

John O'Connell also sought to use the Death Census as a lever to expose the enduring damage caused to the Irish people by the Act of Union. His reference to 'misgovernment [...] in former times' and to the failure of 'present legislation' was an explicit condemnation of the Union and of British policy in response to the Famine. 'Had [the Irish] possessed a Parliament of their own', he told members of the House of Commons in March 1847, 'they would have prevented their country from sinking so low as she now was'.[6] O'Connell reserved his fiercest criticisms of the Union for the receptive crowds which gathered at weekly Repeal Association meetings at Conciliation Hall in Dublin. At a meeting of 19 May 1847, he concluded his reading of that week's Death Census returns with a blistering attack on British rule, telling the crowd that: 'The state of Ireland is well described by those horrible details which I have read to you. Here are a people, the finest on the face of the world, physically and morally, sinking into their graves from actual starvation'. This is the consequence, he exclaimed,

> of the Union with England. This is the condition to which English legislation has brought our country. This state of things must continue, must grow worse, unless they repeal the disastrous Union, and give us back our own Parliament, which alone can save the country from absolute ruin.[7]

The message was clear, if hardly well attuned to the sympathies of British MPs: only through Repeal and the creation of an Irish Parliament could there be any real hope of ameliorating Ireland's miserable condition.

3. See, for example: *Hansard*, 17 February 1846, 83, cc 1050–89; *Hansard*, 13 March 1846, vol.84, cc 980–1010; *Hansard*, 8 February 1847, vol. 89, cc 942–87. Daniel O'Connell also used the Mansion House Committee in 1846 to urge the Government to widen its relief efforts: Christine Kinealy, *Repeal and Revolution: 1848 in Ireland*, Manchester: Manchester University, 2009, 61.
4. *Hansard*, 19 February 1847, vol. 90, cc 251–93.
5. Ibid., vol. 89, cc 1358–1434.
6. Ibid., vol. 90, cc 1343–1414.
7. *The Pilot*, 19 May 1847.

This effort to convince Parliament to do more for the people of Ireland during the Famine proved ineffectual, not least because appeals for aid for Ireland were bandaged in the flag of Repeal. The Death Census, we now know, had no perceptible influence on Government policy. There were many reasons for this, and we discuss these further in Chapter Five, but it did not help that the Repeal Association was no longer, by 1847, the influential, mass organisation it had been only a few years earlier. The banning of the Clontarf Monster Meeting in 1843, a split in the Association in 1846, and Daniel O'Connell's death in 1847 had seriously undermined its effectiveness and status as a political organisation.[8] The senior O'Connell had formed the Repeal Association in 1840 with the intention of uniting Irish people, regardless of religious persuasion or political affiliation, in the common cause of Repeal. The model was similar to that of his earlier Catholic Association, which had proven so successful in the campaign for Catholic Emancipation.[9] While the social and political advancement of Catholics lay at the heart of O'Connell's Repeal agenda, his movement also appealed to a small but significant number of Irish Protestant nationalists whose desire for an independent Irish Parliament was not inconsistent with their religious affiliation. Indeed, Protestants had played a major role in a new, radical intellectual movement popularly known as 'Young Ireland',[10] whose links with the Repeal Association in the early 1840s had given the nascent organisation some much-needed intellectual vigour.[11] Young Ireland consisted largely of idealistic young middle-class journalists and students of mixed religious backgrounds, who sought to promote the Repeal cause through a romantic form of nationalism that celebrated Irish culture and history. Their journal *The Nation*, launched in 1842, soon became the widest circulating newspaper in Ireland, and Repeal Association membership increased considerably over 1842–43 as people were inspired to join the cause by the writings of these confident young thinkers. The increase in membership was such that the Corn Exchange in Dublin, where the Association met for its weekly meetings, became too small for the growing crowds, and so Conciliation Hall, with its 5,000 strong capacity, was constructed. A rejuvenated Daniel O'Connell proclaimed that 1843 would be the 'Repeal year'.[12] Events proved otherwise.

Throughout 1843 the Repeal Association held a series of 'Monster Meetings' at various locations, including historic sites, across Ireland. Some contemporary reports

8. George Boyce, *Nationalism in Ireland*, London: Routledge 1995, 154–65; K. T. Hoppen, *Ireland Since 1800: Conflict and Conformity*, London: Longman, 1989, 24–35; Kevin Nowlan, *The Politics of Repeal: A study in the Relations between Great Britain and Ireland, 1841–50*, London: Routledge & Kegan Paul 1965, 93–124.
9. Boyce, *Nationalism in Ireland*, 145.
10. Young Ireland was a local variant of wider currents of European romantic nationalism. The original inspiration came from Young Italy and the nationalistic ideas of Giuseppi Mazzini. Some Young Irelanders later went on to form the much more militant Irish Confederation in early 1847. Its leading members in turn were responsible for the ineffectual 'rising' of the following year.
11. Richard P. Davis, *The Young Ireland Movement*, Dublin: Gill and Macmillan, 1987, 27.
12. L. J. McCaffrey, *Daniel O'Connell and the Repeal Year*, Kentucky: University of Kentucky Press, 1966.

suggest that hundreds of thousands of people attended these gatherings.[13] These very public displays of Repeal fervour, not surprisingly, caused alarm at Westminster. In October 1843 the Prime Minister, Robert Peel, banned a meeting which was to be held at Clontarf – a battle site famed in Irish annals as the location where Brian Boru defeated the Norsemen (and their Gaelic allies) eight centuries earlier – with troops dispatched to enforce Peel's proclamation. Daniel O'Connell was a strong advocate of non-violent politics. Fearing bloodshed, he cancelled the meeting. In spite of this public climb-down, he was, nonetheless, arrested alongside his son John and several supporters, charged with treason, and sentenced to a year's imprisonment in May 1844.[14] This sequel, though it was not apparent at the time, marked the beginning of the end for the Repeal Association. While O'Connell's sentence was overturned in September 1844 and he was able to return home in triumph, the Repeal movement had begun to move in a different direction in his absence.

At the time of his imprisonment, the elder O'Connell had placed temporary control of the Association in the hands of William Smith O'Brien, a Protestant Irish landlord from County Clare who sat as a Liberal MP in the House of Commons. Smith O'Brien had supported the Catholic Association, and he had been attracted to join the Repeal Association by virtue of his sense of injustice at the arrests of O'Connell and other leading Repealers following the cancelled meeting at Clontarf.[15] However, although he was a political moderate and an admirer of Daniel O'Connell, Smith O'Brien increasingly moved away from the avowedly conciliatory approach of O'Connell and his acolytes to a more radical form of Repeal politics. Young Ireland, for whom Smith O'Brien was becoming the *de facto* father figure, also moved in a more radical direction. Thus, Smith O'Brien's Young Ireland and Daniel O'Connell's 'Old Ireland', as it became known, began to diverge. A shift in O'Connell's own thoughts on Repeal was partly the cause. When O'Connell returned to Dublin in 1844 following imprisonment, his pragmatic response to the failure of his 1843 Repeal campaign was briefly to advocate federalism rather than the outright repeal of the Act of Union.[16] This was at variance with the doctrinaire nationalism espoused by Young Ireland in the pages of *The Nation*, which saw in full Repeal the only way of improving conditions in Ireland and uniting the peoples of Ireland.

The growing rift between Young Ireland and O'Connell was evident elsewhere too. By the end of 1844 O'Connell was again moving closer to the British Whigs in order to obtain concessions for Ireland, which in the eyes of Young Ireland further compromised his Repeal credentials.[17] O'Connell's view was that some form of

13. For example: *Southern Reporter and Cork Commercial Courier*, 13 July 1843; *Freeman's Journal*, 2 August 1843.
14. McCaffrey, *Daniel O'Connell and the Repeal Year*, 117–214; Kathleen Quigley, 'Daniel O'Connell and the Repeal Crisis within the Irish Repeal Party, 1843–1845', *Albion: A Journal Concerned with British Studies* 2, no. 2 (1970): 99–107.
15. Denis Gwynn, 'William Smith O'Brien', *Studies: An Irish Quarterly Review* 35, no. 140 (1946): 448–58.
16. Kinealy, *Repeal and revolution: 1848 in Ireland*. Oxford, 2009, 40; Nowlan, *The Politics of Repeal*, 73–79.

alliance with the Whigs was necessary if he was to have any effective influence on government policy regarding Ireland.[18] In 1846, he committed the Association to propping up Russell's minority Whig government, much to the consternation of Young Ireland who believed he was sacrificing Repeal for minor, short-term concessions. Moreover, sectarianism was also creeping into the Association, as evidenced by the heated exchanges in Conciliation Hall over the Irish Colleges Bill in 1845, which sought to introduce mixed denominational university education. Both Daniel and John O'Connell were strongly opposed to the creation of what the former described as 'Godless colleges', whereas Young Ireland saw in the Bill an opportunity to bring Irishmen together irrespective of their religious persuasion.[19] To Young Ireland, a non-sectarian approach to Repeal was crucial in attracting Protestant supporters, and they also worried that the Association was too closely aligned with the Catholic Church. Yet, these disputes, undesirable though they were, did not seriously threaten the unity of the Association. As one leading Young Irelander, Charles Gavan Duffy, reminisced many years later, Young Ireland knew that to leave the Association would weaken the Repeal movement and that the campaign for an independent parliament would consequently be 'gradually abandoned'.[20]

It was the issue of 'physical force' versus 'moral force' in the summer of 1846 that brought these simmering tensions to a head.[21] Peaceful rather than violent protest had been the foundation of all of O'Connell's political campaigns, and Young Ireland claimed to be committed to this strategy. Yet, the increasingly aggressive rhetoric emanating from *The Nation*, which frequently praised Irish revolutionaries such as those involved in the 1798 Rebellion, suggested otherwise. O'Connell had little time for such rhetoric and felt obliged to re-assert his control over the movement.[22] Hence, on 13 July 1846 he presented a series of resolutions to the Association which he demanded all members commit to.[23] The key point of these 'Peace Resolutions', as they became known, centred on members rejecting physical force as a means of achieving Repeal. This was a direct challenge to Young Ireland. The timing of, and the need for, such a discussion, which was brought forward with little warning by O'Connell, bemused many Young Irelanders, as none of them had expressed any desire to take up arms against British rule. William Smith O'Brien considered the resolutions, which he knew would cause some form of rupture in the organisation, 'exceedingly unwise' and 'utterly unnecessary', and he suggested that it was a test engineered to force out of the Association

17. McCaffrey, *Daniel O'Connell and the Repeal Year*, 10.
18. Nowlan, *The Politics of Repeal*, 108.
19. Ibid., 87–89.
20. Charles Gavan Duffy, *Four Years of Irish History, 1845–1849*, London: Cassell, Petter, Galpin & Co., 1883, 217.
21. Quigley, 'Daniel O'Connell', 99–107.
22. *A History of Ireland: Ireland under the Union, I, 1801–70*, ed. W. E. Vaughan, Oxford: Oxford University Press, 1989, 360; Nowlan, *The Politics of Repeal*, 108–11; Maurice R. O'Connell, *Daniel O'Connell: The Man and His Politics*, ed. with an introduction by Conor Cruise O'Brien Dublin: Irish Academic Press, 1990, 113–14.
23. *The Pilot*, 13 July 1847; 15 July 1847.

'those persons who are identified in opinion with *The Nation* newspaper'. He thought the move 'suicidal' for the Repeal movement, a view that turned out to be prescient.[24]

Discussions took place over several meetings in Conciliation Hall during the last two weeks of July, and then boiled over during a heated adjourned meeting held on 27 July. The Young Ireland view, expressed by Smith O'Brien, Thomas Francis Meagher, John Mitchel and others, was that they agreed with moral force as a matter of principle but could not submit to the notion that physical force was *never* necessary.[25] But John O'Connell and his allies were not prepared to accept any outcome other than the complete repudiation of physical force agitation by every member. Daniel O'Connell was away on business in London during the meeting of 27 July, and in his absence John, more aggressive in tone than his father, led the case for moral force. He responded to a fiery speech by Meagher, in which the Young Irelander defended the use of the sword 'in defence or assertion of a nation's liberty', by stating that such language could not 'be safely listened to by the Association'. O'Connell declared that he and Meagher could no longer be in the same organisation. To Smith O'Brien, this was a threat to expel Meagher. He considered further discussions, which had already gone on for several hours over two consecutive days, futile, and he along with Mitchel, Meagher and other Young Irelanders withdrew from the Association and never returned.[26] The result was a split in the Repeal movement. It left the Association without the influential Smith O'Brien and some of its brightest young members. In the following months, the Association's reading rooms were banned from providing copies of *The Nation*, and those who opposed the treatment of Young Ireland were expelled from the organisation.[27] By the end of 1846 this bad feeling had diminished somewhat, and Daniel O'Connell, recognising the value of a united Repeal movement, attempted to bring Young Ireland back into his organisation. Negotiations, however, broke down once again over the Peace Resolutions, and with no way back the Young Irelanders formed the Irish Confederation in January 1847. There were now two separate parties advocating Repeal in Ireland, even as many of the Irish poor were descending from absolute poverty into destitution.[28] A united Repeal voice, focusing on famine conditions, just might have achieved more generous treatment by the Whig government.

Much of the blame for this has been directed at John O'Connell, both for his role in the split over the Peace Resolutions and for his ineffective leadership of the Association subsequently. In the pages of *The Nation*, Young Irelanders explicitly blamed John, rather than Daniel, for the break-up of the Repeal movement in the summer of 1846, although this was at least partly out of respect for the ageing Liberator;

24. *The Pilot*, 15 July 1846. Denis Gwynn, 'Smith O'Brien and the "Secession"', *Studies: An Irish Quarterly Review* 36, no. 142 (1947): 129–40.
25. *The Pilot*, 15 July 1847; 29 July 1847.
26. *The Pilot*, 28 July 1846; Paul R. Wylie, *The Irish General: Thomas Francis Meagher*, Oklahoma: Oklahoma Press, 2012, 37–42.
27. Ann Andrews, *Newspaper and Newsmakers: The Dublin Nationalist Press and the Mid-Nineteenth Century*, Liverpool: Liverpool University Press, 2004, 94.
28. Nowlan, *The Politics of Repeal*, 114.

after all, it was the elder O'Connell who had initially brought forward the Peace Resolutions in early July, and he fully supported his son's actions in the aftermath of the split.[29] Moreover, few historians have attempted to rehabilitate John O'Connell from the charges of incompetence and opportunism directed at him by the leading Young Irelander, Charles Gavan Duffy, whose later writings on Irish history presented him as an 'incapable pretender' who put party politics above the needs of the Irish people.[30] Kinealy, for example, has argued that the Repeal Association's alliance with the Whigs during the Famine meant John O'Connell supported the government's response to the famine throughout 1847, and that the only Irish MP seriously to challenge the government was William Smith O'Brien.[31] Yet, while it is true that the already weakened Association lost much of its influence following Daniel's death, the accusation that John O'Connell did not challenge the government during Black '47 is misleading. Throughout 1847, at Repeal Association meetings and in Parliament, John O'Connell spoke repeatedly about the desperate situation in Ireland, and constantly criticised the government for not doing more. He spent the best part of four months in London in 1847 and spoke at over forty parliamentary sittings. Most of these were on matters relating to the Famine. William Smith O'Brien spoke at eleven parliamentary sittings. Of the two Repeal leaders, the voice of John O'Connell was the one more frequently heard in Parliament during the worst year of the Famine, and his stance became increasingly critical of the Government as we shall see.

In 1846 and early 1847 John O'Connell (and his father) had implored the government to take a more direct role in the supply of food to the Irish people.[32] Peel's Tory administration had secretly imported grain in early 1846, and O'Connell hoped to convince the Whigs to do the same.[33] He also demanded that restrictions be placed on the exportation of food, a policy which had in fact been implemented during the subsistence crisis of 1800–1801.[34] Such requests were frequently expressed by Irish Repeal MPs during the Great Famine. John O'Connell developed his own longer-term plan for the production of food to feed the population. On 5 March 1847, during a long speech in the Commons, he proposed a major scheme of land cultivation which would see several hundred thousand people then engaged in road building on public works employed instead in tilling the land in time for the next season. This would ensure

29. *The Nation*, 1 August 1846; Duffy, *Four Years of Irish History*, 240–42.
30. Duffy, *Four Years of Irish History*, 408. For a study which questions aspects of Duffy's interpretation of John O'Connell, see Maurice R. O'Connell, 'John O'Connell and the Great Famine', *Irish Historical Studies* 25, no. 98 (1986): 138–43.
31. Kinealy, *Repeal and Revolution*, 110.
32. See, for example, *Hansard*, 2 February 1847 89, cc. 699–764.
33. Christine Kinealy, *Charity and the Great Hunger in Ireland: The Kindness of Strangers* London: Bloomsbury 2013, 22.
34. Liam Kennedy and Peter M. Solar, 'The Famine That Wasn't: 1799–1801 in Ireland', QUCEH Working Paper, no. 19–06, October 2019, Queen's University Belfast.

a good harvest, he believed. 'No time', he warned Parliament, 'was to be lost in taking measures to procure an extensive cultivation.' He continued:

> Whether that would be restricted to merely the green crops, or should extend to wheat, or other such grain, it was not for him to say; but that seed should be supplied to Ireland, and the people set to work cultivating the land, was the proposition which he deemed it his duty to bring before the House.[35]

In response to O'Connell's elaborate plan, Henry Labouchere, President of the Board of Trade, sympathised with the intention but was unwilling to support such a policy. He was 'convinced that it is not merely the duty of Government to do for Ireland that which the hon. gentleman has pointed out as the proper course for us to pursue, but that it is not possible or practicable if we wished it'. For Labouchere, the main sticking point was that it required government interference in the free market. 'To supply seed to a whole people', Labouchere argued, 'is that which no Government can undertake to do. I say that the provision of seed on the part of the Government would cripple private enterprise, and lead to irreparable mischief'.[36] Here we meet one of the biggest criticisms, from contemporaries and historians, of British government policy during the Great Irish Famine: its strict adherence to the doctrines of political economy. Labouchere justified his stance by stating that the government was introducing free food, although this was only a stop-gap measure while an amended Poor Law was introduced. A scheme such as O'Connell's to ensure the 1847 harvest was sufficient was never implemented (though there is evidence from earlier subsistence crises of expanding the crop acreage as an insurance against further harvest failure).[37] While the potato crop in 1847 was largely blight-free, not enough seed had been planted so the output was low.[38] Many died as a result of the inevitable shortages, and large numbers fled the country.

The failure of Parliament to introduce more effective relief schemes in Ireland left John O'Connell disillusioned with Westminster politics. His ideas on what the Government should be doing were far removed from what the Government was willing to do. By March 1847 he appears to have become resigned to the fact that the Whigs were not going to act on the warnings of Repeal MPs as he and his father had proposed. Indeed, John O'Connell reluctantly supported the Government's Poor Law Bill, which placed the responsibility for famine relief on Irish ratepayers, because he saw little prospect of anything better and because it allowed for the provision of outdoor relief. His view was that this was the least worst option available. As he told Parliament on 15 March 1847, 'anything Government had yet done, or what they meant to do, would be insufficient to meet this great calamity, [and I am] [...] ready to snatch

35. *Hansard*, 5 March 1847, 90, cc. 962–80.
36. Ibid.
37. Kennedy and Solar, 'The Famine that Wasn't'.
38. Christine Kinealy, *A Death-Dealing Famine: The Great Hunger in Ireland*, London: Pluto, 1997, 16.

at the poor law as a means of saving even a few lives'.[39] Daniel O'Connell expressed the same disappointed view in his final speech in the House of Commons.[40] As sketched in the previous chapter, the situation was indeed grim. Even at the time, father and son seem to have realised the new measures would not be sufficient to save Ireland from catastrophe.[41] At the end of March 1847, an exasperated John O'Connell returned to Dublin from London after a three-month absence and declared at a Repeal Association meeting that he would not be attending Parliament for the foreseeable future. 'England' he exclaimed, 'as represented by her Parliament, has been niggardly in her relief to the starving Irish people':

> I do not apply [this] to any one party in particular. I apply it to all parties in that House (hear, hear.). They have been niggardly in dealing out with a hard and grinding hand succour and support to that people whom they have so cruelly and foully misgoverned; and their conduct is aggravated by the fact, that they accompanied every step in the inadequate relief which they gave us, with the grossest insults and attacks upon the Irish people (hear.) [...] I have been sickened and disgusted at the inefficient [relief] measures that have been brought forward, and [...] I will not return this session.[42]

Instead of focusing his efforts on Westminster, John O'Connell turned his attention to creating a united voice from within Ireland to challenge the government. Thus, shortly after returning to Dublin he held out an olive branch to Young Ireland in an attempt to 'see the breach in our once united ranks healed'.[43] At a Repeal Association meeting at the beginning of April O'Connell emphasised the importance of a united Repeal movement to exert pressure on Parliament at this time of crisis. 'I am ready and willing', he told members, 'to do anything in my power to serve and save the country, now bleeding at a thousand wounds, steeped in the most dreadful distress, and mocked at by every English party, and mocked at also by the inadequate relief measures brought forward to remove the extreme misery of the people.' To enthusiastic applause, he concluded with an earnest appeal to see all Repealers united in an effort to save his fellow-countrymen from misery and ruin.[44]

O'Connell had learned something from the failed unification efforts of early 1847, taking a more conciliatory approach on this occasion. He expressed remorse over the split with Young Ireland and for the harsh words he had directed towards some of its members. The response of *The Nation* to these overtures was cautious. While it declared itself to be in favour of a union among 'all true Repealers', the wounds of summer 1846 and the events that followed were still raw. Furthermore, it remained critical of

39. *Hansard*, 15 March 1847 90, cc. 1345–1414.
40. *Hansard*, 8 February 1847 89, 942–45.
41. Cormac Ó Gráda, *The Great Irish Famine*, Cambridge: Cambridge University Press, 1995, 38–39; Delaney, *Curse of Reason*; Peter Gray, 'The Triumph of Ideology and Famine Relief', *History Ireland*, 3, 2 (1995): 26–35; Kinealy, *Death-Dealing Famine*, 121–24.
42. *The Pilot*, 31 March 1847.
43. *The Pilot*, 7 April 1847.
44. *Freeman's Journal*, 6 April 1847.

the Repeal Association's continuing association with the Whigs.[45] Smith O'Brien, for his part, was unwilling to reunite the fractured Repeal movement while the association with the Whigs was maintained. In response to O'Connell's overtures, he stated in an inflammatory speech at a meeting of the Irish Confederation that 'the alliance of Repealers with the Whig government has done more to destroy, to demoralise, and degrade the national character of this country [...] than any circumstance which I can call to mind in Irish history.' These were hard words; harder ones were to follow. 'I say further [...] in my conscience I believe that it has been the occasion of the death of thousands of my countrymen'.[46] Smith O'Brien continued in bombastic vein: had the Repeal Association remained united with Young Ireland, the pressure they could have placed on the government would have been 'irresistible [...] and the people would have been fed'. This form of language surprised John O'Connell, who admitted at a Repeal Association meeting the following week that he was 'a good deal depressed' by Smith O'Brien's speech. Nonetheless, he could not resist a retort to the main charge: if the split had indeed caused thousands of deaths, then Smith O'Brien was just as guilty for stubbornly refusing to accede to the Peace Resolutions on a matter of principle.[47]

Despite this unpromising prelude, negotiations did go ahead. Delegates met early in May 1847, headed by John O'Connell and William Smith O'Brien on either side. During the negotiations, O'Connell conceded some territory on the issue of the Peace Resolutions and on taking positions from political parties, such as the Whigs, who were not committed to Repeal. They hit an impasse, however, over the Irish Confederation's condition that any reunion must involve the dissolution of the Repeal Association and the formation of a new Repeal party. Driven by filial loyalty, John O'Connell explained that he could not agree to this while his father, still alive at the time, was out of the country, and the negotiations wound to an inconclusive end.[48] More than a year would pass before the two parties would once again discuss unity proposals, by which time their influence locally and nationally had waned to the point of near insignificance. It is hard to resist the conclusion that their famished compatriots deserved better from their political leaders, irrespective of which of the two opposing camps they favoured.

Around the time that John O'Connell was arranging the negotiations with Young Ireland in April and May 1847, he also began suggesting that all Irish MPs should return from Westminster and work together under a bi-partisan 'Council of National Distress'.[49] Such a council would, he explained, 'communicate to England the real requirements of the suffering Irish people, and the real gravity of the danger which, unless met by measures far more extensive than any yet proposed, threaten to bring a fearful convulsion on the Empire!'[50] In making this suggestion, O'Connell was trying to revive something of the spirit of the short-lived 'Irish Party'. Formed in January 1847,

45. *The Nation*, 10 April 1847.
46. Ibid.
47. *The Nation*, 17 April 1847.
48. *The Pilot*, 10 May 1847.
49. *Dublin Weekly Nation*, 1 May 1847.
50. Ibid.

this was a cross-party coalition of 88 Irish peers and MPs (including such leading figures as Daniel O'Connell, John O'Connell and William Smith O'Brien) who had agreed to work together to bring before Parliament a raft of proposals in response to the Famine.[51] These included providing food to the people rather than relying on private enterprise, and undertaking wider social changes through major construction schemes, land reclamation and by compensating tenants for improvements to their smallholdings. The momentum of the Irish Party was lost following a divide over the Railways (Ireland) Bill in February 1847, and it never recovered.[52] John O'Connell's attempt to re-establish a party coalition along these lines was not immediately fruitful. The death of his father in May, which came as a shock to many including John himself, led to a period of mourning, and parliament went into recess in July for the general election of 1847. O'Connell took up the idea again in August 1847, immediately after an election which saw the number of Repeal Association MPs increase from 20 to 36, by encouraging all Irish MPs to meet in Dublin before Parliament reconvened later in the year. The purpose was to draw up a list of urgent proposals to press upon the Government. The general view of the government at this time was that the worst of the famine was over owing to a blight-free potato harvest, and that the Poor Law would prove sufficient for the needs of the Irish people.[53] To this view O'Connell warned, with grimly accurate foresight, that while the blight was absent not enough seed potatoes had been planted earlier in the year. 'The recklessness of [the government] not doing anything to save the country from the danger with which it was threatened by a recurrence of scarcity', he exclaimed at a Repeal Association meeting, 'is beyond the power of language to describe'.[54]

John O'Connell's efforts resulted in a delegation of Irish MPs meeting under a Council of National Distress and National Safety at the beginning of November 1847, which was widely reported in the Irish press.[55] Over 40 Irish MPs took part in the proceedings which lasted several days. Smith O'Brien was among the delegates, but O'Connell failed to attract many MPs who were not Repealers; unlike the meetings of the Irish Party earlier in the year, no Tories and only a few Whigs felt compelled to take part in this initiative.[56] The Council agreed upon a list of 35 resolutions, not dissimilar to those drawn up by the Irish Party earlier in the year, which was sent to the Prime Minister, Lord John Russell. The resolutions were wide ranging, but the main ones set out proposals to stave off the immediate dangers of famine and to enable longer-term social reforms.[57] Warning that the Poor Law would 'not be sufficient, generally, to meet the distress which must be relieved', the Council's resolutions urged the establishment

51. Nowlan, *The politics of Repeal*, 126–27.
52. Ibid., 135.
53. Kinealy, *A Death-Dealing Famine*, 119–20.
54. *Freeman's Journal*, 10 August 1847.
55. *Cork Examiner*, 5 November 1847; *Freeman's Journal*, 3 November 1847; *Limerick Reporter*, 5 November 1847.
56. Nowlan, *The Politics of Repeal*, 152.
57. *The Pilot*, 15 November 1847.

of food depots 'without delay' and recommended that employment should be provided to finish off the public works projects abandoned earlier in the year. They also urged the government to provide advances to railway companies, which echoed Bentinck's failed Railway Bill earlier in the year, and to support other areas of industry in providing work and stimulation to the economy. A tax on absentee landlords was proposed, and legislative reform of the relationship between landlord and tenant was recommended to give greater security to the latter.

A large deputation from the Council, consisting of 32 Irish MPs, met with the Prime Minister in London at the end of November to discuss these resolutions. Their primary concern was to emphasise the need for immediate relief in Ireland, but it quickly became apparent that on this question Russell's mind was set. Without the support of Irish Tory and Whig MPs, the Council had little influence and Russell was unwilling to grant any concessions. The Prime Minister explained that while the Government recognised that there were 22 'distressed' Poor Law unions in Ireland (all situated along the west coast) which would require additional financial assistance, the rest of the country would have to rely on the Poor Law.[58] By this time the government was of the view that enough had been done for Ireland by way of gratuitous relief, and of course the dictates of political economy to which the government subscribed pointed to the harmful effects of charitable interventions. Indeed, informing the delegation that 'it would be most pernicious to allow the people of Ireland to think that they could rely always on the giving of alms by the United Empire', Russell charged that 'the rations distributed last year induced [the population] not to make the usual exertions for the cultivation of soil, and in the case of fishermen they had been found to refuse going to sea, relying for support upon the bounty of government'. Russell, it seems, was of the view that the soup kitchens had made the Irish population prone to idleness. John O'Connell, in a lengthy reply, told the Prime Minister that the Council did not share his optimism that the Poor Law would provide for the immediate needs of the Irish people, and asked Russell to 'adopt a liberal policy towards Ireland, so as to prevent a recurrence of the late dreadful calamity which had visited that country'. But the government would stick rigidly to its position. Moreover, an unintended consequence of reliance on the Poor Law led to widespread evictions under the Gregory Clause.[59]

The Death Census, we can see, was created at a time when John O'Connell and many others in Ireland had become frustrated by Parliament's inadequate response to the Famine, but still held at least some hope that by revealing the true extent of the crisis the Government might be persuaded to rethink its Irish policy. But there was more to the creation of the survey than this. In fact, the immediate backdrop to what became known as the Death Census was a series of highly politicised and, for the Whig administration, potentially very damaging debates about famine-related

58. *Morning Post*, 26 November 1847.

59. C. Kinealy, *This Great Calamity: The Irish Famine, 1845–52*, Dublin: Gill and Macmillan, 1994, 219. For a different perspective on the Gregory Clause see B. M. Walker, 'Villain, Victim or Prophet? William Gregory and the Great Famine', *Irish Historical Studies*, 38 (2013): 579–99.

mortality which took place in the House of Commons during March 1847. The debates were triggered at the beginning of the month by a motion which asked for:

> a return of the number of persons who have died in each parish in Ireland, during each month since the 1st November 1846, in so far as the same can be ascertained by information derived from the enquiries of the constabulary and from the officiating clergymen of the several religious denominations, specifying the number who have died from starvation, or disease consequent upon insufficiency of food, with a summary for the whole of Ireland.[60]

The mover of this proposal was not John O'Connell (as might have been expected in view of the resemblance to the Death Census), but his political opponent in the Repeal movement, William Smith O'Brien. Not only that, John O'Connell, who was present in Parliament at that moment, commented that clergymen would struggle to make these returns as they were too busy 'attending to the perishing population'.[61] Initially at any rate, O'Connell failed or chose not to recognise the value of the motion also proposed by Smith O'Brien. We shall return to O'Connell shortly; of more significance for now is the discussion that Smith O'Brien's motion provoked in Parliament. He disclosed to the Commons that he felt compelled to present the motion because he wanted to show that tens of thousands of people (O'Brien suggested as many as 240,000) had been 'allowed by the government and parliament to die like vermin' because of Government policy.[62] His motion, therefore, was an unmitigated attack on the welfare strategies employed by the Whigs. Moreover, the motion prompted Lord Bentinck, the leading Protectionist (anti-Peelite) in the Tory Party, to suggest that the returns should not only feature the number of deaths since November 1846, but the number of deaths 'in last year, and the year before'.[63] Bentinck had for some time been one of the most vocal and persistent critics of the Whig's handling of the crisis in Ireland since their return to office in July 1846, and he was particularly opposed to their refusal to interfere in markets regulating the supply of food.[64] He believed that the shift from the interventionist approach of the Tories to an ideologically driven policy of non-intervention and free trade under the Whigs had had disastrous implications. Thus, his suggestion for returns comparing the number of deaths over consecutive years was a deliberate attempt to back up this assertion with evidence. While Bentinck was motivated by more than simple political point-scoring, he would have understood his proposal threatened seriously to undermine his opponents on the other side of the House.

In the event, Smith O'Brien's motion was approved with an amendment which removed the reference to 'clergymen', their inclusion being objected to by Sir George Grey, the Home Secretary, on the ground that the Government had no authority

60. *Freeman's Journal*, 12 March 1847; Hansard, 9 March 1847.
61. *The Nation*, 13 March 1847, 358.
62. Ibid.
63. *The Nation*, 13 March 1847.
64. Christine Kinealy, *The Great Irish Famine: Impact, Ideology and Rebellion*, London: Bloomsbury Academic, 2001, 47–48.

to compel the clergy to provide such information.[65] Smith O'Brien consented to the amendment without much complaint, but it did not satisfy Bentinck who was frustrated by the absence of the comparative dimension he had proposed.[66] As such, he brought the issue up again in Parliament two days later, moving for:

> A comparative return of the number of deaths which have occurred in each parish of Ireland, or from as many parishes as may be practicable, in each of the last three periods of six months, commencing the 1st day of September and ending the 1st day of March, respectively, with a summary for each period.[67]

Bentinck's proposal – the Death Census in all but name – required the involvement of the Protestant and Catholic clergy as, in the absence of civil registration of vital events, such information could only be procured from parish registers. However, the government once again objected to the involvement of clergymen. In the view of Henry Labouchere, Chief Secretary for Ireland, not only did the government not possess the power to compel the clergy to provide the necessary information, but the absence of a system of registration in Ireland akin to that of England and Wales meant accurate mortality figures simply did not exist. It would be dangerous, in his view, to ask the clergy to provide returns as they 'might mislead the House and the country'.[68] By 'mislead', of course, Labouchere meant that they might indicate much higher rates of mortality than the Government was prepared to admit, and he was unwilling to accede to this possibility when the proposer was so avowedly determined to blame the Government for the mortality crisis.

Labouchere's concerns cannot be dismissed out of hand. Exaggerated claims emanating from Ireland, such as those of Archbishop MacHale, the firebrand Repealer from the west of Ireland, who declared that two million Irish had died from famine by September 1847, were not unusual.[69] And as we shall see later, there were grounds for concern about the recording of deaths by Catholic clergymen. Some did not keep death registers while others kept only partial records. Nonetheless, the limited evidence available to us does not show a pattern of deliberate exaggeration of famine mortality by clergymen when, in the spring of 1847, they were requested by the Repeal Association to compile returns for the Death Census. In any case, Labouchere continued to defend the policy pursued by his party, stating that they had done 'all that was in their power to alleviate the distress' in Ireland. Bentinck was unmoved. While he temporarily withdrew his motion to give the government time to inquire into the means whereby the figures might be procured, he again raised the subject in the House several days later. In the meantime, Bentinck had acquired his own evidence, which showed that, contrary to Labouchere's assertion, Church of Ireland clergymen in Ireland did in fact

65. *The Nation*, 13 March 1847.
66. Ibid.
67. *Hansard*, 11 March 1847, 90, cc. 1148–56.
68. *Hansard*, 11 March 1847, 90, cc. 1148–56.
69. *Evening Mail*, 8 October 1847.

keep reliable burial records as was required of them by canon law, and that medical professionals also kept detailed records, although he was advised that 'the Roman Catholic pauper population are in nineteen cases out of twenty consigned to the grave without even a funeral service'. In response, Labouchere doubted that canon law was strictly followed, and he stated that Anglican records were in any case of little value on their own as they only represented a small portion of the population.[70] The matter was dropped, only for Bentinck to revive it once again the following week.[71] This time, he came armed with a letter from Archbishop MacHale, who had written to Bentinck informing him that Catholic clergyman could indeed provide the required information, and that the accuracy of such could be verified by local medical attendants. To this, Labouchere responded with his own findings, asserting that reliable Anglican and Catholic records simply did not exist, at least not for the purposes of obtaining national mortality figures. O'Brien interjected, asking if the government would accept returns compiled by MacHale's priests, but Russell rejected the idea of presenting information 'obtained in any unusual manner'.[72] Bentinck, presumably recognising that the discussion was going nowhere, made no further attempts to promote the idea. Posterity does, however, grant him the final word on the matter. On the same day as this exchange with Labouchere over mortality statistics, Bentinck warned the Government during a debate over the Irish Poor Law Bill that the truth about the true extent of mortality would become known. When that time came, he predicted 'the public, and the world itself, will be able to estimate at its proper value your management of the affairs of Ireland.[73]

A question remains: why was it John O'Connell, whose initial reaction to Smith O'Brien's proposal for clerical involvement in compiling mortality figures was one of scepticism, who ended up adopting the idea? There are a number of possible reasons. It is possible that O'Connell's view was changed by the positive responses to Bentinck's proposal by prominent Catholic figures such as Archbishop MacHale, with whom the O'Connells had a close association. Moreover, one would be surprised if some Catholic clergymen did not write to O'Connell, as the head of the Repeal movement, on the same matter. Indeed, we know that members of the Catholic clergy regularly wrote to John O'Connell informing him of the progress of the famine, as he read out several of these letters during his final speech in Parliament before he temporarily withdrew at the end of March 1847.[74] Alternatively, one might be tempted to view O'Connell's actions more cynically. Doubtless he considered the political capital to be gained from carrying out the census through the Repeal Association, and it is understandable that he might not want the credit to go to Smith O'Brien. However, we should be careful here. O'Connell was at this time making overtures to the Irish Confederation to reunite

70. *Hansard*, 22 March 1847.
71. Ibid.
72. Ibid.
73. Ibid.
74. Ibid.

the two Repeal parties, so it is unlikely that he was purposely trying to undermine Smith O'Brien, its leader, for personal or political advantage. Further, O'Connell was being sincere when he declared in Parliament that he was unsure if clergymen had the time to provide such returns, as he repeated this doubt when he first proposed the plan in Conciliation Hall a few weeks later. Restating his view that 'The clergy [...] who would be the best persons to furnish the information, are overworked', O'Connell left it to a Repeal Association committee to determine the best way of putting the idea into action.[75] It was the committee that recommended the use of the clergy. And there is no doubt that the Repeal Association, as compared to the Irish Confederation, was in a far better position to undertake the Death Census. Unlike Smith O'Brien's minority faction, the Repeal Association had the backing of the mass of Catholic clergymen across Ireland. Had the Repeal Association not enjoyed this close relationship, there almost certainly would have been no Death Census conducted in Ireland in 1847.

75. *Vindicator*, 3 April 1847.

Chapter Four

ESTIMATES OF FAMINE MORTALITY IN THE DEATH CENSUS

The Death Census provides quantitative evidence on deaths in normal times and deaths during the early course of the Famine. This is the statistical spine of the work, and the numbers are potentially of great significance, relating to different parts of the country and different social and economic conditions. But some problems need to be addressed. In the first place, many parish priests were not in the habit of keeping burial registers, which helps explain why so few records are to be found in the archives. Of those that did keep registers, we might wonder if the priests were providing a comprehensive record of burials, even in ordinary times. When famine was ravaging their local communities, it is easy to imagine that overworked clergymen, some themselves weakened by famine-related disease, might feel they had more urgent tasks than keeping a record of deaths and burials. As we noted, John O'Connell acknowledged as much when first introduced to the idea of a mortality count. We might also wonder if some clergymen failed to understand fully the instructions issued by the Repeal Association. Moreover, some might have been tempted to exaggerate famine mortality to score a political point or to secure financial or food aid for the famished amongst their parishioners. Clearly, the validity of the survey needs to be appraised.

The Death Census

Although the Death Census was conceived originally as a national survey, these plans were quickly scaled back; and, in the end, responses were received from one hundred parishes. This represents one in ten parishes, as there were just over one thousand Catholic parishes in the country in the 1840s.[1] Viewed as a *sample* of the total this is quite a respectable sampling fraction. A more significant limitation is that the sample is far from being a representative one. A glance back at Map 2.1 confirms that the returns were geographically skewed. The constituent parts of the western archbishopric of Tuam are well covered – helpful as western parishes suffered heavily – and the south and south-west of the country are reasonably well represented. There are scattered returns

1. The *Catholic Directory and Annual Register for the Year 1838*, London: C. Dolman, 1838, 90–138 lists 997 individual parishes in the 27 dioceses into which Ireland was subdivided. There were 2,508 civil parishes, according to Brian Mitchell, *A New Genealogical Atlas of Ireland*, 2nd ed., Baltimore: Geneaological Publishing 2002, 9.

from the north of Ireland. The striking omissions are parishes from the archbishopric of Dublin. There are no returns at all relating to counties Dublin, Kildare, Carlow, Wexford. This sub-region was one of the more prosperous of the Irish regions.

The queries in the Death Census (see Chapter Two) asked each priest to provide numerical answers to questions about deaths in the parish. In effect the Repeal Association, the instigator of the Census, was asking for figures that would allow the reader or listener to make a comparison between pre-Famine (or 'normal' mortality) and Famine or 'abnormal' mortality (excess mortality). The contrast, if such there was, would indicate the severity of the Famine locally. The period of normal mortality specified in the Death Census was from 1 October 1845 to 1 April 1846. This was reasonable enough as there were relatively few famine deaths before the summer of 1846. Ideally, one might have wished for a longer time span, so as to capture and average out random fluctuations in the normal death rate. This would have complicated the enquiry, particularly for priests who were not in the habit of keeping good records, and almost certainly would have led to some confusion. The second period specified was another six-month time span, from 1 October 1846 to 1 April 1847 when famine and famine-related diseases were driving an escalating death toll.

In assessing the reliability of the demographic information contained in the Death Census, we may begin by looking at the estimates of normal or pre-Famine mortality as reported by priests from the various parishes. On the basis of a wider knowledge of the period and of death rates in other pre-industrial societies, we would expect the implied death rates to lie within the range of 20–30 deaths per thousand of population. Wrigley and Schofield suggest a range of between 20 and 35 deaths per 1,000 per annum in pre-industrial Europe, though they add that mortality rates at the extreme ends of this range were rarely observed 'other than by way of short-term fluctuation'.[2] According to Mokyr, pre-Famine Irish death rates were of the order of 23 or 24 per 1,000, so a range of 20–30 deaths per 1,000 should easily encompass virtually all Irish experience outside times of subsistence crises or major epidemics.[3]

Only two pieces of information are needed to calculate parish-level mortality rates: these are the number of deaths in a particular parish in a year and the size of the parish population. However, as the Death Census was recording Catholic burials only, we also need to know the size of the Catholic population locally. In many parishes of course the Catholic share of the population was overwhelming, and so it is no great issue. For the island as a whole it was three out of every four souls. Quite apart from its overall weight in the country's population, the Catholic experience is of particular interest as the socio-economic composition of the majority denomination left it more vulnerable to subsistence crises.

There are some further complications. There is, first of all, the problem of boundaries. Three types of parish units were in use in mid-nineteenth century Ireland: the civil parish which was used in population censuses and other official documents, the larger

2. E. A. Wrigley and R. S. Schofield, *The Population History of England, 1541–1871*, Cambridge: Cambridge University Press 1997, 181.
3. Joel Mokyr, *Why Ireland Starved*, 33–35.

Church of Ireland parish or union (often a multiple of civil parishes) and the Roman Catholic parish which might be but often was not a multiple of civil parishes. Moreover, the boundaries of Catholic parishes in the 1840s are not as well-known as the boundaries of civil and Church of Ireland parishes. We have drawn on two authoritative sources to plot the boundaries of the Catholic parish unit (which in the case of the Death Census was the recording unit). These are Brian Mitchell's *Genealogical Atlas of Ireland* and the Catholic parish maps displayed on the National Library of Ireland's website.[4] A further challenge, once the boundaries of the Catholic parish had been identified, was to establish the numbers of Catholics within those boundaries. In effect, this meant eliminating the Protestant segment of the local population – often a small minority – from subsequent calculations. As religious affiliation was not recorded in the official population censuses until 1861, this might seem like an impossible task.

We are fortunate, however, in that in 1834 a government commission was set up to inquire into the state of public instruction and religion in Ireland.[5] The remit was broad and included authorising the commissioners to calculate the size of the different denominations in each Church of Ireland parish (or union of parishes) in the country. The method used by the commissioners is itself noteworthy. Enumerators for the 1831 Census of Ireland were re-employed and, armed with a copy of the household returns for 1831, were requested to 'ascertain and insert [...] the particular religious persuasions' of each individual, either from their personal knowledge or by revisiting the houses to make the necessary inquiries. Once the local enquiry was completed, public meetings were convened in each parish, to which the enumerator presented his account of the religious breakdown of the parish. His estimates were open to challenge, not least from the clergymen of the different denominations who had every reason to take a close interest. Corrections were possible at this stage, so we may place a high degree of confidence in the final outcome.[6] The Commissioners estimated the religious composition of each parish or parish union for 1831 and 1834. We favour the 1831 counts as we view them as marginally more reliable. It is worth pausing over the work of the Commission as it is unique in the context of Irish census taking. This was the only time an Irish census was revisited in total, verified, and corrected, which must make it special also in a European context.

The next stage involved the hazardous task of reconfiguring this information so that it related to the parish units of the Catholic Church. It was then a simple matter of extrapolating the 1831 population estimates forward in time to 1841, using the intercensal population growth rate for the locality.[7] A further extrapolation carried the estimated population of each Catholic parish forward to 1845 and the eve

4. Mitchell, *New Genealogical Atlas of Ireland* (2002); https://registers.nli.ie/.
5. *Commission for Inquiring into the State of Religious and Other Instruction in Ireland* (1835), BPP, House of Commons Papers (1834), 356, vol. 43, xliii.399, 1. The Commission was established on 4 June 1834.
6. *First Report of the Commissioners of Public Instruction*, vol. 33, 829, 34, xxxiii.1, 829, xxxiv.1, 2, 3.
7. This might be the civic parish or a cluster of civic parishes, as the case might be, that approximated the Catholic parish.

of the crisis, this time using a uniform growth rate of 1.0 per cent per annum for all the parishes. Ideally, we would have wished to use parish-specific growth rates for this final time interval, but we do not have such detailed knowledge, at least not in most cases.[8]

There is one further complication which relates to the period of actual famine – the second period specified in the Death Census – about which we can do little. This is the problem, as the crisis deepened, of people on the move, of migrants and refugees bringing about a redistribution of population within regions. Captain Edmund Wynne, an Inspecting Officer for Public Works in County Clare, and a well-placed observer of the extent of destitution in one of the worst affected counties in Ireland, was alert to the possibility that the census of population for 1841 might be of limited use in predicting local population five years on.

> The census of 1841 being pronounced universally to be no fair criterion of the present population and consequent destitution, I tested the matter in the parish of Clondigad, barony of Islands [south-west of Ennis], where I found the present population more than a third greater than that of 1841; this I believe to be the case in all the districts along the coast, and to be caused entirely by the sea-weed traffic, which has done an infinity of mischief. Squatters from all the southern counties have settled down and converted the country into one monster cottier farm.[9]

In 1847 the presence, or indeed absence, of workhouses, soup kitchens, Public Works schemes or employment opportunities could all influence local population levels. As an aside, it may be mentioned that some priests in the course of their responses to the Death Census did include estimates of the size of the local Catholic population in 1847. These were often out of kilter with population figures from the 1841 census, possibly for the reasons Wynne enunciates but more likely because counting people of all ages and of varying visibility (some inhabited improvised shelters in out-of-the way places), even in a small locality, was no easy task unless conducted by trained enumerators.

Having estimated the Catholic population for Catholic parishes, we are now in a position to calculate mortality rates and use these to assess the plausibility of the figures for deaths supplied by priests for the pre-Famine period. We may begin with the example of Killedan parish in County Mayo. The local priest reported that 80 people had died between 1 October 1845 and 1 April 1846. We estimate the Catholic population of the parish in mid-1845 at 6,664 inhabitants. If the range of plausible death rates was from 20 per thousand to 30 per thousand inhabitants, as suggested earlier, then we would expect between 76 and 114 deaths in Killedan for this six-month period.

8. It is true the small numbers of surviving Catholic baptism registers, when combined with death registers, would help in approximating local growth rates but this is generally not possible. In any case we have no estimates of local migration.
9. Captain Wynne to the secretary of the Board of Works, 5 December 1846 in: *Correspondence from July 1846 to January 1847 relating to the measures adopted for the relief of distress in Ireland. Board of Works Series*, BPP, Command Papers (1847), 764, vol. 50, L.1, 308–9. Clondagad's population was 5,088 according to the 1841 census; *Report of the Commissioners appointed to take the Census of Ireland for the Year 1841*, BPP (1843) 504, xxiv.1, 158.

This is after taking account of seasonality in deaths.[10] According to Revd John Brennan there were 80 deaths for the half-year, which fits comfortably within the expected interval. The same may be said of Toomore, also in County Mayo. The estimated Catholic population is 3,741 for mid-1845 and the expected interval is from 43 to 64 deaths. Once again, the 48 deaths reported by the Revd John Corley for Toomore appear quite credible. He assures us: 'if my return of deaths be not under, it is not over'.[11]

So far, so good. But the stark finding overall is that the vast majority of the parishes in the Death Census did not return mortality figures for the pre-Famine period that are remotely in line with expectations. In fact, reported deaths fall far below the lower limit of the Wrigley-Schofield range for most of the 55 parishes we tested, implying implausibly low mortality in pre-Famine Ireland.[12] This, by the way, would have the further effect of serving to exaggerate the contrast with Famine times. Unless the priests were lying for political or ideological purposes, we presume they were guided by the burial records in their possession, if they kept such records, or were simply dependent on memory. So how or why were more accurate mortality counts for the pre-Famine period not supplied to the originators of the Death Census?

The answer to this conundrum opens doors onto the social history of the period and has implications for the practice of parish-register demography. An important clue is contained in the return by Revd J. O'Meara for Aglish and Whitechurch, County Waterford. He noted 360 deaths in the parish between 1 October 1846 and 1April 1847, but added that 'we have no regular register of deaths in this parish, nor can we, as several of the children are buried without any notice given to the parochial clergy'.[13] Revd John Halanan, of Ballinhassig, County Cork, listed the names of sixty-two adults who had died. A revealing aside follows: as well as these adults there were 'many young children up to seven years old [...] the account of whom I did not receive, as they were so young and not requiring my personal attendance'.[14] Nor was there any consistency in relation to age in the omission of children. Revd John Ryan's return for Knockany, County Limerick, reported '66 of the age 15 and upwards', whereas Revd Michael Tobin reported 160 deaths in Cahir parish, County Tipperary, though 'no child under twelve years is included'.[15]

10. A population of the size of Killendan would imply between 133 and 200 deaths in a full year. Based on an analysis of mortality figures in eight Catholic parishes (10,451 burials), we conclude that 56.8 per cent of all deaths in a year occurred in the harsh six-month period between 1 October and 31 March.
11. Revd John Corley, Toomore, County Mayo, Part II, pp. 156–7.
12. There are 100 cases in all. Sixteen reports did not include numerical information on mortality, and we were unable to estimate local Catholic populations in another 29 cases.
13. Revd J. O'Meara, Aglish and Whitechurch, County Waterford, Part II, pp. 243–4.
14. Revd John Halanan, Ballinhassig, County Cork, Part II, pp. 196–8.
15. Revd John Ryan, Knockany, County Limerick, Part II, pp. 215–6. A small number of burial registers give the ages of the deceased and even the cause of death now and then. It is evident that children are being omitted when, despite high infant and child mortality, no young ages are being recorded.

Some priests provided rough estimates of child deaths. Revd John Long in Moyvane, County Kerry, stated that the 180 deaths he reported was 'exclusive of children', but added that their number 'could not be less than 40'. In this he was probably right in view of the high incidence of infant and child mortality in this period. He goes on: 'I mean by adults all those who receive the rites of the church in the last sickness'.[16] By contrast, only a handful of priests specified that their mortality counts included children. The return from Revd John Ford of Kilbeacanty, County Galway, included '170 persons, men, women and children', while Revd Michael Gill's return for Kilmaine, County Mayo, included the names of all deaths in his parish, including those of children.[17] But the great majority of clergymen were silent on the matter. Helpfully, a small number of surviving parish registers gives the age of the deceased and typically younger ages are absent from the record, which serves to confirm the point. Of relevance to historians of childhood, the routine exclusion of children from burial registers may also suggest different attitudes in the past to child death and to the rituals surrounding children's interment.[18]

Other factors were at play. Priests charged fees for burial services, so the very poor might well dispense with their services by dint of necessity or even indifference. These deceased would not, therefore, enter the written record. A further, more speculative thought is that the priest-respondent may have been reporting on a part of rather than the whole parish, particularly where two historically distinct territories had been united to form a single parish.[19] Where two clergymen, typically a parish priest and a curate, serviced a parish, there may have been a spatial division of labour.

Thus, we have three potential reasons for the low numbers of burials relative to population in normal times. These are the exclusion of children from clerical records, the exclusion of the poor (or at least some of the poor), and the use of sub-units of parishes in making returns. The quantitative importance of excluding children from the burial count may be gauged, at least in a rough way, from later age-specific mortality figures. Broadly reliable details of age at death did not become available for Ireland until after the Public Health (Ireland) Acts of 1878–9. Of the more than half-million deaths in the period 1880–85, children under the age of 15 accounted for almost 30 per cent. If anything, the proportion may have been slightly higher in the 1840s.[20] Even making allowance for under-recording of the order of 30 per cent, this would still not bring

16. Revd John Long, Moyvane, County Kerry, Part II, pp. 210–11.
17. Revd Michael Gill, Kilmaine, County Mayo, Part II, pp. 147–53.
18. On the treatment of unbaptised babies, often still-births or infant deaths, see Liam Kennedy, 'Afterlives: Testimonies of Irish Catholic Mothers on Infant Death and the Fate of the Unbaptised', *Journal of Family History*, 46, no. 2 (2021): 236–55.
19. In the report on Borrisoleigh, County Tipperary, which united two ecclesiastical territories, and which had two priests and two churches, it seems clear that the Death Census does not refer to the Ileigh portion of the parish. This conclusion draws also on the local knowledge of one of the authors.
20. A total of 555,535 deaths were reported for the six-year period from 1880–85, with 157,620 recorded as under 15 years of age. *Seventeenth Detailed Annual Report of the Registrar-General of Marriages, Births, and Deaths in Ireland, 1880*, London: HMSO, 1881, 94–95; *Eighteenth Detailed*

many of the parish death rates within the expected range. It follows that the exclusion of some of the poor was also part of the story and this proportion is likely to have been higher outside of relatively normal times.[21]

Thus far we have been talking about normal or pre-Famine times, though of course 'normal' in the context of a largely agrarian society is a debatable notion. We may now look more closely at the second time frame used in the Death Census, the half-year of 1 October 1846 to 1 April 1847 when famine conditions were biting deeply. If the reasons for the under-recording of burials remained much the same across time, then we have grounds for comparing the pre-Famine and Famine periods. So it would seem. However, the comparisons (not shown) are worrying. In the more extreme cases we found a ten-fold increase in mortality, and sometimes more. This is simply beyond the bounds of credibility. Moreover, if viewed geographically, the outcomes do not make sense in terms of known regional differences in famine conditions.

It might seem from a close examination of deaths within the two time frames that there are good grounds for dismissing the quantitative information in the Death Census and concluding that the priest-respondents were hopelessly unreliable, as indeed some critics had alleged (see Chapter Five). Pray, let us not rush to judgement in doubting our clergymen witnesses. There is a strong possibility that most respondents to the Death Census were giving figures for pre-Famine mortality based on under-recorded burials (as just discussed) *and* they were then giving more comprehensive accounts of mortality for the later period (as requested by the Repeal Association). In that case, one would not expect the two mortality estimates to bear much relation to each other. In other words, we may not be comparing like with like. Our view is that we can discard the pre-Famine mortality counts for most parishes for one or more of the three reasons outlined earlier but that the estimates of Famine mortality may possibly approximate the terrible reality in the localities. Detailed local studies will do much to tease out these and related matters, bearing in mind also the disruptions accompanying dearth and disease. People were on the move, the proportions impoverished were rising, and funeral arrangements were often improvised in the worst affected areas.

Parish Burial Registers

We can get a firmer handle on the relationship between normal and famine-time mortality – something that is not possible from the Death Census – by examining the small number of Catholic parish burial records that are extant. In effect, we can look

---

Annual Report of the Registrar-General of Marriages, Births, and Deaths in Ireland, 1881, London: HMSO, 1882, 102–3; *Nineteenth Detailed Annual Report of the Registrar-General of Marriages, Births, and Deaths in Ireland, 1882*, London: HMSO 1883, 98–99; *Twentieth Detailed Annual Report of the Registrar-General of Marriages, Births, and Deaths in Ireland, 1883*, London: HMSO, 1884), 88–89; *Twenty-first Detailed Annual Report of the Registrar-General of Marriages, Births, and Deaths in Ireland, 1884*, London: HMSO 1885, 90–91; *Twenty-Second Detailed Annual Report of the Registrar-General of Marriages, Births, and Deaths in Ireland, 1885*, London: HMSO, 1886, 110–11.

21. Relations between priests and laity are discussed in more detail in Chapter Six.

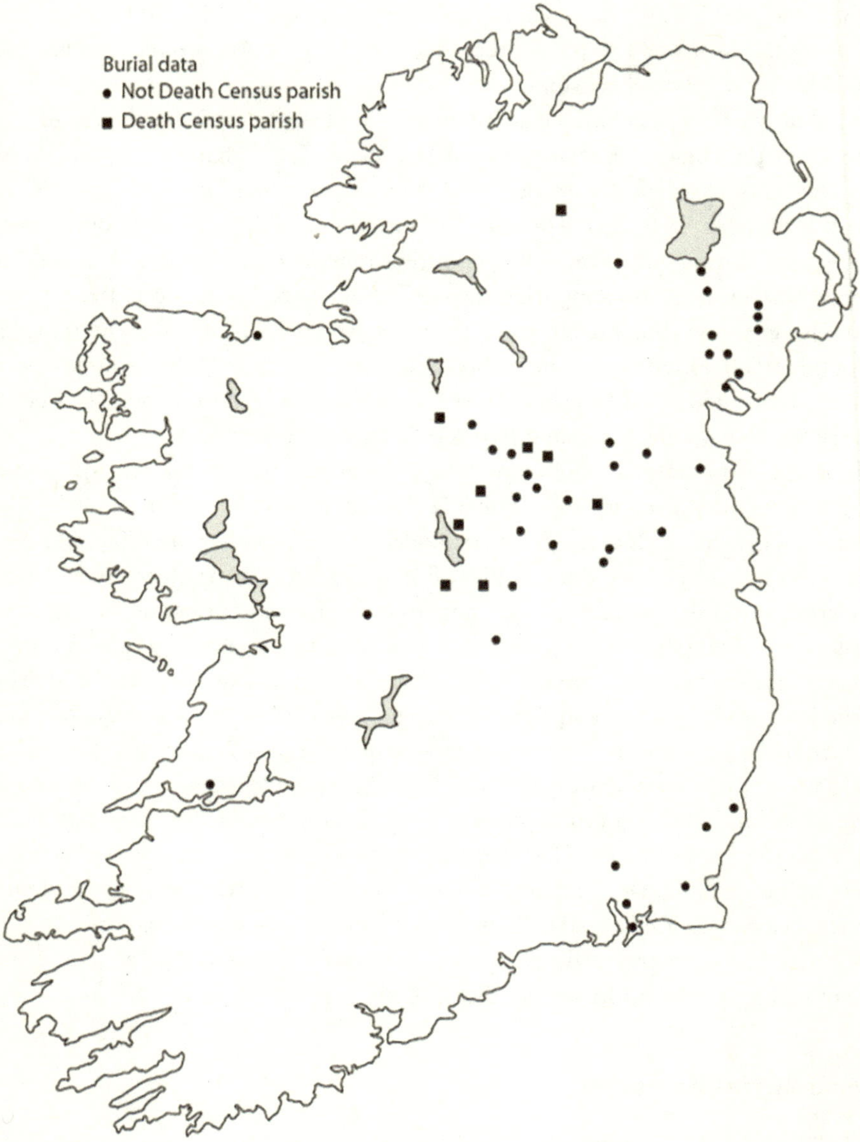

Map 4.1 Spatial distribution of burial registers from 47 Catholic parishes

Source: National Library of Ireland: Online Catholic Parish Registers (https://registers.nli.ie/).

over the priest's shoulder and observe what he actually recorded, focusing our attention on the two critical time intervals specified in the Death Census. Our dataset consists of 47 parish burial registers whose geographical distribution is shown in Map 4.1. These, we believe, constitute most of the surviving and well-kept burial registers for the Famine years. Fortuitously, nine of these cover parishes that submitted reports to the Death Census, so we can do some further checks on the reports for those parishes. The qualifications we entered earlier as to the limitations of burial registers apply here as well, though it might be supposed that a priest noting burials week in and week out would be inclined to stick to much the same pattern of inclusions and exclusions. If so, this would make pre-Famine and Famine entries more directly comparable, though we would still expect some distortion in the relationship between the two because more burials without the offices of a priest are likely in times of dearth.

The sample of 47 parishes (Table 4.1) using actual burial records from parish registers reveals a less dramatic but more plausible picture of the Famine's impact than that which can be derived from the Death Census. All parishes, without exception, show some degree of excess mortality during the six-month Famine period, ranging from minor increases in Mohill and Kilglass in east Connacht to an apparently fivefold increase in Mullagh

Table 4.1 Number of burials for the period 1 October 1845–31 March 1846 compared with those for the period 1 October–31 March 1847, as recorded in parish registers

Parish	County	Pre-Famine	Famine	Ratio
Mohill	Leitrim	58	74	1.3
Kilglass	Sligo	17	24	1.4
St James and Templetown	Wexford	29	42	1.4
Mullingar	Westmeath	78	119	1.5
Killeen	Meath	15	23	1.5
Templemichael and Ballymacormick	Longford	32	50	1.6
Killeeshil	Tyrone	19	30	1.6
Granard	Longford	32	52	1.6
St James and Hook	Wexford	52	90	1.7
Glinn	Wexford	27	48	1.8
Milltown	Westmeath	24	44	1.8
Drumgooland Lower	Down	24	45	1.9
Kilbroney	Down	17	32	1.9
Cappagh	Tyrone	30	57	1.9
Dromara	Down	15	30	2.0
Kiltoghart	Leitrim	16	32	2.0
Aghaderg	Down	18	37	2.1
Collinstown	Westmeath	31	64	2.1
Clonmellon	Westmeath	33	70	2.1
St Peters, Athlone	Roscommon	33	75	2.3
Balliver	Meath	11	25	2.3
Monasterboice	Louth	10	23	2.3
Cappataggle	Galway	12	28	2.3
New Ross	Wexford	116	272	2.3
Colmcille	Longford	17	40	2.4
Monageer	Wexford	11	26	2.4

(*Continued*)

Table 4.1 *(Continued)*

Parish	County	Pre-Famine	Famine	Ratio
Ballygarrett	Wexford	30	71	2.4
Carlingford	Louth	23	56	2.4
Moate	Westmeath	28	71	2.5
Tullylish	Down	29	74	2.6
Drumgooland Upper	Down	10	26	2.6
Carnaross	Meath	16	42	2.6
Clara and Horseleap	King's Co.	22	58	2.6
Mostrim	Longford	17	45	2.6
Drumlish	Longford	21	56	2.7
Drumgath	Down	13	35	2.7
Killine	Meath	13	35	2.7
Balliboy and Killoughy	King's Co.	33	89	2.7
Kilmurray McMahon	Clare	27	79	2.9
Scrabby	Longford	18	54	3.0
Seagoe	Armagh	21	70	3.3
Streete	Westmeath	14	48	3.4
Drumlumman South	Cavan	19	76	4.0
Newry	Down	61	252	4.1
Cashel	Longford	22	118	5.4
Nobber	Meath	13	71	5.5
Mullagh	Cavan	11	66	6

Source: National Library of Ireland: online Catholic parish registers (https://registers.nli.ie/.)

in County Cavan. Between the two extremes, mortality was typically between two and three times the normal level, more or less in line with what we might expect. For the 47 parishes, the median ratio of Famine to pre-Famine mortality was 2.3, while the mean of these ratios was marginally higher at 2.5. By contrast, we find a much higher ratio, in excess of 4 to 1, for the aggregate of the 78 parishes in the Death Census for which we can make a direct comparison.[22]

It may be helpful to place the findings in Table 4.1 in a comparative context. One of the most detailed explorations of local famines is that by Alfani, Mocarelli and Strangio, published in 2017.[23] The authors examined crisis-level rises in burials in more than

22. Adding together all deaths for 78 Death-Census parishes in the pre-crisis period (1 October 1845 to 1 April 1846) we come to a total of 3,740 recorded burials. For the crisis period (1 October 1846 to 1 April 1847) the total comes to 15,598. The ratio between the two is 4.2, which is clearly too high as some of the parishes were located in the less-badly affected eastern parts of Ireland.
23. Guido Alfani, Luca Mocarelli and Donatella Strangio, 'Italy' in Guido Alfani and Cormac Ó Gráda, eds., *Famine in European History*, Cambridge: Cambridge University Press, 2017, 29–31.

200 communes in central-northern Italy over two and a half centuries (1569–1801). The typology used to organise their findings was based on quite stringent rules. In periods when mortality was 50 per cent above normal, they define these as 'small crises'. When mortality was two to three times above normal mortality, they deem these to be 'medium-sized crises'. Beyond that, crises are held to be 'severe'. In the light of these criteria, famine in most of the parishes in Table 4.1 would be characterised as medium-sized crises, though we suspect a degree of underestimation in some instances. Some overestimation is likely in the case of urban parishes containing workhouses such as Newry or Cashel. In the Italian localities most were categorised as small or medium-sized crises, and few qualified for severe status.

Suffering Exaggerated?

As mentioned earlier, we have the original burial records for nine parishes (within the sample of 47) which also happened to supply reports to the Death Census. Six of these are usable in terms of making direct comparisons (others are unsuitable by virtue of having a workhouse in the parish). Using these six matched cases we can check the extent to which the priest-respondent drew on his own burial register in completing his return for the Death Census. The results are shown in Table 4.2. The burial figures for half the parishes, that is the first three in the table, are similar. In two of these cases they are identical. This is reassuring. But it looks as if the method of compilation of burials must have varied as between the two sources for the other three parishes. Why this might be so we do not know, though there may be some clues in our earlier discussion of problems with recording and parish boundaries. This leads us to an important and not very obvious point. Using the widely used ratio between pre-Famine and Famine deaths as a measure of crisis *impact*, shown in Table 4.3, the difference in results between the two sources turns out to be minor in most cases. Thus, for Drumlumman South in County Cavan for example, the two approaches give identical outcomes: Famine mortality was four times the pre-Famine level. Even in the case of Colmcille East and Scrabby, on the Cavan-Longford border, where the counts of burials are very different, the measures of Famine impact turn out to be fairly close, and in fact the Death Census

Table 4.2 Comparing deaths *reported* in the Death Census (DC) against burials *recorded* in the parish registers

	Pre-Famine Register	**Pre-Famine DC**	**Famine Register**	**Famine DC**
Drumlumman South	19	19	76	76
Moate	28	28	71	71
Cashel	22	22	118	125
Clonmellon	33	43	70	102
Templemichael and Ballymacormick	32	40	50	85
Colmcille East and Scrabby	18	56	52	117

Source: Death Census and National Library of Ireland: online Catholic parish registers.

Table 4.3 Impact measure: ratio of Famine deaths to Pre-Famine deaths

	Burial Registers	**Death Census**
Drumlumman South	4.0	4.0
Moate	2.5	2.5
Cashel	5.4	5.7
Clonmellon	2.1	2.4
Templemichael and Ballymacormick	1.6	2.1
Colmcille East and Scrabby	2.9	2.1

Source: Death Census and National Library of Ireland: online Catholic parish registers.

approach points to a lower Famine impact. There is thus little to suggest systematic exaggeration of the Famine impact in Death Census reports, at least for the small number of parishes we can test closely.

There was a legitimate concern at the time, one that historians might also harbour, that the priests exaggerated their body counts for the Famine to make a political point about the inadequacy of government relief, or to impress upon Westminster the need for more support. Many of the reports do indeed have a strong political flavour. But this subsample of parishes from the Death Census suggests that, as far as the quantitative dimensions to the Famine go, exaggeration is not evident. The indications from our external check using the priests' own parish registers is that they consulted their registers and reported accordingly. That said, the subsample is small and it would be unwise to generalise this finding to all of the 94 other Death Census respondents and their parishes in the absence of further testing by means of intensive local studies.[24]

Conclusion

The role of priest is not that of a professional enumerator. A naïve use of the quantitative information contained in the Death Census, such as a direct comparison of pre-Famine and Famine deaths, would lead to seriously misleading results. This is not to say that the data should be discarded, rather it is to recognise that in many cases the construction of the two estimates proceeded on quite different bases. This realisation caused us to examine critically the recording practices in Catholic burial records. This proved rewarding and there may be wider implications for the study of the Irish Catholic worldview. The different religious rites and ceremonies varied in importance: the sacrament of baptism was an almost universal practice within Irish Catholic communities whereas funeral rites were desirable (where affordable), but not critical to salvation.[25] In other words, burial records offer a less comprehensive coverage than, say, baptism records. The apparent insouciance, if it is that, with which child burials were treated may also suggest something of attitudes to child death before the mid-nineteenth century.

24. The methodological approaches deployed in this chapter might offer some guidance to local historians contemplating deeper studies of the Death Census in their particular locality.
25. On Catholic religious practices for the period see S. J. Connolly, *Priests and People.*

Our interest here, however, has been the omissions from and the deficiencies in burial registers and the implications for demographic analysis. Within these limitations, it may be said that the record of pre-Famine deaths found in the Death Census is not as far off the mark as might at first appear, once the three potential weaknesses identified earlier are taken into account. The record of Famine deaths seems to be a more comprehensive measure of death and burial and we have some grounds for cautious optimism regarding the reliability of the estimates from the test applied in Table 4.3. Nonetheless, we would repeat the warning that generalising from the experience of a handful of parishes is fraught with uncertainty. That said, it is worth underlining the fact that the findings from all six parishes point in the same direction.

In addition to interrogating the reports of the Death Census itself, we have also examined the actual burial registers compiled by parish clergy. The sample of 47 parishes reveals widespread and severe excess mortality across Ireland. Indeed, there is almost certainly an element of underestimation of the Famine impact, partly because of the pressure on clergymen during the crisis leading to under-recording but also because of the rising proportions of destitute within Irish society who could not afford burial fees. Some corpses were buried without charge, it is true, but the small number of surviving burial registers that give information on fees do not suggest that this was common practice.[26]

Much that we need to know can only be established by detailed local historical endeavour, drawing not only on parish registers but on local newspaper reports, graveyard inscriptions, oral history and other sources. The Death Census supplies an impetus to that work but the testimonies of the clergymen cry out to be supplemented by other sources. Fuller understandings of the Famine experience in the localities and its manifold faces are dependent on the knowledge and expertise of local historians. In a sense, they follow in the footsteps of the priest-scribes who were writing at the time about their own congregations and to whom we are indebted for their pioneering reports of death, destitution and the extremes of human misery.

26. See, for example, burial records for New Ross and St James and Templetown, County Wexford, Drumgooland Upper, Drumgath and Seapatrick, County Down, Cashel and Clongish, County Longford and Moate, County Weatmeath (National Library of Ireland: Catholic Parish Registers).

Chapter Five

EYEWITNESS ACCOUNTS OF BLACK '47

Introduction

The year 1847 has gone down in history and memory as Black '47.[1] It was the second year of the Great Famine. Hunger, destitution and death were everyday occurrences. Among those best placed to convey a picture of the unfolding tragedy were the priests of the Catholic Church who ministered to three-quarters of the population. Living among people, many of whom were illiterate, particularly so in the Gaelic-speaking areas west of the Shannon and in south Munster, they were articulate witnesses for their people.[2] They saw the Famine at its worst and some of them died in the course of their duties, mainly from epidemic fevers. This was true also of clergymen of other denominations, medical doctors and poor-law administrators, whose professions brought them in close contact with the disease-infected victims of hunger.[3] We have seen in the last chapter that the Death Census was fundamentally a statistical survey, though one that needs to be handled with care. Its proponents wanted to quantify the effects of famine on mortality across Ireland by comparing the number of deaths between October 1846 and April 1847 against the same period a year earlier. However, in addition to providing this information most of the respondents included vivid testimony, often running into many hundreds of words on conditions in each of their parishes. They wrote about hunger, disease, swollen stomachs, insanity, emigration, death; a few even included lists of the names of the dead. Some spoke critically of political economy, proselytism, outrages, inadequate soup rations, tight-fisted rate payers, and of course of landlords, particularly if absentee. Some wrote haunting individual stories of the suffering they had witnessed, of parishioners unburied by the roadside, of workers collapsing on the public works, of families dying in the filth and cold of their cabins. They might also acknowledge acts of

1. Neil Buttimer, 'The Great Famine in Gaelic Manuscripts' in John Crowley, William J. Smyth, Mike Murphy, eds., *Atlas of the Great Irish Famine*, Cork: Cork University Press, 2012, 460–72. The term *an drochshaol* (the bad life or bad times) was commonly used in Gaelic-speaking areas to describe famine times.
2. The counties of Sligo, Mayo and Galway in Connacht, and of Kerry in Munster, all had illiteracy rates in excess of 60 per cent in 1841. Female illiteracy levels were higher still. The barony of Ross in County Galway reported the highest illiteracy rate in Ireland in 1841, a figure of 87 per cent for its inhabitants. See Liam Kennedy et al., *Mapping the Great Irish Famine*, Dublin: Four Courts Press, 1999, 94–95.
3. D. A. Kerr, *'A Nation of Beggars'? Priests, People and Politics in Famine Ireland, 1846–1852*, Oxford: Oxford University Press, 1994; Peter Froggatt, 'The Response of the Medical Profession to the Great Famine' in *Famine: Irish Experience*, ed. E. Margaret Crawford, 134–56.

charity and benevolence, and profess loyalty to their 'gracious Queen'. The panacea of repeal of the Union found frequent expression, as well as words of heartfelt devotion to the 'Liberator', Daniel O'Connell. Politics aside, these eyewitness accounts offer unique, personal, and frequently harrowing insights into the ravages of the Great Famine at one of its worst stages. These are the human stories that are often lost in the administrative and political records that underpin much of the historiography.

The subject of this chapter is what was seen through the eyes of these priests as reflected in the reports they submitted to the Repeal Association. They had much to say on a whole range of topics that also resonate with accounts of famine in societies other than Ireland. The chapter concludes with a discussion of the reception of the Death Census in the printed media and, more importantly, at the seat of power in Westminster. Can we, in the end, say that the Death Census made a difference?

Eyewitness Accounts

By the time the priests wrote their accounts for the Death Census in April and May of 1847, it was clear that the prevailing crisis was not a subsistence crisis of the kind that periodically visited Irish society. The second and almost complete failure of the potato crop threatened an unprecedented famine, the effects of which were already being felt. Hunger and disease had been ravaging much of the south and west of the Ireland since mid-1846, and mortality in many parishes subsequently surged as earlier chapters have demonstrated. By February 1847 the workhouses, erected under the Irish Poor Law Act of 1838, were recording upwards of 2,000 deaths per week, a roughly fivefold increase on the previous year (Figure 5.1). These are astonishing levels of mortality in institutions established to provide succour and to save lives. Many people who entered the workhouse were in a desperate physical condition, having endured many months of hunger and illness. 'Many from this parish', wrote the priest of St. Mary's in Athlone, County Westmeath, in his Death Census return 'when in the lowest state of exhaustion from famine and disease, were admitted [to the workhouse] and died there in a few days.'[4]

The famine, of course, did not affect all parishes equally, and it is interesting to note that even at this time of national crisis some of the priests reported that the famine had not materially affected their locality. Thus, Revd Patrick Nowlan of Stamullen parish, County Meath, situated some 22 miles north of Dublin city, wrote: 'Not a single individual has suffered in this union from famine'.[5] Similarly, at Faughanvale, County Londonderry, the priest reported that the 'total number of deaths [is] not known, but they are not more than other years. No deaths by famine'.[6] The priest at Rossglass, in east County Down, was able to report the same, stating that 'neither the famine nor disease has occasioned any remarkable increase of mortality in this parish'.[7] Such positive commentaries were, however, the exception, and they are all exclusively

4. Revd K. Kilroe, St Mary's parish, County Westmeath, Part II, pp. 292–4.
5. Revd Patrick Nowlan, Stamullen parish, County Meath, Part II, pp. 284–5.
6. Revd Michael Hughes, Faughanvale parish, County Londonderry, Part II, pp. 265–6.
7. Revd John McKenna, Rossglass Parish, County Down, Part II, p. 260.

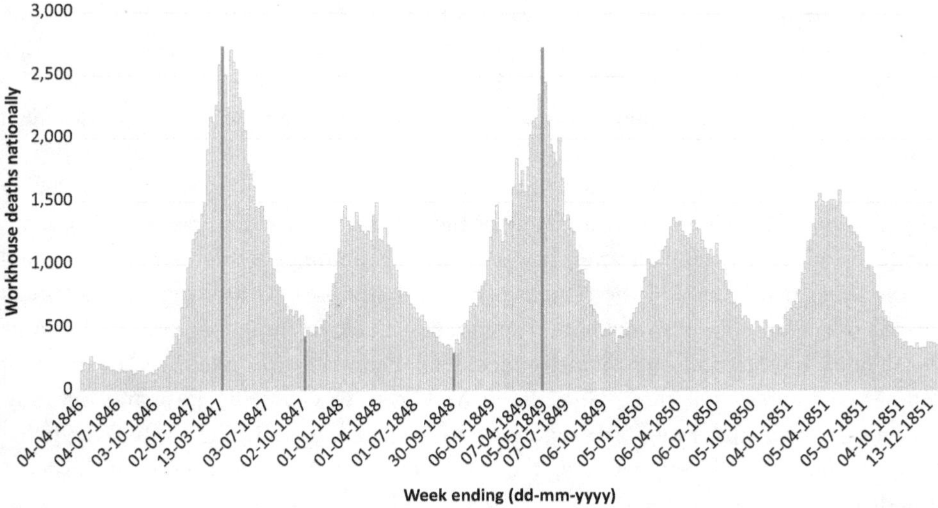

Figure 5.1 Workhouse deaths recorded nationally, per week, 4 April 1846–27 December 1851

Source: *Thirteenth annual report of Poor Law Commissioners, with appendices*, BPP, Command Papers (1847), 816, vol. 28, xxviii.1, 26; *First annual report of the Commissioners for administering the laws for relief of the poor in Ireland, with appendices,* BPP, Command Papers (1847–48), 963, vol. 33, xxxiii.377, 16; *Second annual report of the Commissioners for administering the laws for relief of the poor in Ireland,* BPP, Command Papers (1849), 1118, vol. 25, xxv.87, 2; *Third annual report of the Commissioners for administering the laws for relief of the poor in Ireland,* BPP, Command Papers, (1850), 1243, vol. 27, xxvii.449, 2; *Fourth annual report of the Commissioners for administering the laws for relief of the poor in Ireland,* BPP, Command Papers (1851), 1381, vol. 26, xxvi.547, 2; *Fifth annual report of the Commissioners for administering the laws for relief of the poor in Ireland,* BPP, Command Papers (1852), 1530, vol. 23, xxiii.155, 2.

from parishes located in the north and east of Ireland which, on the whole, avoided the worst of famine. The vast majority of parishes responding to the Death Census were situated in the south and west, and they paint a very different picture. 'The most heart-rending scene imaginable occurred here last week', wrote Revd Michael Gill of Kilmain, County Galway, who recounted finding a woman dead by the roadside, 'her child, aged, I should think, about seven years, lying asleep over the corpse of her poor mother!'[8] Many other priests commented on a blasted landscape, finding people dead along the roads or abandoned beside bushes and ditches.[9] Elsewhere, Revd Cleary, of Lorrha and Dorrha, County Tipperary, recounted a recent exchange between himself and a young boy in his townland. Attending at a house having heard of a man being seriously ill, he asked the young boy who answered the door where his father was. 'He is sick, sir', the boy replied. 'Where is your mother?', Cleary inquired. 'She is sick,

8. Revd Michael Gill, Kilmaine parish, County Mayo, Part II, pp. 147–53.
9. See, for example, returns for Revd James McKernan of Cloone-Conmaicne, County Leitrim, Part II, p. 127. Revd D. O'Kane of Carracastle, County Mayo, Part II, pp. 140–1. Revd Michael O'Flynn of Attymass, County Mayo, Part II, pp. 137–9. Revd John Sheehan of Ennistymon, County Clare, Part II, pp. 180–7. Revd K. Kilroe of St Mary's, Athlone, County Westmeath, Part II, p. 293. Revd John Halanan of Ballinhassig, County Cork, Part II, pp. 196–8.

sir', was the boy's response. 'Where are your brothers?' 'They are all dead, and one is dead in the corner', came the boy's melancholy reply. 'This unhappy family', the return continued, 'consisted of seven on last week; now they are only three'.[10]

The prevalence of sickness and disease is evident in many of the accounts. Revd Thomas M'Inerney, of Feakle parish County Clare, recorded an additional 400 deaths in his parish between October 1846 and April 1847 compared to the same period during the previous year. He noted that 'Many of those persons have died of fever, dysentery, and dropsy, which diseases are yet very general'.[11] Testimonies of this kind are replicated many times over. Some of the returns offer local glimpses of the social-psychological effects of epidemic fever. Neighbours, normally sociable in rural communities, became wary of each other and kept their distance. Understandably, people feared contracting highly contagious maladies. Thus, Revd McGavar of Colmcille East and Scrabby, counties Cavan and Longford, reported cases of people suffering from fever being given 'drink off a shovel, reached into their huts, lest the person who administered the drink should inhale the contagion'.[12] Revd O'Gorman of Clareabbey and Killone, County Clare, recalled that one family of eight, all suffering from sickness and lying on damp straw, had 'little communication with neighbours, who apprehended contagion'.[13] In effect, they were abandoned to face death alone. Such descriptions evoke images of the great plagues, when victims were confined to their homes awaiting certain death.

The extent of descriptive information contained in the Death Census returns varied, but most of the priests provided commentary on three issues which command attention: first, the deficiencies in and the inadequacy of state relief measures; secondly, the amount of land that had been tilled; and thirdly, the extent of emigration from their parishes. These issues are good indicators of not only the consequences of the famine up to that time, but also of how ill-prepared communities were to deal with the crisis during the months that lay ahead. Most of the returns convey not only a grim picture of suffering at the time but also a foreboding sense of worse to come.

The timing of the Death Census is important here. The census occurred just as the public works schemes, which had provided employment to over 700,000 people as late as March 1847, were being closed.[14] Soup kitchens, which were to provide a free meal each day, were to be opened in their place under the Temporary Relief Act. Unfortunately, the transition from the public works regime to the soup kitchens was far from seamless (Table 5.1). Often, the works were closed before the kitchens opened, leaving many people without relief. 'The people are perishing since the public works ceased', stated Revd John Meagher from Toomevara, County Tipperary, who condemned

10. The return for Lorrha and Dorrha was completed by Revd Cornelius O'Brien, who recounted these grim details after being informed of them by his assistant, Revd Cleary. See Part II, pp. 234–6.
11. Revd Thomas M'Inerney, Feakle, County Clare, Part II, pp. 186–7.
12. Revd Thomas McGavar, Columcille East and Scrabby parish, County Longford, Part II, pp. 279–80.
13. Revd. O'Gorman, Clareabbey and Killone parish, County Clare, Part II, pp. 175–8.
14. Kinealy, *A Death Dealing* Famine, 98–106.

Table 5.1 The gap (in weeks) between the official termination of Public Works (1 May 1847) and participation in direct feeding under the Temporary Relief Act, 1847

	Number of Electoral Divisions	1841 Population
Before 1 May	631	2,682,763
On 1 May	73	244,726
<1 week	238	864,849
1–2	284	1,128,229
2–3	157	625,556
3–4	194	928,649
4–5	40	168,412
5–6	79	414,206
6–7	21	94,501
7–8	45	149,010
8–9	7	25,792
9–10	12	46,495
10–11	4	17,560
11–12	5	14,535
13–14	6	17,396
Not Under Act	225	666,164
Unknown	28	95,805
Total	**2,049**	**8,184,648**

Source: *Temporary Relief Commissioners, Seventh Report, supplementary appendix*, London: HMSO, 1848, 22–86.

the 'murdering delay in putting the relief system into operation'.[15] In the parish of Ballymachugh and Drumlumman South, County Longford, the priest reported that 'the public works were closed in the middle of this week. There is little or no employment; no issue of food, cooked or otherwise, from the rates'.[16] At Castlemore and Kilcolman, County Roscommon, soup kitchens had yet to be established, and the priest feared that 'hundreds – I may say thousands – of the people will starve!'[17] So too at Ardfert and Kilmoyley parish, County Kerry, where the priest stated that 'half the poor of my parish will not survive the present year, as there are only a few now employed on the public works, and no outdoor relief is given at present'.[18]

15. Revd. J. Meagher, Toomevara, County Tipperary, Part II, pp. 242–3. To make matters worse, large-scale evictions followed. See Helen O'Brien, *The Famine Clearance in Toomevara, County Tipperary* (Dublin, 2010).
16. Revd. P. Murray, Ballymachugh and Drumlumman South parish, County Cavan, Part II, pp. 252–4.
17. Revd Denis Tighe, Kilcolman and Castlemore, County Roscommon, Part II, pp. 158–60.
18. Revd Jeremiah O'Sullivan, Ardfert and Kilmoyly parish, County Kerry, Part II, pp. 202–4.

Conditions in these parishes must have been appalling during the transition period, but they were far from unique. Several of the priests wrote of starving parishioners resorting to the most desperate measures imaginable, attempting to survive on nettles, watercress, and seaweed. As we know from famines elsewhere, a resort to inferior and sometimes harmful foods is a common response to prolonged hunger and can serve to produce further death.[19]

According to Table 5.1, 631 electoral divisions, containing 2.7 million people in 1841 or almost exactly one-third of the population, had come under the Act before 1 May 1847. Another 73 electoral divisions came under the Act on 1 May. We cannot assume that public feeding had begun by that date for these electoral divisions as the necessary infrastructure and compliance with the conditions set out in the Act may not have been put into effect by then. Reading down through Table 5.1, these are the earliest points in time from the 1 May, the date at which state-funded soup kitchens could have been opened in these various localities. As we know, there were many complaints in the Death Census, and elsewhere, of slowness in opening these feeding stations and the lethal consequences of any time gaps between the phasing out of public works schemes and the switch to direct feeding of the poor. The minority phenomenon of 225 electoral divisions, most of them in Ulster, not coming in under the Act (N.U.A.), is noteworthy. Even where the Temporary Relief Act and its direct provision of food had been implemented locally, priests were often critical of the adequacy of the sustenance. The new system of relief was in operation in Castletownroche, County Cork, where:

> Rations of meal are given out every day, but these are not sufficient to support life [for] long. There is no allowance made for cooking. The people would rather work; they say they have pains in their bones from being idle. All the [Public] Works here, with a single exception, were discontinued, leaving the poor people in a very miserable state.[20]

In the parishes of Aglish and Whitechurch, in west County Waterford, the rations from the soup kitchen were described as 'too scanty, and are sufficient only to prolong life', while at Desertmartin and Kilcronaghan, County Londonderry, the priest described the food rations as 'very unwholesome' and complained that some parishioners had to walk up to seven miles to receive this 'sham relief'.[21] Circumstances in Kilbeacanty, County Galway, were 'deplorable' according to Revd John Ford, who noted that, in a parish which 'contains very near 700 houses, poor and very poor', 'during the last fortnight there were 2,889 persons served with a pound of Indian meal, merely to keep the life in them'.[22] Seven hundred houses would correspond to about 3,500 people.

19. Stephen Devereux, *Theories of Famine* (Hemel Hempstead, 1993).
20. Revd James Fitzpatrick, Castletownroche parish, County Cork, Part II, pp. 199–202.
21. Revd J. O'Meara, Aglish and Whitechurch parishes, County Waterford, Part II, p. 244. Revd James Collins, Desertmartin and Kilcronaghan parishes, County Londonderry, Part II, p. 265.
22. Revd John Ford, Kilbeacanty, County Galway, Part II, pp. 111–12.

This suggests four out of every five of Ford's parishioners required urgent aid.[23] Conditions were no better in neighbouring Beagh parish, where Revd O'Shaughnessy observed that 'there was little or no food, and, if possible, worse clothing. The present state of the parish is very bad; no arrangements unless giving out Indian meal very scantily'.[24] Cheap Indian meal became a substitute, staple foodstuff in Ireland during the Famine but the change to an unfamiliar diet, if not thoroughly cooked (and this in turn depended on an adequate supply of peat), gave rise to stomach pains and in some instances aggravated vulnerability to disease and death. In nutritional terms its quality was not comparable to that of potatoes.

It is true that Indian meal was not wholly new to Ireland. It had been imported to some port towns during the near-famine of 1800–1 but was not generally known in Ireland.[25] Revd Patrick Mullins of Killeely, County Galway, noted that 'many who were in comfortable circumstances were carried off by diseases occasioned by the sudden transition to a meal diet, which in great measure explains the vast disproportion between the mortality of the latter [75 deaths] and the corresponding previous period [5 deaths]'.[26] Revd Patrick Nowlan of Stamullen, County Meath, reported similar problems, observing that 'the deaths from Oct., 1845 [*sic.* should be 1846], to 1st April, 1847, have been somewhat more than for the same period of the previous year among the aged and the very young children, arising, in my opinion, from the change of diet – from the substitution of Indian meal, imperfectly cooked, for the potato and the oatmeal stirabout'.[27] We notice that the very old and the very young were being disproportionately affected, again a feature of other famines, though the twist here seems to be not the lack of food as much as the switch to an unfamiliar diet.

Few of the priests expressed any hope that the availability of food would improve during the year ahead, for circumstances dictated that much of the land at this time remained untilled. John O'Connell, we may recall, had proposed to parliament in March 1847 a government-funded scheme of land cultivation in Ireland, though his proposal was short on detail. However, the adherence of the Whigs to fiscal rectitude and the principles of *laissez faire* meant they refused to interfere actively in the rural economy.[28] The Death Census sheds light on the consequences. 'The general prospects for the coming year are of a very gloomy character', wrote Revd Patrick MacLoghlan of Ballynakill, County Galway, 'in consequence of a great space of the land being left

23. *Report of the Commissioners appointed to take the Census of Ireland, for the year 1841*, 1843 (504), 24, 378.
24. Revd M. O'Shaughnessy, Beagh parish, County Galway, Part II, p. 110.
25. Liam Kennedy and Peter M. Solar, 'The Famine That Wasn't: 1799–1801 in Ireland', QUCEH Working Paper, no. 19–06, October 2019, Queen's University Belfast, 1–33.
26. Revd P. Mullins, Killeely union, County Galway, Part II, pp. 113–14. For reasons explained elsewhere, the ratio between first period and second period deaths should not be taken literally.
27. Revd Patrick Nowlan, Stamullen Parish, County Meath, Part II, pp. 284–5.
28. Gray, *Famine, Land and Politics*, passim.

untilled for the want of food, and of the means to procure it'.[29] In Kilmeen, County Cork, the priest stated that 'not one fourth of the land as compared with former years [is] cultivated – the prospects for the ensuing year cheerless in the extreme'.[30] The inability of the poor to obtain seed was one problem. Another was that the customary bonds linking farmers and labourers – bartering labour for access to potato-growing land – were breaking down. In addition, the gnawing hunger meant some people were eating the seed potatoes rather than sowing them. 'The land is tolerably well tilled (with the exception of what is held by the one or two-acre tenants, who had no seed to sow [...])' wrote Revd Timothy Newell of Oranmore and Ballynacourty, County Galway, 'but', he continued, 'I am sorry to say that the starving poor have in many instances picked up the seed under the pressure of their hunger'.[31] The famishing poor of Kilchrist and Clondagad, County Clare, were doing the same, as Revd Timothy Breen observed:

> In compliance with our earnest exhortations and advice, the poor people tilled almost all the land fitted for wheat, before 1st of January, and as four fifths and more of the soil of the parish is not suited to the production of wheat they were vigorously proceeding with the culture of oats, barley &c., up to the beginning of April, when the vast numbers thrown out of employment by the reduction of the labourers on the [Public] Works entirely paralyzed their energies by throwing them on their own resources. Many were afterwards obliged to consume the seed they had reserved. [...] More than a third of the available soil will remain untilled.[32]

In Breen's parish, the Temporary Relief Act had been operating for about three weeks when he transmitted his return, but he described the support as scanty, and complained that the relief administrators were more concerned about 'fear of increasing taxation' than they were about feeding the people. In this parish there existed 'wretched poverty', and the failure of many small cottiers to cultivate their land held out little prospect of improvement. Such must have been the case across much of Ireland. More than three-quarters of the returns observed that land had been only partially tilled during the first half of what became known as 'Black '47'. The re-orientation of the rural economy away from tillage crops, which was more fully revealed in the post-Famine decades, was underway.

The weight of circumstances encouraged many people to leave the country. Emigration during the Famine accelerated from late 1846, and contributed to the greatest demographic decline in Ireland's history.[33] Between 1846 and 1850 roughly as many people left Ireland as died from famine-related causes. Before the Famine less

29. Revd Patrick MacLoghlan, Ballinakill parish, County Galway, Part II, pp. 108–9.
30. Revd Hartnett, Kilmeen parish, County Cork, Part II, pp. 201–2.
31. Revd Timothy Newell, Oranmore and Ballynacourty parish, County Galway, Part II, p. 120.
32. Revd Timothy Breen, Kilchrist and Clondagad, County Clare, Part II, pp. 189–91.
33. *Famine Demography: Perspectives from Past and Present*, eds T. Dyson and C. Ó Gráda, Oxford: Oxford University Press, 2002.

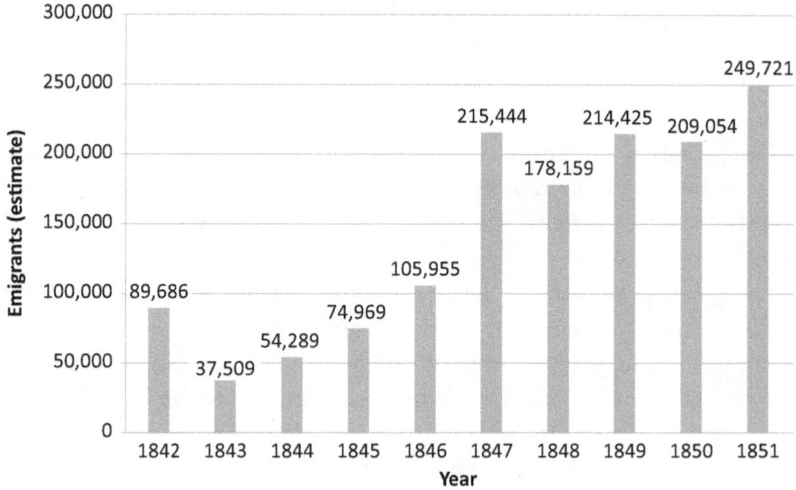

Figure 5.2 Emigration from Ireland, 1842–1851

Source: Vaughan and Fitzpatrick, *Irish Historical Statistics: Population*, 260.

than 100,000 emigrated annually; between 1847 and 1851 the annual outflow was of the order of 200,000 (Figure 5.2). Emigration was a form of famine relief, as has been persuasively argued by Ó Gráda and O'Rourke.[34] Most found their way to North America, but large numbers also settled in Britain.[35] Yet, in the worst hit areas of Ireland those who stayed in the country tended to be from the very class in greatest need of relief, which was the multitudes of cottiers and labourers. As sources of food and income dried up, they found themselves caught in a poverty trap, unable to afford to exit, with the workhouse as the place of last resort. Though transatlantic fares had fallen during the 1840s to a typical steerage fare of £3 to £4 per person, this still meant that those without land, capital or other assets to dispose of were unable to escape to America.[36] The cost of moving a family was a multiple of the individual cost. The cheaper fare to Britain beckoned, favouring also the individual migrant, while family groups multiplied

34. Cormac Ó Gráda and Kevin H. O'Rourke, 'Mass Migration as Disaster Relief: Lessons from the Great Irish Famine', *European Review of Economic History* 1, no. 1 (1997): 3–25. See also David Arnold, *Famine: Social Crisis and Historical Change*, Oxford: Blackwell, York, 1988: 70–72.
35. Lewis Darwen, et al., '"Unhappy and Wretched Creatures"', 589–619; Arthur Gribben ed., *The Great Famine and the Irish Diaspora in America*, London: University of Massachusetts Press, 1999); K. A. Miller, *Emigrants and Exiles: Ireland and the Irish Exodus to North America* New York: Oxford University Press, 1998; Frank Neal, *'Black '47': Britain and the Irish Famine*, Basingstoke: Macmillan, 1997.
36. John Killick, 'Transatlantic Steerage Fares, British and Irish Migration, and Return Migration, 1815–60', *Economic History Review* 67, no. 1 (2014): 170–91. Pre-paid tickets from kinfolk in Canada or the United States could break this deadlock, as was increasingly the case as the stock of relatives in the New World built up.

the cost and hence the barrier to leaving Ireland. Moreover, those who had held on longer into the Famine years, hoping in vain for a return to normal times, might, in a subtle variant of the 'poverty trap', find themselves too debilitated and demoralised to move.

The Death Census captures the scale and social composition of the emigrant streams, as well as the barriers to migration. 'The middling and poorer classes all determined to leave this country – the first all going to America, and the second off to England or some other place', wrote Revd. James Hughes of Kilcolman (Claremorris), County Mayo.[37] 'Emigration has been on a large scale this spring', reported Revd Murray for Ballymachugh and Drumlumman South, in south County Cavan, 'and it would have been greater still if the people had means of going where, as they say, 'they would get plenty to eat and plenty to do, and fair play and liberty into the bargain'.[38] Similarly, from Castlemaine, County Kerry, it was stated that 'the greatest rage prevails to emigrate, but thousands willing have not the means'.[39] In Toomore, County Mayo, there was 'a great many who emigrated to America', and the priest, Revd Corley, thought 'none would remain [in his parish] if they had the means to take them from the wreck of a country'.[40] Thus, while psychological resistance to emigration was being broken, even in Gaelic-speaking areas of the country, nonetheless in many parishes there remained a large pool of destitute people who required support. The return of Revd M'Craith of Ballinahinch and Killoscully, County Tipperary grimly observed that emigrants

> consisted of a class of holders of from five to ten acres or more of land, which they gladly sold to enable them to emigrate. Many others of the same class would follow them if only they could do so; but they cannot sell their small farms and must reluctantly remain. So also must remain a population of at least 2,000 without land! without food! whose whole earthly reliance is on the continuance of work to employ them; or on the provision of the new poor relief bill to feed them.[41]

Killoscully was an impoverished, mountainous district in the west of the county. As elsewhere, the poor faced a poverty trap in terms of emigration and accessing livelihoods abroad.

On the whole, the Death Census paints a picture of abject misery during the first quarter of 1847. Yet, reading the evidence one gets the sense that many of the priests felt something could still be done to save their starving parishioners, if only effective remedial measures were taken. Some of the priests were contemptuous of absentee landlords, who contributed little or nothing to local relief efforts and were beginning to evict tenants from their smallholdings. Revd Tighe of Castlemore and Kilcolman, now in County

37. Revd James Hughes, Kilcolman (Claremorris), County Mayo, Part II, p. 144.
38. Revd P. Murray, Ballymachugh and Drumlumman parish, County Cavan, Part II, pp. 253–4.
39. Revd Thomas Carmody, Castlemaine parish, County Kerry, Part II, pp. 209–10.
40. Revd John Corley, Toomore parish, County Mayo, Part II, p. 158.
41. Revd John M'Craith, Ballinahinch and Killoscully parish, County Tipperary, Part II, pp. 219–20.

Roscommon, then County Mayo, reported that in the week before he completed his return for the Death Census a total of 19 families, consisting of 128 individuals, had been evicted by a landlord resident in Dublin, and their houses had been pulled to the ground; somewhat unusually he provided the names of those evicted who, he stated, were 'still clinging to what they once called their 'happy homes'.[42] In other cases, the priest noted how vital a resident landlord had been to the local population. Patrick MacLoghlan from Ballynakill, County Galway, for example, wrote that the 'present state of the parish would be truly melancholy, were it not that a great portion of those thrown off the Public Works were employed by Sir M. D. Bellew, and he pointed to this instance as being 'illustrative of the beneficial effects of a resident proprietary'.[43]

Other priests made it clear that they held Westminster responsible for the unfolding crisis. 'If the present government does not exert itself better than it has heretofore', wrote Revd Burke of Kilchreest, County Galway, 'I will have to record double the number of deaths [in the next six months]'.[44] Elsewhere, the government's relief policies were variously described as 'murderous', 'heartless' and 'demented'. We can see here the seeds of John Mitchel's contention that the English caused the Famine, as also of other genocidal interpretations of the catastrophe, with priests referencing 'the murderous edict', 'the murdering edict', 'the murderous rule', 'the murderous policy', the 'cruel and murdering delay', and such like. We cannot ignore the deeper political context here. In the early nineteenth century Catholic priests had stood aloof from politics,[45] but Daniel O'Connell's political drives from the 1820s had changed attitudes among the clergy and many of them stood full-square behind the Repeal movement. 'We are a nation of beggars, and will remain so until we have our own Parliament', lamented Revd William Heffernan of Clerihan, County Tipperary.[46] 'Shame on the English government [...] to tolerate such a state of things', observed Revd Patrick Horan of Kildysart, County Clare, who asked rhetorically if 'any one be found so cold-hearted, so anti-Irish, as not to cry out for Repeal?'[47] Some priests expressed hope, in vain as it turned out, for the return to Ireland of a fit and healthy Daniel O'Connell. Revd Quin of Ardrahan, County Galway was 'delighted to find that our beloved Liberator [Daniel O'Connell] is getting better; may the God of Mercy restore him to us, and counsel those who have in a great measure been the means of breaking his heart'.[48] Others, who completed their returns later, mourned the news of the Liberator's death, in some instances with melodramatic expressions of sorrow.

42. Revd Denis Tighe, Castlemore and Kilcolman parish, County Roscommon, Part II, pp. 159–60.
43. Revd Patrick MacLoghlan, Ballynakill parish, County Galway, Part II, pp. 108–9.
44. Revd Michael Burke, Kilchreest parish, County Galway, Part II, pp. 112–13.
45. Thomas Newenham, *Natural, political, and commercial circumstances of Ireland, appendix*, 22–33.
46. Revd William Heffernan, Clerihan parish, County Tipperary, Part II, p. 231.
47. Revd Patrick Horan, Kildysart parish, County Clare, Part II, pp. 192–3.
48. Revd B. Quin, Ardrahan parish, County Galway, Part II, p. 106.

Contemporary Perceptions of the Death Census

The Death Census was created, primarily, to influence government policy at a time when many people in Ireland thought Westminster was failing to recognise the seriousness of the crisis. It was therefore crucial that British politicians and policymakers were made aware of its contents. More than this, the survey needed to convince them to do more for the people by way of relief. There were various channels through which this might have been effected. One was through the press. We already know that the pro-Repeal *Pilot* newspaper reported extensively on the parish returns that make up the Death Census. Had they not done so, the census would no longer survive. Another way the government might have been influenced was by Irish MPs reading out the reports in parliament. However, when John O'Connell brought the idea of the Death Census to the attention of the Repeal Association in April 1847, he had already decided not to return to Westminster during the current session as he was frustrated by government inaction. He did, however, state on more than one occasion that he hoped the publication of the returns in the Dublin newspapers would be enough to attract the attention of Westminster. 'I do hope that the government will at once consider the fearfully important matter to which it [the Death Census] relates', he told the crowd at a Repeal Association meeting at the end of April 1847.[49]

Whether English MPs actually read some of the returns is another matter. They cannot but have been aware that an informal census of mortality had taken place. Officials at Dublin Castle almost certainly relayed information on the survey to Westminster, and copies of the Repeal newspapers which published the returns found their way into the hands of opponents in London. Members of Parliament so inclined would have been able to get hold of copies to read the accounts. But we have no direct evidence to suggest that any did. Indeed, some priests who participated in the Death Census questioned why more effort was not made to ensure that the returns were seen by MPs in London. John O'Connell spoke at length on this matter at a Repeal Association meeting at the beginning of May 1847:

> One of the reverend gentlemen who have sent us these returns has asked – 'Why is there not some Irish member in the House of Commons to make these details public?' [...] I thank the reverend gentleman for his address to me; but I have to assure him that I am endeavouring in every way that lies in my power to call the attention of the three kingdoms, and of the nations of the world, to these frightful details of suffering, privation and death [...] It was for this purpose that I originated an address from the Association to the clergy throughout the country, in order to get from them the veritable details before the world, and call on the world to say whether there was ever such a scene of misery as that which now exists in Ireland, or such criminal apathy in not providing relief, as that which has been displayed by the English government [...] The Committee of the Association have postponed several matters for the purpose of making public this [Death] census. They have postponed addresses and other documents, which were to be read in the Association today, in hopes that the newspapers which are rendering us such valuable services at present would

49. *The Pilot*, 28 April 1847.

> give insertion to those melancholy returns. It is our intention to collect all these returns into a small book – and send the handbook of English crime to every member of parliament and to our friends in America and elsewhere, as an impeachment of the English parliament for the inefficient relief it has afforded to the Irish people.[50]

There must be more than a little suspicion that this fiery rhetoric, which played well with the crowd, concealed a certain defensiveness on O'Connell's part. It may be at this early stage that he planned on publishing the documents in printed form. Circumstances, however, made this difficult. At a Repeal Association meeting a couple of weeks later, O'Connell reiterated his desire to see the returns disseminated to a wider audience but explained that the Association's lack of funds prevented them doing so. Thus, 'The [Repeal] Association has not the means now of giving any publicity to these details, beyond that to which the proprietors of newspapers [...] are giving'. 'Of course', he continued, 'the publicity thus given is insufficient. If the Association was not in its present distress, in consequence of the awful condition of the country, we could spread these horrific details through every town and city in England [...] and thus bring to the minds of every individual the consequences of the old mis-policy of England'.[51] In the event, the returns were never published by the Repeal Association.

Supporters of the Repeal Association, including the pro-Repeal newspapers, certainly viewed the Death Census as a necessary initiative to highlight the critical condition of the Irish population and of the government's inadequate response to the events. The *Dublin Weekly Register*, for example, trumpeted its own coverage of the Death Census, viewing the condition of Ireland as an indictment of the half-century old union:

> Each week they [the Death Census returns] augment in fearfulness and horror. What matter of indignant impeachment they supply to the future historian against the policy of which our people are the victims! What incentives do they not afford to Irishmen to join in one firm and compact body, to end that policy which makes millions of their brethren its immediate victims, crushing the poor into unmade graves, trampling the industrious into pauperism, and bringing down the most opulent to poverty![52]

From the west of Ireland, the *Galway Mercury* commented favourably on the importance of the Death Census to keep the Famine in the public eye: 'The "Death Census" continues to unfold horrors greater than men imagined to exist. This series of papers will do more, we are convinced, to place the famine and its awful effects tellingly before the world, than could be effected by detached correspondence.'[53] For others, however, the Death Census was of little import. When the *Belfast Commercial Chronicle* and the London based *Morning Post*, for instance, reported on a Repeal Association

50. *The Pilot*, 5 May 1847.
51. *The Pilot*, 19 May 1847.
52. *Dublin Weekly Register*, 15 May 1847.
53. *Galway Mercury*, 22 May 1847.

meeting in May 1847, the part of the meeting in which John O'Connell read out the Death Census was not included. It was:

> [...] *neither very interesting nor particularly important* [our emphasis]. Mr John Reynolds abused the Irish Members [of Parliament] for not supporting the Dublin Improvement Bill; Mr Town Clerk Ford called upon the liberal citizens of Dublin to register their votes; and Mr John O'Connell accused the Government of being the 'moral murderers of the people of Ireland by not adequately supplying them with food in this dreadful period of scarcity'. He then read a number of letters from Roman Catholic clergymen, being a continuation of the 'Death Census' which the [Repeal] Association has been for some time preparing.[54]

Somewhat surprisingly, no pro-Repeal newspaper outside of Dublin published the returns of the Death Census in full. This may explain in part their general neglect by historians.

We can but conclude from all this that the Death Census, if it was read by English, Scottish or Welsh MPs at all, had a negligible effect on government policy. It certainly failed in its primary aim of bringing the horrifying events in Ireland to the attention of the English government and the wider population. But would things have been different if more effort had been made to bring the Death Census to the attention of the government? What, we might ask, would have happened if John O'Connell or another Repeal MP had read the returns out in Parliament? It is, of course, impossible to know with certainty, but some indication can be obtained by considering the response in Westminster to a similar survey, called the 'Destitution Census', which *was* read out in Parliament by John O'Connell in November 1847. The Destitution Census was the direct successor of the Death Census and was conducted by parochial clergy in the west of Ireland a few months later. Devised by Archbishop MacHale of Connacht, a fiery Irish nationalist known as 'The Lion of the West', the Destitution Census was a regional survey which asked Catholic clergymen to answer a series of questions about the extent of destitution in their parishes. More limited in its coverage than the Death Census, and carried out in September 1847, the Destitution Census consists of 46 surviving returns (there might have been more, although it is unlikely) from four of the five counties of Connacht.[55] MacHale asked O'Connell to read out parts of this census in the House of Commons when Parliament reconvened in late 1847, and on 23 November O'Connell duly obliged. In doing so, he brought the grim details of this survey into the heart of Westminster politics for the first time.

This was the first meeting of the new parliament following the July General Election. A few weeks earlier, a Council of National Distress and National Safety had met

54. *Morning Post*, 12 May 1847; *Belfast Commercial Chronicle*, 12 May 1847. The newspapers were commenting on the Repeal Association meeting of 10 May 1847, which recounted the returns for parishes in Cork, Galway, Kerry, King's, Leitrim, Sligo, and Longford. *The Pilot*, 12 May 1847.

55. It is the intention of the authors to publish the Destitution Census, with accompanying commentary, in the future.

in Dublin and had agreed on a series of emergency proposals that demanded, amongst other things, immediate relief interventions in Ireland.[56] Henry Grattan, MP for County Meath, who had attended the Council meeting in Dublin, was present in Parliament on the opening day and he spoke before John O'Connell. Pressing the case for urgent relief in Ireland, Grattan moved that an amendment be made to a proposed address to the Queen so that it included the following words: 'That though the present Poor Law may materially alleviate the existing distress in some districts of Ireland, yet as it must be quite inadequate in others, it will be absolutely necessary to devise immediate measures to avert famine and pestilence from a large number of Her Majesty's subjects in that country'.[57] In response, Sir George Grey, the Home Secretary, objected to the inclusion of the amendment, and his reasoning neatly encapsulates the prevailing position of the Whigs on this issue. The amendment, Grey argued, was,

> directly opposed to the spirit evinced by the speech of the hon. Gentleman who moved [the address]; for I am sure it is his desire, as it is the desire of the Government and of every gentleman in England and Ireland, to excite the spirit of self-reliance among the people of Ireland, and to put an end to that degrading system of reliance on extraneous aid which I believe would be prompted and encouraged by an acquiescence in the Amendment which has been proposed.[58]

Grey's stance was clear: Ireland was to support itself; dependency was to be discouraged. As Grey sat down, John O'Connell rose to speak. He argued, like Grattan, for the need for immediate relief, stating that Ireland could not support its own people at present, and he used some of the Destitution Census returns to demonstrate how desperate the situation in the country had become. 'Surely', he asked, having read out the returns, 'such a state of things required the immediate attention of Government and of Parliament'.[59] Yet, it received little support in the House. Sir Benjamin Hall, Whig MP for Marylebone, London, and no friend of Irish Repealers, attacked the speech in a condescending and antagonistic retort during which he assailed the character of O'Connell and some of the Catholic clergy, and defended the government's record during the Famine. Hall claimed that he was

> exceedingly surprised at what had fallen from the hon. Gentleman [O'Connell], who took to himself the title of the leader of the Irish people (Mr. J. O'Connell: No.) At all events the hon. Gentleman put himself in that position, whether he assumed the title or not. The hon. Member said that no measure of a conciliatory character had during the last eighteen months been adopted in respect to Ireland. The hon. Member who made that sweeping accusation must have forgotten what was done in the last Session. He (Sir B. Hall) had taken a prominent part—too prominent for the ability he possessed—in endeavouring to reform the abuses in Ireland; and whenever he heard statements like those made by the hon.

---

56. See above, pp. 48–9.
57. *Hansard*, 23 November 1847, 95, c. 86.
58. Ibid., c. 94.
59. Ibid. c. 106.

> Gentleman he would endeavour to show up those abuses, and to show that those statements made by persons who had had everything from this country was not founded on fact. Was the sending 8,000,000 or 10,000,000 of money to Ireland nothing? Had England not done everything in her power to stay the famine, the plague, and the pestilence with which it had pleased Providence to afflict Ireland? And was not all the necessary money cheerfully granted by the people of this country? Had they not at the commencement of the last Session of Parliament entertained the hope that the labouring classes of this country might be relieved from some portion of taxation, and did not the people patiently submit to all that money being granted for the sake of Ireland, without ever asking a single Member of the House of Commons to demand the reduction of a single tax? Was the House then to be told that it had done nothing for the people of Ireland?[60]

Hall went on disingenuously to accuse some Catholic clergymen of encouraging recent assassinations in Ireland, and pledged support for an Irish Coercion Bill. While few MPs were as outspoken as the representative for Marylebone, his words nonetheless represented the feelings of many in the House towards the end of 1847. Tellingly, Hall's pugnacious speech 'elicited the applause of the House'.[61] No MPs, during this or subsequent sittings, commented on the evidence from the Destitution Census presented by O'Connell, and despite the presence of several senior government ministers during the debate the government saw no reason to change its approach to distress in Ireland. It fell to a later prime minister, Tony Blair, to offer an apology for the reluctance of the then government to do more.[62]

The Destitution Census met a similarly hostile response in the English press. The London *Evening Mail*, for example, was scathing in its review of the Destitution Census, stating that the Connacht bishops were trying to foster a lie that two million people had died as a result of famine while the 'Protestant Government of England [sat] idly by'. The newspaper alleged that MacHale had set a target of two million deaths nationally for the priests in his region to consider when compiling their returns; each priest would duly return a quarter of their parishioners as having died during the crisis. The main text is worth relaying in detail:

> The Roman Catholic bishops of Connaught, presided over by the veracious M'Hale, met the other day and passed a resolution, first affirming that the famine had 'slaughtered' about two millions of the people of Ireland, and then inviting the clergy of the communion to supply the particulars for their several parishes. Here is the resolution:- That, with a view of furnishing the Government with a seasonable knowledge of the extent and depth of the public misery, and that they may not labour under the lamentable ignorance on which Ministers relied last year as an apology for their not meeting in time the terrible famine *that has slaughtered about two millions of our people*, the clergy be respectfully requested to answer the annexed queries.
>
> And here is the first of the annexed queries:- What has been the reduction in the number of your parishioners by famine and its consequence, epidemic disease, since last October?

60. Ibid. c. 114.
61. Ibid. c. 121.
62. *Irish Times*, 2 June 1997.

Friend, first thou tellest a lie, and then 'thou askest a question'. Does anybody doubt how an inquiry will be conducted that has begun under these honest and charitable auspices? Does anybody doubt that the reply will justify the question? Let it be remarked that there is no such thing as trustworthy statistics in Ireland. They are impossible. The 'population returns' themselves confess they have been rendered comparatively worthless by the prejudices, delusions, and dishonesty of a people who will always give any answer rather than the right one. In the perpetual haze that necessarily envelopes such a state of society, the parties appealed to in this instance will be able to make any statement they please. They will take care that it shall be impossible to check it. The parish priest will include in his return all the deaths for the last five or ten years, whether from starvation, or fever, or ague, or asthma, or gout, or smallpox, or whooping cough, or any other disease; or by rifle, or blunderbuss, or by stoning, or burning alive, or drowning, or drunkenness, or any other casualty. Then, if it be possible to return any body two or more times, the opportunity will not be omitted. A death will be entered at the place of burial, at the place of death, at the place of previous residence, at the place of former residence, where the deceased was known, where his friends resided, where his cart and horse occasionally stood, where he sometimes took a drink of poteen, and, in fact, wherever his death was known; and if there have been other deaths in the family within four or five years, they will be multiplied by all these localities. Famine and pestilence have made their chief havoc among the mendicant class, who are a large portion of the people, and who, in the absence of an effective Poor Law, have hitherto subsisted by going daily or weekly rounds of considerable extent, and filling their scripts with small contributions of food, a single potato, or a handful of meal from every hovel they came to. Of course, every poor creature who had gone a round of twenty parishes, and who last winter found every house as empty as her own, and who then lay down to die, will count twenty times over – twenty at the very least. In this way it will be no difficult matter to make either two millions, or four millions, or ten millions. Last winter it was no uncommon thing for the relief lists presented to the officers of the Board of Works to exceed the whole population of the district. That error, of course, will be avoided in this question. The cue is given. It is to be about two millions, say for decency 1,927,309. That is about a quarter of the whole Irish population. So the priest of every ordinary parish will take care to return 'about' a quarter of his people.

The imagination of the *Evening Mail* scaled even greater heights when it prophesied the use to which these informal censuses would be put in times to come, though it also bears stating that MacHale's irresponsible use of the figure of two million deaths served to undermine the credibility of the whole exercise for outside audiences:

The object is transparent enough. It is to give a seeming authenticity and a universal currency to the impudent and diabolical assertion, that Her Majesty's Ministers wilfully allowed two millions of the Irish people to perish by famine and its natural consequences in less than a twelvemonth. We say 'wilfully', because the resolution insinuates that the 'lamentable ignorance' spoken of was only a pretence and by way of 'apology', and that the Minster deliberately refused to meet the famine in time in order that the 'two millions' might perish. The statement made therefore by the bishops, and bolstered up by the clergy, is to be palmed on the whole world as an authentic census, made by the most competent authorities, after the most careful research. It will be food for ages to come in the controversial and elementary books of the Roman Catholic Church in every quarter of the world. Wherever

> the name of England is known, as a great 'heretical' power, priests will be found carefully instilling the 'fact' into the minds of the tenderest innocents. 'In the dreadful winter of 1846', it will be written and taught, 'when the only food of the Irish Roman Catholics had perished, the Protestant government of England refused to take any measures to convey food to that miserable population, and sat with folded arms while two millions died. That any survived is owing to the bounty of America and other foreign nations. The number of the victims is authenticated by a return made after the most minute inquiries by the parochial clergy of Ireland, and not contradicted, for it could not be contradicted at the time'. Such, we venture to predict, will be the form of the lie destined to continue for ages as part of the stock in trade of the Romish controversialists.[63]

This lengthy, contemptuous editorial concluded with the promise that the newspaper would 'keep an eye' on the priests' mortality figures in the coming weeks and expose any fallacies therein. In the event, they need not have bothered. As the returns came in the evidence hardly pointed to a great conspiracy. Indeed, only once did the *Evening Mail* refer to the Destitution Census again, and then only to mock some minor statistical errors unrelated to mortality.[64]

It was not only the London newspapers that sought to downplay the scale of the crisis. The *Dublin Evening Packet*, a conservative (anti-Repeal) newspaper, also attempted to expose the fallacious nature of the priests' returns. It drew upon a single example, that of Revd Owen Feeny of St John's, Coolderra and Calry parish, County Sligo, to denounce the veracity of the whole survey, which it claimed was trying to 'mislead the government and defame the national character'.[65] The newspaper argued that Feeny's return so wildly exaggerated the extent of mortality and suffering that 'not a single individual, of any age or sex, out of a population of 22,277, can be expected to be alive at the close of next February [1848]'. Feeny's brief return had identified 872 families with no more than three months provisions, 1,353 families who were 'totally destitute', and 1,513 families possessing a cabin and no more than a rood of land. These were grim figures indeed, but the *Packet* had failed to appreciate, be it by accident or design, the full meaning of the account. St John's Catholic parish was coextensive with the four civil parishes of Calry, Killaspugbrone, Kilmacowen and St John's, and included the town of Sligo. In 1841, these four parishes were reported to have had a population of 23,620, inhabiting 4,173 houses (4,477 families).[66] Although we cannot know the population of the four civil parishes in October 1847, Feeny did not, as the *Packet* had presumed, claim that every family in his parish was on the verge of starvation. In fact, the 2,225 families that he identified as either destitute, or with provisions for three months or less, represented about half of the numbers in his parish, a situation that some other priests in the West of Ireland might have envied. Certainly, criticisms can be made of the Destitution Census, but there is little evidence to suggest

63. *Evening Mail*, 11 October 1847.
64. *Evening Mail*, 3 November 1847.
65. *Dublin Evening Packet and Correspondent*, 28 October 1847.
66. *Census of Ireland, 1841*, BPP, 1843 (504), 416. Strictly speaking, these are households rather than families but the difference is slight in most cases.

that Feeny's return was purposely misleading. The *Packet* concluded its report with a call for information from Feeny's parish to show that his data were exaggerated. We find no evidence that this appeal met with any success.

As noted, O'Connell had hoped to publish the returns of the Death Census and to provide a copy to every member of the Westminster parliament. For various reasons this did not happen, but now, nearly two centuries later, the Death Census has finally made it into print in composite form in this volume. This is a belated tribute to the many Catholic priests who, in the face of unprecedented horror, took the trouble to write the reports that make up the Death Census in the vain but laudable hope of influencing government policy. Of the many who toiled among the disease-ridden poor, we might single out Revd William Hanrahan, curate of Ennistymon parish, in the County Clare, who died of Famine fever in April 1847, some two months before Revd Sheehan prepared his Death Census report for the parish.[67] In an eloquent obituary his parish priest described him as one who dared to enter 'the haunts of pestilence', bringing the comforts of religion to the dying, until he martyred himself in the cause of charity'.[68]

67. *Dublin Weekly Nation*, 17 April 1847; *Tipperary Vindicator*, 17 April 1847.

68. Revd John Sheehan, Ennistymon, Part II, p. [X].

Chapter Six

FAMINE, PRIESTS AND PEOPLE

> We have this day to announce the death at Cootehill, in the 25th year of his age, and the 5th of his ministry, the Rev. John Smith, R.C.C. of Drumgoon, deservedly regretted by all who came within the compass of his ministration. Stricken by typhus fever whilst in the discharge of his duties to which so many of the faithful clergy of the people have fallen martyrs, he expired on the 22nd instant, in the fervent hope of a blessed Resurrection.[1]

> How is all this desolation to be accounted for? Surely it was not caused by the visitation of an angry Providence, but by the crying injustice of our earthly rulers.
>
> Revd P. Mullins, Killeely, Galway[2]

The botanical image that so transfixed the Irish public in the autumn-winter of 1845 was that of the putrefying tuber. The sense of foreboding and despair this inspired was captured in a contemporary oil painting – 'The discovery of the Potato Blight' – by the Cork-born artist, Daniel McDonald (1821–53). It has graced the cover of several histories of the Irish Famine.[3] Yet the image of the mess of potatoes was symptomatic of a deeper malaise, of a social system that accommodated runaway population increase, leaving its people vulnerable to harvest failure. George Nicholls' hastily compiled reports on a Poor Law for Ireland in 1838 spoke of a 'reckless disregard of the future'.[4] Weak landlordism, which might be seen as a consequence, though not a necessary consequence of seventeenth-century colonialism, had accepted or acquiesced in the proliferation of cottier and labouring households, most notably in mountainous localities and west of the Shannon.[5] Strong landlordism would have meant a more interventionist ruling class exercising tighter control over household formation, accompanied by periodic evictions of squatters and smallholders

1. *The Pilot*, 26 July 1847. Another account supplies a little more detail of his last days: 'On the 8th ultimo, when attending four persons in one miserable bed, who were labouring under typhus fever, he was seized with the malignant and fatal malady, in which he remained until the 22nd instant in extreme agony, when his pure spirit departed from this vale of tears, a martyr to the duties of his sacred ministry'.
2. Report to the Death Census by the Revd P. Mullins, Killeely union, County Galway, 1847.
3. Mokyr, *Why Ireland Starved*; Póirtéir, *Great Irish Famine*. See also Niamh O'Sullivan, *In the Lion's Den: Daniel McDonald, Ireland and Empire*, Hamden, CT: Quinnipiac University Press, 2016.
4. *Poor Laws – Ireland: Three Reports by George Nicholls Esq*, 11.
5. Liam Kennedy, 'The Irish Population Explosion in Long-Run Perspective', Unpublished paper, Queen's University, Belfast, 2018.

as market conditions changed. To take a nearby comparator, this would have meant a tenurial regime more akin to that of Scotland where landlords were vigilant in controlling access to land and housing.[6] This had a ruthless edge, so the Scottish historical alternative had its downside, particularly in the shorter term.[7] Apologists for the system would argue that it was the longer term that really mattered, and that over much of rural Scotland it prevented the build-up of great reserves of underemployed labour, expanding cumulatively through time, of the kind that would eventually weigh down Irish society and leave it vulnerable to an existential threat following a massive failure of the staple food crop. As a consequence, many parts of Ireland in the 1840s had the features of a bloated rural slum. Below the level of the landlord, Irish rural families possessed their own agency. Indeed, some, at least, had emigrated to Britain and America before the famine. However, with the exception of the middling-sized and large farmers, the rural Irish were only slowly adjusting family strategies to narrowing economic prospects, even at the cost of subsisting on watery potatoes.[8] Though age at marriage was not low by European standards on the eve of the Famine, access to marriage was nearly universal among the rural poor and fertility had been high for generations.[9] This despite a darkening economic climate and deflationary pressures following the end of the French Wars in 1815. The century-long gap in famines (but not hunger) since the 1740s helps explain this demographic vitality and is interrelated with extreme dependence on a single, cheap source of food. Still, none of this meant that a cataclysm was inevitable. Irish society could withstand one bad harvest, be it of cereals or potatoes. Moreover, few if any largely agrarian societies in mid-nineteenth century Europe could have withstood repeated failures of its principal foodstuff. In that sense Ireland was unlucky in its dealings with the natural world and heavy mortality was inevitable during the course of four or five years of a shrunken domestic food supply. Finland, some fifteen years later, suffered harvest failures of *shorter* duration, possessed its own home-rule parliament, treated its poor in a niggardly fashion, and ended up with heavy excess mortality.[10] That said, much more could have been done to alleviate the sufferings of the people, by the British government, by Irish landlords, by Irish farmers and property holders, and by Irish political representatives.

---

6. W. A. Crawford, 'Ulster as a Mirror of the Two Societies,' in *Ireland and Scotland, 1600–1850: Parallels and Contrasts in Economic and Social Development*, T. M. Devine and D. Dickson, eds. Edinburgh: John Donald, 1983, 60–69.
7. See T. M. Devine's study, *The Scottish Clearances: A History of the Dispossessed, 1600–1900*, London: Penguin, 2018.
8. Kevin O'Neill, *Family and Farm in Pre-Famine Ireland: The Parish of Killashandra*, Madison: University of Wisconsin Press, 1984.
9. Joel Mokyr and Cormac Ó Gráda, 'New Developments in Irish Population History, 1700–1850', *Economic History Review* 37, no. 4 (1984): 473–88.
10. Andrew Newby and Timo Myllyntaus, '"The Terrible Visitation": Famine in Finland and Ireland 1845 to 1868: towards an agenda for comparative Irish-Finnish Famine Studies', in *Famines in European Economic History*, Curran et al, eds., 145–66.

The Death Census and Repeal Politicians

The Death Census was an Irish politicians' initiative and yet it leaves many questions unanswered. Dioceses rather than counties or baronies may be the more relevant spatial unit in explaining the uneven take-up. The archbishopric of Dublin stands out as a region from which the clerical response was strangely silent. The response rate to the Death Census must also give rise to questions about the commitment of the Repeal Association to the initiative and its effectiveness in executing it. The role of John O'Connell and his close associates is central here. Much of the historiography, it has to be said, has been unduly influenced by the febrile recollections of their critics within the Irish Confederation, which was a breakaway faction from the broad Repeal movement. John O'Connell has been portrayed by his opponents as the architect of the split in the Repeal ranks, as weak and ineffectual in his leadership role, and too close to the Whigs to challenge their handling of the Famine. The last is clearly untenable as his speeches inside and outside of parliament testify. One has only to think of his many impassioned addresses to parliament in the spring of 1847, conveying grim news of the progress of distress in Ireland. We might also enter into the scales John O'Connell's attempts to forge unity across the ranks of Irish MPs, all the better to press the cause of Ireland. Still, the cause of Ireland in 1847, at least among the rural poor, was famine, famine, famine.

While he had a significant role in relation to the Death Census, the assessment of O'Connell's effectiveness was moot. It is certainly the case that the Repeal Association struggled under severe financial constraints at the time the Death Census was being conceived. But the postal expenditure, for instance, at less than £10, can hardly have been prohibitive, though of course there were associated costs. Might more energy have been committed to boosting the response rate through reminders and exhortation? Might the findings have been more vigorously publicised in Britain or was public opinion there already tiring of dismal news from Ireland? Most puzzling of all, John O'Connell made no mention of the Death Census in his political memoir published some two years later.[11] Apart from a few vague references to famine in Ireland there is no discussion of the calamity. It is a remarkable omission.

The political representatives of Ireland did not have a 'good famine' in the sense of articulating constructive ideas for relief and pursuing appropriate strategies. The Young Ireland dissidents were fiercely critical of the Repeal Association, and of John O'Connell in particular, but some of the arguments propounded by this radical clique could be less than helpful. The youthful revolutionary, Thomas D'Arcy McGee, was hardly speaking for many of the rural or urban poor when in late 1845 he spurned the idea of American aid for Ireland. However, *political* assistance was acceptable in his view, given that the only cure for Ireland's ills was independence. These sentiments may not have resonated

11. John O'Connell, *Recollections and Experiences during a Parliamentary Career from 1833 to 1848*, London: R. Bentley, 1849.

in the hungry back lanes of Skibbereen.[12] Moreover, neither faction was prepared to concentrate its energies exclusively on the national calamity that was the Famine. To do so would have meant parking the constitutional question for the duration of the crisis. This seems to have been too much to ask, even as the famine pits opened and graveyards filled to overflowing, even in a leading town such as Belfast.[13] In Britain, associating demands for famine relief with the hugely unpopular demand for the return of an Irish parliament hardly helped in terms of gaining a sympathetic hearing at Westminster. Or from the wider British public.

The counterpoint however is that a united front might have made little difference. Charles Wood at the Treasury worried about the stability of the British economy in the face of financial and trade dislocations, and, absurd as it may seem, some Whigs, and even some Catholic clergymen, obsessed about the moral dangers of public relief fostering dependence among the Irish poor. All we know for sure is that an alternative approach was not tried.

How Many Died?

The issue of how many people died during the Great Famine, and whether the government could have saved more lives, has long occupied the minds of historians, polemicists and the general public, both in Ireland and in the Irish diaspora. What this volume brings out strikingly is that similarly challenging questions were being asked during the Famine itself. Calculations as to the numbers dying in different parts of Ireland were supplied by a range of commentators and fed into divisive political debates round the handling of the Famine. At one point in early 1847 parliament debated the possibility of a national, state-sponsored mortality census, as independently proposed by William Smith O'Brien and George Bentinck. O'Brien accused the British government of allowing the Irish people to 'die like vermin' while the leading Tory MP Bentinck believed that the Whigs were trying to 'conceal the truth' about the number of Irish deaths caused by famine. Government ministers resisted. It would have been too embarrassing politically to quantify too much; instead they fashioned some technical arguments to evade the question. The Death Census is the product of these anguished debates, and of the politicisation of Famine mortality more generally.

The reports that made up the Death Census tended to fuse political and humanitarian concern, so there is a wealth of social commentary of value to

12. See David A. Wilson's magisterial two-volume biography, *Thomas D'Arcy McGee*, 2 vols, I: *Passion, Reason, and Politics, 1825–1857*, Montreal: McGill-Queen's University Press, 2008), 120–21. 'Not only would it [aid] "force this disagreeable feeling of pauperism upon Ireland" but it would blunt the political struggle.' (McGee later became an apostle of moderation in his adopted country of Canada but that is a later story).

13. Eamon Phoenix, *Two Acres of Irish History: A Study through Time of Friar's Bush and Belfast, 1570–1918*, Belfast: Ulster Historical Foundation, 1988.

historians and others. Sometimes it is the small, local detail that takes the reader closer to *an droch shaol* (the hard life):

> The poor of this parish are relieved only once a week or once a fortnight; only one pound of meal is allowed for each individual adult for the week, and half a pound for those under nine years, and this proportioned to time will only allow an ounce a day to each adult, and half an ounce to those under age, and to add to this misery, the public works are stopped; the consequence of this is that the poor are dropping as fast and as numerous as the leaves of the forest.[14]

It is impossible not to empathise with the plight of the compilers of these reports, working away at the front line of the crisis. The Revd Francis Arthur of Kinvara, County Galway, declared that he was 'nearly exhausted in body and spirits'. Mindful of his spiritual duties, there was not 'an hour of the day or night that I am not giving the sacraments to my doomed parishioners'. He goes on to mention that his colleague, the Revd Mr Forde, had been 'hurried to an untimely grave, broken-hearted at the frightful scenes he had witnessed'.[15] This was far from exceptional. In the diocese of Kilmore, in the north of Ireland, of the 64 priests serving there, seven died in 1846–47.[16] Farther south, in the diocese of Killaloe, five priests died in 1847–48, one of cholera and four of famine-related diseases.[17] Obituary notices in the *Irish Ecclesiastical Register* for 1848 named 31 priests across Ireland who died of 'fever' or 'typhus fever' during the preceding year.[18] These men, and they are all men, were as close as it gets in terms of witnessing at first hand and over a continuous passage of time the afflictions visited on neighbours, friends, kinfolk. Had there been female priest-witnesses, other or different aspects of the Famine might have been highlighted. But there were not.[19] Lest it be forgotten, the priests were reporting on their own congregations only, and most of the parishes included in the Death Census were overwhelmingly Catholic.

The *bete noir* of later historians and balladeers, Charles Trevelyan, is not mentioned in the reports, which is a point of some interest. Neither is Sir Robert Peel, prime minister at the beginning of the Famine, nor is Charles Wood who held tightly the strings of the Exchequer during the worst years. Their Whig colleague and prime minister, Lord John Russell, does come in for fleeting critical acknowledgement. There is a single damning reference to Randolph Routh, the superintendent of famine relief, and his 'advocacy of political economy'. This lack of specificity in relation

14. Return by the Revd. Mr O'Connor, Straide and Bohola, County Mayo.
15. Return by the Revd Francis Arthur, Kinvara, County Galway.
16. Donal A. Kerr, *'A Nation of Beggars'?*, 43.
17. Ibid, 43.
18. *Battersby's Registry … or the Complete Catholic Directory, 1848*, 341–44. According to the compiler the registry is not complete, so this may be an underestimate (page 341).
19. This in turn suggests that attention to the testimonies of Catholic nuns might open up fruitful lines of comparison. The eyewitness accounts of the Sisters of Charity (Grey Nuns), working among Famine refugees in Montreal come to mind. See http://faminearchive.nuigalway.ie/eyewitness-accounts/grey-nuns [accessed 5 June 2022].

to key figures mirrors what has been observed in relation to oral traditions of the Famine.[20] However, good, generally resident landlords are given names and spoken of appreciatively; oppressive landlords, usually absentee, who were demanding rents, tumbling houses and evicting tenants are frequently referred to but not usually by name. What is noticeably absent from these narratives are references to collective action or other forms of resistance. Social differences within local communities are mentioned but class tensions do not get a look in. Family disintegration is a rarity, as when 'a poor man in Ballynalligan became insane from want, and attempted the life of his wife'.[21] The mood of the reports generally is of a destitute people but also of a passive people enduring terrible sufferings – a reaction consonant with clerical attitudes and a Catholic world view. Only occasionally is the threat of hungry crowds mentioned – 'neither life nor property is safe, and no magistrate can control the fierce instincts of a famishing multitude' – but this is counterbalanced by the image of the priest as mediator.[22]

While urging restraint on their congregations yet acting as the local leaders of the people, this highly politicised clergy felt empowered to voice bitter criticism of the government of the day. This could be quite unrestrained. We recall some of the phrases: 'this monstrous cruelty' (Killedan), the 'murderous policy of the government' (Ennistymon), the 'cruel and murdering delay in putting the relief system into operation' (Toomevara), and 'the murderous edict of stopping the public works' (Carracastle). There are more in this vein. Suffice it to say we can see here a prefiguration of later polemical writings that presented British government policy, either by omission or commission, as genocidal.[23]

Not that such charges were reserved for the Irish Great Famine only. Another great European famine, the Ukrainian famine of 1932–33, has been cast in genocidal terms, and perhaps with more justification.[24] Nearer home, in the case of Scotland, some historians have not hesitated to summon up images of the Jewish Holocaust to condemn estate clearances (mass evictions of tenants) in the Scottish Highlands. To take but one absurdly exaggerated example, that of F. G. Thomson: 'The Victims of the [Scottish] Clearances [were] subjects of intense hatred such as the gypsies and the Jews were to experience under the Nazis and other groups in the Western World'.[25]

20. Cormac Ó Gráda, *Black '47 and Beyond*, 197.
21. Return for the Death Census of the Revd Mr O'Gorman, Parish Priest of Clarecastle, County Clare.
22. See the commentary on the parish of Ardrahan, County Galway in Part II, pp. 105ff.
23. Mitchel, *Last Conquest of Ireland (Perhaps)*; Tim Pat Coogan, *The Famine Plot: England's Role in Ireland's Greatest Tragedy*, New York: St Martin's Press 2012; Aengus Ó Snodaigh, 'An Droch Shaol: The Irish Holocaust', *An Phoblacht*, 11 September 1997.
24. *Holodomor and Gorta Mór*, Christian Noack, Lindsay Janssen and Vincent Comerford, eds. London: Anthem, 2012. For an overview of competing interpretations of the Ukrainian famine see Stephen Devereux, *Theories of Famine*, New York: Harvester Wheatsheaf, 1992, 140–42, and Liam Kennedy, 'Famine as Genocide? Ukraine and Ireland' in Stephen Velychenko, Joe Ruane and Ludmilla Hrynevych eds., *Ireland, Ukraine and Empire*, New York: Columbia University Press, 2022.
25. Devine, *Scottish Clearances*, Annex A: 'The Highland Clearances as Holocaust', 365.

Most historians, however, would shy away from anachronistic arguments of this kind. Of more immediate relevance is the question of how much confidence we can repose in the parish-level reports that constitute the Death Census.

Priests and People

The compilers of the Death Census were priests. They were all men, following a common vocation in life. The relationship of priests to people is therefore crucial in assessing the Death Census as a historical source. How familiar were priests with the conditions of life of the people they purportedly served? Did their social origins preclude them from close identification with the sufferings of their parishioners? Perhaps their elevated status within Irish rural society and the deference accorded to the wearers of clerical garb served to insulate them from the trials and tribulations of their congregations. Perhaps many of their parishioners were only nominally connected to the local church, with some indifferent or even hostile.[26]

The social origins of the Catholic clergy have long been a source of fascination for historians and indeed others.[27] In Pre-Famine times and subsequently few came from the ranks of the rural or urban poor. At the end of the eighteenth century, in the view of Daire Keogh, 'clerics came from families ranging from the modestly comfortable to the well off'.[28] Under the impact of rapid population expansion, as discussed earlier, the ratio of priests to people continued to deteriorate in the pre-Famine decades. It may be that the social groups supplying priests had broadened by the 1840s, though this is far from clear.

The great historian of Irish population change and of Irish rural society, K. H. Connell, maintained that priests were drawn from the peasantry.[29] However, this is to neglect that rural society was stratified along social lines. There seems little doubt that a majority of those ministering during the Great Famine came from the farming class, to which may be added a sprinkling of other backgrounds in shopkeeping, trading and the minor professions. The farmer designation, however, covers a range of social and economic gradations. The likelihood is that most of these priests were the sons of middling-sized or larger tenant farmers.[30] Thus, they came neither from the rural poor of cottiers and labourers nor from the more privileged tiers of society. As the sons of farmers, traders and shopkeepers they knew well the rhythms and routines of making a living from the land, as well as the vicissitudes of the rural economy. Some even farmed

26. On instances of anti-clericalism in earlier time periods see Daire Keogh, *'The French Disease': The Catholic Church and Irish Radicalism, 1790–1800*, Dublin: Four Courts Press, 1993, 24–25.
27. See, for example, Connell, *Irish Peasant Society*, 122–27; Keogh, *'The French Disease'*, 7–8; Connolly, *Priests and People in Pre-Famine Ireland*, 35–47; James O'Shea, *Priest, Politics and Society in Post-Famine Ireland: A Study of County Tipperary, 1850–1891*, Dublin: Wolfhound Press, 1983, 13–16; Kevin Whelan, 'The Catholic Church in County Tipperary, 1700–1900' in William Nolan ed., *Tipperary: History and Society*, Dublin: Geography Publications, 1985, 244–45.
28. Keogh, *'The French Disease'*, 8.
29. Connell, *Irish Peasant Society.*
30. Connolly, *Priests and People*, 35–40.

in their own right.[31] In a loose but also in an intimate sense, they were *of* the people and embedded in the local community. Unlike state-supported clergy, they were dependent on the donations of their parishioners for their subsistence, which also meant living among the people. Absenteeism was not an option, as it might have been for some clergy from the established church, the Church of Ireland.

Priests were not only independent of the social establishment, they were often also the best-educated members of local society, proficient in the language of the public sphere which was English, and so in a position to write and report on the effects of the Famine in their localities. Still, we need to bear in mind that clerical control of the Catholic laity was less assured in the 1840s by comparison with the later nineteenth and twentieth centuries. Alternative supernatural understandings, either of pagan or of corrupted Christian origin, sustained popular traditions round patterns and wakes that clashed with orthodox Catholic beliefs and practices. Attendance at church was often irregular, though poverty and poor clothing was part of the explanation. David W. Miller reckons that in rural areas attendance at Sunday mass varied from 60 per cent of the Catholic population to as low as 20 per cent in some parishes.[32] Not only were low levels of church attendance evident but the pattern varied regionally. In Gaelic-speaking districts, particularly in the poorer western regions of the island attendance was especially low. These were the areas where the consequences of the Famine were at their most dreadful.

Might this suggest that priests were not well positioned to report on the plight of the poorest and the most vulnerable? The stinging remark by the Bull McCabe, the principal protagonist in John B. Keane's melodramatic play, *The Field*, comes to mind: 'No priest died during the Famine.'[33] This is of course untrue. Many priests, as well as doctors, nurses and workhouse attendants, contracted disease in the course of ministering to the poor; priests wrote anguished letters to local and national newspapers appealing for aid; many were involved in local relief committees.[34] While it is true that regular church attendance was low by later standards, rites of passage were mostly marked by religious ceremony.[35] Baptism seems to have been almost universal, irrespective of social status, and clergymen frequently officiated at weddings and funerals.[36]

We also know that members of the Catholic clergy were coming to be recognised and consulted as authoritative figures on Irish social and economic conditions by the opening decades of the nineteenth century. Worried by reports of food scarcity and

31. In County Tipperary at mid-century, according to O'Shea, at least 40 of the county's parish priests rented farm holdings. See his *Priest, Politics and Society*, 21.
32. David W. Miller, 'Irish Catholicism and the Great Famine', *Journal of Social History*, IX (1975), 81–98.
33. John B. Keane et al., *The Field*, Cork: Mercier Press, 1991.
34. Kerr, *'A Nation of Beggars'*.
35. Connolly, *Priests and People*, 91.
36. This is our judgement from a survey of more than 50 parish registers from the 1830s and the 1840s. While payment might be a barrier to a church wedding or funeral, there was no necessary charge for baptism. Records of baptism fees in parish registers show that some parents paid no fees at all and non-payments rose during the Famine itself.

hunger, the *Cork Mercantile Chronicle* undertook a survey of conditions across the baronies of County Cork in 1812. Its sources were Catholic clergy who were held to be closer to the people than state officials or clergy of the Church of Ireland.

> We knew that their constant residence in their several parishes, and their daily intercourse with their parishioners, must have given them such opportunities of collecting local information, as are not enjoyed by any other individuals [...] we felt perfectly satisfied that we could rely with the most unbounded confidence on their well-known regard for their several flocks, and the poor in general [...][37]

In the matter of filling in forms and communicating social observations many of the Catholic clergy had been initiated into such practices as evidenced by the massive response of priests to the detailed questionnaires circulated by commissioners investigating Irish poverty in the 1830s.[38] Also dating from the mid-1830s, the Commission of Public Instruction involved clergymen of all denominations from across the island in the task of checking the religious affiliations of their local congregations.[39] There are even scattered instances of priests conducting their own local religious censuses.[40] So detailed inquiries and reporting were hardly unfamiliar practices to clergymen when famine broke out in 1846.

The reports from the localities, as we have already noted, were generally critical of government relief measures. This is hardly surprising in view of the limitations of state relief and the existential threat confronting the priests' congregations in many parts of Ireland. There was sometimes an ideological edge to the writing, a point we will come back to. But it should not be assumed that priests were invariably hostile to the British state, either then or earlier. If we refer back to the harvest failure and subsistence crisis of 1822, we find very different clerical attitudes. During the course of that crisis, in addition to substantial government aid, huge volumes of charitable aid flowed across the Irish Sea from Britain to Ireland. These combined efforts averted a major regional crisis. The Catholic bishop of Killaloe spoke for many when in the autumn of 1822 he expressed his appreciation of 'this unheard-of munificence, in favour of the destitute population of our unfortunate country'. He continued

> In the history of the world is there to be found an instance of such benevolent feelings as are now manifested, and by whom? by the illustrious English protestants, in favour of the destitute Roman Catholics of Ireland.'
> Heavenly God! can those wretched poor people ever forget such kindness.[41]

37. Ó Ciosáin, *Ireland in Official Print Culture*, 114.
38. *First report from His Majesty's Commissioners for inquiring into the condition of the poorer classes in Ireland*, BPP, House of Commons Papers (1835), 369, xxx; 1836 (43) *Third report of the Commissioners for inquiring into the conditions of the poorer classes in Ireland*, BPP, House of Commons Papers, vol. 30, xxx.1, xxx–xxxiv.
39. *First Report of the Commissioners of Public Instruction*, vol. 33, 829, 34, xxxiii.1, 829, xxxiv.1.
40. Brian Gurrin, et al., *Irish religious censuses of the 1760s.*
41. Quoted in Timothy P. O'Neill, 'The Famine of 1822', MA dissertation, University College Dublin, 1965, 28–29.

This historic moment may well have been the high point in feelings of accommodation between Catholics and Protestants in Ireland, and between Britain and Ireland. By the late 1840s such clerical voices were either muted or absent. The mass mobilisation of Catholics in the Catholic Emancipation campaign of the later 1820s, the 'tithe war' of the 1830s, the Second Reformation (a Protestant evangelical crusade to banish 'popish superstition'), and the campaign for Repeal of the Union meant that popular and clerical attitudes were very different from those of a generation earlier. The majority denomination on the island was moving in a new political direction that would have momentous consequences for the evolution of politics in Ireland and hence for Anglo–Irish relations in the long run.

All this might suggest that there are grounds for being suspicious of the mindsets of the clergymen reporting to the organisers of the Death Census. Moreover, the organisers of the survey were Repeal MPs, so the priest–politician nexus suggests further grounds for wariness. But, setting aside references to the Liberator and Repeal, the content of the reports is reassuringly in line with other eyewitness accounts. Indeed the priests do not dwell on the more grisly scenes picked up by visitors and newspaper reporters at the time. They seem more inclined to highlight the magnitude of the crisis. As hundreds of thousands of families faced the abyss in 1847, it was virtually impossible to exaggerate the scale of the disaster. Rather the problem was one of how to convey the scale and intensity of hunger, disease and deprivation to the wider audience on the neighbouring island where political power resided.[42] When assessed alongside other sources that document experiences of hunger and death during Black '47, the Death Census has the ring of authenticity.[43]

The theme of evictions may be selected to illustrate the wider point. 'It was indeed a harrowing scene to witness the widow and orphans (the day after the husband's remains, who died of want, were hurried to the grave) levelling to the ground their miserable cabin for some trifling compensation proffered to them by the agent, who refused the day before to advance the price of a coffin for the departed husband till the work of eviction would be fully compensated'.[44] It is a cruel scene sure enough but hardly more emotively drawn than dozens of other contemporary depictions of clearances during the Famine.

The psychological effects on priests of attending to the spiritual and temporal duties attaching to their ministry in the midst of hunger, and the indignities of hunger, are conveyed by a number of the respondents to the Death Census. Unsurprisingly, priests who died of famine-related disease as a consequence are mentioned, and by name. Once

42. On the challenge of famine representation see Margaret Kelleher, *The Feminization of Famine: Expressions of the Inexpressible*, Durham, NC: Duke University Press, 1997.

43. As noted in Chapter Four, in the admittedly small number of cases where it is possible to check estimates of the mortality impact of famine from the Death Census against surviving death registers, there is a reassuring degree of concordance.

44. The account is from the report of Revd Patrick Lyons, Kilmeen, County Galway.

or twice the disturbed mental states of parishioners are observed, though this is unusual. The report for Aglish and Whitechurch in County Waterford is an exception:

> It is remarkable that the poor people here are more pleased than afflicted when one of their family dies! I have known a poor man who buried two of his children, and thanked God that a third was dying. The poor fellow was a loving father and an excellent member of society – sober, industrious and religious, and appeared delighted that his child was taken away before he should witness the distress of such times.[45]

So much for what the Death Census tells us. The detailed contents of the reports are unfolded in Part II of this volume. But what of the dimensions of the Famine that are excluded or overlooked in the Death Census? Inevitably, the picture supplied by this census is not a comprehensive one as it is framed within the limits set by the questions being asked. Gradations of social class for instance are not highlighted, other than occasional references to landlords and absenteeism. The closest one comes to a recognition of social inequalities below the level of the landed elite is the distinction sometimes drawn between those who could afford to emigrate and those who could not. More generally, it was community rather than class that held the priests' gaze. In parishes in the West of Ireland there was little social differentiation to speak of but this was certainly not true of parishes in much of the north and east of the country. Language as a social marker – Gaelic-speaking areas were generally poorer in terms of literacy and income; many were disadvantaged geographically as well as socially – is an issue left unnoticed though the language spoken might carry material consequences in terms of gaining workhouse admission, employment on public works schemes or finding employment abroad. Gender gets occasional recognition but only in vague terms and infrequently. Attention to violent assaults taking place within families and communities under the pressure of extreme hunger, while not absent, is slight.[46] But then the reports were never intended to be comprehensive. The format of the questionnaire precluded that, although helpfully the detail supplied sometimes spilled over these boundaries. What we can say is that the Death Census, within the limitations of its brief, is replete with detail as to the lived experience of the times.

Much more might be said about the returns themselves. The demographic materials in particular will be most effectively exploited through the medium of local and regional studies. But that is only the beginning. Revealing references may be found to inferior foods (water cresses, weeds, nettles, seaweed), distended stomachs, diseases rampant, ragged clothing, shame, evictions, landlord and tenant relations, church attendance, the poverty trap and emigration. To these may be added observations on public works, soup kitchens, workhouses, burials and the failure of different relief measures

45. Return by Revd J. O'Meara, P.P. of Aglish and Whitechurch. *The Pilot*, 21 May 1847, p. 244.
46. Ó Gráda, *Black '47 and Beyond*, 39–41. An exception is the return by Revd P. Murray, P.P. of Ballymachugh and Drumlumman South, County Down, who speaks of a husband who got into 'a gloomy state of mind' and poisoned himself by taking arsenic. Then, in the grip of frenzy, he turned on his wife and cut her throat.

to connect in time. Raymond Gillespie, the editor of the most successful local history publishing series in Ireland (Maynooth Studies in Local History), chides us: 'local history is too important to be left to the professionals'.[47] Or as the British historian Pene Corfield succinctly puts it: 'History belongs to everyone'.[48] We concur readily with these judgements. The Death Census opens possibilities for dialogue between national, regional and local historians of Ireland.

In the end, the story of the Death Census is one of tragedy and irony. The tragedy is that in the region of a million women, men, and children died of hunger and famine-related disease, often under the most squalid conditions, sometimes abandoned by family and neighbours, and left to their fate by landlords and the state. The irony is that the Death Census, in a moment of hope, seemed to hold the key to more generous government provision for the Irish poor. It was not to be. It is the well-fed descendants of these famine victims, five or six generations later, and in particular the historians among us, who are reaping the benefit of these intimate encounters with almost unimaginable suffering.

47. *A Various Country': Essays in Mayo History, 1500–1900*, Raymond Gillespie and Gerard Moran, eds. (Westport, Foilseacháin Náisiúnta Teoranta,1987), and the essays therein.
48. https://www.penelopejcorfield.com/PDFs/6.2.3-PJC-2016-01-No61MonthlyBlog.pdf [accessed 25 January 2022].

Part II

Chapter Seven

THE DEATH CENSUS: TESTIMONY IN CONTEXT

Contents

PROVINCE OF CONNACHT

Summary of the returns for Connacht

County	Parish	Deaths		
		Oct. 1845– Mar. 1846	Oct. 1846– Mar. 1847	from famine
Galway	Ardrahan	16	61	37
	Ballinakill	10	56	30
	Beagh	20	100	
	Kilbecanty	60	170	30
	Kilchreest	10	140	'greater portion'
	Killeely union	5	75	55
	Kilmeen	NA	27 or 30	14
	Kinvara union	52	148	98
	Oranmore and Ballynacourty	20	240	200
Leitrim	Cloone-Conmaicne	27	260	230
	Drumreilly Lower	12	64	26
	Drumreilly Upper	51	132	75
	Glenade	143	173	129
	Killenummery and Killerry (Sligo)	36	171	130
	Kiltoghart	98	320	150
Mayo	Addergoole	55	240	180
	Attymass	72	320	240
	Backs	24	189	158
	Carracastle	'very few'	300	75% of total
	Clare Island	20% of famine period	82	two thirds of total
	Kilcolman (Claremorris)	'No record'	156	123
	Kilcommon and Robeen	49	934	909
	Killedan	80	650	400
	Kilmaine	NA	220	NA
	Straide and Bohola	NA	375 (Oct.–May)	300 (Oct.–May)
	Toomore	c. 48	384	20
Roscommon	Castlemore and Kilcolman	86	420	290
	Kilglass	'No registry'	1,000	950
	Loughglynn	65	189	103
	St Peter's and Drum	30	192	50
	Tarmonbarry	'No registry'	300	c. 200
Sligo	Achonry	10	51	32
	Bunninadden	28	232	125
	Dromard	20	100	50
	Kilfree	40	256	206
	Skreen	20	160	90

County Galway

Ardrahan, Kilmacduagh Diocese

Commentary

The Catholic parish of Ardrahan was in Kilmacduagh diocese at the time of the Death Census. The Catholic parish was coextensive with the civil parish of the same name.[1] Its population was reported in the statutory censuses at 3,805 in 1831, and 4,191 in 1841 (about 1,000 more than the 3,200 inhabitants that Revd Quin estimated for his parish in 1847). This implies a rate of increase of about 1 per cent per year between 1831 and 1841.[2] In 1841, 44 per cent of the housing was classified as fourth class and the female illiteracy rate was 81 per cent. These two measures of poverty and disadvantage are included in this and later commentaries to give a rough indication of living standards in the localities. It should be noted, however, that it is not always possible to map data precisely from civil parishes, as in the population censuses, on to Catholic parishes. This qualification is unlikely to make much difference in practice to the patterns of literacy or housing quality locally.

Patrick Bodkin Quin had long-standing connections with Ardrahan. Arriving from Peterswell parish, he had been parish priest of Ardrahan from at least as early as 1834, when he is recorded as contributing £1 to the O'Connell annuity that year.[3] He farmed locally, was a supporter of the Repeal Association, was a prominent advocate of Catholic rights, and was a member of the Ardrahan Relief Committee during Black '47, when he signed a memorial to the Lord Lieutenant protesting at the temporary termination of Public Works (the memorial is replicated below).[4] It seems reasonable, therefore, to infer that his knowledge of the locality was extensive, and he was a prime candidate to report on Famine deaths in the area. Quin did not live long beyond the submission of his report, for in early September 1847 the *Galway Mercury* announced his death:

> We sincerely regret to be obliged to state, that another of the venerated Priesthood of Ireland has fallen a victim to that most dreadful malady, fever, and yielded up his soul into the hands of his Creator, on the morning of Sunday last [29 August]. The Very Reverend Mr. Quin, P.P. of Ardrahan, in this County, and one of the Vicars General of the united dioceses of Kilmacduagh and Kilfenora, expired at his residence, to the inexpressible regret of his attached and now truly afflicted parishioners. Mr. Quin was an able theologian,

1. *Thom's Irish almanac and official directory, 1850*, Dublin: A. Thom, 1850, 343.
2. *Abstract of Population Returns for Ireland, 1831*, BPP, House of Commons Papers (1833) (634) vol. 39, xxxix.59, 294, 296, 300; *Report of the Commissioners appointed to take the census of Ireland, for the year 1841*, BPP, Command papers, (1843), 504, vol. 24, xxiv.1, 376, 378, 380.
3. *The Pilot*, 29 December 1834.
4. 'Robert Gregory, esq., of Coole [...] granted [1840] the longest lease he could give to Rev. Patrick B. Quin, P.P. of Ardrahan, for his farm, the term of which was expired last May, and gave him timber, slates, and glass, for building a suitable residence thereon'. *Freeman's Journal*, 18 September 1840; *The Nation*, 12 August 1843; *Freeman's Journal*, 24 January 1844; *Galway Mercury, and Connaught Weekly Advertiser*, 8 May 1847.

> a profound scholar, a zealous Priest, and a most charitable man. After serving religion in the capacity of curate for many years, he was appointed Administrator of the mensal parish at Kinvarra, whence he was collated to Peterswell, and afterwards to Ardrahan. where his unostentatious piety and his strict attention to the duties of his ministry, won for him the respect and regard of all knew him. May he rest in peace.[5]

The Public Instruction Commissioners reported the parish to be predominantly Roman Catholic; they identified only 61 Protestants (1.6 per cent) in the 1831 census population.[6] We estimate the Catholic population at about 4,298 in mid-1845, falling to about 3,745 by mid-1847.

Return by Revd P. B. Quin, PP for Ardrahan:

Number of deaths from 1st October, 1846 to 1st April, 1847? 61.
Number of same known to be caused by famine? 37, six of whom died of starvation, and thirty-one of fever and dysentery, brought on for want of nourishment.
Numbers of deaths during the same period last year? 16.

I am half my time all out mad by the state of my poor parishioners, and my curate in fever. During the present month twice as many have died as in the same time in winter. The population of my parish is about 3,200. May God bless them; my heart is broken at the scenes around me. If we had our parliament this would not be so. Our unfortunate country is doomed, I fear. I am delighted to find that our beloved Liberator is getting better; may the God of Mercy restore him to us, and counsel those who have in a great measure been the means of breaking his heart.

Source: *The Pilot*, 7 May 1847, 1.

Memorial from Relief Committee of Ardrahan to Lord Lieutenant, May 1847

> The Relief Committee of Ardrahan forwarded a memorial to the Lord Lieutenant, of which we subjoin an abstract: The Committee view with feelings of intense apprehension the discontinuance of the public works until the 20th May, Special Sessions now been held in the Baronies of Loughrea, Dunkellin and Ki[l]tarton, for the purpose of finishing and completing the roads now dangerous and in many cases impassable, preventing the conveyance of produce, to and from the several markets.
>
> Impressed with the exigencies of the times, memorialists earnestly entreat the Government at once to rescind the order suspending these works, and to sanction the finishing of these roads without delay. This measure is more imperatively called for by the awful destitution prevailing in the parish, now considerably the increase, hundreds being thrown upon the world without food or employment.

5. *Galway Mercury, and Connaught Weekly Advertiser*, 4 September 1847; *Battersby's Registry*, 343.
6. *First report of the Commissioners of public instruction, Ireland*, 4d.

Considerable excitement exists in the neighbourhood, and on Saturday, 1st May, numbers assembled at Ardrahan, had they not been restrained by the Rev: Mr. Watson,[7] would have committed serious depredation, as it happened the Relief Clerk was violently assailed, the Police Barrack menaced, and the cattle in the surrounding pastures threatened with destruction.

The Committee apprised of these facts, feel it their duty to direct your Excellency's attention to this melancholy state of affairs; neither life nor property is safe, and no magistrate can control the fierce instincts of a famishing multitude.

Memorialists beg to observe, that hitherto they have supplied the wants of the poor chiefly from private funds, now exhausted, but although they have fully complied with the instructions of the new Relief Act, and sent up the required estimates, &c., no steps have been taken to carry out the provisions of said measure, in consequence of which the state of the population, especially the female portion thereof, is quite appalling to every Christian feeling.

With respect to the employment of the able bodied, the Committee humbly submit, that the resident Landlords have without exception, continued to employ the people to the utmost of their ability. The Spring business will soon be brought to a close, and those persons who have hitherto laboured their own land will be idle until harvest, many of these honest, industrious and decent men, with numerous families, and means exhausted by the exorbitant price of food.

The only employment available, is a small portion of the General Drainage, which runs along the north side of the parish, and is the means of employing the most indigent who travel several miles daily, in order to obtain subsistence by the work thus afforded, but in the south-western extremities, there can be no drainage, and the population is overwhelming.

The Committee humbly and anxiously solicit your immediate attention the state of this large electoral division, as there is reason to dread the recurrence of a similar outrage to that which already took place near Gort.

Hitherto, the resident Clergy and gentry have used most strenuous efforts to restrain the starving people, but the prospects of the ensuing week are such, that the Committee are compelled to throw off the weight of the responsibility resting upon them.

Since October, memorialists have unflinchingly discharged their duty to the public and to the poor, seeking to maintain public order, and endeavouring, at the same time, to hold out a helping hand to the perishing paupers; but the crisis is such, they cannot risk their health, perhaps, their lives, in a hopeless struggle, which, if unassisted by Government, must end in the destruction of the parish. Therefore, memorialists humbly pray, that the Public Works now suspended may be renewed without delay, for the convenience of the of the public at large, and the support of the famishing poor.

J. S. Lambert, Chairman, John Martyn, Tullyra; James Daly, Castledaly;
F. M. Shawe Taylor; P. Quin, P.P.; Arthur Vincent Watson, Clk.

---

7. Arthur Vincent Watson, Church of Ireland curate of Ardrahan D. W. Crooks, ed., *Clergy of Killaloe, Kilfenora, Clonfert and Kilmacduagh, biographical succession lists compiled by Canon J. B. Leslie*, Belfast: Ulster Historical Foundation, 2010, 267.

Ballynakill, Tuam Diocese

Commentary

The parish of Ballynakill is located in east Galway, in the barony of Killian. There are four civil parishes named Ballynakill in County Galway, including this parish in Killian barony, one nearby, to the north, in Ballymoe barony (Elphin diocese), another near Clifden, and a fourth, bordering County Clare. We can identify this parish as the Ballynakill in Killian barony because of the mention of Ballinlass townland, and of the Bellew family in the return.

We have been unable to reconstruct the pre-Famine populations of the parish from the statutory censuses, although Revd MacLoghlan mentions about 220 families, which would suggest a population of around 1,200 people. In 1841, 89 per cent of the housing in the *civil* parish of Ballynakill (not coterminous with the Catholic parish of Ballinakill) was classified as fourth class and the female illiteracy rate was 90 per cent.

In his return MacLoghlan, a supporter of the Repeal Association and a collector of the Repeal Rent in the Mount Bellew area, was critical of the parsimony of landlords in the parish, with the single exception of Baronet Sir Michael Dillon Bellew.[8] He mentions the notorious Ballinlass evictions, when 61 families, consisting of nearly 300 people, were evicted from the Gerrard estate near Mountbellew on 13 March 1846. These evictions received extensive coverage in Irish newspapers, including the *Freeman's Journal* which published the names of those evicted.[9]

Return by Revd Patrick MacLoghlan, PP for Ballynakill:

Number of deaths from 1st October 1846 to 1st April, 1847? 56. This should be considered a large number out of a district not containing much more than 220 families.

Number of same known to be occasioned by famine? 30. Remotely or proximately, in some instances, there were inquests held, at which verdicts were brought in of their having died of starvation. The entire of the above number died of starvation and its effects.

Number of deaths during the same period last year? 10.

Some of the persons known to have died of starvation here were strangers passing through the parish, who took suddenly ill and died. Others who died were of the number of those poor people who were about this time last year ejected from the lands of Ballinlass.

To the credit of the inhabitants of this town, not one even of those helpless and friendless strangers was permitted to be buried without a coffin and other requirements. The present state of the parish would be truly melancholy, were it not

8. *The Pilot*, 23 September 1846.

9. *Freeman's Journal*, 27 March 1846; *Freeman's Journal*, 28 March 1846.

that a great portion of those thrown off the public works were employed by Sir M. D. Bellew, Bart., both on his own work and on drainage under Mr Labouchere's letter, no matter whose tenants they were – a fact of itself illustrative of the beneficial effects of a resident proprietary. He is the only resident landlord in my district; all the others are absentees, some of whom refused to subscribe one penny to our local relief fund! The machinery of the new relief measure [Soup Kitchen Act] is so complicated that I fear it will be some time before it can be brought to work here. Even if it were in operation this very day, the quantity of relief it professes to give is so stingy and niggardly that very little good can be expected from it. The general prospects of the coming year are of a very gloomy character in consequence of a great space of the land being left untilled for the want of food, and of the means to procure it. The landlords in general give no aid of any kind to their poor struggling tenants; on the contrary, some are, it is said, likely to follow the noble example of the proprietor of Ballinglass. The extent of emigration from this parish is trifling, for a very good reason – because they have not the means. Three or four families of the best means in the parish have emigrated, as also some stout able-bodied young men, who by labour and industry laid by some money.

Source: *The Pilot*, 7 May 1847, 1.

Beagh, Kilmacduagh Diocese

Commentary

Named 'Beogh', this is the return for Beagh parish, in Kiltartan barony, in south County Galway. The parish was in Kilmacduagh diocese at the time of the Census.[10] Beagh Catholic parish was coextensive with the civil parish of the same name. The statutory censuses reported its population at 5,343 in 1831 and 5,751 in 1841; suggesting a yearly increase of about 0.7 per cent during the 1830s.[11] In 1841, 67 per cent of the housing was classified as fourth class and the female illiteracy rate was 84 per cent. The area was overwhelmingly Catholic; the Public Instruction Commissioners reported only 46 Protestants (0.9 per cent) in the parish in 1831.[12] We estimate the Catholic population to have been about 5,943 in mid-1845, falling to about 5,046 by mid-1847. Revd Michael O'Shaughnessy, who had been parish priest of Beagh since at least the 1820s, was well placed to provide an accurate commentary on the critical state of his parish in 1847.[13] In his return he claimed that deaths in the period from October 1846 to March 1847, at 100, were five times the number which had occurred in the equivalent period a year previously, but in our judgement both figures grossly underestimate the true number of deaths occurring, for the kinds of reasons highlighted

10. *Thom's Irish almanac, 1850*, 343.
11. *Abstract of Population Returns for Ireland, 1831*, BPP (1833), 634, 296; 1843 (504) *Report of the Commissioners appointed to take the census of Ireland, for the year 1841*, 378.
12. *First report of the Commissioners of public instruction, Ireland*, 4d.
13. *Dublin Evening Post*, 15 October 1829.

in part I of this volume. A return to the Death Census also issued from the neighbouring parish of Kilbeacanty.

O'Shaughnessy was a strong supporter of O'Connell, collecting money in the parish for the Liberator's Compensation Fund in 1843, and contributing £1 to his bishop's Repeal collection in the same year (see Death Census return for Kilbeacanty), as the press reported that, in Beagh, County of Galway, 'The adherents of the Liberator in this patriotic locality have supplied to the fund for 1842 the sum of 8*l.* 8*s.* 6*d.*, by the hands of the exemplary and efficient Catholic Rector, Rev Michael O'Shaughnessy, who has at the same time kindly supplied the names of the [...] estimable co-operators, so worthy being associated with him and his reverend and patriotic curates in the good work of justice and wisdom.' These individuals, numbering over 30, contributed from a shilling to a pound each.[14]

Return by Revd M. O'Shaughnessy, R. C. R. for Beagh.

Number of deaths from 1st October 1846 to 1st April 1847? 100.
Number of same known to be caused by famine? Greater part of the above deaths caused by use of bad food and want of food.
Number of deaths during the same period last year? 20.

I have seen many cases where there was little or no food, and, if possible, worse clothing. The present state of the parish is very bad; no arrangements [for relief] unless giving out Indian meal very scantily. The land is partially tilled – the prospects for the coming year are very dismal. The wheat crop looks well in many places, the oat crop very poor, generally speaking. As to potatoes, very few sown, and as to the chance of a good growth, it is more than doubtful. On the whole, unless through the interference of Providence, the coming prospects are rather awful.

Source: *The Pilot*, 16 June 1847, 2.

Kilbeacanty, Kilmacduagh Diocese

Commentary

Named 'Kilbiaconty', this is the return for Kilbeacanty parish, located in Kiltartan barony. It was in the diocese of Kilmacduagh at the time of the Death Census.[15] The boundaries of the Catholic parish were coterminous with those of the civil parish. The statutory censuses reported its population at 4,544 in 1831 and 4,575 in 1841.[16] In 1841, 80 per cent of the housing was classified as fourth class and the female illiteracy rate was 88 per cent. The parish was virtually exclusively Catholic. The Public Instruction Commissioners reported only 3 Protestants for 1831.[17]

14. *Dublin Weekly Register*, 22 July 1843.
15. *Thom's Irish almanac, 1850*, 343.
16. *Abstract of Population Returns for Ireland, 1831*, BPP (1833), 634, 296; *Report of the Commissioners appointed to take the census of Ireland, for the year 1841*, BPP (1843), 504, 378.
17. *First report of the Commissioners of public instruction, Ireland*, 4d.

Revd John Ford, who submitted the return, had been parish priest of Kilmacduagh since at least 1838, so he would have known his parish intimately, and was well placed to comment on conditions in the local community.[18] He was a strong supporter of O'Connell and the Repeal Association, contributing £1 to Bishop Edmond French's collection for the Association in 1843. It is notable that returns were received from six parishes in Kilmacduagh diocese (Ardrahan, Beagh, Kilbeacanty, Kilchreest, Killeely Union and Kinvara Union), which may point towards diocesan support for the Repeal Association's initiative:

> Gort, 19th April, 1843,
> My Dear Sir – I feel, indeed, great pleasure in being the medium of sending you the enclosed order, amounting to 15*l.* 10*s.*, with a list of the subscriptions of the venerable clergy of Kilmacduagh, and myself. May I beg you will have the kindness to propose us as avowed Repealers. The sum is trifling, but I hope it will be accepted as a sincere expression of our thorough conviction that our country never can be prosperous or happy until she is allowed to legislate for herself in a domestic parliament. Please do accept the sincere regards and gratitude on the part of my clergy and myself. I have the honor to be your very faithful and humbl[e] servant,
> Edmond Ffrench, R.C. Bishop.

The eleven parishes contributed from 10s to £2 each, and the priests and other religious officers were named in the submission.[19]

Ford was explicit in saying that the number he gives for deaths in his parish in the period October 1846–March 1847 included children. He does not state this for the deaths during the earlier period, but it seems safe to assume that children are included in that total too. We estimate the Catholic population of the parish in 1845 at about 4,750, so 60 deaths between October 1845 and March 1846 for a population of that size represents a mortality rate of about 24 per 1,000, comfortably within expected parameters (see the discussion in the Introduction to this volume). The implied mortality rate in the famine period was about three times higher, or about 82 per 1,000 people in a full year.

Return by Revd John Ford, P.P. for Kilbeacanty:

Number of deaths from the 1st October 1846 to 1st April 1847? 170 persons, men, women and children.
Number of same known to be caused by famine? 30. Of those died of disease brought on by famine – three in one village; ten of great want in another; eight by fever in another village, brought on by indigence; four in another place by perfect want; three in another locality; and three out of this parish, who went into the workhouse and died. Total, 61.

18. *Catholic directory and annual register for 1838*, 136.
19. *Dublin Weekly Nation*, 29 April 1843.

Number of deaths during the same period last year? 60.

The present state of the parish is deplorable; it contains very near 700 houses, poor and very poor – some few rich, but very few. During the last fortnight there were 2,889 persons served with a pound of Indian meal, merely to keep the life in them. There is very little ground tilled; as for potatoes, not 40 acres sown, for the want of seed. There is wheat pretty forward. Fifty or sixty persons left this parish, men and women, for different parts of America. The prospects of next year are very bad, and how it will end the Lord only knows.

Source: *The Pilot*, 12 May 1847, 4.

Kilchreest, Kilmacduagh Diocese

Commentary

Kilchreest parish is located in south Galway, near Loughrea town. It was situated in Kilmacduagh diocese when the Death Census was being compiled.[20] In 1841, 37 per cent of the housing in the *civil* parish of Kilchreest (not coterminous with the Catholic parish of Kilchreest) was classified as fourth class and the female illiteracy rate was 90 per cent. The return for the parish was compiled by Revd Michael Burke, the parish priest of ten years standing.[21] Burke, who succeeded Revd Patrick Mullins as parish priest (see Death Census return for Killeely Union), was a firm supporter of the Repeal Association, contributing £1 to Bishop French's Repeal fund in 1843, to secure membership of the Association (see Kilbeacanty parish), and collecting the Repeal Rent for the Repeal Association.[22] Despite Burke's public political leanings, his contribution is not very informative regarding circumstances at the local level, and he limits himself to a staid, generic criticism of a government which should 'exert itself better than it has heretofore done'. Gratuitous food supplied locally was insufficient.

The numbers he provides on deaths in his parish would suggest that mortality during the Famine period increased fourteen-fold, but this is not credible. The most likely explanation for this extraordinary ratio is that all deaths in the pre-Famine period were not being recorded.

Return of Revd Michael Burke, C.C. of Kilchreest:

Number of deaths from the 1st October 1846 to 1st April 1847? 140.
Number of same known to be caused by famine? The greater portion of the above number died of actual want, and the rest of the given number struggled with death through a longer period, who had the good luck to have doled out to them some small portion of food, but insufficient to satisfy their craving appetites.
Number of deaths during the same period last year? 10.

20. *Thom's Irish almanac, 1850*, 343.
21. *Catholic directory and annual register for 1838*, 136.
22. *The Nation*, 30 September 1843, 16.

The reverend gentleman remarks – If the present government does not exert itself better than it has heretofore done, I will have to record double the number of deaths within the same given period.

Source: *The Pilot*, 12 May 1847, 4.

Killeely Union (Kilcornan, or Clarenbridge), Kilmacduagh Diocese

Commentary

The Catholic union of Killeely, located east of Galway Bay, included the parish of Stradbally and part of Killeenen parish. The union was in Kilmacduagh diocese at the time of the census.[23] In 1841, 47 per cent of the housing in the *civil* parish of Stradbally (not coterminous with the Catholic union) was classified as fourth class and the female illiteracy rate was 73 per cent. The return was compiled by Revd Patrick Mullins, parish priest. Mullins had been parish priest in Kilchreest parish, but had been stationed at Kilcornan or Clarenbridge for about a decade by 1847.[24] A new marriage register was opened for the parish in mid-1837, with Mullins' name on the title page, so it is reasonable to presume that his tenure as parish priest commenced at that time.[25] Mullins was a supporter of O'Connell and Repeal. He collected the Repeal Rent for the Association, and contributed a substantial £2 10*s*., 'the personal subscription of the public-spirited Catholic Rector' to the O'Connell Tribute in 1845, with another £1 10*s*. donated shortly afterwards. His curate, 'another patriotic admirer of the Liberator', contributed to the Tribute too.[26] According to Mullins' return, the number of deaths occurring in the union was only five in the period between October 1845 and March 1846, rising to 75 in the same period the following year. There is no doubt that the figure of five deaths for the pre-Famine period greatly underestimates 'normal' mortality. In light of Mullins' political sympathies it is hardly surprising to see him place the blame for the catastrophe on 'the crying injustice of our earthly rulers'.

Return by Revd P. Mullins, P.P. for Killeely union:

Number of deaths from the 1st October 1846 to the 1st April 1847? 75.
Number of same known to be caused by famine? 55.
Number of deaths for same period last year? 5.

My fellow-labourer having been confined by fever those weeks past, brought on by over exertion in attending the sick, and my feeble endeavours to supply

23. *Thom's Irish almanac, 1850*, 343.
24. *First report of the Commissioners of public* instruction, 60; *Catholic directory and annual register for 1838*, 136.
25. https://registers.nli.ie/registers/vtls000634156#page/3/.
26. *The Nation*, 29 July 1943; *Dublin Weekly Register*, 2 August 1845; *The Nation*, 3 January 1846.

his place have not until now allowed a moment's leisure for a reply to your well-advised circular relative to the death census. Besides as no registry has been kept in the parish, I deemed it right to make due inquiry, of which the above return is the result, and which may be relied on. The number of deaths in this parish in ordinary times might average eight annually – seldom amounted to ten, infants of course excepted. I may here observe that many who were in comfortable circumstances were carried off by diseases occasioned by the sudden transition to a meal diet, which in a great measure explains the vast disproportion between the mortality of the latter and the corresponding previous period.

The present system of relief [soup kitchens] is but partially in operation here – in one entire electoral division it is not as yet available, although its conditions were complied with a fortnight ago. Many in and throughout the parish would be added to the dead list were it not for the small rations doled out by the good Sisters of Charity stationed at Claranbridge.

With respect to tillage, at least one third of the surface lies waste, particularly of an extensive tract held under the Courts, commonly called the estate of Betagh and Concannon. I am not aware of any landlord having supplied his tenantry with seed, except a small quantity by Mr. Redington. A great number of the able-bodied of both [estates] have bidden farewell to their homes, and many more would had they the means. How is all this desolation to be accounted for? Surely it was not caused by the visitation of an angry Providence, but by the crying injustice of our earthly rulers.

Source: *The Pilot*, 12 May 1847, 4.

Kilmeen, Tuam Diocese

Commentary

Kilmeen is located east of Loughrea, in south County Galway. In 1841, 42 per cent of the housing was classified as fourth class and the female illiteracy rate was 78 per cent. Its return was made by its parish priest, Revd Patrick Lyons. Lyons was a noted Repealer, and was one of 124 clergymen from the diocese of Tuam contributing a combined £126 to the Royal National Repeal Association fund in early 1845.[27] At the close of 1846 Lyons saw the impending cataclysm, prompting him to appeal, through the newspapers, to landlords to 'go hand in hand with his fellow-man to save his country from inevitable ruin'.

To the Editor of the *Galway Mercury*
Kilmeen, Loughrea, 24 December 1846.
Dear Sir,
The awful and universal calamity with which the Almighty has been pleased to visit his people for his own wise and mysterious purposes, has forced the Catholic clergy unwillingly to take

27. *The Nation*, 8 March 1845.

notice of facts which may be erroneously construed into desire of promoting individual aggrandisement, or wilfully intending an act of malicious vituperation. This criticism on their conduct should not deter them from laying before the public the sad and mournful, but alas, too true picture of the unparalleled distress and destitution of a people, the most patient in their sufferings, and the most resigned in their afflictions on the face of the earth. While famine, with all its evil concomitants is, with rapid strides and irresistible progress, laying the entire country desolate – while the pitiful cries and mournful yearnings for food of numberless families are penetrating the very clouds and reaching the throne of Heaven— while the Angel of death, with careborn and ghastly figure, marks with unerring aim its victims for destruction, the hard-hearted and unrelenting Pharoah issues his cruel edicts, and swears that the chains which bound the incorrigible Irish serfs must be rivetted more closely, and the lash held over them to be an awe and a check to their future disaffection. The rents must be enforced from a starving people. Human ingenuities is [are] put to the test, and lo, a stratagem, as unwise in its policy as it is new in its invention, is had recourse to. The public driver, the harbinger of evil to the poor is no longer fit for office; he is forced to resign his mean but profitable employment in favor of a crafty solicitor. A letter of attorney is sent through the post-office, addressed to the care of the Priest, to the starving tenant threatening "to bind him hand and foot and cast him into exterior darkness unless he pays the last farthing". Rents thus exacted are carried away to support the extravagantly supplied board and gorgeous display of worldly pomp and splendour of an absentee landlord. But the day of retribution is at hand – the cries of the emaciated father, of the starving child, and of the helpless mother, have reached the throne of Heaven – while the guests are seated in the banquet hall enjoying the full measure of their sensuality and revelling in wine and drunkenness, some mysterious hand is seen writing on the wall their inevitable doom, not requiring the prophetic spirit of a Daniel to exemplify its meaning – "They have been weighed in the balance and found wanting, and their properties handed over to the management of others".

There still remains for the starving millions one ray of hope that lightens in the distant horizon. There still appears to float over the vast abyss of human inconsistencies one plank by which the landed proprietors can save themselves and their properties from utter annihilation. "Forty days and Nineveh will be destroyed". One grand effort must he made to avert the impending danger. Let the individual (after the example of the King of Nineveh) divest himself of the variegated mantle of aristocratic pride and political prejudice, and put on the garb of national sympathy, and go hand in hand with his fellow-man to save his country from inevitable ruin, and protect the people from the ravages of a widespread famine. While the great bulk of the gentry are placed in the embarrassing position of gross apathy and wilful inactivity, it is gratifying to see that there are some still to be found who are alive to the interests of the poor, and manifest a deep sympathy for their sufferings by acts of charity and benevolence. Some are buying Indian Meal at their own expense and selling it under value, in order to save the people if possible, from the exorbitant market prices. While others are giving donations in money in order to add some additional comfort to the poverty-stricken board of the destitute poor during the Festival of Christmas.

Ten pounds have been placed in hands for distribution among the poor of my parish by Mr. Tully, of Rathfarn [Rafarn], who feels that he could not with comfort enjoy the fruits of his industry, on this festive occasion, while the people around him were literally starving. Such acts of benevolence will have their own merit from Him who allows not the giving drink of water in His name to pass unrewarded.

> Deaths from starvation, of late, are of such frequent occurrence as not to elicit from depraved human nature any extraordinary exertion to arrest their progress. It is my painful duty to record one of those melancholy scenes that occurred, a few days ago, in this parish. 1 was called on to administer the last rites of religion to a dying man whose haggard face, wrinkled brow, and shrivelled cheek bespoke the awful ravages of hunger. He died the victim of starvation, and many families in the parish are fast approaching the same fate. Thanking you for your kindness in giving publicity to this melancholy tale in the pages of your truly honest and independent journal, I remain, dear Sir, with great respect, yours very faithfully,
> Patrick Lyons, P.P.,
> Kilmeen, Loughrea.[28]

Lyons produced two returns for the Death Census, describing his parish as a small parish, with a population of about 1,000 in 1847 in his second report. His first return reports 27 deaths between October 1846 and March 1847, with 11 of these caused by famine. His second commentary boosts both figures by 3. Although 11 or 14 deaths in a six-month period that can be directly ascribed to famine represents a grave situation, it is difficult to marry those figures with Lyons' comment in his Christmas Eve letter to the *Galway Mercury* that 'deaths from starvation, of late, are of such frequent occurrence as not to elicit … any extraordinary exertion to arrest their progress'. Although many families were in great distress, he puts the number of families who were in a state of 'utter destitution' at just 12. Unfortunately, Lyons does not include the number of deaths for the earlier six-month period in his returns, as had been requested, but if we assume that the 11 deaths from starvation out of 27 total deaths represents excess famine mortality, then the normal mortality would have been around 16 in a typical six-month period between October and March. It is worth noting, however, that in his first return Lyons names the dead, and notes the number they left behind in their families. These are implicitly adult deaths, so the actual mortality level must have been above the 11 that he notes in his return.

Return (number 1) by Revd. Patrick Lyons, P.P. of Kilmeen:

Number of deaths from 1st October 1846 to 1st April 1847? 27.
Number of the same known to be caused by famine? 11, *viz*:- Michael Connelly, leaving seven in family; John Daly, five; Kitty Mahony, three; Michael Silk, six; Mary Flaherty; Morgan Kenny, two; Bridget Lyons, two; Winney Burke; Widow Martin, three; Bridget Forde; and a traveller, who died suddenly from exhaustion.

There is a great mass of misery and destitution in the parish at present, occasioned in a great measure by the removal of the poor from the public works, before the new relief bill, with all its multitudinous preliminaries, be in full operation. There is a good breath of land under grain sown by persons of means, but the land of the poor intended for the grain crop is a perfect waste, no seed

28. *The Galway Mercury*, 26 December 1946.

supplied from the landlords. There are some proprietors giving some trifling compensation to the poor to leave their homes, and turn them adrift on the world's wild waste. Six pounds is an ordinary offer made to a family of seven, to leave the home of their fathers either to die by the highway, or become a burthen on the public. There are seven families in one village in a parish whose lease is expired and against whom a decree of eviction has been obtained, though they were prepared to pay the arrears due on the land, and to submit to an advanced rent. They are to be turned off, and some little money given them in order to give up the quiet possession of their houses and land. The poor people have been threatened with a visit from the sheriff for some weeks past; but I believe the above manner of treating them is the most plausible at the present time.

Source: *The Pilot,* 21 April 1847, 4.

Return (number 2) by Revd Patrick Lyons, P.P. of Kilmeen:

Number of deaths from 1st October 1846 to 1st April 1847? 30.
Number of same known to be caused by famine? 14 died of actual want, and a great many more by disease, occasioned by want, out of a population of 1,000 in this small parish.

I deem it imprudent to delay for any considerable time, any necessary information which might lead to a perfect elucidation of that sad tale of woe and destitution, so glaringly depicted in the emaciated countenances of the people. One townland in particular (the property of a nobleman whose character as a good and kind landlord stands very high in the estimation of the public, and who holds at present a distinguished place in the ministry) presents the most melancholy picture of the awful privations of the unfortunate poor. Seven human beings, slain by the desolating sword of famine, bequeathing no other legacy to their wives and children, but to drink of the cup of bitterness and affliction which hurried themselves to the grave. This village (Racecourse) which was once the scene of gaiety and the irresistible source of amusement to the gentry of the entire province, is now become a field of desolation – seven human beings dead in it of starvation, and five families (twenty-three persons) turned adrift on the world's wide waste, without home, without shelter, without the means of emigrating, without any compensation but a few pounds, that will scarcely support their starving and naked children for a few weeks, and then be immured within the walls of a contagious workhouse, or prefer the alternative of dying of starvation by the highway.

It was indeed a harrowing scene to witness the widow and orphans (the day after the husband's remains, who died of want, were hurried to the grave) levelling to the ground their miserable cabin for some trifling compensation proffered to them by the agent, who refused the day before to advance the price of a coffin for the departed husband till the work of eviction would be fully completed.

You will not think it possible that a person who calls himself a minister of the Christian religion, would be a party to this wholesale and barbarous eviction. Are the worst days of penal enactments again to be revived? Is it thus that Protestantism maintains its vaunted character of independencies? Are the poor to be unhoused in order to establish a residence for a Protestant clergyman to entitle him to the tithes of a parish, where there has been no resident rector – no church – no congregation.

The tithes of the parish of Kilmeen are at present vested in the Ecclesiastical Commissioners, and the above unholy means are had recourse to in order to place them under the control of a Christian minister without a residence, a church, or a congregation in the parish.

Source: *The Pilot,* 7 May 1847, 1.

Kinvara Union, Kilmacduagh Diocese

Commentary

Described as the united parishes of Kinvara, Killian and Duras, this return covered the civil parishes of Kinvarradoorus and Killinny in south County Galway. The union was in Kilmacduagh diocese at the time of the Famine.[29] The statutory censuses reported the population of the two civil parishes at 5,430 in 1831 and 7,751 in 1841.[30] In 1841, 39 per cent of the housing was classified as fourth class and the female illiteracy rate was 88 per cent. The Protestant community was miniscule; the Public Instruction Commissioners identified only 20 Protestants in the 1831 census list.[31]

The return for the Union of Kinvara was signed by Revd Francis Arthur. Although Arthur had only recently been appointed parish priest, he had been curate in Kinvara for a number of years.[32] He was a staunch repealer, organising the collection of £21 2*s.* 3*d.*, the parish's contribution to the O'Connell Tribute in 1843, that sum 'forwarded by Rev. Francis Arthur, the highly patriotic and effective treasurer', who subscribed £1.[33]

Arthur may have inspired confidence as a treasurer, but his credentials regarding demographic analysis are less convincing. His numbers for deaths occurring in the periods October 1845–March 1846 and October 1846–March 1847 are deficient. The figure for deaths during the former period (52 deaths, or about 100 in a full year) implies a crude death rate of 11 per 1,000, given that the Catholic population of the parish was about 8,000 in mid-1845 (as our projection suggests). This death rate is far too low and suggests once again the kinds of problems with recording deaths that we

29. *Thom's Irish almanac, 1850*, 343.
30. *Abstract of Population Returns for Ireland, 1831,* BPP (1833), 634, 294, 296, 298; *Report of the Commissioners appointed to take the census of Ireland, for the year 1841,* BPP (1843), 504, 378. Killenhy parish is Killinny.
31. *First report of the Commissioners of public instruction, Ireland,* 4d.
32. *Dublin Weekly Register,* 2 December 1843.
33. *Dublin Weekly Register,* 23 December 1843.

noted earlier. Our population estimates for the parish in 1845 (about 8,000 Catholics and a total population of 8,100) is well off the 10,000 that Arthur speaks of in his return.

Although he would have known that his return was likely to be published in the press, as others were, he used the main points in his return in a desperate letter he wrote to the *Freeman's Journal* at the same time. Tantalisingly, he refers to 'a black registry of deaths' kept in the parish and used to detail 'the number that fell victims to the principles of political economy'. His reference to the importance of having a resident Protestant clergyman in the area to assist with poor relief is also particularly noteworthy.

To the Editor of the *Freeman*
Kinvara, County Galway, 24 April 1847.
Dear Sir,
As your good journal is so often the medium of calling public attention to where distress exists, I beg leave to request, on behalf of my famishing people, that you would be please'd to insert the following:-

This parish is as poor as any in the western part of Ireland – there are many causes to account for this poverty. In the first place, there is not a resident landlord, one weak old gentleman excepted, living in an union of three parishes, and hence no private employment. The people in ordinary years depended solely for support on potatoes, and the selling of sea weed – the former has totally failed, and the weed in consequence of the disappearance of the root, is of little or no value – the boat which usually sold for £1 10*s*., is now freely given for two or three shillings. Again, we have no resident Protestant clergyman to assist, as they so nobly do in other places, in the great work of charity.

From these and other causes arises the peculiarly unfortunate state of this locality, and which have reduced the people to the greatest possible degree of destitution. It is my opinion that out of a population of ten thousand, there won't be four hundred who will not be fit objects for relief. God only knows how prostrated we are in mind and body at this frightful state of things, and from not knowing how two thirds of the population can be kept alive for the next three months. Deaths here from positive starvation, and from dysentery arising from bad food, such as nettles, and sea weed, from October last up to the present time, amount to 148.

The mortality would be much greater but for the extraordinary exertions of Doctor Hynes, of this place (who in fact is, I am sorry to say, the only person to look on this mass of human beings). He sacrificed his time, professional duties, and the interests of himself and family for these poor neglected creatures.

By his exertions, both public and private, life was kept in many who otherwise would be numbered in the black registry of deaths now kept by us to show the number that fell victims to the principles of political economy. Many a time have I been called to give the sacraments to creatures dying by the roadside, where they used to fall from exhaustion. Not many days ago I went to see a family at Claddagh, one of whom wanted a priest. Oh! what a sight there presented itself. There were five, the mother and four children, in one litter of straw, all nearly dead for want of food. When some nourishment was then brought in the only exertion they could make was when they saw the food to open wide their mouths like so many unfledged birds!
I remain, dear Sir, your obedient servant,
Francis Arthur, Adm.[34]

34. *Freeman's Journal*, 28 April 1847.

Return by Revd Francis Arthur, P.P. for Kinvara union:

Number of deaths by starvation from 1st October 1846 to 1st April 1847? 148.
Number of deaths occasioned by eating bad food – such as nettles, seaweed? 98.[35]
Average number during the same period last year? 52.

We are in an awful state in this locality. No public works going on – what the imperial ukase left undone was crowned by the money which I must say was so niggardly voted by the gentlemen of the barony being run out. In one week 1,130 were thrown off the roads without any resource in the world, and the consequence was the deaths of many of them. It is now a fortnight since a session was held in Gort, but as yet not a soul employed. The new relief [Soup Kitchen] act for the gratuitous distribution of food is commenced, but it is sought to find out many who should not get any. But the fact is, out of a population of 10,000 there is not 100 who would not be ranked under the first class paupers.

How, I ask, could they be in any other state? In a union of three parishes there is not a single resident landed proprietor, one old feeble gentleman excepted; no resident Protestant rector to assist in the great work of charity – in fact, not a human being to take the slightest interest in the lives of this mass of wretched, and landlord forsaken creatures, but Dr. Hynes of this town and myself. There must remain of necessity a large quantity of land untilled. No seed, no money, no encouragement from their landlords.

I am nearly exhausted in body and spirits by having for some time past to attend to these parishes. Not an hour of the day or night that I am not giving the sacraments to my doomed parishioners. My late dear co-operator, Rev. Mr Forde, was hurried to an untimely grave, broken-hearted at the frightful scenes he had witnessed.

Oh how often do I pray the giver of all good things to restore health and spirits to our beloved O'Connell, that he may once more send his voice through the land to have one universal shout of execration raised against a ministry that won't give food or employment to the loyal subjects of our Queen.

Source: *The Pilot*, 7 May 1847, 1.

Oranmore and Ballynacourty, Galway Diocese

Commentary

The Death Census return for Oranmore was submitted by Revd Timothy Newell, curate of the Union. Newell was a recent arrival in Oranmore, being transferred there from St Nicholas East city parish in 1845. His first appearance in the parish's baptismal register was on 7 August 1845, so his familiarity with the parish may have been limited.[36]

35. The *Freeman's Journal*, 15 May 1847, presents a synopsis of this return, which commences 'deaths by famine, 148, in addition to 98, occasioned by a melancholy subsistence on sea weed, nettles, "bliskane", &c.'.
36. *The Nation*, 13 January 1844, 1; https://registers.nli.ie/registers/vtls000634198#page/23/.

He was a firm supporter of O'Connell and the policy of Repeal, paying £1 for membership of the Association in 1844, and, alongside many other Galway priests, opposed the government's Colleges Bill, signing a declaration to that effect as 'Administrator of Oranmore' in November 1845.[37] He also wrote long, detailed letters to the newspapers, outlining the critical state of his district, of which two are presented below. Ironically, Newell's letters provide us with greater details on conditions in Oranmore than his Return does, including stories, witnessed by him, of bloated bodies, and bodies decaying and putrefying before death.

To the Editor of the *Galway Mercury*
Oranmore, 5 January 1847.
Dear Sir,
On a late occasion your kindness afforded me what I fear, was too considerable a space in your journal, to detail some of the melancholy consequences, resulting in this locality from starvation, and the apathy of public functionaries, would to God, that circumstances of a like horrifying character did not again force me, to trespass upon you for a similar indulgence, and to become once more the herald of sorrowful tidings. Another victim of gaunt hunger and want, the Widow Logan, of Balinacourty, has been sacrificed to the theory of political economy, which our rulers are determined, it would appear, to carry undeviatingly into execution. The poor creature's husband died about three weeks ago from starvation, and she has herself now followed to 'that bourne whence there is no return, where the wicked cease trouble and the weary are at rest'.

I fear, Sir, the tragical drama is only beginning for those most helpless members of society – the destitute widows and orphans, the aged and the infirm – classes for whom the paternal benevolence of government has made no provision. It may be asked, why do they not go to the Poor House? But you, Sir, can well answer that by informing the querist, that the workhouse of this Union is filled to overflowing, so much so that the propriety of closing it, for want of funds, was discussed at the Board of Guardians the last meeting day. The only alternative left therefore for such unfortunate creatures in this quarter, is to perish in their helplessness. Oh! if the cold hearted economists were but to hear their agonising supplications for relief, they would have some other than human nature or they would he induced to change this course of policy in their regard. But, perhaps, I may not be far-sighted enough to see the beauty of the policy of the government, or able to fathom the depth of their benevolent intentions in regard to the above named classes. The instinct of nature, I know, urges the brute creation to procure necessaries for their helpless progeny, and makes them foster them the more and guard them from evil, in proportion to their inability to aid themselves. Perhaps, it may be some beautiful social instinct bearing an analogy to the other, that impels our political protectors to keep provision away from the most helpless members of society, namely, the widows and orphans, the aged and infirm, lest, perhaps, they might be tempted to gorge themselves with food and kill themselves with repletion. I must confess I was silly enough to think that in a calamity like the present, it was most consonant to the principles of political economy, to provide in particular, for such as were unable to help themselves, but, I should suppose, our enlightened rulers think it would be better on all accounts, to let such excrescences on the social body drop off, by the stimulant of food being withheld

37. *The Nation*, 26 October 1844; *Freeman's Journal*, 14 November 1845.

from them,– perhaps the State Doctor may be right, but, I must acknowledge, I cannot bring myself to approve of such a system. But I shall not proceed further philosophising on their principles of action but relate some more of my experiences, which, I trust, in their sad and strange characters, will speak for themselves.

On Sunday last I was called to see a sick family in this parish, consisting of a widowed mother and three children, and though I have met in my clerical ministrations, with several cases of affliction and wretchedness, I have never seen so frightful a scene of living misery, as came then under my observation. The three children, who were afflicted with either the smallpox or measles, were literally a mass of filth and suppuration, huddled together upon a litter straw that was perfect dung; their little bodies were shivering with the cold, having only the few rags they were in the habit of wearing by day, covering them, and when I entered the house, I found the woe-worn mother, with the instinct that impels the hen to cover over her chickens, stooping over the afflicted children to screen them from the piercing blast! Not a spark was there, to illumine the dreary and cheerless hearth – not even the shelter of a roof had the wretched creatures; for it was pervious to the winds and the rain of Heaven, and worse than all, they had nothing to take in the shape of nourishment for the day or two previous to my visit except the cold water, which the poor little sufferers were ever and anon calling to their mother in weak and enfeebled accents to moisten their parched lips with. In the horror of the scene, I prayed to the Almighty, that I might never again see such another.

But the above is no solitary instance of widow and orphan suffering in this quarter; hundreds of cases are to be met with, it not possessing such an intensity of misery as the one I have detailed, still presenting features of horrifying suffering and privation. Many of these unfortunate creatures are to be met with looking for relief, more like walking skeletons, than beings possessed of living flesh and blood. There are no less than Three Hundred destitute widows in this parish, with an average of about two or three children each, and about Two Hundred aged and infirm persons; and, in the name of the God of Heaven, what will become of them? It is true some of them would be able earn a scant subsistence for themselves, if they were to be employed on the public roads; but, besides the demoralising tendency of females being put to labour on the public works, I regret to state that public employment in this locality is nearly extinct. There are at least, at the present moment, about One Thousand destitute unemployed labourers here, each with his quantum of family depending him for maintenance. We are to have, forsooth, a Baronial meeting on Saturday next, to shape our work for the people; but I must confess, I am beginning to look upon such proceedings as "a solemn humbug – a farce upon a monster scale". The old adage of "the mountain being in labour and bringing forth but a mouse"[38] is perfectly exemplified in such sessions, where the fuss and bustle of magistrates, rate-payers, country gentlemen and priests, met together to devise employment for the starving poor, eventuates in almost nothing at all. At the last Baronial meeting held at Claranbridge, presentments were passed for £38,000, and out of that amount their high-mightinesses, the commissioners of public works, in their munificent liberality towards a starving people, condescended to sanction about £4,000, to be expended in employing the poor of a very large Barony!! I fear some similar consummation will be the result of the next meeting.

38. Revd John Brennan's Death Census return for Killedan, County Mayo, included a reference to this same adage.

The people who have long enough lived upon "the hope deferred" are beginning now to listen to the promptings of despair, and I fear, that the links which religion bound round the peasant's heart hitherto, will be loosened, if not severed, bv the dreadful cravings of hunger. Depredations upon property, so far as the killing of sheep and taking corn and turnips are, notwithstanding the remonstrances of the ministers of religion, becoming matters of frequent occurrence, and the poor having (as they think) tried far enough the process of maceration, are now beginning to have recourse to another system of livelihood. God in Heaven mend this state of things, and save the people from such sentiments becoming general. But, I fear by my lengthened observations that I am trespassing too much upon your indulgence, and therefore shall cut short further commentary at present, and beg to assure you, Mr. Editor, that I remain sincerely your's,
Timothy Newell, R.C.C.[39]

To Editor of the *Galway Mercury*
Oranmore, 23 February 1847
Dear Sir,
The wholesale destruction of human life, occurring here from want of the necessaries of life, is fast approximating to what we have read and heard of Scull and Skibbereen, a few weeks ago, and we shuddered to have to record deaths from starvation, by 'units', but now, alas! we have to compute them by 'dozens.' No less than 54 individuals (men, women, and children), have perished of want, since December last, in the parishes of Oranmore and Ballinacourty; and if the Government, from any compunctious feelings, shall require to ascertain, through their 'Relief Commissioners', the number of starved wretches provided for in the grave, I shall be able furnish to them with a truly black list, well authenticated, showing the names and residences of the persons victimised here, to the so much spoken of political economy of our rulers. Hitherto, the relief committee here have given coffins for the interment of the starved dead – but they are becoming so numerous now, that it has been resolved, instead of procuring the common decency of burial for the dead, to reserve the relief fund for the support of the living. I fear much that the want of coffins for the burial of the dead will cause them to be unburied, to generate infection, more disastrous to human life than the want of food itself. The unusual occurrence here of a human being having been interred without the decency of a coffin, took place (as I have heard) in the parish of Ballinacourty a few days ago, when the corpse, after being 5 or 6 days unburied, was at last sacked up in coarse canvass, and deposited in its parent earth. Another horrifying circumstance occurred near Oranmore, of a poor wretched woman named Redington, perishing unfelt during the night time, and in the morning the lifeless body was found partially devoured by rats. It is impossible for me to give you anything like an adequate description of the harrowing scenes of misery which the discharge of my clerical duties brings daily under my observation, and the sight of which I need not tell you, aggravates in a very great degree to me, the toilsome and very harassing labour which the attendance upon the dying and famine stricken poor has at the present imposed. I shall detail to you only a few of my melancholy experiences, and from them your readers will be able to judge the appalling character and intensity of the distress prevailing in this district. Oh! that some charitable Christians, some good Samaritans may be induced by the perusal, to pour oil and balm, by their benevolent contributions, into the wounds of the woe-worn children of affliction here.

39. *Galway Mercury and Connaught Weekly Advertiser*, 9 January 1847, 3.

On Thursday last, I was called to administer the last rites of religion to a sick female named Hynes, in the village of Carmoniest, in this parish, and on entering the hovel where she was, I found the wretched woman with her three children stretched on the same pallet straw, in the last stage of exhaustion from hunger. They had no fire to warm – no covering, save the rags they wore, to screen them from the blast – and food, l believe, they had none for the two previous days. Never can I forget the agonised, woe begone, and convulsive working of the afflicted father's countenance, as he stood, wringing his hands, looking on the misery of his dying family. A few hours after my departure, the eldest child went to its God, and the day following the second. The wife and the other child still linger, but I fear there are little hopes of their recovery. On the same day, I was called to attend another sick family, named Walsh, at Newtownbutler, and there I found the man of the house's sister, in the last agony, her body inflated to an amazing size, from air taking the place of other nutriment in the system – a common symptom of persons in the last stage of suffering from inanition. Beside this poor creature were stretched four emaciated children, more like tenants of the sepulchre than human beings. It was, in truth, a harrowing sight to witness, the poor little innocents particularly, in their want and misery. The adult mentioned above and one of the children, have since perished, and the rest are still in a very precarious way. Same day I was called to attend what a few weeks ago was the stout and the stalwart man, Patt Connell, of Newtownbutler, and I found him, on his wad of straw, borne down by the fell influence of hunger to such a degree of exhaustion as to be unable to speak. The starving wife and three or four shivering, half-starved children were grouped around the pallet of the dying man. Shortly after I attended him, he breathed his last. I attended a poor woman named Nancy Shaughnessy, of Oranbeg; who was labouring under dysentery, and the poor creature being left without attendance or cleanliness, had such a mephitic atmosphere about her, that several times, while I was giving her the sacraments, I was obliged to go out to inhale pure air. The misery of that poor creature's bed of sickness and death (for she died shortly after my visit), was enough to shock the most iron-hearted spectator. Without fire, without food, without covering or attendance, stretched on her pallet of straw, devoid of all consolations save those which religion afforded, she slept the sleep which knows no waking.

On Friday last I was called see a family named Christian, of N.T.Butler, and there were the five or six children half naked and shivering over a few embers that were on the hearth, while the father himself and another child were stretched together in sickness on a litter of a straw; not an article of furniture of any kind was to be seen in the house, and the desolate appearance of everything around, was enough to strike a chill on the heart.

Yesterday I administered the rites of the Church to a sick person – in the opposite corner was the corpse of a victim of starvation with only a sack covering it. But I shall not trespass upon you by any more of these painful details ; oh! what a number of them could I not furnish you with. The destroying Angel, in the shape of famine, is devastating the country, and still the remedial measures of foreign legislation drag their slow length along, and Heaven only knows when we shall have the benefit (if ever we have any) of their application. But for the charitable relief dispensed to the poor here, in however small quantities individually, the number of the dead would by this time, in all likelihood be trebled....

I have great apprehensions, though now that the ratio of starvation deaths will be frightfully augmented, as about 500 individuals have been thrown out of employment here,

by works being suspended for want of funds. God in Heaven help the poor, for dismal is the prospect before them. Begging your indulgence for being more diffuse than I intended in this communication, and thus trespassing too much on your space,
I beg to remain, dear Sir, Yours very truly,
Timothy Newell, R.C.C.[40]

Newell's figure of 20 deaths for the October 1845–March 1846 period is far too low. We estimate that the Catholic population was around 11,800 in 1845, and hence, deaths should fall somewhere in the range of 135–200 in a parish of that size. Nonetheless, the number of deaths during the October 1846–March 1847 period, at 240, is well above the likely upper limit in normal times, indicating significantly elevated mortality during the Famine.

Return by Revd Timothy Newell, curate for Oranmore and Ballynacourty:

Number of deaths from the 1st of October 1846 to 1st April 1847? 240.
Number of same known to be caused by famine? About 200 individuals, men, women and children, have perished for the effects of want in this parish.
Number of deaths during the same period last year? 20.

Several instances have occurred in this parish of almost all the members of families being carried off from the effects of famine. I have known some families where five members perished, others in which three, many in which two. I regret to have to state that fever is now unfortunately superadded to famine and dysentery here, and numbers are suffering from it. The evil is likely to be very much extended and aggravated from the want of a local fever hospital. I know instances of all the members of families being laid sick in fever, and no one to attend them. The food supplied by relief committees suits not the condition of the sick; so the poor wretches are in an awful state of want and misery. I fear that this infection (if it spread) will be the most dreadful ingredient in the vial of God's wrath that is being poured out upon the poor. The new relief act (Soup Kitchen) has not as yet come into operation here, and the gentry do not seem over solicitous to work it; whilst, on the other hand, the labour rate act is so far set aside, that very few, comparatively speaking, of the destitute population are deriving any alleviation of their want from it. The land is tolerably well tilled (with the exception of what is held by the one or two-acre tenants, who had no seed to sow and were not able to procure it). Potatoes have been sown to a greater extent than people expected; but I am sorry to say that the starving poor have in many instances picked up the seed under the pressure of their hunger. Emigration has taken place to a great extent from this parish, and mostly of those classes of persons who were the most thriving, industrious and well behaved in general.

40. *Galway Mercury and Connaught Weekly Advertiser*, 27 February 1847, 2.

As if the cup of misery of the poor were not sufficiently charged with 'gall and vinegar', some landlords here are serving their tenants with notices of ejectment, so that lest famine should not kill its victims, extermination will be added.

Want of space does not allow me to say more, and I beg therefore to subscribe myself yours,

Timothy Newell, R.C.C.

Source: *The Pilot*, 28 April 1847, 3.

County Leitrim

Cloone-Conmaicne, Ardagh Diocese

Commentary

The Death Census return for Cloone-Conmaicne parish, in south County Leitrim, was prepared by the parish priest, Revd James McKiernan. McKiernan had been stationed in the parish since 1828, and in 1831 he can be found sending £8 5*s.* to the O'Connell Tribute, collected from his parishioners.[41] He was a supporter of the Repeal movement while loyal to the monarch, Queen Victoria, and was one of 74 Ardagh priests to counter-sign in 1841 Bishop William O'Higgins' letter (below) to T.M. Ray, the Secretary of the Association, seeking membership of the Association:

> Ballymahon, 28 January 1841.
> My dear Sir,
> The enclosed sum of £74 is from portion of the clergy of Ardagh, who, in common with their other brethren of this diocese, have been taught, by long and sad experience, that the only reasonable hope of justice for their beloved but oppressed country must rest upon repeal of the unconstitutional and tyrannical enactment commonly known by the absurd name of the Legislative Union. Their names and addresses will be found in the annexed list, and they desire me to request that you will, at your earliest convenience, have them enrolled members of the Loyal National Repeal Association. Others of our priests have already joined that patriotic and respected body, and within a few days you will have received the names and subscriptions of the 'hundred Ardagh priests' to whose political influence and determination I gave feeble expression at the Repeal meeting in Mullingar.
>
> For my own part, although I must respect their motives, I cannot but feel grieved at the fatal credulity of some honest Irishmen, who would still look for justice to an English parliament. England, to the amazement of civilised Europe, has too long exercised, under the name of law, cruel and barbarous sway over this ill-fated country; and should the foul and daring conspiracy of the Tories succeed in vesting itself with the hypocritic garb of legislation, heaven alone can foresee the consequences. Such a final disaster might force the country to seek remedy in that energy which often arises from despair, and it would be for those in whom the injured and insulted millions justly place their last and only hope, to consider such steps as the true spirit of the constitution, the experience of the past,

41. *Dublin Morning Register*, 13 April 1831.

and the justice of their cause might suggest for self-preservation, consistent with the most inviolable attachment to our good and gracious Queen.

Most ardently wishing that Englishmen may, in the spirit of common justice and common sense, accede to a speedy repeal of the detested Union, and thus avert every possibility of civil commotion, or a dismemberment of the empire.

I am, my dear Sir, yours truly,
W. HIGGINS.[42]

Thereafter, he regularly appears, along with his curate, Revd P. O'Farrell, in Repeal Rent lists.[43] McKiernan's report on Cloone-Conmaicne describes an area devastated by famine. He claims that deaths during the six-month period from October 1846 to March 1847 were nearly ten times the level that they had been a year previously, and that the number was accelerating. There is little doubt that his figure for the pre-Famine period does not include all deaths in the parish. In 1841, 39 per cent of the housing in the *civil* parish of Cloone (not coterminous with the Catholic parish of Cloone-Conmaicne) was classified as fourth class and the female illiteracy rate was 70 per cent.

Return by Revd James McKiernan, P.P. for Cloone-Conmaicne:

Number of deaths from 1st October 1846, to 1st April 1847? 260.
Number of same known to be caused by famine? 230.
Number of deaths during the same period last year? 27.

Men, women and children have perished from the effects of hunger in this parish. Fever and dysentery are very prevalent in this parish, and mortality rapidly increasing. The shrieks and cries of the poor are disheartening – their squalid and emaciated appearance indicative of approaching death. Many of them have dropped dead in the public roads and private passes, and several have been interred without coffins. I fear the relief granted by the legislature is not sufficient to save them from starvation. There is a great deal of land prepared for a crop, but remains unsown for the want of seed, &c.

A great number have emigrated to America, leaving their fatherland without any compensation. No resident landlords, nor any to afford relief to our starving poor.

Source: *The Pilot*, 19 May 1847, 2.

Drumreilly Lower, Kilmore Diocese

Commentary

Drumreilly Lower parish straddles the border between north Leitrim and south County Cavan. In 1841, 45 per cent of the housing in the Carrigallen barony part of the *civil* parish of Drumreilly (not coterminous with the Catholic parish of Drumreilly Lower)

42. *Dublin Morning Register*, 2 February 1841.
43. *Freeman's Journal*, 2 May 1845.

was classified as fourth class and the female illiteracy rate was 64 per cent. The return was prepared by Revd B. M'Conochy, curate of the parish. This is Bernard Conaty, who was ordained in 1845, and had been appointed curate of Drumreilly Lower after his ordination, under Philip Freeman, parish priest, remaining in the parish until 1849, when he transferred to Templeport.[44] Conaty describes serious distress in the parish. His estimate of the number of deaths between October 1846 and March 1847 is five times the number he reported for the same period a year previously, and the mortality rate was said to be increasing with some of his parishioners dying in the open.

Return by Revd B. M'Conochy, R.C.C. for Drumreilly Lower:

Number of deaths in this parish from 1st October 1846 to 1st April 1847? 64.
Number of same known to be caused by famine? 26.
Number of deaths during the same period last year? 12.

There were two very sudden deaths since 1st April; one, Patrick Kelagher, who kept travelling till he fell in the field, and was carried in dead. The other, Thomas Aypell, was working up to his death on the relief works.

The present state of the parish is alarming; the deaths from the 1st of April up to this amount to 15, all but two caused by starvation. The outdoor relief will never save us from starvation and death. We have no public works; had but few during the winter and spring. The new arrangements only increase and aggravate our distress, as our parish is cut up in small farms, which, by the working of the new act here, excludes the small farmers from the outdoor relief. Such a law will never stay the spread of famine.

There are lands – townlands I mean – in the parish of 100 acres, not having ten acres under grain crops. There are hundreds of acres tilled and prepared for crops that cannot be cropped this season. Our wheat, rye, and bere crops of last winter's sowing are all gone, and our early sowing of this year is nearly all gone too. Our late crops, which are limited, are promising pretty well.

Emigration was rather limited here from want of means, not of will. But we have a land-clearing – house-levelling – lattitatting, ejecting system here, our great curse is absenteeism. Our only resident proprietor is Wm. C Percy, esq. Garridice [Garadice]. But the patience of our people – their submission to the will of God in this awful visitation – their respect for the laws of the land – their strict attention to the advice and soul-saving instructions of their priests, had no parallel in the world's history. How long will this state of things continue? How long will the father sit by and see his children fall and die by the wall, like the spider when his slender thread is broken? Once the pride of his heart – the support and stay of his declining years, and consolation of his death bed.

44. Francis MacKiernan, *Diocese of Kilmore, Bishops and Priests, 1136–1988* (Breifne Historical Society, 1989), 66, 133, 194.

Should our rulers and the Board of Works delay much longer in re-opening the relief works [Public Works], all the advice of the priests, all their influence and instructions, will be lost on the now obedient and starving people; their voice will no more be heard than the cry of the drowning mariner in the roar of the tempest; nor would the Egyptian granaries save thousands from death before the 1st of August, if the able-bodied get no employment, or the small farmers get no outdoor relief, unless they give up their little holdings to tyrant landlords, without compensation for seed and labour.

I regret I did not receive this in time to have it filled and returned to you for last Monday. The absence of the parish priest, and heavy duty on my part, rendered it almost impossible to be attended to sooner.

Source: *The Pilot*, 11 June 1847, 4.

Drumreilly Upper, Kilmore Diocese

Commentary

Named as Drumvilly Upper in the return, this submission is for Drumreilly Upper parish in south-east County Leitrim. In 1841, 45 per cent of the housing in the Carrigallen barony part of the *civil* parish of Drumreilly (not coterminous with the Catholic parish of Drumreilly Upper) was classified as fourth class and the female illiteracy rate was 64 per cent. The parish priest was Revd Michael Smith, who had been in that role since 1819. Revd John Maguire was the diocesan administrator and had previously been appointed curate of Kildallan (1829) and Oughteragh (1838). He became curate of Drumreilly Upper the year following the Death Census, and parish priest of Killasnett in 1849.[45] Maguire reported a near tripling of deaths between October 1846 and March 1847 in comparison with the same period a year previously. Interestingly, he notes that he received relief from the brother of Irish M.P. William Smith O'Brien, a leading figure in the Young Ireland movement.

Return by Revd John Maguire, Adminstrator, Drumvilly Upper:

Number of deaths from 1st October 1846 to 1st April 1847? 132.
Number of same known to be caused by famine? 75.
Number of deaths during the same period last year? 51.

Answer to 1st query – All the cases remarkable for their forbearance under their severe destitution.

State of the parish most deplorable; no resident gentlemen; principal part in the Court of Chancery; not even a Protestant clergyman residing in it; has a meal store and boiler, and were it not for the more than human exertions of the Rev Henry O'Brien, brother to Smith O'Brien, M.P., who comes from

45. MacKiernan, *Diocese of Kilmore*, 64.

the neighbouring parish to my assistance, we would all perish. If the Board of Works could be prevailed upon to complete the works and roads unfinished, it would be the most speedy relief. The land partially tilled, and where tilled, prospects favourable. Emigration was extensive before the famine, but those who would emigrate are unable for want of means.

I have the honour to be, your most obedient servant,

John Maguire, Administrator.

Source: *The Pilot*, 23 June 1847, 3.

Glenade, Kilmore Diocese

Commentary

The Catholic parish of Glenade straddles the border between counties Sligo and Leitrim, near Donegal Bay. In 1841, 34 per cent of the housing in the *civil* parish of Rossinver (not coterminous with the Catholic parish of Glenade) was classified as fourth class and the female illiteracy rate was 69 per cent. The return for the parish was prepared by Revd Francis O'Reilly, P.P., who had been transferred to the parish from nearby Killinagh parish in 1839, replacing Hugh De Lacy, who became parish priest of Killinagh, replacing Laurence Mawn, deceased.[46] O'Reilly joined the Repeal Association in August 1841, one of a dozen Kilmore priests to sign up at that time. Notably, they hoped that O'Connell himself would propose their membership if he was in attendance. He was, and his motion for the 12 to be admitted passed unanimously.[47]

Mr. Ray read the minutes of the last day's proceedings and then proceeded to read the correspondence which had been received since the last day of meeting. Among them was the following letter from the Rev. J. Rogan, P.P., Manorhamilton:

> Manorhamilton, August 16, 1841.
> Dear Sir, I enclose half notes for £12 10*s*., the subscriptions of the undernamed twelve clergymen of the diocese of Kilmore, who request the honour of being proposed Repeal members by the Liberator, should he happen to be at the next meeting of the Association. They have taken an active part in by-gone struggles; and for past exertions, or any services to be rendered on the present eventful occasion, they shall be amply recompensed should this expression of their feelings in anywise contribute to cheer and support him in his arduous career. May God bless and protect him is our ardent prayer, and. that of the, millions of his warm hearted admirers Our zeal in the cause will appear manifest from the remittances to be shortly made by the wardens appointed in our respective parishes [...] [The eleven priests were then named].
> Your very obedient and humble servant,
> J. Rogan.[48]

46. MacKiernan, *Diocese of Kilmore*, 74, 94, 186.
47. *Freeman's Journal*, 18 August 1841.
48. *Freeman's Journal*, 18 August 1841.

By 1843, O'Reilly was being described as 'an old and valued member of the Association', when sending remittances totalling an impressive £21 11*s*. from 'the poorest parish in Ireland'. The parish may not have been able to fund a curate, as O'Reilly noted in his Death Census return, but it would not be found wanting when national pride was at stake. Ironically, though, the following year the Association publicly noted that Glenade was one of a number of County Leitrim parishes which failed to collect Repeal Rent in 1844.[49]

O'Reilly's figures for the number of deaths reported in his Death Census return are out of step with the returns received from many other parishes. He claims that the deaths in Glenade during the six-month period October 1846–March 1847 totalled 173, compared with 143 deaths during the same period a year previously. This represents a rise of just 30 deaths, or about 20 per cent, a far lower proportion than was reported for most other parishes in his county.

Return by Revd Francis O'Reilly, P.P. of Glenade:

Number of deaths from 1st October 1846 to 1st April 1847? 173
Number of same known to be caused by famine? 129 [likely meant 29].
Number of deaths during the same period last year? 143.

I am parish priest of the poorest parish in Ireland. I am placed in the bogs of Leitrim, where the plough was never stretched. No Protestant church – no resident gentleman – no magistrate – no respectable person to co-operate with me. The parish is small, and the people are so very poor, that we could not support a curate.

The land here consists of reclaimed bog. No wheat. The poor people chiefly depended on the potato – the potato perished, and the poor are perishing for want of them. We have no soup. For God's sake, in the name of humanity, can you point out to me where, when, and how, I could procure some relief to help us to wade through those few trying scenes.

Observe that in all cases where old people were employed on the public works, that they could not procure for themselves and family a sufficiency of food. They sank exhausted and died.

Source: *The Pilot*, 28 May 1847, 4.

Killenummery and Killerry, Ardagh Diocese

Commentary

The union of Killenummery and Killerry straddled the border between Leitrim and Sligo; Killenummery parish is in Leitrim, Killerry in Sligo. In 1841, 38 per cent of the housing was classified as fourth class and the female illiteracy rate was 72 per cent. The return for the parish was made by Revd Daniel MacGill, parish priest. MacGill

49. *Tipperary Free Press*, 16 September 1843; *Weekly Freeman's Journal*, 24 August 1844.

had been curate of the parish, serving under Revd Peter Magauran, but following Magauran's death in December 1837, aged 65, he succeeded as parish priest.[50]

Well known in the locality, he was a prominent member of the North Leitrim Agricultural Society,[51] and a firm supporter of O'Connell's drive for Repeal. The *Freeman's Journal*'s reported a 'magnificent Repeal demonstration in Sligo' in October 1845, reputedly attended by 200,000, that is, 20,000 above the population reported for the County by the national census four years previously. MacGill's attendance at the 'Monster Banquet' held to celebrate the event was noted.[52]

> The Monster Banquet was held in the Repeal Reading Room, New Bridge Street [...] From the walls were suspended several banners with appropriate inscriptions – 'The memory of Grattan and Flood'; 'Repeal and No Surrender'; 'Ireland for the Irish'; 'O'Connell, the Father of his Country'; 'Repeal of the Union'; 'Never give up'; 'For a nation to be free she only has to will it'; 'Peace and Perseverance'; 'Old Ireland'; 'Civil and Religious Liberty'.
>
> At the head of the room where the President's table stood was erected a canopy supported by two Ionic pillars, and on the pediment rested a well-executed painting of Drumcliffe Bay, with a round tower in the distance. Over the entrance door was a gallery, set apart for the accommodation of ladies, about one hundred of whom were present. The windows on either side of the grand entrance were ornamented with two transparencies representing the old parliament house, 'God save the Queen' being inscribed above and 'It was and shall be underneath' [*sic*]. The *tout ensemble* was strikingly picturesque. The green and gold uniforms of the members of the '82 Club, contrasted with the more homely garb of the citizens, and the gay dresses of the women, imparted additional charms to all.[53]

Prophetically, the same edition of the newspaper (18 October 1845) contained the following worrying report on 'the potato crop in the West', cautioning, in language that must have appeared sensationalist to many readers, that the failure of 'the people's crop' might be a looming prospect.

> THE POTATO CROP IN THE WEST (from our own correspondent)
> As the potato crop begins to be gathered in a feeling of insecurity, not yet amounting to panic, begins to manifest itself throughout the province. The true state of the crop is not yet known, and I feel that it is my duty, however the statement may savour of the 'alarmist', to state that, from what I have seen and learned from others, the true state will, I much fear, prove more alarming than the Worst anticipations have already reached. In truth, the alarm is at present confined to the reflecting few, the many neither investigating the facts, nor calculating the probable results of those which they have ascertained.

50. There is a reference to Magauran's death in the registers for the parish. (https://registers.nli.ie/registers/vtls000632439#page/59/mode/1up, 17 December 1837).
51. *Sligo Champion*, 20 September 1845.
52. *Freeman's Journal*, 18 October 1845, 3–4.
53. *Freeman's Journal*, 18 October 1845. The meeting was attended by more than 60 persons, with J.P. Somers as president. More than 50 of those listed were clerics.

I do not think the crop is as much affected by the rot as the writers of some of the agricultural articles in the public journals seem to imagine, yet I am persuaded that there exists a false sense of security in many districts where the plague has not yet shown itself. I say yet, for such is the character manifested by it in the several localities I have visited, that the field - the plot - the very ridge which today *seems* safe, may, within two days, be found to be thoroughly infected. I have before me as I write a dish of potatoes, some of them as fine looking, firm, and well-coloured, presenting to the casual observer all the appearances of sound and good potatoes, yet, on close examination, these healthy looking potatoes present the early stages of the incipient and rapidly advancing rot. In fact they appear sound, and would sell in the market as sound potatoes, if the purchaser were not well acquainted with the disease. An examination of this dish of potatoes leads me to conclude that the disease is more general than is supposed, and in some measure, at least, accounts for the *apparently* sudden infection alluded to above. In fact, the labourers will dig out tubers affected by the rot in its incipient stages and not be aware of the presence of the disease. Yet in a short space of time – perhaps not over four-and-twenty hours – those potatoes, so recently healthy looking, will be found rotten to their very centre.

This peculiarity of the disease is one cause – a manifest one – of the uncertainty that prevails as to the state of the crop. Another cause is that the general crop has not yet been dug out. In Mayo the farmers are beginning to complain. A most intelligent clergyman tells me that in his parish, situate about five miles south of Castlebar, the injury sustained is extensive. His calculation is that every third potato is bad. In the neighbourhood of Westport a similar report has been made to me, while in the vicinage of Ballina there seems to be no cause of complaint. But I do not place too much reliance on the confidence felt in this latter and more northern district, for as I passed along through it I saw that the general crop was yet in the ground and the stalks seemed still unfaded in most of the fields.

Indeed all through Mayo the general crop yet remains undug, and from what I have already stated, you will at once perceive that the digging of a few baskets in different parts of a field is no test of the presence or absence of the fatal malady, It may be *apparently* absent to day, or for aught at present I know of the pathology of the disease, really absent, and within a few days the tubers may be far advanced in decay. In the fair-green of Screen, about half-way between Ballina and Sligo, I conversed with many of the farmers from different parts of the county. They manifested uncertainty, but not alarm. I hope they may not have cause for alarm, but I confess that the result of careful and extensive inquiries through the three counties of Mayo, Sligo, and Roscommon, leads me to fear that their confidence is the result of ignorance of the character of the disease. The fully developed malady they cannot fail to recognise, even the incipient they are beginning to know; but the fact that a potato will appear healthy one day and diseased the next, though learned by many from sad experience during the past week, seems to be not yet universally known. In the immediate vicinage of the town of Sligo the disease has appeared and created much anxiety. The expediency of holding a public meeting to discuss the propriety of memorialing [memorialising] the Privy Council to take measures to preserve the corn for the use of the people has been canvassed, and I believe only deferred till further information should be obtained. In Boyle, the place from which I now write, a large proportion of the crop is damaged, but there is a sort of compensation as if providentially provided, in the quantity of the tubers. Here the disease is as prevalent in the high as in the low damp ground.

I write this, for the purpose of giving you, without delay, as much information as I could collect on this important subject. My deductions may appear to be rather more alarming

> than the facts would warrant. Would to God they may prove so! But, I write to you without reservation, and candidly confess that the rapidity with which the disease passes through its several stages – its sudden appearance, in a previously healthy-looking potato, and the, impossibility of knowing to what extent it has already, or may hereafter reach, has produced a feeling of alarm which the contemplation of the prospect – of even the possible failure – of the people's crop, cannot fail to excite.[54]

The *Journal*'s correspondent could hardly have foreseen what unfolded in the area over the following six years. The Famine was devastating in this region. MacGill's Death Census reported 171 deaths during the period October 1846 and March 1847, against 37 during the same period in the previous year. His return is undated, but he claimed that another 50 deaths had occurred in the weeks since 1 April. These figures indicate that deaths in the Famine period were running at nearly five times the normal level. However, we estimate the Catholic population in mid-1845 at about 7,100, and a population of this size would typically experience between 81 and 122 deaths in the six months between October and March in normal times. Hence, the 36 deaths reported by MacGill for the October 1845–March 1846 period is far too low.

Return of Revd D. MacGill, P.P. of Killenummery and Killerry:

Number of deaths from 1st October 1846 to 1st April, 1847? 171. And if it had not been limited to 1st April, 1847, I could place on record 50 more deaths.
Number of same known to be caused by the famine? 130.
Number of deaths during the same period last year? 36.

Very few outrages; preparations for supplying rations of soup, rice, and bread to the destitute poor; grants of money were given to a large amount by the boards of works; from 7 to 800 persons [i.e. 700–800] were employed during several months, but the wages being only 10*d.* per day seldom 1*s.* – hence, not only individuals, but entire families died of exhaustion, caused by an insufficiency of food, or by the bad quality of it.

Typhus fever and dysentery are rife in this district; there are daily victims; and the purport of the verdict of each inquest is, death occasioned by the monopoly of bread stuffs allowed to the merchants by Lord John [John Russell, P.M.], and the advocacy of political economy by Sir R. Routh [Randolph Routh, superintendent of famine-relief].

Cropping of the soil is pretty fair, but not to such an extent as would supply food to whatever miserable population may be in existence next harvest.

Emigration to a vast extent is prevailing here; some are unceremoniously deserting houses, land &c., and repairing to the seaport town of Sligo in order to embark for America.

Source: *The Pilot*, 12 May 1847, 4.

54. *Freeman's Journal*, 18 October 1845.

Kiltoghart, Ardagh Diocese

Commentary

The Catholic parish of Kiltoghart covered the southern part of the civil parish of Kiltoghert, County Leitrim.[55] In 1841, 54 per cent of the housing in the *civil* parish of Kiltoghert (not coterminous with the Catholic parish of Kiltoghart) was classified as fourth class and the female illiteracy rate was 64 per cent. Revd Felix Slevin had been appointed parish priest of Kiltoghart in July 1832, replacing Revd John McKeon. Slevin, vicar general of the diocese of Ardagh, remained parish priest until 1846, when Peter Dawson, 'respected and Irish hearted Catholic rector' of Rathcline, succeeded him.[56]

Dawson was a supporter of O'Connell, contributing to the O'Connell Tribute in 1846, and collecting his parish's Repeal Rent during that year.[57] It is no surprise, therefore, to see him participating in the Association's Death Census inquiry. According to Dawson, the number of deaths in the period October 1846–March 1847 was above three times the normal level. Indeed, he stated that the real death rate was much higher, but the presence of the workhouse, where many more deaths were occurring, reduced the official numbers in his parish. In some instances, people entered the workhouse when death was imminent for the purpose of obtaining a coffin for burial. Bodies were disposed of without recourse to a priest.

Return of Revd P. Dawson, P.P. of Kiltoghart:

Number of deaths from 1st October 1846 to 1st April, 1847? 320. Awfully great as this mortality is, the return would be much larger but that the district workhouse being in this parish very many go in to die, that they may ensure coffins. In the workhouse built for 800, 469 died between 1st October, 1846, and April, 1847, and 295 last month.
Number of same known to be caused by the famine: 150 died of actual starvation and of the remainder fully one half by disease produced by hunger.
Number of deaths during the same period last year? 98.

The state of the whole parish is such that it is impossible to select particular cases – father, mother, and children have been carried off in many cases. I will send you the names of those who died of starvation in a few days, with the names of the proprietors and middlemen under who they lived, as also what those have done to relieve their dependents. Every day makes things worse; fever spreading – no employment, as we had no resident proprietors, and our prospects for the next four months still more gloomy. Four grown persons died this day (2nd May) of actual starvation in one townland, yet our committee will afford no relief to grown (or, as they say, to able bodied) persons, nor to any person holding over two

55. There were variant spellings of parish names, e.g., Kiltoghart and Kiltoghert.
56. *The Pilot*, 6 May 1846; *Battersby's Catholic Directory*, 341.
57. *The Pilot*, 6 May 1846; *Dublin Weekly Nation*, 8 August 1846.

acres of land although the land will not be taken from them, and in some cases the whole family is in fever. The people are in such a state of alarm (or rather utter despair) that many adults die and are buried without the priest ever hearing of it. My return therefore is considerably under reality. A son was asked 'why he did not bring the priest to his father,' he answered 'I was seeking something to keep the life in seven children myself and wife.' Think of sending two lbs, of meal, four half rations to the younger four in a family of eight, four being adults and so of all families whatever their number.

Source: *The Pilot*, 7 May 1847, 1.

County Mayo

Addergoole, Killala Diocese

Commentary

There are two parishes called Addergoole in the west; one in Killala diocese in central Mayo, the second in north Galway, in Tuam diocese.[58] This return is for the Mayo parish, and it presents one of the more disturbing accounts from the Death Census. In 1841 74 per cent of the housing was classified as fourth class and the female illiteracy rate was 91 per cent – unmistakeable signs of economic and social deprivation. The parish priest of Addergoole was Patrick MacHale, transferred to the parish from Kilfian parish in 1840, to replace John Hopkins, who was moved to Skreen parish, in County Sligo.[59] MacHale submitted the return for Addergoole, and Hopkins the report for Skreen.

MacHale notes that some parishioners had been reduced to consuming weeds to stave off hunger, and reports that bodies were lying unburied for extended periods. According to MacHale, deaths had increased significantly, from 55 in the period October 1845–March 1846, to 240 in the same period a year later.

Return of Revd Patrick MacHale, P.P. of Addergoole:

Total number of deaths from 1st October 1846 to 1st April 1847? 240.
Number of same known to be caused by famine? 180.
Number of deaths during the same period last year? 55.

In many instances I have known persons to have lived on weeds for five days. A boy, by name Anthony M'Loughlin, of Castlehill, had the jaw literally fallen off him by famine and disease. A stouter young man [there] was not in the parish.

The remains of the dead are left often for a week without interment, the inhabitants of the village not having strength enough to carry them to the grave. Many die without the attendance of a priest, they fall off so suddenly. Hugh Moffitt

58. *Thom's Irish almanac, 1850*, 344.
59. *Freeman's Journal*, 21 February 1840.

and a grown child of his died within half an hour most suddenly. I attend in many places where all the members of the family have nothing but the appearance of spectres, actually crawling on all fours, or stretched out for death.

Description is impossible.

On a large extent of property held under James Anderson, of Mossbrook, there is no tillage. Colonel Knox's property is very badly tilled, comprising the fourth of the parish.

I had not an opportunity of making the above return earlier.

Source: *The Pilot*, 19 May 1847, 2.

Attymass, Achonry Diocese

Commentary

Attymass is a small parish located in east County Mayo, near the border with County Sligo, and south of Killala Bay. It borders Backs parish to the west, from which parish a return also emerged. In 1841, 87 per cent of the housing was classified as fourth class and the female illiteracy rate was 95 per cent. The Death Census for Attymass parish was prepared by the parish priest, Revd Michael O'Flynn. O'Flynn was a recent arrival in Attymass, transferred there from Colloony, in Sligo.[60] He made an appearance in the newspapers in January 1846, proposing a possible miraculous remedy for the disease of the tubers:

> The Potato Disease – Among the many unaccountable things connected with the disease in potatoes related to us, we have learned from the Rev. Mr O'Flynn, P.P. Attymass, a most respectable and well-informed gentleman, that one of his parishioners, having dug out his potatoes found them all affected with the disease, and considered them perfectly useless. The man, however, made a heap of them and covered them with a little straw and a few spades of soil, leaving them almost entirely exposed to the late rains and storm. After being in this state for ten or fifteen days, curiosity induced him to look at them, and, to his great astonishment, discovered that they had all become sound and fit for use. It is also a well known fact that potatoes which had been covered with water for weeks, and those left undug to the present, have continued undamaged, though exposed to so much wet. Which, then, is it better to allow them to be damp or to keep them free from moisture?[61]

O'Flynn's next known venture into print was his Death Census submission, published in May 1847, which appears to have had more substance than his elixir for the disease. The population of his parish had been recorded in the statutory censuses at 3,276 in 1831, rising only slightly to 3,435 by 1841.[62] Most of its inhabitants were Catholics; the Public

60. *Freeman's Journal*, 12 March 1844.
61. *Saunders News-Letter*, 3 January 1846.
62. 1833 (634) *Abstract of Population Returns for Ireland, 1831*; 1843 (504) *Report of the Commissioners appointed to take the census of Ireland, for the year 1841*, 398.

Instruction Commissioners noted only 36 Protestants enumerated by the 1831 census.[63] We estimate the Catholic population of the parish in mid-1845 at about 3,500, from which we would expect to see between 40 and 60 deaths in a normal October–March period. The 72 deaths reported by Revd O'Flynn for the October 1845–March 1846 period must, therefore, represent a return of all deaths which had occurred. By our estimates, Attymass is one of nine parishes which attempted to enumerate all deaths for the period October 1845 to March 1846. According to O'Flynn, circumstances in his parish were deteriorating rapidly, and unless something drastic was done 60 per cent of the population would die by November 1847. On average, five people per day were dying in the parish.

Return by Revd Michael O'Flynn, P.P. of Attymass:

Number of deaths from 1st October 1846 to 1st April 1847? 320.
Number of same known to be caused by famine? 240.
Number of deaths during the same period last year? 72.

Of several families from one to five died of actual starvation, and were from three to five days waiting for coffins, and ultimately buried in their rags, the only substitute for coffins. I feel perfectly at ease any day and night that I have not more than five or six sick calls to attend.

The stopping of the public works leaves this parish a perfect mass of destitution; at present there are to my perfect knowledge 250 cases of dysentery. Many previous cases proved fatal; about 400 are swelled in limbs and faces to an alarming extent. The tillage is not quite up to the six tenth of what it was last year – the potato crop one-fiftieth of last year.

I have no hope whatever of one-fortieth of the support necessary for my parish being so much, say thirty-nine-fortieth, of what it was last year; yet it is evident how far short we are of the amount of support for this year. Emigration is not to any considerable amount for want of means. The soup kitchens may stop the famine partially, but my opinion is, that they will increase dysentery.

I have to apologise for not having answered your letter ere this, on account of the extraordinary duties I have both day and night to perform, in consequence of dysentery brought on by starvation. It is painful to me to state that for want of provisions famine has increased 20 per cent since the 1st April, 1847, and I am perfectly conscious that the six-tenths of its present population will not survive until 1st November next.

Typhus fever is also raging and committing a great havoc. It is a very rare thing to see more than eight or ten persons at the burial of the corpse. A few days ago there were two little boys found dead on the road side at Bohalla [Boyhollagh], in my parish; these were three days dead before I heard of it on the evening of the third day. They were buried thus: - their coffins were the rags of clothes

63. *First report of the Commissioners of public instruction*, 52d.

they wore, and their graves a sandpit, into which they were thrown without my knowledge. A third has been thrown in since.

The mortality of my parish averages daily five deaths since the 1st April last, 1847. Unless immediate steps be taken by the government to stay the destroying sword that is depopulating the land, it will be once more the valley of eagles, and not the homes of Christians. May God in his mercy remove this calamity.

Source: *The Pilot*, 28 May 1847, 4.

Backs, Killala Diocese

Commentary

Backs Catholic parish, in Tirawley barony, north-east Mayo, was coextensive with the two civil parishes of Ballynahaglish and Kilbelfad. It borders Attymass parish to the east, for which a detailed Death Census return was also made. The population of Backs parish grew slowly it seems during the 1830s, rising marginally from 8,904 in 1831 to 9,078 by the time of the 1841 census.[64] In 1841 38 per cent of the housing was classified as fourth class and the female illiteracy rate was 90 per cent. The parishioners were almost exclusively Catholic; the Public Instruction Commissioners identified a mere 173 Protestants (1.9%) in the two civil parishes in the 1831 census list.[65]

The Death Census return for Backs was prepared by Revd Patrick J. MacHale, the parish priest. MacHale, not to be confused with Revd Patrick MacHale, parish priest of Addragoole parish, and signatory for that parish's Death census, was a supporter of O'Connell and the Repeal drive. He signed his name to a petition requesting a public meeting on the matter in August 1840,[66] and attended a Repeal Banquet in Castlebar in 1843 where 'the dinner, which was such as to please the most fastidious palate, was served up in a style of great elegance, and the wines were of choice vintage'.[67] It is to be hoped that the diet at the Repeal Banquet was of better taste than that described in an 1847 advertisement, from which we learn, while Famine mortality was rising, 'Ireland's greatest difficulty [...] is that of getting good tea'.[68]

We estimate the mid-year Catholic population of the Catholic parish at about 9,281 in 1845, collapsing to 7,842 in 1847. A population of that order in 1845 would typically witness between about 105 and 158 deaths in a normal October–March period, so MacHale's reported 24 deaths between October 1845 and March 1846 is too low. His figure for the Famine six-month period indicates that mortality in the parish was well above normal rates.

64. *Abstract of Population Returns for Ireland, 1831*, BPP (1833), 634, 318, 320; 1843 (504) *Report of the Commissioners appointed to take the census of Ireland, for the year 1841*, BPP, 398, 400.
65. *First report of the Commissioners of public instruction*, 52d. The Public Instruction Commissioners total for Kilbelfad civil parish is 3 less than the 1831 census figure.
66. *Freeman's Journal*, 11 August 1840.
67. *Nation*, 5 August 1843.
68. *Mayo Constitution*, 12 January 1847.

Return by Revd Patrick J. MacHale, P.P. of Backs:

Number of deaths from 1st October 1846 to 1st April, 1847? 189.
Number of same known to be caused by famine? 158.
Number of deaths during the same period last year? 24.

The present state of the parish is awful to contemplate, many without food for three days, except some meal and water they get instead of soup. The government arrangements [soup kitchens] will fall short in giving relief to half the destitute. The land is but very imperfectly cropped, and, I really think, next year will be more frightful. All that could or had means to emigrate have done so.

Source: *The Pilot*, 28 May 1847, 4.

Carracastle, Achonry Diocese

Commentary

Described as a return for the 'parish of Carracastle, half only of [the civil parish of] Killebrah', this parish is located in east County Mayo, bordering counties Roscommon and Sligo. In 1841, 81 per cent of the housing in the *civil* parish of Kilbeagh (not coterminous with the Catholic parish of Carracastle) was classified as fourth class and the female illiteracy rate was 88 per cent. O'Kane had arrived in Carracastle from Attymass in 1844, on the eve of the Famine, replacing the Repeal supporter, Revd Thomas M'Nicholas.[69] O'Kane, too, was a Repealer, paying £1 for his membership in 1844.[70] The description he gives of his parish in his Death Census response is harrowing, with people dying in the open and burials without coffins. He claims 300 deaths in the parish between October 1846 and March 1847, well above the unquantified total for the same period a year previously. The closure of Public Works was, according to O'Kane, a 'murderous edict'.

Return of Revd D. M. O'Kane, P.P. of Carracastle:

Number of deaths in this parish from 1st October 1846 to 1st April, 1847? 300.
Number of same known to be caused by famine? Three fourths of these have died of famine, and of fever and dysentery occasioned by famine.
Number of deaths during the same period last year? Very few deaths same period last year.

Several have perished on the high roads, and numbers in their hovels who would only be visited by the clergyman. At length we were obliged to commence burying them without coffins. The present state of the parish, owing to the advance of fever and dysentery, is most deplorable. Numbers are dying, and deaths have increased 20 per cent since government issued the murderous edict of stopping

69. *Freeman's Journal*, 12 March 1844; *Dublin Morning Register*, 30 September 1842.
70. *Freeman's Journal*, 9 July 1844.

the public works. A trifle of out door relief is being given, which is not sufficient to stay one third of the famine. About one-fourth of the land is tilled; for want of seed or support, no more could be done. Our prospects for the ensuing year are poor. Emigration to the next world is most extensive in this district. The people would emigrate if they had means. There are no coroner's inquests held now. I believe it was not considered necessary to be reporting the deaths of the mere Irish, however they might perish. But there is a God!

Source: *The Pilot*, 19 May 1847, 2.

Clare Island, Tuam Diocese

Commentary

Located off the coast of County Mayo, Clare Island had a population of 1,616 in 1831 and 1,615 in 1841. Populations of 554 and 577, respectively, were reported for Inishturk for the same years.[71] The religious breakdown of the island in 1831 is not available, but it is safe to assume based on anecdotal evidence that Catholics comprised the vast majority of the population.[72]

The parish priest at the time of the Death Census was Peter Ward, who had been stationed on the island since at least 1843.[73] He also subscribed to the Repeal Association that year.[74] Ward's return is one of the few responses which provides a complete listing of the names of the deceased within his parish in the period October 1846–March 1847, and we can have confidence that he was not exaggerating the death toll on the island, as there seems little likelihood that he went to the trouble of fabricating names that he knew would be available publicly.

The island's population was probably about 1,700 by mid-1845, so the 96 deaths reported by Revd Ward in the October 1846–March 1847 period, which is equivalent to a yearly total of about 165 deaths, equates to a very high mortality rate of nearly 100 per 1,000 people, more than three times greater than what we would normally expect. Ward appears to suggest that one-third of the population of Inishturk island had also died during the same six-month period, although his statement is ambiguous. According to Ward, mortality on Clare Island was about five times the level that it had been a year previously.

Ward wrote to the *Castlebar Telegraph* in April 1847, stating that coffinless burials were occurring on the island, because of the extreme situation they were dealing with, and 'for want of any fund'. It is surprising, therefore, that he failed to mention this in his Death Census response.[75]

71. *Abstract of Population Returns for Ireland, 1831*, BPP (1833), 634, 318; *Census of Ireland 1851: Part I, area, Population and number of houses, by townlands and electoral divisions, county of Mayo*, BPP, Command Papers (1852–53), 1542, vol. 92, xcii.453, 161.
72. *First report of the Commissioners of public instruction*, 49d.
73. *Southern Reporter and Cork Commercial Courier*, 4 May 1843.
74. *The Nation*, 6 May 1843; *Freeman's Journal*, 2 June 1846.
75. *Freeman's Journal*, 9 April 1847.

Return of Revd Peter Ward, P.P. of Clare Island:

Number of deaths from 1st October, 1846 to 1st April 1847? 82.

Lecarrow Village – Charles Malley, Hugh Malley, Dominick Bradshaw, Cicily Malley, Mary Moran, senior, Mary Moran, jun., John Grady, Austin Kean, Bridget Grimes.

Cappanagour – Pat Barrett, Margaret Barrett, Honor Malley.

Kill – Sarah Malley, Michael Malley, Mary Malley, Michael Scholefield, Pat Malley, Margaret Grady, Mary Ruddy, Honor Ruddy, John Ruddy, Letitia Barrett, Mary Barrett.

Founglass [Fawnglass] – Honor Toole, Ann Madden, Patrick Bradshaw.

Glen – John Grady, Mary Grady, James Grady, John McNabb, Bridget Malley, Michael Malley, Michael Kean, Mary Kean, Honor Burns, Alice Burns, Anne Lavell, Thomas Ruddy, Bridget Bradshaw, Michael Ball, Michl Scholefield, Bridget Bradshaw, jun, Pat Connor, Thomas Budds, Margaret Kirby, Pat Ruddy, Edmund Kerrigan, Michael Kerrigan.

Toormore Village – John Grady, Catherine Grady, Catherine Ruddy, Mary Gordon, Pat Malley, Bridget Gibbons.

Streak Village [Strake] – Charles Malley, Austin Gibbons, Mary Gibbons, Peter Murray, Pat Murray, junior, Anne Murray, John Murray, Pat Murray, sen., Bridget Murray, Michael Malley, John Malley, Bridget Malley, Anthony Malley, Honor Malley, Pat Malley, Winifred Malley, Pat Barrett, Anthony Cannon, Pat Murray (Michael), Martin Murray, Winifred Barrett, Mary Barrett.

Ballytouhy – Mary Cannon, Pat Malley, Bridget Malley, Margaret Toole, Catherine Malley, James M'Namara.

Number of same known to be occasioned by famine? 14 – viz. John English, John Malley, Margaret Molloy, James Kirby, Catherine Molloy, Michael Ruddy, Catherine Malley, jun., Mary Toole, Michael Madden, Peter Salmon, Mary Salmon, John Toole, Thady Malley, and Martin Malley. In fact, two-thirds of the above mortality lists are cases produced by failure of food. The same is to be recorded of the island of Tunisturk [Inishturk], amounting to the third of the census of this island.

The number of deaths during the same period last year bear a proportion of 20 per cent to this year's mortality.

It is almost miraculous how these islands got over with the above number of cases of mortality, when it is recorded that they have been without a relief committee since the commencement of the famine, till it's being included with Westport division a month ago. Its connexion with that division is like that of the shark with its prey – all devouring as it is and consumptive in itself – not the slightest thanks did I receive from the executive. After being told that, for lack of funds, save the generous sympathy of the Indian relief fund, to which I am indebted for 50l., and for which humanity I thought a trifling donation might be forwarded, no other available resources or channels lay before me or them in that quarter. Be it so; the days of Whiggery, hypocrisy, and all that, are nearly numbered. Open foes any day to disguised, hollow, and would-be time-killing, treacherous friends.

Source: *The Pilot*, 7 May 1847, 1.

Kilcolman (Claremorris), Tuam Diocese

Commentary

The Catholic parish of Kilcolman (Claremorris) was coterminous with the civil parish of Kilcolman, in Clanmorris barony, in south-east Mayo. In 1841, 62 per cent of the housing was classified as fourth class and the female illiteracy rate was 84 per cent. Revd James Hughes was parish priest there for eight years, transferred from Ballintubber in 1839.[76] Hughes was political, involving himself in the anti-tithe movement and in O'Connell's Repeal drive.[77] He attended the 'dinner to Mr O'Connell' at the Great Repeal meeting in Mayo in July 1840, and was a member of the Repeal Association.[78]

In 1844, while O'Connell was in prison, rumours were rife that the Queen would pay a visit to Ireland. No visit would take place until 1849, but Hughes took to the pen in 1844, writing to the Repeal MP, Robert Browne, advising the Association that its proper course of action should be 'sullen and discontented silence':

> Claremorris, August 31 [1844].
> My dear Mr. Browne, I beg to remit, as this year's first repeal rent instalment from this parish, £3. The association will not, I hope, forget that the repeal rent resources of the principal and most populous districts in Connaught are only now beginning to become available, this province being chiefly agricultural. This is the cause why the remittances to the association have been this year up to this from our county so comparatively few. Connaught did its duty last year. It will do the same this year, now that its proper season is coming on. The remittances from this parish shall be in future monthly, till all have contributed.
>
> I presume to offer in this manner, with great respect to the association, my opinion on what should be the demeanour of the Repealers of Ireland on the occasion of the Queen's rumoured visit to this country.. [...] Whilst O'Connell and the repeal martyrs are consigned to dungeon, and suffering under irons, are the Repealers of Ireland to take any part in the Royal pageant which is contrived and intended to exult over their servitude and degradation? Eternal infamy and shame on any who would recommend such a course! By this, do I mean to countenance or encourage any demonstration of disrespect to the Royal visitor? By no means. What I intend to recommend during the Royal sojourn

76. *Dublin Monitor*, 7 March 1839; The *Globe and Traveller*, 23 March 1839.
77. *Londonderry Journal*, 14 August 1838.
78. *Londonderry Journal*, 14 August 1838; *Dublin Morning Register*, 30 July 1840; *Freeman's Journal*, 14 May 1844.

> in our country, would be sullen and discontented silence, and a perfect abstinence from all manifestations of any public feeling. [...].[79]

Hughes' parish of Kilcolman had a reported population of 8,391 in 1831 and 9,451 in 1841, suggesting a yearly growth rate of about 1.2 per cent in the decade after 1831.[80] The parish had a small Protestant community, with most of these probably living in or close to Claremorris town. The Public Instruction Commissioners put the community at 170 strong, or two per cent of the population in 1831.[81]

We estimate the Catholic population of the parish at about 9,650 in mid-1845, falling to about 8,580 by mid-1847. In normal conditions a population of about 8,500 would experience between about 97 and 146 deaths in a normal October–March period, so the 156 deaths reported by Hughes between October 1846 and March 1847 appear at first sight to indicate that the parish had avoided the worst of the Famine. Yet, his descriptive testimony point in the opposite direction. Furthermore, in a second report from the parish later in November that year Hughes puts the deaths in the period from 'last October to the 10th of last April' at 350 'from famine and epidemic', with an additional 250 deaths between April and November.[82]

Return of Revd James Hughes, P.P. of Kilcolman:

Number of deaths in this parish from the 1st October 1846 to 1st April 1847? 156. Number of same known to be caused by famine? 123.

No record of the deaths of this parish for the corresponding period of last year.

All the cases of starvation are very remarkable. The present condition of the parish is most wretched; the new relief measure [Soup Kitchen Act] is in very slow progress – no potato tillage, not half the usual quantity of oat tillage. I consider the condition of this parish must be infinitely worse next year than this. The middling and poorer classes all determined to leave this country – the first all going to America, and the second going off to England or some other place.

Source: *The Pilot*, 7 May 1847, 1.

Kilcommon and Robeen, Tuam Diocese

Commentary

Kilcommon and Robeen is located in south-east Mayo, bordering County Galway near Claremorris Town. The parish was coextensive with the two civil parishes of Kilcommon and Robeen. The 1831 census put the parish's population at 9,700, rising

79. *Evening Mail*, 4 September 1844.
80. *Abstract of Population Returns for Ireland, 1831*, BPP (1833), 634, 316; 1843 (504) *Report of the Commissioners appointed to take the census of Ireland, for the year 1841*, BPP, 396.
81. *First report of the Commissioners of public instruction*, 40d.
82. *The Pilot*, 17 November 1847.

to 11,000 in 1841.[83] In 1841, 70 per cent of the housing was classified as fourth class and the female illiteracy rate was 90 per cent. The parish was predominantly Catholic; with only 329 Protestants counted in the Public Instruction Commissioners' report.[84] We estimate the parish's Catholic population by mid-1845 to be about 11,080, dropping to perhaps 9,740 by mid-1847.

The Death Census return was prepared by Archdeacon James MacHale, the long-time parish priest of Kilcommon.[85] MacHale was a strong supporter of the Repeal cause. He was a chief organiser of a 10,000-strong Kilmain barony Repeal demonstration, held in the chapel-yard of Ballinrobe in 1840, where he proposed the secretary for the meeting.[86] In 1843 he, along with others, campaigned for the repeal of the new Poor Law system, appealing, instead, for 'some wise and well-worked enactment for the relief of the aged and inform'.[87] The 934 deaths he gives in his Death Census return for the six months after 1 October 1846 is nearly 20-times the number for the equivalent period a year previously. In a population of this size, we would expect to see 126–189 deaths between October and March in normal times.

Return by Revd J. MacHale of Kilcommon and Robeen

Number of deaths from 1st October 1846 to 1st April 1847? 934, in the parish of Kilcoman and Robin, 25 of which were from old age, &c., all the rest from starvation.
Number of deaths during the same period last year? 49

Source: *The Pilot*, 19 May 1847, 2.

Killedan, Achonry Diocese

Commentary

The Death Census for Killedan parish was made by Revd John Brennan, curate of the parish. Killedan parish is coextensive with the civil parish of the same name in Gallen barony, east County Mayo, and Brennan's submission is one of a number of commentaries compiled for parishes in the area. In 1841, 76 per cent of the housing was classified as fourth class and the female illiteracy rate was 86 per cent.

The population of the parish expanded by about 1.5 per cent per year between 1831 and 1841, climbing from 5,741 to 6,410.[88] The Protestant population was miniscule; the Public Instruction Commissioners reported only 16 Protestants in the entire parish. We estimate the Catholic population of the parish at about 6,700 in mid-1845, falling

83. *Abstract of Population Returns for Ireland, 1831*, BPP (1833), 634, 318; 1843 (504) *Report of the Commissioners appointed to take the census of Ireland, for the year 1841*, BPP, 398.
84. *First report of the Commissioners of public instruction*, 40d.
85. *Catholic directory and annual register for 1838*, 132.
86. *Freeman's Journal*, 25 September 1840.
87. *Freeman's Journal*, 10 February 1843.
88. *Abstract of Population Returns for Ireland, 1831*, BPP, 318; 1843 (504) *Report of the Commissioners appointed to take the census of Ireland, for the year 1841*, BPP (1833), 634, 398.

to perhaps 6,100 two years later. From a population of this size, we would expect to see between about 76 and 114 deaths in October 1845–March 1846. Brennan's figure of 80 for the six months after October 1845 lies within this expected range, and his figure for the later six-month period indicates an eightfold increase in mortality.

Return of Revd John Brennan, curate of Killedan:

Number of deaths in this parish from 1st October, 1846 to 1st April, 1847? 650.
Number of same known to be caused by the famine? 400.
Number of deaths for the same period last year? 80.

In making this statement I am not under the actual number; I am sure I don't exaggerate. As for remarkable cases of destitution, I regret to state that they are innumerable and of daily occurrence. But to mention one or two of the many: I was called upon last week to a village named Carranteeane [Carrownteeaun], to attend an entire family who were dying from the twofold horrors of fever and starvation. The father of the family died two days previously, and on entering the miserable dwelling, I found one child dead, and five more just expiring, and huddled together on the bare ground with scarcely any covering. And on leaving this house I was called upon to attend three other families in succession in the same village, who were, if possible, in more misery. And I found such of the children as could crawl about gather around a labourer (who was cutting stubble land) eagerly watching the weeds and roots. And on my way on this day to attend a call, I witnessed a most appalling sight – a dead body thrown one side of a ditch with a child in her arms – and upon inquiring the cause, I was told by a bystander that she was found dead on the streets this morning from actual starvation.

The water cresses and nettles are already consumed here; the land is badly cropped, and this parish will soon be a complete waste, both from deaths and the rapacity of landlords. As to emigration, such as had the means have left the country, and the prospects of the coming year are dark and gloomy. Mortality has rapidly increased since the murdering edict of the 20, and subsequently 10, per cent of the public works. There is scarcely a day but insult is added to injustice by the conflicting and contradictory orders of either the Board of Public Works or its subordinates; for on one day the starving poor are called upon to work, and next day denied employment, and are frequently deprived of their miserable earnings, for to my own knowledge, several hundreds of the labourers have nine days due to them, which the engineer in charge has refused to return for payment. This I can prove, and defy contradiction. Consequently, the public may judge if this conduct, considering the times and circumstances, is not well calculated to drive the people to madness and despair.

Cheering hopes were held out, and flattering promises made, on the event of the cumbrous machinery of outdoor relief coming into operation; but bitter experience proves that these hopes were only imaginary, the promises delusive, and the entire bungling a 'partuviunt montes et nassetur ridilulus mus' [*sic*. 'parturiunt montes, nascetur ridiculus mus'[89]]. For the inspecting officer of this district, as I am informed, frequently told the committee that they would be accountable for the deaths from starvation if they did not give in their estimates at once. Now, the estimates have been returned for the last eighteen days, and the starving poor have only got four days' rations, for which they are solely indebted to charitable institutions, and I have seen them on this day congregating in hundreds amidst the heaviest rain into this village (Kiltimagh), and some coming the distance of five miles for one pound of Indian meal; and for their rations they got the sad intelligence that the order previously given by the government inspector for meal, has been counteracted. The shrieks and cries of the almost lifeless expectants, upon witnessing the sad reality of the carts coming home empty from Westport, twenty miles from this town, would shock humanity; and unless the government adopt some immediate and effective means to remedy this monstrous cruelty, the consequences will be terrific and alarming in the extreme.

Source: *The Pilot*, 28 May 1847, 4.

Kilmaine, Tuam Diocese

Commentary

Kilmaine parish is located in south Mayo, bordering County Galway. The parish was served by Revd John McHugh, parish priest, and his curate, Revd Michael Gill. It was Gill who compiled the returns for the parish. Remarkably, he submitted three reports for Kilmaine.[90] The first report incorrectly located the parish in County Galway, but the second identified it as a Mayo parish. In 1841, 75 per cent of the housing was classified as fourth class and the female illiteracy rate was 93 per cent.

Concern had been growing in the county during 1846 and Gill was one of sixteen priests to put his name to an August 1846 appeal for support 'in consequence of the total loss of the potato crop'. He was also a collector of the Repeal Rent in the area.[91]

DISTRESS IN MAYO

The following petition for the adoption of some measures to meet the present distress and impending famine has been forwarded to the House of Commons by the patriotic clergy of the deanery of Ballinrobe. It supplies a melancholy confirmation of the facts which we elsewhere publish with regard to the spread of destitution in Mayo:

89. 'The mountains are in labour; a ridiculous mouse will be born' (Aesop's Fables). Note that Timothy Newell's letter to *Galway Mercury*, 5 January 1847, also included reference to this fable.
90. We know that Gill is referring to Kilmaine, County Mayo, because he refers to a tragic incident which occurred on the road between Tuam poorhouse and Ballinrobe; this road passes through Kilmaine parish, County Mayo.
91. *Freeman's Journal*, 26 January 1847.

Ballinrobe, August 24, 1846.

"To the Knights, Citizens, and Burgesses of the United Empire, in Parliament assembled.

"The petition of the undersigned Roman Catholic clergymen of the deanery of Ballinrobe, in the county of Mayo,

"MOST HUMBLY SHOWETH – That in consequence of the total loss of the potato crop, starvation and pestilence, its necessary concomitant, stare us in the discharge of our ministerial duties. That we apprehend the consequences will be appalling if timely precaution be not taken by the parliament to avert its direful effects. That we therefore pray your honourable house to adopt such measures as you in your wisdom deem necessary to meet this awful emergency.[92]

Gill's three returns are among the most detailed of the various returns. By listing the names and addresses of his dead parishioners, they starkly outline the scale of the catastrophe in this south Mayo parish. His mortality figures seem to cover the period from 1 November 1846, not 1 October 1846 as requested. They suggest that mortality was around three times higher between November 1846 and October 1847 than during the same period a year earlier.

An issue regarding the return for Termonamongan, County Tyrone, requires explanation. At the end of the return for that parish a list of more than 100 names of Famine dead is presented, organised by townland. Although the method of presentation appears to suggest that the list refers to Termonamongan parish, in fact it is Gill's third report of deceased for Kilmaine parish. In the transcriptions below the death-counts by townland are not given in the returns; so the figures represent our interpretation of Gill's lists.

Return of Revd Michael Gill (first report), curate of Kilmaine:

I send you a list of the persons who died of starvation in a few villages of the parish; and when I tell you that I attended about 80 persons, and also attended confessions, you will not say that I was negligent at complying with the request of the Association. Of these 80 persons about 65 died. To the best of my knowledge about 50 of these died of starvation and its attendants, to wit, fever and dysentery.

Here follows the list, with my observations: -

Croughcusane Village – From November to May, died – Peggy Ford, Michael Ford and wife, and left two children; Peggy Munster, two children belonging to Michael Jennings; Judy Faraher, John Forbes, Mary Jennings, Ned Jennings, Wat Walsh and his wife; a poor woman name unknown, who died by the road side; Pat Joyce. Making 14 in this village. [14]

Kilkeran Village, died – Thomas Ryan, left six in family; John Lyons or Lee, left four in family, was buried in a mat; Davy Ryan and his mother and child, died suddenly, and were buried without coffins in the house they lived in – April 16th; Mrs Ryan, wife of said David, and another child, were buried on 29th April (I provided coffins for these). [7]

92. *Freeman's Journal*, 28 August 1846.

Ardmoran – Thomas Corcoran. [1]

Knocknagubee – Pat Doyle and wife, fever; Peggy Reilly, a beggarwoman (contributed to buy a coffin for her); Thomas Nalty, dysentery (provided coffin for him); Mary Sheridan, do; Peter Hyland, do; contributed towards coffins for them. [6]

Knocknaploga – Michael and Biddy Naughton; Thos Meenehan, Mary Meenehan, dysentery both. [4]

Knockmeelwood – Michael M'Donnell, Mrs M'Donnell, Pat M'Donnell and his daughter, all out of one house by fever, brought on from want of food, left behind them five in family; James Cuffe, Mrs Cuffe, Peter Cuffe, left three children; I contributed for coffins for the above; Mrs Connor, left four in family; Stephen Kyne, left four in family. [9]

Cahir Kilernan – Peter Kielty and wife, left four orphans; Thomas Haynaghan; J. Biggans and daughter, left six in family; Pat Flanagan and wife, left five in family; F. McDonogh. [8]

Kilmain – William Noone and five children, all died of starvation; John Connor, dysentery; the daughter of the above woman also died at Croughcussane, name unknown; a man named Duddy buried by the roadside; Ellen Donoghoe, I provided a coffin for her, a poor beggar woman.

There were several others who died of starvation in Kilmain, whose names I will send in next week. Almost all of these were cottiers, with only a garden, and depending on labour. They are not the persons who were located in the poorest part of the parish. These will fill the list of the next and succeeding weeks.

The most heart rending scenes imaginable occurred here last week. The man named Duddy, in Kilmain, died by the roadside: he and his family were standing under a hedge. They were sent from the poorhouse in Tuam, and were on their way to Ballinrobe, their own district. Mr Kirwan, of Dalgan [Shrule parish], chairman of the committee, two days after the man's death, on passing by the road, and seeing their state, ordered the police of Kilmain to have the family sent to the poorhouse of Ballinrobe, but took no regard of the dead body. The police humanely removed them, also interred the body where it lay, lest the dogs should come and devour it.

I witnessed another shocking scene on the same day as I was passing on my duties. A poor woman, name unknown (and not included in foregoing list), died by the roadside, and had there lain dead three days! I saw her child, aged, I should think, about seven years, lying asleep over the corpse of her poor mother! Before I was able to get home to procure a coffin for her, she was buried in a mat; a painful and demoralising act, if it could be helped.

The same week Davy Ryan and his mother died the same night suddenly, they were interred in the house they died in. I attended Davy Ryan's wife in fever a few weeks ago; she recovered, but all her family were so reduced by starvation, that for the previous week they were totally unable to leave the house, and, alas!

she herself, poor woman, and her child fell victims this week to starvation! I leave the reader to imaging the scenes I had to encounter in this abode. The police also visited this house the same or previous day. The scenes of misery and starvation in this parish are awful. I give you the words of the ex-chairman of this union, that in no part of Ireland is there more misery and starvation, though I think while chairman he acted with a great deal of apathy towards the poor. And for the present committee they are doing nothing, though the people are dying. They have funds to the amount of about 200l. They could have these funds available for the support of the poor if they liked, either to have meal purchased and sold at first cost or given gratuitously. I am sure the central relief committee when sending it meant to give it in either of these ways, and that they did not desire to see the people starving and meal rotting in the stores. I am telling facts no man can contradict.

The very first moment the Rev Mr. McHugh had recovered from a fit of sickness, which he caught in his great anxiety for the relief of the people he sat in the store, and distributed 50l worth of meal which he and the Protestant curate had got for the relief of the poor of this parish.

May I beg of the Association to impress on the government the necessity of sending a commissioner here to carry out the act of Parliament – to supersede the do nothing committee of this parish. I make no exception – all are doing nothing. Or if the government will not do this, let the central relief committee, and all other committees who subscribed, send down persons to distribute the monies and meal immediately, and they will earn the blessings of hundreds of starving poor.

There is not a stream growing water cresses, nor an old garden growing nettles, that is not filled with persons gathering them for food. There is not a ploughman or labourer in the field that hasn't a flock of children gathering 'bliskanes' after him.[93]

There is more distress in this parish than in any on the west coast of Ireland, for there are more farms in it, and consequently more cottiers – more than three hundred families all depending on labour. That source is dried up.

I must apologise for the length of this awful detail of human misery, and appeal to the humane public for some means to get coffins for the dead. I despair of relieving the people with the aid of the committee we have in Kilmain. I coffined ten or twelve persons myself, and contributed to more than forty coffins more since November last to the amount of from one to three shillings each, and must say that alien legislation, absentee landlords, and resident fools, with a few honourable exceptions, are the fruitful source of all our misery.

Source: *The Pilot*, 5 May 1847, 4.

93. Bliskanes are 'poisonous weeds of the dock species', *Freeman's Journal*, 8 May 1847.

Return of Revd Michael Gill (second report), curate of Kilmaine:

Here follows a list of forty one persons in addition to the former names sent by me to the Association on last week who died of starvation and its attendants, to wit, fever and dysentery, since 1st November last, making, in both weeks, the total number of ninety-five, and I am sure when I have the entire death census taken, the present number will be double, and am sure, please God, I will be able to close the census of this parish next week. I have no remark to make in addition to my remark last week, save that the committee of Kilmaid [i.e. Kilmain] are giving soup or porridge gratuitously since Monday last [i.e. 10 May 1847], and also some meal. May God infuse into their hands/hearts[94] the disposition to give it generously.

At Clyard – Pat Gaynard, of dysentery. [1]

At Caramore – Michael Curreen, left five in family. [1]

At Lecarrea – Pat Brenan, Biddy Brenan, Mrs M'Namara and sister. [4]

At Ballybocagh – Pat Fahy, left two in family; Peter Feeny, left four in family; John Shaughnessy and his son Thomas, both died suddenly of starvation. [4]

At Knockroe – Two children of Ned Ruave, Thomas and Luke; two children of Michael Walsh. [4]

At Clenadeen – Mrs Duddy, left four children; Catty Noon, left two children; Rose Hart; John Hart, left five children; Pat Maguire; a poor beggarwoman, name not known; Pat Kennedy, Catty Walsh. [8]

Ballyfagnagh – Catty Hughes, left three in family; Thomas O'Dea, left six in family; Mary Glynn, left three in family; Catty Flanagan, Rebecca Cannavan, Sally Flanagan. [6]

At Clonadeen – Biddy Rowland, Sally and Susan Loftus. [3]

At Islandmore – Two children of a man named Buckley, who was transported for cow stealing at the last quarter sessions of Claremorris, and left six in family. [95][2]

At Caramore – Geoffrey Martin, Pat Hohagan, left five days without a coffin, and left eight in family. [2]

At Lecarrow – Pat Brennan, left three in family; Kate Cunnerren. [2]

At Keelas – Michael Cunnereen, Andrew Trimmings. [2]

At Lanoe Village – Pat Walsh, Pat Hughes. [2]

At Caranoe – Michael Curreen, left three in family. [1]

At Kilkeran – A child of a man named Lee. [1]

Source: *The Pilot*, 14 May 1847, 4.

94. *Freeman's Journal*, 12 May 1847 says 'hearts'. The *Pilot*, 12 May 1847 says 'hands'.

95. James Buckley was sentenced to 10 years transportation for cattle-stealing at the Claremorris quarter-sessions, March 1847 (*Mayo Constitution*, 6 April 1847).

Return of Revd Michael Gill (third report), curate of Kilmaine:

I send you my third list of names of those who died of starvation, and its attendants – to wit, fever and dysentery, in this parish, amounting to 120 persons, in addition to my two former lists – amounting to all 215 persons since November last.

There died in this parish during the same period about 60 persons, not of hunger, but according to the ordinary course of nature – a fair average number for any year, taking the population of this parish into consideration, the population being between 1,000 and 1,100 families. The ghastly countenances of the poor creatures who are daily seen suing a quart of porridge at the porridge shop, loudly proclaim that the same number will be doubled ere the summer is over – were they to get the greatest luxuries, their life blood is almost fled.

With regard to the cultivation of the lands in this parish, all the cottiers were unable to sow any of their gardens; the holders of a few acres, scarcely as much as will satisfy the landlord's claim, being, in most cases, when paying rent, promised seed, but which promises were not fulfilled, with very few exceptions; some landlords giving the sum of 4l. to the tenant to *tumble his house*, and go where he liked, so that the prospects for next year look gloomy in the extreme. Settled despair is in every countenance, yet with the patience of martyrs they are awaiting their time, to be summoned to another and better world.

Oh! that the brave, the loyal, the pious, and resigned people of this country, should be thus mowed down by the heartless policy of the brutal Whigs.

As for the committee here, they are still doing nothing, or, at least, next to nothing – one day giving porridge, two days idle, or half idle.

I cannot close these few remarks without detailing an almost incredible case. A man, named Michael Sheridan of Knocknoguhee, died on last Thursday week. His son and grandchild were sleeping on the same wad of straw with him. The grandchild died on Wednesday last. The son was living up to Thursday night last, with the dead corpse of the father unburied. That is eight days the living and the dead were on the same wretched wad of straw in a wretched hovel, not eight feet square, for the want of a coffin!

I cannot say whether the wretched creature was since buried, as I was confined to my room from sickness and fatigue. Humanity recoils at the bare idea of such a scene – yet, alas! the case is too true.

Should this state of woe meet the eye of our legislators, the small still voice of their consciences must warn them that the house of their retribution must surely come.

[Note: At the end of the return for Termonamongan parish, County Tyrone, a list of famine dead by townlands is presented. In fact, this list of deceased is not associated with Termonamongan parish, but is Gill's list of deceased for Kilmaine, in his third report. Hence, we present this list below, in its rightful place.]

The following persons have perished from famine in the subjoined localities: -

BALLINITEA – Mrs O'Brien, left three in family; Pat Tierney, two d[itt]o; James Johnson, four d[itt]o; Mrs Peter Donnellan, four d[itt]o. [4]

CAHIRKILLERNAN – Thomas Haynaghan, Peter Murray, Mrs Anstro; two children of Pat Murray; a second child of Bigans's. [6]

LISIS – Pat Walsh, three in family; Pat Casey, four do; Michael Costello three do; John Freehan, found dead in an outhouse; Katty Godwin, Margaret Reilly, Sally Reilly, Pat Reilly, a boy; Margaret Hereran, John Herehan, Thomas M'Donough, Owen and Bryan Gaynard, Widow Sweeny, John Lorken, Mrs Lorken. [16]

CREGMORE LYNCH – Two children of William Brother; Thomas Meally, five in family; Thomas Sheridan, six do. [4]

KALGRAMAHER – James Bahy, Mrs Hart, John Hart, Sibby Loughneen, Judy Loughneen. [5]

LOGNASUMEY – John Duddy, Peggy Munster, Patrick M'Dermott*, Michael Hagnaghan, Mrs Hagnaghan, John Tracy; a child of Mrs M'Guire. [7]

PARKNAKNOCKANE – John Gibbons, Catty Doherty, Pat Henly, John Henly, John Shaughnessy, Mary Conry, Anthony Conry, Biddy Conry, Catty Cody, Biddy Kine. [10]

DOOBOY – John Kelly. [1]

CLYARD – John Hogan left three in family; Luke Varaly, six do; John Connor, one do; Thomas Connor, nine do; James Lally, one do. [5]

CAHIR – Ned M'Tighe, found dead in a hut; Pat M'Tighe, Mary Carty, Thomas Walsh, Peggy Walsh. [5]

CARANA, DALGAN, AND DERREEN – John Size, James Lavelle, left three in family; John Lavelle, Daniel Reilly, John Greany, Pat Callaghan, a child; Owen Berreen, left five in family; Mary Kevin, Mary Kelaghan, Mary Hogan, Lilly Hogan, Katty Grimes, Mrs Gibbons, Thos Lynch, and a child of Owen Hay. [15]

CLOONMEALTOGUE, CAHIR, AND CARTOONS – Mary Hughes, Catty Hughes, Pat Killeen, Mary Killeen, Pat Rigne, Mrs M'Gagh, Pat Staunton, Catty O'Hara, Peter Costello, John Shaughnessy, Thady Carty, Larry Hynes, William Killeen, Martin Casey, Biddy Walsh, Thomas Walsh, Catty Walsh, M. Costello, Pat Casey, Pat Walsh, Martin Gibbons, left one child; James Gibbons, Luke Tyne, Pat Schahel, John Schahel, M. Murphy, Bridget Murphy, left six behind; Thomas Hyland, Michael Walsh, sen.; Michael Walsh, jun.; Michael Walsh jun., a second child of Michael Walsh; Thomas Devily, Mrs Devily, and one child; Mrs John Devilly left two in family; Pat Martin, one do. [36]

CARANTURLY – Ned Curry; a child of Thomas Reilly; Rose Naughten. [3]

Source: *The Pilot*, 28 May 1847, 4.

* Another coroner, Mr Rutledge, held an inquest at Kilmaninemore, barony of Kilmain, on the body of Patrick M'Dermott. Verdict – died of starvation. Several other persons died of starvation in this barony, on whom no inquests have been held.[96]

96. *Freeman's Journal*, 23 January 1847, 4.

Straide and Bohola, Achonry Diocese

Commentary

The Revd O'Connor, curate of Bohola, in Gallen barony, County Mayo prepared a return not only for Bohola but also for the neighbouring parish of Straide (Templemore). The return does not follow the standard pattern as it records famine deaths over the period 1 October 1846 to 1 June 1847, an eight-month period rather than the half-year prescribed by the Repeal Association. O' Connor admits no registry of deaths was maintained in either location, and adds with 'disease so prevalent and deaths so numerous that we have not one minute to spare'. His numbers were approximate at best, he says. This account is among the most eloquent and heart-wrenching to be found in the collection of reports that constitute the Death Census.

According to O'Connor, conditions were considerably worse in Straide parish, than in neighbouring Bohola. The parishes were of similar size. The 1841 census reported 4,301 inhabitants in Bohola, and 4,251 in Straide. We estimate the Catholic population to have reached about 4,500 in the parish of Bohola and about 4,450 in Straide by mid-1845. Populations of these orders of magnitude would lead us to expect between 67 and 100 deaths in both parishes in a typical eight-month period between October and May. O'Connor's estimate for deaths – 375 in the two parishes – was at least four times normal mortality. By 1851 the population of both parishes had plummeted, declining to 2,901 in the case of Bohola and 2,387 in Straide. Population decline was more severe in the case of Straide, with a loss of 44 per cent as against 33 per cent in Boholo. This is consistent also with famine mortality estimates. If our estimate of the population of each of the parishes in 1845 is roughly correct, and if O'Connor's mortality figures can be relied on, then Straide was experiencing 50 deaths per 1,000 people as compared to Bohola's 33 per 1,000.

Our pre-Famine indicator of housing poverty points in this direction also. In Straide in 1841 the proportion of fourth class housing was 65 per cent as compared to 58 per cent in Bohola, though in terms of female illiteracy there was little to choose between the two (87 per cent and 88 per cent respectively). How one might explain the contrasting fortunes of the two parishes is grist to the mill of local historians

O'Connor's account of his parish conjures up tragic images of despair and anguish. He gives scant detail of relief measures in his own parish, but is scathingly critical of support in Straide, where 'the poor are treated [...] barbarously'. Public works had been suspended, and gratuitous relief was insufficient, and only sporadically doled out. 'An ounce a day' of meal went no further than 'securing deaths from starvation', and not well enough at that, given the mortality figures. Forty-nine deaths from starvation in Lakill townland (its population was 289 in 1841 and was less than half that in 1851 when only 135 souls were enumerated) is shocking, as is the report of 13 deaths in a single day in O'Connor's parish, in spite of the more efficient provision of relief there. His account of the burial of a child named O'Neill, uncoffined, in the floor of her cabin is among the saddest of the many stories of death to be found in the Death Census. That the corpse lay unattended for nine days, the neighbours fearing to help, speaks volumes of the disintegration of community or *comhar na gcomharsan* (mutual co-operation among neighbours) when weakened by hunger and terrified of contracting typhus or one of the other contagious diseases coursing through the community.

Return of Revd Mr O'Connor, curate of Bohola:

I hope you will not consider that it was through any neglect we retarded the return of the number of deaths in the parishes I am appointed to as curate. No; disease so prevalent and deaths so numerous that we have not one minute to spare; and also we have no registry of deaths kept in these parishes, and this occasioned more injury and created more delay; and notwithstanding the strict inquiry I have made, I could not ascertain the exact number. Still, I have ascertained that in the parish of Straid or Templemore we had 225 deaths since the 1st of October up to 1st of June, and of these 200 died of actual want and starvation; and I am certain that before the expiration of one fortnight we will have at least 100 more to add to the gloomy catalogue of deaths from starvation. Die they must inevitably, the poor are treated so inhumanly, so unjustly, and I may say so barbarously in Straid parish, the system of relief there is so inadequate.

The poor of this parish are relieved only once a week or once a fortnight; only one pound of meal is allowed for each individual adult for the week, and half a pound for those under nine years, and this proportioned to time will only allow an ounce a day to each adult, and half an ounce to those under age, and to add to this misery, the public works are stopped; the consequence of this is that the poor are dropping as fast and as numerous as the leaves of the forest. In one townland in this parish, called Salull [Lakill?], 49 human beings have died of starvation, and in one day last week I attended with the consolations of my religion 13 persons who were real victims of starvation. I found them stretched on wads of straw, quite feeble and unable to stir, all from want and real destitution. In Europe there is no parallel for Straid parish, or any place where charity should direct her steps sooner, and on that account I hope you will, if possible to you, have me enabled to relieve the many and very many who are in want in this parish. There is no person really interested for it. I, of course, as Catholic Curate, am excluded, and cannot be of any assistance to my starvelings in the other parish. I am appointed to Bohola: we had 150 deaths from October last, and of this number 100 have died of actual want and destitution, and even in this parish shocking cases and gloomy scenes have occurred, such as being compelled to bury a great many without coffins; and in one instance a poor girl of the name of O'Neill died of fever, she remained unburied and unheeded for nine days. They could not procure a coffin: the neighbours were unwilling to go near her, and on the ninth day her aged mother was compelled to dig a pit in the cabin floor and have her buried therein. The relief is carried out in this parish punctually and regularly; much gratitude is due to the officer in charge, and the members of the committee, for their exertions in aid of the destitute. Still the pittance allowed is not sufficient to support nature. One pound of meal is not adequate sustenance, and, in my opinion, it is only retarding life for a little, and securing deaths from starvation. I must conclude by hoping you will exert your talents and influence in behalf of Straid, and direct me what steps to follow, or some means to adopt, so as to be of some assistance to my starving flock.

Source: *The Pilot*, 16 June 1847, 2.

Toomore, Achonry Diocese

Commentary

The Catholic parish of Toomore (Foxford), in the barony of Gallen, in east Mayo, was coterminous with the civil parish of the same name. The return for the parish was compiled by Revd John Corley, parish priest. Corley had been writing to the newspapers to raise awareness of the situation in Foxford in the early months of 1847, recounting incidents of people consuming rotting horse flesh, and un-coffined corpses.

Foxford, January 18th, 1847
Dear Sir, Your [editor of *Dublin Evening Post*] deep concern for the wants and sympathy for the sufferings of your countrymen embolden me to trouble you with a few lines, which I hope you will publish in the next number of your invaluable journal. Our wants here hourly increase, and the cry of our famishing people in the streets and villages is most distressing. The police yesterday, in searching for stolen meat, happened to discover one of the most awful, and even incredible, cases of shocking destitution in the history of any people. On entering a house they perceived some meat boiling in a pot on the fire, and supposing it to be part of the stolen meat, they examined the pot, and the contents turned out to be part of the flesh of a diseased horse, which they preserved for the purpose of eating it. This fact proves, Sir, to what extremes this wretched people are reduced, and it could not be the effect of design, or the result of deliberation, as they did not expect a visit from the police.

We suffered much here from the beginning of this awful visitation; but the wants and sufferings of our people are much increased by the delays occasioned by the studied and complicated forms insisted on by the engineer department. It is impossible for the clergymen and clerks to procure continuous employment for the people.
I remain, dear Sir, your very humble and obedient servant,
John Corley, P.P., Toomore.[97]

97. *Dublin Evening Post*, 21 January 1847.

Foxford, March 9th, 1847.

Dear Sir, In the mountainous parish of Toomore there are six thousand souls, who are all, with few exceptions, without seed, and many of them without the supply of one day's food. Deaths are so frequent, that the Rev. Mr. Hyland and I can scarcely attend all; and it sometimes happens that one member of a family remains uncoffined, for want of means, whilst we are administering sacraments to others, in the same apartment. We have not received, from the commencement, more than fifty or sixty pounds, to assist us to meet the distress of the most wretched locality in Ireland.

There are some contributions at present in the hands of Colonel Jackson [Chairman of Board of Guardians of Swinford Union], but the want of a boiler keeps even this relief from famishing thousands. We succeeded up to this period, through the charity of an English prelate, to afford the decency of human interment to our poor people; but, I fear, for the future, that we must bury them without coffins, or, what is worse, endanger ourselves by having them long time unburied.

Your obedient servant,

John Corley, P.P. Toomore.[98]

The 1831 population of the parish was 3,576, rising to 3,744 by 1841. This was a modest rate of increase, being less than 0.5 per cent per year during the 1830s.[99] In 1841, 50 per cent of the housing was classified as fourth class and the female illiteracy rate was 81 per cent. The vast majority of the inhabitants were Catholics. The Public Instruction Commissioners reported the Catholic population to be above 95 per cent in 1831. It is likely that most of the 148 Protestants in the parish in 1831 were living in the market and post-town of Foxford.[100] We estimate the Catholic population of the parish to have been of the order of 3,750 by mid-1845, and perhaps about 3,200 by mid-1847. A population of this order would expect to witness about 43 and 64 deaths between October 1845 and March 1846, so Corley's estimate of about two deaths per week fits well within that range.

Corley's numerical data indicate that the Famine was impacting catastrophically in Toomore. The number of deaths in the six-months after 1 October 1846 was roughly six times greater than the number in the equivalent period a year previously. If our Catholic population estimate for mid-1847 (3,224) is tolerably accurate, this would mean that the mortality rate in the October 1846–March 1847 period was about 200 deaths per 1,000 people.

98. *Dublin Evening Post*, 13 March 1847.

99. *Abstract of Population Returns for Ireland, 1831*, BPP (1833), 634, 318; *Report of the Commissioners appointed to take the census of Ireland, for the year 1841*, BPP (1843), 504, 398.

100. *First report of the Commissioners of public instruction*, 62d; Samuel Lewis, *Topographical Dictionary of Ireland*, 2 vols, London: Lewis & Co., 1847, ii, 597.

Return of Rev. John Corley, P.P. of Toomore:

Number of deaths from 1st October 1846, to the 1st April 1847? 384.
Number of same known to be caused by the famine? They were all mediately or immediately caused by famine, but over twenty caused by famine without any disease.
Number of deaths during the same period last year? About two a week, or 48 in all.

The reverend gentleman says – The constitution of the people is very much impaired; there is a very malignant typhus fever and dysentery, together with inflammation. The government measure, 10th Victoria [Soup Kitchen Act], will do a great deal if its machinery were once perfected, but I fear the people will suffer in the interim. Tillage is much neglected, or rather unavoidably postponed, for the people have not seed or means to purchase it, and the prospects of next year are most disheartening, unless something be immediately done. There were a great many who emigrated to America, and more who intend going. I think none would remain if they had means to take them from the wreck of the country. If my return of deaths be not under, it is not over. I fear we will shortly have a much greater mortality.

Source: *The Pilot*, 28 April 1847, 3.

County Roscommon

Castlemore and Kilcolman, Achonry Diocese

Commentary

The return for the union of Castlemore and Kilcolman, on the borders of north-west Roscommon was compiled by Revd Denis Tighe, parish priest of the union since at least 1835.[101] Tighe was a supporter of The Liberator's Repeal drive, contributing to collections in support of O'Connell, and, notably, he was one of the many thousands who signed the 'Leinster and Charlemont Address to the people of Great Britain' in 1840, appealing for support for Catholic appointments to public office.[102] Accompanying Tighe's annual subscription to the Repeal Association in 1841, was a note stating that 'his patriotic people [of Castlemore and Kilcolman] are determined to persevere legally until they have their parliament in College Green'.[103]

Tighe's union was coextensive with the civil parishes of the same name. The administrative history of these parishes is complicated. The parishes were formerly in counties Mayo and Sligo, but were subsequently transferred to County Roscommon. They are in Achonry diocese, but another parish called Kilcolman, also in Mayo and

101. *First report of the Commissioners of public instruction*, 63.
102. *The Vindicator*, 22 April 1840; *Dublin Weekly register*, 16 May 1840.
103. *Freeman's Journal*, 3 February 1846.

proximate to this union, is in Tuam diocese. The 1831 census reported a population of 8,521, rising to 10,187 by 1841, representing an average rise of 1.8 per cent per year.[104] In 1841, 41 per cent of the housing was classified as fourth class and the female illiteracy rate was 80 per cent. The Public Instruction Commissioners recorded a small Protestant community in the parish; only 88 (1.1 per cent) of the 1831 population were identified as Protestants, compared to a Catholic population of 8,027 (adjusted to 8,433).[105] We estimate the Catholic population in mid-1845 at about 10,500, falling to about 10,100 by mid-1847. Notably, our Catholic population estimate is about 2,000 below Tighe's estimate of 12,400. If we favour our estimate over Tighe's number, we would expect to see between about 120 and 180 deaths in the October 1845 to March 1846 period, well above the 86 that Tighe reported. The number of dead during the later six-month period, at 420, was far above the expected range. In November 1847 Tighe claimed that

> The population of this parish at the commencement of last year [1846] was near 12,000; it is now reduced to 9,860 persons – 478 died of famine and its immediate consequences since the 1st of October 1846. There are at present 138 families [about 800 people] suffering from fever [...] There are at present 470 families, consisting of 2,246 persons, in extreme want, living on turnips and a little Indian meal; no language can describe the miserable condition of most of them.[106]

Return of Denis Tighe, P.P. of Castlemore:

Number of deaths from 1st October 1846, to 1st April 1847? 420.
Number of same known to be caused by famine? 290.
Number of deaths during same period last year? 86.

Over half the population in this extensive parish are in a great want of food; fever and dysentery are much on the increase, and carrying off great numbers; the poor are found dying by the road side; tillage is greatly neglected; the landlords have done little or nothing to assist them to crop the land; some of them, far from alleviating the miseries of the poor, are adding to the general distress by evicting their tenants from their holdings. On the week just ended nineteen families, or 128 individuals, were turned adrift on the 'world's wild waste' from the estate here of a landlord resident in Dublin, and their cabins levelled to the ground. I will give their names: - Pat Dor, six in family; Michael Bishop, six do; John Dunn, ten do; John Mahon, six do; Roger Cregg, four do; Pat Cooney, eight do; Pat Sweeny, eight do; John Mahon, four do; Larry Casey, seven do; James Dillon, eight do; Thomas Dillon, three do; Martin M'Donnell, six do; Thomas Gibbon,

104. *Abstract of Population Returns for Ireland, 1831*, BPP (1833), 634, 316, 330; *Report of the Commissioners appointed to take the census of Ireland, for the year 1841*, BPP (1843), 504, 408, notes.
105. *First report of the Commissioners of public instruction*, 60d. The 1831 census recorded 5,427 in Kilcolman parish in 1831; the Public Instruction Commissioners' figures account for only 5,021; a discrepancy of 406 persons. Because the Protestant population was so small we adjust the Catholic population upwards by these 406 missing people.
106. *Freeman's Journal*, 17 November 1847.

seven do; John Conway, six do; Wm Flynn, nine do; James Quinn, five do; William Sharkott, seven do; and Wm Coleman, nine do.[107]

The most of the above are in great want; some of them are still clinging to the ruins of what they once called their 'happy homes,' and are now suffering all the agonies of hunger. The temporary relief [Soup Kitchen] act did not come into operation as yet, and I fear hundreds – I may say thousands – of the people will starve!

Source: *The Pilot*, 7 May 1847, 1.

Kilglass, Elphin Diocese

Commentary

Kilglass Catholic parish is located in north-east County Roscommon, bordering counties Leitrim and Longford. The parish was likely coextensive with the civil parish of the same name. Its population was reported at 9,118 in 1831, rising to 10,053 by 1841, a yearly increase of about 1 per cent.[108] In 1841, 53 per cent of the housing was classified as fourth class and the female illiteracy rate was 76 per cent. Few Protestants lived in the area; the Public Instruction Commissioners noted only 61 in 1831.[109] We estimate that the Catholic population may have reached about 10,400 by mid-1847, before plunging to about 7,700 by mid-1847.

The return for Kilglass was compiled by Revd Henry Brennan, parish priest. Brennan was actively campaigning in favour of his suffering tenants during 1847. Early in the year he issued an address to the landed proprietors in the parish appealing to the non-residents to visit the area to see the devastation with their own eyes:

> The Rev. Henry Brennan, P.P., of Kilglass, has forwarded to us an 'Address to the Landed Proprietors of the Parish of Kilglass', in which he suggests that they should visit their property in the parish, and thus 'have the advantage of a personal observation of the peculiar situation of each tenant – give them the seed best suited to each man's holding, and assist them to make their spring crops'. The rev. gentleman states that famine and pestilence prevail to an alarming extent – 'the deaths are fearfully on the increase every week – almost half the dead are buried without coffins. The people have no seed to put in the ground, and if they had they would require to be fed while doing their spring business'.[110]

Later in the year he was actively appealing for administrative changes to the local relief system which was, he believed, frustrating local relief efforts. In a published letter he recounts a sorrowful tale of dead bodies being discarded in ditches and abandoned

107. Tighe notes 19 families (128 individuals) evicted but lists only 18 families (119 individuals). Perhaps one family, with 9 individuals, is omitted.
108. *Abstract of Population Returns for Ireland, 1831*, BPP (1833), 634, 324; *Report of the Commissioners appointed to take the census of Ireland, for the year 1841*, BPP (1843), 504, 406.
109. *First report of the Commissioners of public instruction*, 22d.
110. *Dublin Evening Post*, 2 March 1847.

cabins in his parish, with dogs chewing on the bones of his dead parishioners. Neither Brennan nor his curate would risk catching fever themselves, relying, instead, on others, former fever suffers – even 'little girls' – to take the risk:

> Kilglass, Rooskey, County Roscommon, July 14th, 1847.
> Sir, There is not in Ireland any parish where fever and destitution prevail to so fearful an extent. We have about 800 sick of fever just now, without the advantage of an hospital, a medical officer, or, I may say, a committee, to stay the progress of disease or coffin the dead. By the bungling of some government official one half of this parish is annexed to the Elphin Committee, which meets, near twelve miles distant therefrom – whilst the other is joined to the Kilmore Committee, that meets near eight miles off. Little or nothing is doing to relieve the sufferers. By this time fever has made its way into almost every house – the poor wretches are wasting away and dying of want. In very many instance the dead bodies are thrown in waste cabins and dykes, and devoured by dogs. In some parts the fields are bleached with the bones of the dead that were previously picked by dogs. About a month since two have died in a waste house near my residence. I have made many fruitless efforts to get persons to take these bodies out of the infected cabin – they were so much afraid of going into it, they would not, even for money, comply with my wishes. About two days ago my curate and myself succeeded in getting two little girls, who are recovering from fever to drag out the second body. Both the bodies are now lying in a drain to the rere of the house, with a slight covering over them. The body was covered with worms, and had one of the thighs devoured by dogs. On behalf of the parishioners I have been all the season applying to the government and the Relief Commissioners for a local committee in Kilglass for these two electoral divisions, into which our parish is divided. We held a meeting, at which we adopted three petitions – one to the Lords Justices, one to the Commissioners, and the third to the House of Commons. The two former we forwarded to their proper destination. We sent off the third petition also – I posted it to Mr [John] Collett, the [Liberal] member for Athlone, to whom we entrusted it for presentation to the House. But, strange to say, Mr Collett has neither acknowledged the receipt of our petition, nor has he as yet presented it, nor even replied to two letters I have addressed to him on the subject within the last fortnight. Since the Earl of Clarendon has come over to Ireland, I wrote to him to request that the just and necessary demand of the parishioners would be acceded to, but his Excellency has not condescended to reply.
>
> Had we got the desired committee, we would undertake to remedy the evils complained of, and endeavour to have the Temporary Relief Act *administered pursuant to its spirit and letter* – and that in a retired, miserable locality, where the poor are neglected, famine and disease stalk abroad with uncontrolled sway, and death most successfully doing its work of desolation. The only alternative now left to us is to appeal to public sympathy, through the columns of your excellent journal – the faithful mirror of public opinion in Ireland. I shall repair to London with the humble address of the poor afflicted sufferers of Kilglass, and with it lay before our gracious Queen the wants and tribulations of this ill-fated portion of her Majesty's dominions.
>
> I have the honour to be your most obedient servant,
> Henry Brennan, P.P. of Kilglass.[111]

111. *The Pilot*, 19 July 1847, 4.

In normal times a population of about 7,700 would witness between about 87 and 131 deaths, and Brennan's estimate of 1,000 dead for the period October 1846–March 1847 vastly exceeds this range. It may not be far wrong, however, as by 1851 the parish's population had collapsed to almost 6,000 below the 1841 census-figures.[112]

Return of Revd Henry Brennan, P.P. of Kilglass:

Number of deaths in this parish from 1st October 1846 to 1st April 1847? 1,000. Number of same known to be caused by famine? 950.

No registry of the number of deaths for same period last year.

The astounding news of the illustrious and ever to be lamented Liberator's death, which so completely unmanned me, prevented me sending this earlier. That disastrous event completes the unprecedented calamity it appears destined to befall Ireland this memorable year.

However, we have one consolation left in our bereavement, that he has bequeathed his indefatigable son, John O'Connell, to his country, whom I hope at no very distant day will be styled the regenerator of Ireland, as his noble and never to be forgotten sire was the emancipator. You may perceive by this report, which I assure you is not at all exaggerated, that nearly 1,000 persons in this parish have fallen victims to the famine.

Its present state is truly deplorable, there being seven hundred and thirty eight people sick; in many instances three or four in one family. The great number seized with this desolating epidemic, fever and dysentery, which now, alas! ravages this ill-fated country from its centre to the sea; the remainder affected with dropsy and emaciation, or famine disease, as it is called.

On an average from 20 to 30 are daily carried off by these fatal diseases to a premature and untimely grave. Their lifeless corpses frequently remain for days uninterred, saturating the surrounding neighbourhood with the noxious and infectious halitus arising from the decomposition of these putrid bodies.

There is no district or fever hospital here where the sufferers could be received. No medical aid afforded, nor means for encoffining and burying the dead.

Kilglass parish is divided between two committees - one meets 12 miles from it - the other eight. The poor starving creatures, who are hardly able to drag their legs after them, must travel to these places of meeting, else their grievances will not be redressed.

Tis utterly impossible for me to attend these committees, having to administer the last consolations of religion to these famine-stricken creatures in their dying moments.

112. *Census of Ireland 1851: Part I, area, population and number of houses, by townlands and electoral divisions, Part VI, general report*, BPP, Command Papers (1856), 2134, vol. 31, xxxi.1, 584, 586.

I represented all this over and over again to the government, demanding a committee in Kilglass. My communications were politely acknowledged, but the committee which was and is indispensably necessary for Kilglass was never since granted to us.

The public works are discontinued altogether. As no person having a cow, though in extreme want, as many such are, will be assigned the rations allowed by the temporary relief [Soup Kitchen] act, now coming into operation, it would be of the utmost importance if the able-bodied poor were to have employment for the next three months, at least, either in these or the drainage works, which are so much wanted, and which ought to be commenced immediately.

As many of the small landholders as possible could have fled to America and elsewhere – but the compensation given here by the landlords for possession of such holdings is so trifling that it is not sufficient to enable them to emigrate.

There is very little tillage, I may say, made throughout the parish, the poor occupants not being able to procure seed oats in any quarter. So, should any of them survive this year, will they not be ten-fold worse next year?

'Tis melancholy to reflect on the present state of things; and worse to contemplate the sad and cheerless prospect of a future. Where all this will end, God only knows.

Source: *The Pilot*, 11 June 1847, 4.

Loughglynn, Elphin Diocese

Commentary

A return was received from Revd Owen Madden, parish priest of Lisacull, Ballaghderrin. Madden's parish, also known as Loughglynn, is located in north-west Roscommon, on the border with County Mayo, and close to Ballaghaderreen town. It covered the western side of the civil parish of Tibohine, in Frenchpark barony. In 1841, 63 per cent of the housing in the *civil* parish of Tibohine (not coterminous with the Catholic parish of Loughglynn) was classified as fourth class and the female illiteracy rate was 82 per cent.

Madden's response to the Association's inquiry was one of the briefest received. He claimed that deaths in the parish in the period October 1846–March 1847 were running at three times the level that they had been a year previously, and most of those he attributed to the Famine.

It is possible that the parish was not as badly hit by the crisis as other areas in the immediate vicinity. The population of the civil parish of Tibohine, for example, declined from 17,804 in 1841 to 13,718 by the 1851 census, representing a population loss of about 23 per cent. But Lisacull parish, which was essentially the western part of Tibohine, declined from 6,976 to 6,076 in the same period – a decline of 13 per cent – while the eastern part of Tibohine, centred on Frenchpark Town, declined from 10,828 to 7,642, a much higher fall of nearly 30 per cent.[113]

Return of Revd Owen Madden, P.P. for Lisacull, Ballaghaderrin:

Total number of deaths from 1st October 1846 to 1st April 1847? 189.
Number of same known to be caused by famine? 103.
Numbers of deaths during the same period last year? 65.

Some of those who die of starvation are left many days unburied for want of coffins. The present state of my parish is most deplorable, there is only a small portion of the land tilled, for all who have any means are preparing to emigrate.

Source: *The Pilot*, 28 May 1847, 4.

St Peter's and Drum (St Peter's, Athlone), Elphin Diocese

Commentary

St Peter's and Drum parish is located in Athlone barony in south County Roscommon, close to the border with County Westmeath. It is co-extensive with the two civil parishes of Drum and St Peter's. In 1841, 38 per cent of the housing was classified as fourth class and the female illiteracy rate was 70 per cent. The return for the parish was prepared by Revd Martin O'Reilly, the long-time parish priest of the parish, and later vicar-general, then archdeacon of Elphin.[114]

O'Reilly was a figure of some influence in Athlone Town. He was a supporter of the Liberal Party in the town in the 1830s, and was a firm O'Connellite when Repeal moved to the forefront of Irish politics, organising the collection of the Compensation Fund for O'Connell in 1840 and joining the Repeal Association in the 1840s. He was Chairman of the Town Commissioners in 1851.[115] He took an active part in the general election of 1841, as contested in the Athlone borough.

113. *Census of Ireland, 1851, Roscommon*, BPP (1856), 2134, 204–5. The calculation is based by assigning the following townlands to Lisacull parish: Aghaderry, Aghadrestan, Aghalour, Ballyglass East, Ballyglass West, Breanamore, Caher, Carrowbehy, Carrownaknockaun, Cloonacolly, Cloonagh, Cloonard, Cloonargid, Cloonbunny, Clooncah, Cloondart, Cloonmaul, Cloonmullin, Cloontowart, Coolagarry, Corracoggil North, Corracoggil South, Corrcommeen, Creevy, Cuiltyboe, Curraghard, Curraghsallagh, Derreenamackaun, Derrinea, Derry, Derrylahan, Driney, Druminagh, Drummad, Errit, Figh, Glebe West, Gortaganny, Kilroddan, Kilrooan, Kiltybanks, Kiltymaine, Lecarrow, Lissydaly, Loughglinn, Loughglinn Demesne, Loughglinn Town, Meelick, Tawnyrover, Tully, Urrasaun.

114. O'Reilly was parish priest by 1834; *First report of the Commissioners of public instruction*, appendix, 64; *Freeman's Journal*, 12 November 1849; *Weekly Freeman's Journal*, 22 January 1870.

115. *Freeman's Journal*, 13 December 1839; *Freeman's Journal*, 17 February 1840; *Freeman's Journal*, 5 March 1844; *Tipperary Vindicator*, 22 June 1844; *Dublin Evening Mail*, 20 August 1851.

A petition presented in parliament a few years later, on behalf of a James Reveille, claimed that 'the Rev. Martin O'Reilly, parish priest of Athlone, had denounced him; that he was paraded in effigy throughout the town; and that the effigy was then burnt; that a party broke into his house; and that his family were obliged to escape as they could, and ultimately to come to England.' It was also claimed by Reveille that he was unable to return home because of threats made against him by the Revd O' Reilly.[116]

The population of the parish of St Peter's and Drum was likely about 12,000 by mid-1845, so the 30 deaths reported by O'Reilly for the October 1845–March 1846 period is clearly a vast underestimate, as are the 32 deaths recorded in the parish's register.[117] Nonetheless, the 192 deaths reported for the later Famine period represented a considerable increase over normal years. Over 80 per cent of the deaths in the parish in the year after 1 October 1846 were said to be linked to the Famine.

Return by Revd Martin O'Reilly, P.P. for St. Peter's and Drum:

Number of deaths from 1st October 1846 to 1st April 1847? 192.
Number of above known to be caused by famine? 50.
And of fever and dysentery occasioned by want of nutriment? 112.
Number of deaths during the same period last year? 30.

It is impossible for me in a brief space to describe the many melancholy cases of persons found either in their wretched cabins, or prostrate on the cold ground on their way to the public works in a state of perfect exhaustion. But the present state of these parishes is most awful. Those who hitherto were enabled to prolong a precarious existence are now without resources of any kind. What a heartrending scene to behold persons who not long since possessed feelings of honour and shame, now with tears trickling down their pallid and emaciated cheeks, crying for breads, and none to be had.

But I shudder at what may happen in a few days, when those employed on the public works may be dismissed.

No rate has been yet struck. No arrangements will be complete until half the population die of starvation!

In these parishes the land is to a great extent tilled, yet there are many acres untilled for the want of means to purchase seed. The prospects of the coming year are by no means cheering. The extent of emigration is very great, but hundreds of families are prevented from emigrating for the want of means.

Source: *The Pilot*, 19 May 1847, 2.

116. *London Evening Standard*, 18 August 1843.
117. https://registers.nli.ie/registers/vtls000633873#page/193/.

Tarmonbarry, Elphin Diocese

Commentary

The return for Tarmonbarry Catholic parish, in east County Roscommon, bordering County Longford, was compiled by Revd Peter Gormley, curate of the parish, under Revd James McNally, parish priest. Gormley was a Repealer, and the organiser of the Repeal Rent collection in his parish.[118]

The Catholic parish appears to have been coextensive with the civil parish of Termonbarry. The statutory censuses reported populations of 4,048 in 1831 and 4,279 in 1841 in the civil parish of Termonbarry.[119] In 1841, 14 per cent of the housing was classified as fourth class and the female illiteracy rate was 62 per cent. There were few Protestants in the area; the Public Instruction Commissioners identified only 81 in the 1831 census list.[120] We estimate that the mid-year Catholic population may have been about 4,370 in 1845 and perhaps 3,850 in 1847. Unfortunately, Revd Gormley provided no pre-Famine mortality figure, but the 300 deaths he reported for the October 1846–March 1847 period, 200 of whom, Gormley informs, died from famine related causes, vastly exceeded the 44–65 deaths that we would expect to observe in a population of about 3,850 under normal social conditions.

Return of Revd Peter Gormley, curate of Tarmonbarry:

Number of deaths from 1st Oct., 1846, to 1st April, 1847, 300.
Number of same known to be caused by famine? about 200.
Number of deaths during the same period last year? No registry of deaths for same period former years.

In this parish it is a very common thing to see dead bodies left abandoned without a person to bury them for many days: from three to six days. Dead bodies are often seen on the highways, where they sink from exhaustion, and there lie. The present state of this parish is very pitiable; famine, starvation, dysentery, and various kinds of fever are doing the work of destruction. The arrangements on foot at present (the outdoor relief system) will by no means save our poor from starvation and death. Tillage is considerably diminished this year, the prospects of the coming year are very gloomy. If landlords claim rent there will be no support for the people whatsoever. Very little emigration as yet for want of means.

Source: *The Pilot*, 28 May 1847, 4.

118. *The Pilot*, 16 May 1845; *Freeman's Journal*, 10 April 1846.

119. *Abstract of Population Returns for Ireland, 1831*, BPP (1833), 634, 324; *Report of the Commissioners appointed to take the census of Ireland, for the year 1841*, BPP (1843), 504, 406.

120. *First report of the Commissioners of public instruction*, 28d.

County Sligo

Achonry, Achonry Diocese

Commentary

Achonry Catholic parish is located in south-west Sligo, and comprises the eastern part of the civil parish of the same name. In 1841, 49 per cent of the housing in the *civil* parish of Achonry (not coterminous with the Catholic parish of Achonry) was classified as fourth class and the female illiteracy rate was 83 per cent. The report for the parish was compiled by its parish priest, Revd. James Gallagher. Gallagher, like many of the clergy of Achonry deanery, was an ardent O'Connellite and he attended the 17 June 1847 meeting of Achonry clergy to sympathise on the death of O'Connell. It is notable that the priests of the deanery were unanimous in their opposition to the Young Ireland party:

> On Thursday, the 17th instant, the clergymen of the Deanery of Achonry, assembled at the Chapel of Ballymote to celebrate the obsequies of our much lamented Liberator. The Rev Michael M'Cauley, R.C.C. celebrant; the Rev James M'Kew, P.P. Clonard, Deacon; the Rev James Henry, P.P. Bunnenadin, Master of Ceremonies. The chapel was crowded by sorrowing thousands from the surrounding parishes, and their joint prayers intermingled with sighs and lamentations at their bereavement ascended high as a sweet odour for the eternal repose of the soul of the illustrious dead.
>
> After the celebration of the solemn obsequies, the clergymen of the deanery held a meeting, which adopted a series of motions 'expressing our heartfelt grief for the death of our dear departed Liberator', renewing commitment to his teachings and policies, as well as one specific to one of their own number: 'we cannot separate on this solemn occasion without giving humble expression to our feelings of abhorrence and humiliation, that the Rev Mr Kenyon, a member of our body, who has acquired an unenviable notoriety by his unaccountable advocacy of the Young Ireland party, should asperse the memory of Him who has been the emancipator of our altars.'[121]

Gallagher's return claims that nearly a quarter of the population had emigrated in the previous few years, and the parish's proximity to Sligo port would have facilitated that removal. These comments contrast starkly with Peter Dowdican's submission for neighbouring Dromard, however, where his parishioners had 'no means' to emigrate. The *Freeman's Journal*, summarising this return, noted that 'Achonry is one of those districts where relief has been accompanied by attempts at proselytism, and benevolence deprived of its purity by allowing one portion of the population with the bounty of "soup, bread, rice and clothes", to corrupt the other.'[122]

121. *Freeman's Journal*, 22 June 1847, 3–4.
122. *Freeman's Journal*, 8 May 1847.

Return of Revd James Gallagher, P.P. of Achonry:

Number of deaths from 1st October 1846 to 1st April 1847? 51.
Number of same known to be caused by famine? 32.
Number of deaths during the same period last year? 10.

The parish is in a most deplorable state for sustenance. The arrangements on foot are far from being adequate to meet the wants of the people. About two-thirds of the land is untilled, therefore the prospect of support for the next year is truly limited. Nearly one fourth of the population have emigrated either to America or England.

Source: *The Pilot*, 5 May 1847, 4.

Bunninadden (Kilshalvey), Achonry Diocese

Commentary

Like James Gallagher in Achonry, Revd James Henry, parish priest of Bunninadden in southern County Sligo also attended the June 1847 meeting of clergy of the Achonry deanery to eulogise Daniel O'Connell following his death. Henry, a member of O'Connell's Repeal Association,[123] had been parish priest of Toomore (Foxford) parish, County Mayo, from 1833 until 1840, before he was transferred to the Sligo parish. It is notable that the earliest surviving parish register for Bunninadden, a marriage register, records marriages conducted in Toomore parish between 1833 and 1840, and marriages in Bunninadden from 1840 onwards, indicating that it was Henry who introduced sacramental registration in both parishes, and that he considered the register his personal property, removing it when he was transferred.[124]

Bunninadden Catholic parish was coterminous with the civil parishes of Cloonoghil, Kilturra, and Kilshalvey, an area which suffered catastrophic population decline between 1841 and 1851. In 1841, 69 per cent of the housing was classified as fourth class and the female illiteracy rate was 81 per cent. By 1851, the national census was reporting the population of Bunninadden Catholic parish at about 5,100, almost one fourth less than had been recorded for the area 20 years earlier, so Henry's accounts of sudden deaths have some credibility. He reported an impossible 232 deaths in the six-month period between October 1846 and March 1847, about eight times greater than the same period the previous year. Death by fever was running at three per day at the time he was compiling the account.

123. *The Nation*, 14 February 1846.
124. NLI Catholic Registers online (https://registers.nli.ie/registers/vtls000632312#page/4/).

Population of Bunninadden Catholic parish, 1831–1851

Parish	**1831**	**1841**	**1851**	**Change, 1841–51**
Cloonoghil	2,241	2,588	1,662	–36%
Kilshalvy	2,034	2,411	1,570	–35%
Kilturra, Sligo part	1,282	1,263	889	–30%
Kilturra, Mayo part	1,199	1,350	1,023	–24%
Bunninadden Catholic parish	6,756	7,612	5,144	–32%

Source: *Census Irelsnd, 1831*, 316, 330; *Census Ireland, 1851, Mayo*, 142; *Census Ireland, 1851, Sligo*, 225, 227, 228.

Return of Revd James Henry, P.P. of Bunninadden, Ballymote, for 'Parishes of Cloonaughill, Kilturra and part of Kilshalvey:

Number of deaths (as registered) from 1st October, 1846 to 1st April 1847? 232. Number of same known to be caused by starvation? 125. Want of food was the remote cause of all the rest.
Number of deaths during the same period last year? 28

There were some instances of labourers at public works dying in an hour or two after returning home; some found dead in their own cabins by their neighbours. Fever prevails at present to a frightful extent – deaths for the last fortnight, from fever alone, average 3 daily. No medical attendance, or other means of any sort, to arrest or mitigate the further ravages of this epidemic. Dysentery is very general, though not so virulent or fatal as some time ago. Rations under the present system of relief [Soup Kitchen Act] are now in operation; but on account of the breaking up of all the public works here, I have no doubt of witnessing more destitution and deaths from starvation for the next month than even in any previous one. Many holdings remain entirely untilled from inability on the part of the holders to procure seed. The landlords, so far from assisting, harassed them by civil bill decrees for rent, by [im]pounding and seizing cattle, that many who might struggle to till their land were dispirited from doing so. A rule of the Sligo Finance Committee, precluding all whose 'holdings' are rated under the poor law valuation at 3*l*., from any (if I may say so) of the ration relief, forced many, after having their holdings tilled, to throw them up to their landlords. The possession in every case is eagerly accepted, provided they can get hold of the house as well as their land. No crop of any sort here but oats. Half the breadth of land is not under this crop this year as last.

Source: *The Pilot*, 28 May 1847, 4.

Dromard, Killala Diocese

Commentary

[See John Hopkins' report for neighbouring Skreen parish].

Dromard Catholic parish is situated on the west coast of Ireland, coterminous with the civil parish of the same name. It is located to the east of Skreen parish, from where a return was also submitted.[125] The 1831 census recorded a population of 2,613 there, but its population had contracted to 2,445 by 1841.[126] This was not exceptional during the 1830s; many districts in close proximity to ports witnessed population declines between the 1831 and 1841 censuses. In 1841, 44 per cent of the housing was classified as fourth class and the female illiteracy rate was 77 per cent. The parish was predominantly Catholic, with a small Protestant minority; the Public Instruction Commissioners identified 229 Protestants (8.9 per cent) and 2,331 Catholics in the 1831 census returns.[127]

The return from Dromard was submitted by Revd Peter Dowdican, parish priest, who had been placed in the parish since at least 1828, in which year he was recorded in the Tithe Applotment Book for the parish, on a small farm in Carrowgilpatrick townland. Dowdican was a Liberal, supporting Daniel Jones, a losing candidate, in the 1837 general election.[128] His submission, somewhat unusually, included the deaths of children in his figures for deaths. We estimate the parish's Catholic population by mid-1845 at about 2,300, and a population of this size would typically experience between 22 and 40 deaths in a normal October to March period. Dowdican's reported figure, 20 deaths, is close enough to the lower limit of the expected range. By mid-1847 the Catholic population may have declined to about 1,900. If this was the case then the 100 deaths reported by Dowdican represent a mortality rate of 93 per 1,000; about three times the normal rate. In Dowdican's view the provision of gratuitous food relief represented the best chance of staving off the worst effects of the food shortages. Tensions between him and the rector, Lewis Potter, are evident, whom he criticises for engaging in unscrupulous proselytising.

Return by Revd Peter Dowdican, P.P of Dromard:

Number of deaths from the 1st October 1846 to 1st April 1847? 100, including old and young, out of a population not exceeding 2,600.
Number of same known to be occasioned by the famine? 50.
Number of deaths during same period last year? 20.

Present state of this parish, appalling destitution; the only prospect to stay the raging famine, soup; and the prospects of support for the coming year lamentable.

125. Lewis, *Topographical dictionary of Ireland*, I, 504.
126. *Abstract of Population Returns for Ireland, 1831*, BPP (1833), 634, 332; *Report of the Commissioners appointed to take the census of Ireland, for the year 1841*, BPP (1843), 504, 416.
127. *First report of the Commissioners of public instruction*, 54d.
128. *Sligo Champion*, 9 September 1837, 1.

A great portion of the public charitable money, clothes, food &c. &c., transmitted to the Reverend Lewis Potter, Protestant rector of Drimard, is appropriated to proselytising purposes, who has employed some old renegade Catholics to allure by soup, rice, bread, and clothes, the famishing children of the Catholics of the surrounding parishes, who must attend his Protestant schools, where Protestant doctrine is expounded either by himself or his apostate Protestant teachers; and also Protestant worship on Sundays and other state days, or fall victims to starvation.

It is expected that the Association will take up this case, and have it exhibited to public reprobation, and that the Hon. Member for Kilkenny, or some other patriotic member, will draw the attention of the House of Commons to so flagrant an abuse of the public funds.

Emigration not extensive, the people having no means.

Source: *The Pilot*, 5 May 1847, 4.

Kilfree, Achonry Diocese

Commentaery:

Kilfree parish is located in south Sligo. The Catholic parish was coextensive with the two civil parishes of Kilfree and Killaraght, both located in Coolavin barony. The statutory censuses depict a rapidly growing population in the area, climbing from 5,188 in 1821 to 7,089 in 1831, and 8,277 in 1841.[129] In 1841, 44 per cent of the housing was classified as fourth class and the female illiteracy rate was 78 per cent. The inhabitants were overwhelmingly Catholic; the Public Instruction Commissioners enumerated 166 Protestants (2.3 per cent) in a population exceeding 7,000 in 1831.[130] We estimate the parish population was of the order of 8,600 by 1845, with about 8,400 of those Catholic.

The return for the parish was compiled by Revd Peter Brennan, parish priest there since at least the first half of the 1830s.[131] Brennan was a notable O'Connellite in the county, contributing to the Compensation Fund in the early 1840s, and was subsequently described as 'the ardent friend of O'Connell'.[132] An April 1844 meeting in favour of Repeal in the parish was chaired by Brennan, to the favour of the attendees,

> who well knew his fearless devotion to the cause of liberty, and his zealous attachment to their own darling measure, Repeal. In calm, clear and eloquent language, he expatiated on the objects of the meeting [...] by imploring the people to attach themselves still more firmly

129. *Abstract of answers and returns, pursuant to act 55 Geo. 3, for taking an account of the population of Ireland in 1821*, BPP, House of Commons Papers (1824), 577, vol.22, xxii.411, 366; *Abstract of Population Returns for Ireland, 1831*, BPP (1833), 634, 330; *Report of the Commissioners appointed to take the census of Ireland, for the year 1841*, BPP (1843), 504,. 416.
130. *First report of the Commissioners of public instruction*, 62d.
131. Ibid., appendix, 63.
132. *Weekly Freeman's Journal*, 3 April 1841; *Dublin Weekly Register*, 22 July 1843.

to O'Connell, to cling to the Repeal, so would then legally and perseveringly struggle for it to the last moment of victory. The Reverent gentleman was loudly and enthusiastically cheered by the congregated multitude, who felt justly proud of him, as one who had joined the Repeal Movement in the earliest period and had since clung to it with unalterable devotion [...] A large number of Repealers were enrolled, headed by the Rev Peter Brennan, whose third annual subscription of one pound was, with a large sum handed over to the treasurer.[133]

Return of Revd Peter Brennan, P.P. of Kilfree:

Number of deaths from 1st October, 1846 to 1st April 1847? 256.
Number of same known to be caused by famine? 206.
Number of deaths during the same period last year? 40.

Widow Horan, of Drumlushana, lay for four days dead before her neighbours discovered that she had expired. The wife of Dominick Gavan, of Meelroe, and her two children, remained for the space of a week unburied; the neighbours could not be induced to enter the hovel where their remains lay, such is the malignant nature of the contageon [*sic.*] with which they were attacked. Fever and dysentery rage most frightfully in this parish. Relief committees are established here; some members of those committees will not give outdoor relief to any person who may be possessed of a yearling calf. They also state that a claimant for relief if possessed of land which he cannot crop – cannot receive any assistance till he gives up his farm to his landlord. Are they correct in taking this view of the law? One half the quantity of land usually tilled will not be cropped this year. Of course our prospects of support for next year are most disheartening. Landlords are giving no encouragement to their tenants. The undernamed individuals have been dispossessed and turned out and their houses thrown down:

Thomas Cosgrove, eight in family; Widow Cosgrove, four do; Patrick Cosgrove, eight do; Patrick Cunningham, eight do; Widow Wynne, two do; Widow Kavanagh, eight do; William Meehan, seven do.

Source: *The Pilot*, 14 May 1847, 4.

Skreen, Killala Diocese

Commentary

[See Peter Dowdican's report for neighbouring Dromard parish].

Skreen parish is a coastal parish in west County Sligo, bordering Dromard parish. As in the case of Dromard, Skreen's population had shrunk during the 1830s, quite possibly because of its proximity to the port of Sligo. The parish's population was reported at 4,567 by the 1831 census, but had declined to 4,103 a decade later.[134] In 1841 35 per cent of the housing was classified as fourth class and

133. *Sligo Champion*, 11 May 1844.

134. *Abstract of Population Returns for Ireland, 1831*, BPP (1833), 634, 332; *Report of the Commissioners appointed to take the census of Ireland, for the year 1841*, BPP (1843), 504, 416.

the female illiteracy rate was 77 per cent. The parish was predominantly Catholic, but was home to a not insignificant Protestant community; the Public Instruction Commissioners reported 595 Protestants (13 per cent) and 3,972 Catholics in the 1831 census returns.[135]

The return for Skreen was compiled by Revd John Hopkins, the parish priest. Hopkins was a respected Repealer. When submitting his £1 remittance for Association membership he was described to the meeting of the Association as 'as pure, as noble, and generous-hearted a patriot as Ireland can boast of'. Hopkins was proposed for membership that year by Daniel O'Connell junior.[136]

Hopkins' return describes a parish ravaged by scarcity, with little available by way of relief. Curiously, Hopkins notes that people were fleeing the area in vast numbers – 'one third of the inhabitants have emigrated' – but Peter Dowdican's report from neighbouring Dromard, closer to Sligo port, observed that 'emigration [was] not extensive, the people having no means'. Ultimately, of the two neighbouring parishes, it was Dromard that experienced the greater proportionate population decline (Table 7.1). Hopkins claimed that deaths had increased by a factor of eight between the two reporting periods, whereas a five-fold increase in mortality was reported from Donard. According to Hopkins, most of the excess deaths were caused by famine.

Table 7.1 Population change in Dromard and Skreen parishes, County Sligo, 1841–1851

Parish	1841 population	1851 population	Change
Dromard	2,445	1,468	–40%
Skreen	4,103	2,963	–28%

Source: Cen. Ire., 1851, Sligo, 233, 236.

Return of Revd John Hopkins, P.P. of Skreen:

Number of deaths from the 1st October 1846 to 1st April, 1847? 160.
Number of same known to have been caused by famine? 90.
Number of deaths during the same period last year? 20.

The present state of this parish is most awful, the new system of relief [Soup Kitchen Act] not having come into full operation as yet.

Prospects of support for the coming year very poor, one half of the land usually tilled neglected this season and one third of the inhabitants have emigrated, and many preparing to be off.

Source: *The Pilot*, 14 May 1847, 4.

135. *First report of the Commissioners of public instruction*, 45, 56d.
136. *Freeman's Journal*, 20 February 1844, 3.

PROVINCE OF MUNSTER

Summary of the returns for Munster

County	Parish	Deaths		
		Oct. 1845– Mar. 1846	Oct. 1846– Mar. 1847	... from famine
Clare	Clareabbey and Killone	12	72	36
	Clonrush and Insihcaltra	23	95	86
	Ennistymon	50	425 + 352 in workhouse	355
	Feakle	400	1,000	600
	Kilchrist and Clondagad	65	352	20
	Kildysart	NA	150	80
	Kilfenora	10	59	40
Cork	Ballybricken	15	45	19
	Castletownroche	NA	116	99
	Kilmeen	40	156	104
Kerry	Ardfert and Kilmoyley	*c.* 208	*c.* 910	*c.* 416
	Ballylongford and Tarbert	*c.* 260	780	> 50%
	Ballybunnion	25	120	80
	Castlemaine	NA	NA	NA
	Moyvane	40 adults	180 + *c.* 40 children	106 adults
Limerick	Killeedy	NA	NA	NA
	Knockany	22, age 15+	NA	66, age 15+
	Pallasgreen	NA	NA	NA
Tipperary	Ballinahinch and Killoscully	30	104	40
	Ballingarry (Slievardagh)	60	170	80
	Ballyneale	16	152	3
	Boherlahan and Dualla	50	200	150
	Borrisoleigh (Glenkeen)	25	100	Perhaps none.
	Cahir	50, age 12+	160, age, 12+	80

(*Continued*)

County	Parish	Deaths		
		Oct. 1845–Mar. 1846	Oct. 1846–Mar. 1847	... from famine
	Clerihan	13	30	12
	Donohill and Kilpatrick	22	71	18
	Fethard	30	185	120
	Lorrha and Dorrha	40	143	100
	Mullinahone	20	40	20
	Thurles	70	Nearly 300 + *c.* 500 in workhouse	*c.* 300
	Toomevara	20	50	30

County Clare

Clareabbey and Killone (Clarecastle), Killaloe Diocese

Commentary

The Catholic parishes of Clareabbey and Killone (Clarecastle), were coterminous with the two civil parishes of the same name. The population of the benefice was 5,128 in 1821, rising to 6,235 by 1831, but it then declined marginally to 6,057 by 1841, perhaps as a result of emigration. In 1841, 54 per cent of the housing was classified as fourth class and the female illiteracy rate was 66 per cent.[137] The non-Catholic population was miniscule in the pre-Famine period; the Public Instruction Commissioners reported 104 Protestants [1.7 per cent] and 6,131 Catholics [98.3 per cent] among the 1831 population.[138]

The return was compiled by Revd Patrick O'Gorman, parish priest of the parish since 1834.[139] O'Gorman was an O'Connellite, regularly contributing sums to O'Connell Tributes and compensations during the 1830s and 1840s and collecting the parish's Repeal Rent.[140] A substantial £22 12*s.* 1*d.* was contributed from the parish in Tribute in November 1843, received at the Repeal Association's office from 'Rev. Patrick O'Gorman, the efficiently-patriotic Catholic rector of these parishes, eminent for their love of country. The present greatly surpasses in amount preceding contributions'.[141]

137. *Abstract of answers and returns*, BPP (1824), 577, 142; *Abstract of Population Returns for Ireland, 1831*, BPP (833), 634, 130; *Report of the Commissioners appointed to take the census of Ireland, for the year 1841*, BPP (1843), 504, 158.
138. *First report of the Commissioners of public instruction*, 45, 220c, 236c.
139. Ibid., 59.
140. *The Pilot*, 9 November 1835. b; 25 January 1836; *Freeman's Journal*; 30 December 1839.
141. *Dublin Weekly Register*, 25 November 1843.

Clare, Ennis, 8th April, 1835.
My Dear Sir – I beg leave to send you the order on the other side in your favour, the amount which you will have the kindness to hand to the treasurers of the O'Connell Tribute. It is the contribution of the Union of Clare-abbey and Killone for 1834. Of this sum I have contributed £1 10*s*; Rev. John OBrien, RCC, 10*s*; Messrs Pat Lynch, Thomas Kelly, Michael M'Inerney, and Michael Lilliss, 5*s*. each, £1; Messrs Michael Glasby, John Cahil, James Moran, Pat Donohoe, Richard O'Shaughnessy, John O'Brien, Mrs. Laffan, Thomas Lynch, Mr. Burke, and Tim Daly, 2*s*. 6*d*. each, £1 5*s*. The remaining portion was given in smaller sums. You will have the goodness to acknowledge this in your *Pilot*.
I am, my dear Sir, truly yours,
Patrick O'Gorman
To Richard Barrett, Esq., Dublin.[142]

Revd O'Gorman's figures for deaths in the two periods are too low and probably represent only a partial count of deaths. We estimate the Catholic population of the parish at about 6,200 in mid-1845, and a population of this size would typically witness between 70 and 105 deaths in normal economic conditions, well beyond the 12 deaths that O'Gorman noted for the October 1845–April 1846 period. He spoke of 'one fourth of our people' dying of want in 1847, which does not gel with a total of 72 dead in the six-month period to April 1847. A meeting of the 'magistrates, clergy and respectable farmers' in the parish on 6 March 1846 provides additional useful information on the desperate conditions in the area. The press reported:

At a meeting of the magistrates, clergy, and respectable farmers of the parish of Killone, held in the national school-house of Newhall, on Friday, the 6th instant, John MacDonnell, Esq., of Newhall, in the chair, for the purpose of urging on the members of the scarcity commission, the necessity of affording immediate relief to the destitute unemployed poor of the district, the following statement was unanimously agreed to:

That there are in this parish one hundred families and upwards, in great want;- the failure of the potato crop, the high price of potatoes in Ennis market (5*d*. yesterday), the want of resident gentry to employ the people – all combine to spread distress and misery throughout the neighbourhood.

That about one hundred acres of the rich alluvial corcas land adjoining the estuary of the river Fergus, have been cultivated during the past year by the labourers of this parish – *the entire produce of which has been lost.*

That at the present moment there are in this parish more than *fifty families in a state bordering on extreme destitution*, or in other words, that they frequently cannot procure even one meal in the twenty-four hours of the cheapest food, as is they are without money, credit, or employment.

142. *The Pilot*, 13 April 1835, 3.

That in *another month* we will have an additional number of *fifty families* and upwards in *similar destitution*, and that before the 1st of next May, *more than the third part of the inhabitants of this parish will have to depend, in order it to sustain life, on the employment afforded by public works, or the relief given by humane landlords.*

That the extensive farmers of the parish have lost almost the entire of their potatoes - hence the poor are excluded from the extensive charities hitherto given in the agricultural districts – hence likewise a great diminution of the employment heretofore afforded by the farmers to the neighbouring poor

That there are not in this parish provisions sufficient, at an average, to *feed the inhabitants for a month.*

That several very useful public work could be undertaken in the parish, *viz.*-one hundred acres of land adjoining Tiermaclane and Cragbrien are covered with water during the greater part of the year, though it could be easily drained and rendered the most productive land in the parish; several new lines of road could be opened; there are a great many roads to be repaired, and some hills to be lowered on the public roads.

John MacDonnell, J.P & D.L.; Charles Mulville, J.P.; Patrick O'Gorman, P.P., Killone [several other signatures follow here].[143]

Return of Revd Mr O'Gorman, P.P. of Clareabbey and Killone:

Number of deaths from 1st October 1846 to 1st April 1847? 72.
Number of same known to be caused by famine? 36.
Number of deaths during the same period last year? 12.

John M'Namara, of Clare village, died under heart rending circumstances. He was confined to his bed for the last two months rather from debility than any sickness; every member of his family (eight) were also confined, or rather stretched on damp straw. They had, consequently, little communication with the neighbours, who apprehended contagion. Having no persons employed in the public works they had no means of procuring any food unless what was supplied occasionally by one individual, but not in sufficient quantities to sustain them. The poor man died; his wife and two children were lying in the same bed with the corpse until the neighbours, who knew nothing of it for ten hours, came in and removed them. I brought Mr O'Brien, MP,[144] to visit the scene; it was literally a 'Skibbereen case'. Mr O'Brien did everything to relieve the family under the circumstances.

143. *Freeman's Journal*, 12 March 1846.
144. Cornelius O'Brien, MP for Clare County.

We have no arrangements to stay the famine; on the contrary, all the people, with the exception of a fractional part, are disemployed. The rations given in outdoor relief is only 1½d. for every adult.

You may be prepared to hear of a hundred cases similar to John M'Namara's in the course of a few months, in the parish of Clare Abbey and Killone.

The symptoms of mortality and emaciating hunger are more alarming now, and during the past week, than ever; but the murderous rule of all is this, that any man known to have constant employment, even though the wages may be the ordinary one of 8 ½d. per day, will get no relief for any member of his family, no matter what may be the number. The law makes provision for this description of persons, it entitles them to cheap food. But the relief inspector, when remonstrated with says that they can get only cooked food, and when requested to supply this cooked food, he replies that he has 'no boiler ready'; a poor man in Ballynalligan became insane from want, and attempted the life of his wife; one fourth of our people are doomed to die of want this year, thousands in every parish see nothing but certain death by starvation haunting them at every step.

Source: *The Pilot*, 28 April 1847, 3.

Clonrush and Inishcaltra (Mountshannon), Killaloe Diocese

Commentary

The parishes of Clonrush and Inishcaltra (or Mountshannon) were located primarily in County Galway, but were transferred to Clare in 1898. They are in Upper Tulla barony, and were coterminous with the civil parishes of the same names. The census recorded the population of the union at 5,282 in 1831, and 5,493 in 1841.[145] In 1841, 45 per cent of the housing was classified as fourth class and the female illiteracy rate was 66 per cent. The parishes had a small but significant Protestant community; the Public Instruction Commissioners reported 795 Protestants [15.1 per cent] in the union in 1831, most of them living in Inishcaltra parish, probably in the vicinity of Mountshannon town.[146] The Catholic population would have been about 4,850 by mid-1845, and about 4,000 by mid-1847.

The report for the parishes was a cross-denominational effort, it being compiled by the vicar, Hugh Brady Huleatt, and the parish priest, Revd Patrick O'Brien. At a time when inter-denominational tensions were heightened by proselytising in some areas, the Protestant and Catholic communities in Clonrush apparently worked well together. A parish relief committee was established in the union in April 1846, and at its first meeting Huleatt was appointed chairman with O'Brien installed as secretary. Among the first resolutions of the new committee was one to open a subscription list to 'purchase

145. *Abstract of Population Returns for Ireland, 1831*, BPP (1833), 634, 132, 298; *Report of the Commissioners appointed to take the census of Ireland, for the year 1841*, BPP (1843), 504, 160, 378, 380.
146. 1835 (45) *First report of the Commissioners of public instruction*, 222c.

India Corn Meal as quickly as possible' and another to authorise O'Brien to write to the Lord Lieutenant 'requesting immediate aid from the government' as the subscribed sums were 'totally inadequate without such assistance to meet the extensive distress which now inevitably exists in many areas'. The committee also resolved to contact the Relief Commissioners, requesting 'India Corn Meal at cut price to be distributed for work or money as the Committee may deem advisable'.[147]

It is striking that the Catholic parish's registry book was used to record the minutes of the Relief Committee, 4 April–23 October 1846, so Huleatt regularly signed his name in the Catholic register, hardly a common experience for a mid-nineteenth-century Protestant pastor. The local relief committee's meeting of 14 May 1846 appointed Huleatt and O'Brien as contractors for the repair of roads in the parish,[148] though three weeks later it was resolved: 'That our Committee find with regret it is reported that some individuals have been employed on the Public Works in this district while others more empoverished have recd no employment, and our Committee are determined to remove such discrepancies and not permit their recurrence'.[149] No interdenominational tensions are evident in any of the recorded minutes.

A Catholic population of almost 5,000 would typically experience 55 deaths or more in a normal October–March six-month period. Thus, the 23 deaths reported for the October 1845–March 1846 period are too low. Since this return is one of the few to have been compiled with the assistance of the Protestant clergyman it is likely that the mortality numbers being reported included the deaths of Protestants as well as Catholics. If the estimated population of the parish (all denominations) was about 5,700 by mid-1845, we would expect a minimum of 65 deaths in the October–March six month period. Still, the 95 deaths given for October 1846–March 1847 indicate considerably elevated mortality, even if that, too, was an underestimate. The use of the term slaughter house to sum up the threat to life resonates.

Return of Revd H. B. Huleatt, vicar, and Revd P. O'Brien, P.P. of Clonrush and Inishcaltra:

Number of deaths from 1st October 1846 to 1st April 1847? 95.
Number the of same known to be caused by famine? 86.
Number of deaths during the same period last year? 23.

Fathers and sons are interred in the same graves at the same time; some exhausted, and dying while a bit of stirabout was preparing for them; some falling on the public works, carried to their huts by the people, and dying immediately after; nothing effectual to stay the progress of famine but the 10th Vic. cap.7 [Soup Kitchen Act], if fairly carried into operation.

A great deal of land untilled in the possession of persons who have nothing to put in the soil.

147. https://registers.nli.ie/registers/vtls000634685#page/50).
148. https://registers.nli.ie/registers/vtls000634685#page/52.
149. https://registers.nli.ie/registers/vtls000634685#page/53.

The prospects for the coming year are extremely gloomy, numbers having a little capital are fleeing from this slaughter house!

Some of our parishioners who died were protracting a miserable existence on half diet; the rest, carried off by a quick process, became victims in a few days.

Source: *The Pilot*, 28 April 1847, 3.

Ennistymon (Kilmanaheen and Clooney), Kilfenora Diocese

Commentary

Ennistymon parish, in west County Clare on the Atlantic seaboard, was in Kilfenora diocese at the time of the Famine.[150] In 1841, 44 per cent of the housing was classified as fourth class and the female illiteracy rate was 74 per cent. We estimate the Catholic population (exclusive of the workhouse) at about 9,900 in mid-1845, from which we would typically expect to see between about 112 and 168 deaths. The 50 deaths reported in the Death Census for this period were well below the lower-bound threshold used in this volume.

The return for the parish was compiled by Revd John Sheehan, the parish priest. Sheehan was actively embedded in the community, organising events ranging from public meetings to celebrate the life of local grandees,[151] to inviting 'the apostle of temperance', Fr Matthew, to preach to his community on the evils of alcohol consumption.[152] A Repeal organiser, he was firmly committed to O'Connell's political approach, directing the organisation of the Association in the parish, and collecting funds for the O'Connell Tribute in his chapel.[153] In 1841 he brought the £12 10*s*. that was raised locally (including his own contribution of 30*s*.) to public notice by way of a verbose letter to the *Freeman's Journal*. He wrote on 12 January 1841:

> Enclosed you have half notes for £12 10*s*., being the amount of the O'Connell Tribute at the chapels of Ennistimon and Clouna. This sum includes my own subscription of 30*s*., together with 10*s*. from Rev. William Hanrahan, and £1 from T. F. Comyn, Esq., Reneen Lodge, a steady contributor to this fund, who, true as the needle to the pole, is at his post on every occasion since the establishment of this national annuity, to contribute his mite and forward a measure which merely acknowledges the services, great and splendid, of a man whom a nation has long since resolved to honour. The making of this collection I consider a sacred duty, amounting to the importance of a religious obligation; for what is it but promoting the cause of morality, of religion, of justice, in the person of the long-tried champion of liberty, whose indomitable energies are directed to the immortal Purpose of raising the destinies of an injured country, and restoring the former glories of her people; than which motive of action what can be more dignified, more ennobling, more calculated

150. *Thom's Irish Almanac, 1850*, 343.
151. *Freeman's Journal*, 21 December 1842.
152. *Dublin Morning Register*, 27 August 1842.
153. *Freeman's Journal*, 19 June 1841.

to bring into play every generous emotion of patriotic sentiment, of national feeling, of public virtue? I have only to regret that the amount is not larger – more in character with the ardour of my own wishes, more in accordance with the importance of the occasion, more worthy of the occasion, more worthy of the cause, and of O'Connell, the advocate of universal freedom, the assertor of popular rights, the vindicator of the ways of God to man, the apostle of peaceful agitation, exhibiting the superiority of moral power over physical force, a secret never more gloriously developed, a mystery never so wonderfully brought to light, or fetched forth from the depths of eternal truth, by any of the sages or heroes of ancient or modern times. 'Tis criminal, I think, to omit this public duty, 'tis a crime disgusting in itself, ungrateful and ungenerous in its tendency, anti-national in its nature 'tis a sin against whatever is just, whatever is honest, whatever is of good repute, whatever is due to the praise of virtue, of distinguished merit, of exalted worth, whatever is great in efforts for a nation's happiness, whatever is unpurchable in sacrifices for a nation's good. To be guilty of this omission year after year, on occasions calculated to kindle all that is most glowing in enthusiasm, to touch every fibre vibrating through the heart of an Irishman, to be guilty of such dereliction, under such circumstances, is enough to have the locality or district where such indifference, or apathy, or omission occurs, branded with disgrace, stamped with the ugly stigma of universal censure and public disgust, as it is evident that no patriot pulse beats there a proof that no individual heart is in the right place, an argument that public spirit not only sleeps, but is dead, and that it stands in need of some process of resuscitation to restore it again to breathing, and the throbbing of life. Why is not something done to draw forth from the parishes and places still, and always in default, something like a response to this call of universal measure of justice-some- thing to wipe away the stain, and rouse the slumbering patriotism of the outstanding districts, and remove the shame of lagging eternally behind? For, is not such conduct, such unhallowed apathy and backwardness, deeply tinged with all the characteristics of vice, which to be hated needs but to be known and seen, involving a moral turpitude, which, though a Christian may not hate, a lover of his country can most heartily despise? In a day or two I shall send the other half notes, and by this post shall send another remittance from a neighbouring parish.

I am your's, &c. John Sheehan, P.P.[154]

Sheehan was firmly set against the government's niggardly approach to famine relief, convinced that 'in England such things would not have happened, so much barbarism would not have existed, without bringing about a revolution in a day'.[155] In February 1847 he was claiming 80 to 100 deaths each month in his parish,[156] and he confirms these figures in his return to the Death Census. Sheehan's return was one of the most detailed commentaries on the crisis from any contributor to the survey, providing vivid descriptions of suffering, disease, and death. Deaths totalling 777 had occurred, he claimed, during the six-month period between October 1846 and March 1847, including 352 counted in the local workhouse.

154. *Freeman's Journal*, 27 January 1841.
155. *Limerick Reporter*, 26 February 1847.
156. *Limerick Reporter*, 26 February 1847.

Return of Revd John Sheehan, P.P. of Ennistymon:

Number of deaths from 1st October 1846 to 1st April, 1847 (including 352 who died in the workhouse)? 777.
Number of same known to be caused by famine? 355.
Number of deaths for same period last year? 50.

[Sheehan accompanied his return with the following letter detailing the prevailing circumstances in his parish.]

Ennistymon, 17th June, 1847.

Dear Sir – I herewith send on the printed form an account of the deaths in those parishes of Ennistymon and Clouny, for the six months ending 1st April, 1847. Between the workhouse and all the deaths are 777. Some of those returned for the workhouse came in from other parishes in the union. I don't know just now how many. That, sir, is a great number of victims already devoured by the famine – many great battles were lost and won, while the dead and wounded did not exceed this amount. The capture of Vera Cruz,[157] and the dismantling its impregnable fortress, did not call for such dismal waste of human life. It is an immense sacrifice of human beings in one little district, to the fatal working – to the destroying abominations of the thrice-blasted Union. Though overworked, attending the sick and dying, I could not believe the mortality was so great until the death census was accurately taken. I can now tell the names, the time, and place where each one died, and I defy the most determined sceptic to find an error in the returns. If there is a mistake at all, it is not in ascertaining the entire number of those who perished.

In this gloomy catalogue some families have been entirely swept away – and in several instances three or four, and up to seven and eight of a family are known to have died of cold, and want of sufficient food, or of the diseases brought on by them – some of the above died in the workhouse of a few days illness. They used to enter the [work] house generally so far gone, and so starved, that no care could bring them about; a little food could never rally such attenuated frames – such feeble constitutions – or repair the effects of their previous destitution. They never thought of entering the workhouse until every other resource abandoned them. Then they brought dysentery and inflammation, and famine-fever with them, and in spite of medical attendance, and all the aids of nursetending, they rapidly sunk and died.

Sometimes, during the hours of my attendance at the workhouse here last winter, I often witnessed scenes melancholy enough – often saw poor creatures brought in on carts like wounded men from the battle field, nearly dead from cold and frightful privations. They merely had symptoms of life – mere remnants of mortality – sad spectacles of humanity – a woeful sign of the times. In this way used they be brought to the workhouse from the road side, or from their wretched cabins, after suffering much misery and several days' fasting, and a course of

157. This Mexican fortress was captured following a siege by American forces in March 1847.

suffering that would kill hundreds. Often I did ask myself on those occasions were we in a Christian country – was this the Ireland of whose fertilising showers, and genial climate, and productive soil, so much was said? Often did I ask was this the dear island so praised and beloved by O'Connell – where the valleys were so fertile, the hills so green, the rivers so meandering and so beautiful, and the landscapes in his eyes, so charming? Was it the dear land he wooed and toiled for, where the staff of life was so abounding, the corn of every kind so prolific, and the yellow harvest so groaning with its golden crops and remunerative tillage? Often did I ask what curse had come upon us, or how did we deserve it?

Many of the above were the tenants or small farmers of those parishes, once apparently comfortable enough, but now the merest paupers, with their little means exhausted, their prospects blighted, several gone the way of all flesh, and their survivors not having the slightest chance of making a rally or recovering their former position. Thus, after one short season did the potato blight knock up the cottier tenants, who, as a class, and they were the principal in those districts on whom all others depended, are now threatened to be absolutely and irrevocably extinguished. In those parishes the landlords did nothing for them – they neither employed them themselves nor made any effort to get them on the public works. They did not stand by those devoted tenants any way, but stood quietly aloof with folded arms, and allowed them to sink away and be victimised. They, the landlords, did not give seed, or any encouragement, to till and sow the ground, or if they did, the instances of such generosity are so unknown, so few and far between, that they hardly deserve counting. The apathy of the landed proprietors is thought to be unaccountable, as by withholding the assistance which may not cost them much, they forfeited the rents which by the smallest aid could be secured to them as usual. The tenants, if assisted, if encouraged and cheered on, would keep on their legs – real though all their difficulties – pay their rents, and make the most determined struggle to keep their position. But they were left to themselves – some of them eat the seed – some were afraid if by any effort they sowed they would not reap, that all would be taken for the rent and taxes, and the consequence is, that many gardens have remained untilled. Some plough lands are entirely left a complete waste, bearing nothing but an abundant crop of weeds and thistles. Those who hitherto kept their ground are now panic stricken – they are giving up in despair, leaving their little holdings and taking away what stock they had, afraid of the levy, and taxes, and poor rate.

Such is the state of the small farmers here. Could the [Repeal] Association devise any plan to save them from fatal ruin? Some of these poor people have made singular efforts to keep their place and put down a little tillage. I know a poor widow who pawned her bedclothes to buy some barley to sow a quarter of ground, the only portion of land she had in the world. Her only son, a little boy, who tilled and dug this garden died last week of hunger. He came to the soup kitchen here for the usual allowance of gruel, or wet meal, but was not fortunate enough in the crowds of applicants to get it. He had, after spending the livelong day waiting for his rations to return home with a heavy heart, an empty piggin as well as an empty stomach, without them – picked up and ate some sorrel, was benighted and found dead in a field through which he was passing in the morning with the earthen vessel near him, containing, instead of gruel, some sorrel which he was eating, when death came to the rescue and put an end to his life and the gnawing of hunger together. Yet the mother of this starved youth has a quarter of ground, her sole farm, under barley; so much for the calumnies of those who asperse the character of the poor, who say that they are idly inclined and willing to make no exertion at all, but depending on outdoor relief and running to those execrable soup depots.

In those parishes there is but small breadth of potatoes planted; but in some localities that happened to be more favoured, and by the most surprising efforts, there is a tolerable share of corn. The crops, with a partial failure of the oats, look well and encouraging, and would go a great way to feed the people, if we are left them. That is another great difficulty just now apprehended. Are those crops to be immediately carried away from our shores, fresh from the sickle, and from the threshing machine, and the flail, and the growers left again to starve or feed on Indian meal, no matter how tainted or rotten. He would have been a benefactor who could tell us how we could keep the produce of our fields for the sustenance of those by whose labour it was grown, on the principle of the Scripture sentence, which says 'thou shalt not muzzle the mouth of the ox that treads the corn'.

There was never such a disposition to emigrate - the better class of farmers have sold, and are every day selling off, and setting out for America, where they hope industry will be more rewarded, and their labour more blessed with the dews of heaven above, and the abundance of the earth beneath – where they expect to be out of the reach of the clearance system, and notice to quit, and landlord exactions. Hundreds of families would have gone away if they had the means. Last year they could sell their little holdings to advantage, but would get nothing for their interest for the tenant-right at present. Those who had no idea of emigration one week are full of it the next – when they see the driver coming for the levy, or the rent, or the poor rate, they get alarmed – they sell off their little stock in a hurry and make a run for the next seaport, flying from their devoted country, from pestilence, and famine – from the bailiff and sheriff together. Some who could scrape together money enough a month ago to emigrate cannot now stir, their little store having been exhausted by the high price of food, and are heard regretting their luckless fate that they did not go away before a month's support made such ravages in their little supplies. Many who last week had the milk of a cow to make the Indian meal, if not a luxury, at least somewhat palatable, are minus that milk this week, the poor cow being in the meantime in *durance vile* [imprisoned], driven to [the] pound, never to return to the owners, for the levy or the poor rate. Such scenes as these I witness every day – they are enough to make one melancholy, and fill him with sadness.

Whatever way the thought of the death census originated, it is worthy of the [Repeal] Association. It could do no greater service to a fallen country than expose those mysteries of horror to the public gaze, and place this awful waste of life, these dreadful records before the world. They will trumpet forth to the earth, in curses of hate and hisses of scorn, the baleful effects of the Union. They will exhibit the monstrous anomaly of "the first flower of the earth and first gem of the sea" [i.e. Ireland], of the poet, a continuous lazaretto [i.e. a quarantine station for disease] – a land of plague and desolation under the withering domination of sway and power. They will exhibit to the wonder of mankind naturally one of the fairest regions of the globe, blighted and blasted, and every field a sepulchre, and two million threatened to be immolated, not in time of war, but profoundest peace, under the destroying sway of the British government. The battle of the Horatii and Curattii in Livy – the retreat of ten thousand in Xenophon – the taking of Constantinople in Gibbon will be read for ever with great interest; but the death census of 1846 and 1847 will form a new and astounding era in Irish history, and will be transmitted through generations yet unborn with increasing execrations of the present period and its policy, until the dead are summoned to rise again, and come to judgement.

Not alone are the poor famine-stricken people dying, but our countrymen of every grade and class are falling like October leaves – the ablest and most charitable of our citizens are mowed down, and consigned to an early tomb by the spreading epidemic – the best of our priests are falling victims to this political economy – to the murderous policy of the government. I have myself lost a dear friend, an able assistant, the Rev. William Hanrahan, as ardent an Irishman, as devoted a patriot, and as good a priest as Ireland could take pride in or boast of in this day of her distress. Like a ministering spirit he was moving eternally through the haunts of pestilence, bringing the comforts of religion to the dying, until he died himself a martyr, the victim of charity, like a Christian hero for the love of Christ, and at his post. He was a Repeal Warden and Volunteer – I have his cards. He had them framed and kept carefully hung up, as mementos of nationhood, in the apartment where he principally spent his time at study, when disengaged from missionary duties. He was devotedly attached to the Liberator, the enthusiastic admirer of his peaceful policy, his incorruptible honesty, his glorious patriotism, and incomparable wisdom. O, those devoted priests, flinging themselves, like Curtius of old, into the dread gulph,[158] to save their country, to cheer up the dying moments of their countrymen – those noble spirits and heroic ecclesiactics who have and are offering themselves up as holocausts to appease the Almighty's wrath – who have

158. Marcus Curtius, who, to appease the Roman gods, sacrificed himself by riding into a chasm, which immediately closed over thus saving the city.

stood between the porch and the altar, making atonement to Heaven for the sins of their nation – can anything be done to perpetuate their deeds and their virtues, to snap their memory from oblivion? Could medals be struck, or a column raised, with their names thereon engraved, in connection with that of the Liberator, who all have died in the same cause, that they all may go down together praised and blest, and remembered to the latest posterity.

I was engaged in making out this census when the news of the Liberator's death came upon us, startling and horrific, somewhat like the sound of the last trumpet on the resting places of the dead. The sad intelligence delayed those returns – there could not but be a pause – the shock, though expected, was terrible – a painful nerve was touched – and the sensations vibrated through the hearts of many. America was independent when the star of Washington [i.e. George Washington] was no more, but 'Sarmatia groaned when Kosciusko fell'.[159] O'Connell is dead and the Union not Repealed – O'Connell dead, and the triple curse of dissension, and famine, and pestilence on Ireland! – O'Connell gone, and his own loved Erin so bewildered, so bothered and so ruined. But the glorious spirit he evoked still lives – the organisation he left behind will work on – the faithful clergy, whose altars he liberated, will never be base enough to change their faith from his teachings and principles. The people whom he schooled so long, and loved so well, will long remember his lessons, and the veneration for his memory, and magic of his name, and influence of his counsels on the present and future generations, will still raise Ireland above what the present famine and misgovernment made her, a nation of beggars starving on gruel, and make her what he lived, and laboured, and died for – a great and prosperous self governed country – I am &c., &c.,

John Sheehan, P.P.

Source: *The Pilot*, 23 June 1847, 3.

Feakle, Killaloe Diocese

Commentary

Feakle Catholic parish covered the eastern part of the civil parish of Feakle; the remainder of the civil parish was covered by the Catholic parish of Caher Feakle. In 1841, 49 per cent of the housing in the *civil* parish of Feakle (not coterminous with the Catholic parish of Feakle) was classified as fourth class and the female illiteracy rate was 74 per cent. It appears that this return covered both Catholic parishes and hence also the civil parish of Feakle. The return for the parish was compiled by Revd Thomas McInerney, parish priest, and Revd Martin Foley, his curate. McInerney was a long-standing O'Connell supporter. During the 1828 Catholic Emancipation election in the county he led a band of Feakle freeholders into Ennis to vote for O'Connell in the historic by-election defeat of William

159. From Thomas Campbell's poem, 'The pleasures of hope', part II.

Vesey-Fitzgerald, and was acknowledged by O'Connell as 'one of the patriotic clergymen who worked hard to secure my return for Clare'.[160] It is noteworthy that in the 1830s McInerney was the recipient, on an order of the Lord Lieutenant, of 'an elegant chalice, price 25 guineas [...] in testimony of his successful interposition, by which the lives of the policemen's wives in that village [Feakle] were saved from an infuriated mob'.[161]

We are sceptical about the accuracy of the mortality figures returned in McInerney's and Foley's return. We estimate the parish's Catholic population at about 10,600 by mid-1845, so 400 deaths in the six-month period between October 1845 and March 1846, amounting to about 700 deaths in a calendar year, suggests a mortality rate of above 65 per 1,000 people per year. A crude mortality rate of that order is well above any reasonable mortality rate in normal economic circumstances, and has to be discounted. McInerney indicated that mortality more than doubled in the famine six-month period between October 1846 and March 1847, which is certainly credible even if the actual numbers cited are of doubtful validity. McInerney died at Lahinch in September, a few months after submitting his return.[162]

Return of Revd Thomas M'Inerney, P.P. and Rev. Martin Foley, C.C. of Feakle:

Number of deaths from 1st October, 1846, to 1st April, 1847? About 1,000.
Number of same known to be occasioned by famine? About 600.
Number of deaths in the same period last year? 400.

Many of those persons have died of fever, dysentery, and dropsy, which diseases are yet very general. No arrangements have been yet made calculated to relieve the distressed state of this parish. The committee now in existence for the last month have done nothing of any use to the people.

About one-half of the land tilled, the prospects of relief for the coming year are alarming. A great many have emigrated, and many more are preparing to do so next month.

Source: *The Pilot*, 7 May 1847, 1.

Kilchrist and Clondagad, Killaloe Diocese

Commentary

The Catholic parish of Kilchrist and Clondagad in south-west County Clare was coterminous with the civil parishes of Kilchreest and Clondagad. The return for the parish was compiled by Revd Timothy Breen, parish priest. Breen had arrived in the parish the previous year, having previously been stationed in Kilrush, as curate.[163]

160. *Newcastle Courant*, 12 July 1828, 2; Morning *Chronicle*, 15 November 1828.
161. *Morning Post*, 6 April 1831.
162. *Battersby's Registry*, 343.
163. *Dublin Weekly Register*, 6 June 1846 (curate in Kilrush); N.L.I. Catholic parish registers, Kilchrist (https://registers.nli.ie/registers/vtls000634679#page/4/mode/1up).

He was a supporter of O'Connell, and Repeal. A Monster Meeting for Repeal held at Ballyket, County Clare, on Sunday, 4 July 1841, attracted a reputed 130,000 and was addressed by Breen in fiery language:

> The Rev. Timothy Breen, C.C., Kilrush, in proposing the next resolution was received with loud applause. He said – Fellow-countrymen, the time has come when Ireland requires that every man should do his duty, and the thousands assembled here, as well as the aggregate millions that have assembled and are preparing to assemble through all Ireland to petition for a Repeal of the Legislative Union, is a sufficient guarantee that every man will do his duty. I know that some hypocritical Philpot of Exeter, some *pious* Roden will turn up their eyes to Heaven, while their hearts are as black as the eyes are. I am aware that such hypocrites will exclaim, and the exclamation will be echoed by every ranting Bible-reading granny in England and Scotland, and even by every paltry Orange Catholic in Ireland, 'Oh, what a profanation is this! Here is a minister of religion, and on the Lord's day, too, helping that great agitator O'Connell, to Repeal the Union and exciting the people to sedition – going to destroy your blessed and holy institutions'. But we know the sacred sanctity of the cause in which we are engaged, and we will persevere. We can see the absurdity of their idle taunts and we despise them. For, if to relieve the oppressed and lessen the oppressor's power – if to love one's country and lessen the number of her enemies – if to shelter the houseless, to clothe the naked and feed the hungry – yea more, to prevent our fellow-countrymen from falling into that sad state of destitution – if such acts be in accordance with the dictates of religion, and the functions of a minister of the Most High, then I will say that it cannot be discreditable to the priest to co-operate with the liberator of his country, nor a desecration of the sabbath day to hold a Repeal meeting on a Sunday (hear, hear).
>
> No country on the face of the earth so urgently requires the zealous aid of her children as the ill-treated land we live in. Her resources neglected, her mines unexplored, her fertile soil uncultivated, her people unemployed, her manufactories ruined, her energies cramped, her commerce unprotected, her harbours without shipping. But no. I mistake. There is sometimes shipping in her harbours. Whoever approached the banks of that majestic and beautiful, but much neglected, river some time ago, may see that her harbours are not always unoccupied. The stout and gallant ship stood forth in bold relief on the bosom of the water – her curling pennants floated gaily in the breeze – the heavy hum of living beings on board – the frequent passing and repassing of the boats, that like sea-wasps returned to and from the shore, giving an opportunity to surrounding friends to say the sad farewell to the dear companions of their childhood – all this bespeaks a vessel bound for a foreign land. But what is her traffick? Is she carrying away the superabundant produce of our well cultivated fields in order to bring us back, in return, those luxuries that may bring cheer to the fireside of a cottager, and render his home happy? No. She is freighted with human beings. She carries away the youth, and vigour, and enterprise of our country – leaving behind but the indolence, and poverty, and old age of the remnant of their families. They depart from an ungrateful land, that refuses sustenance to her children, because the fostering care of a domestic legislature has ceased to watch over her interests. May God be with them; our best blessings attend them; they tear away with them half our hearts, because they go away desolate and friendless – loneless, cheerless, and almost hopeless – from the land of their birth. And yet they go unstained by a crime; and yet the exterminator lives unmolested in the vicinity, perhaps, of their widowed friends; for, alas! the deep

> ocean is now the grave of many of them: friends that brood in silence and in peace over that miserable state of things that enforces exile from one's country without being guilty of any crime against God.
>
> Oh! curse on the minion that calls you disloyal - Thou' fierce to the foe, to your friends you are true.
>
> The Rev. gentleman continued, amidst loud applause, to address the meeting at considerable length.[164]

The pre-Famine statutory censuses show a growing population in the parish, rising from 7,219 in 1831 to 8,062 by the time of the 1841 census.[165] In 1841, 54 per cent of the housing was classified as fourth class and the female illiteracy rate was 72 per cent. The parish was almost exclusively Catholic: the Public Instruction Commissioners identified only 51 Protestants there in 1831.[166] We estimate the parish's Catholic population by mid-1845 at about 8,300. A population of that order would typically experience about 95 to 142 deaths, so the 65 deaths reported for October 1845–March 1846 is on the low side. The ratio between deaths in the pre-Famine period compared to the six-month period during the Famine is nearly 6:1 which is hardly credible.

Although Breen supported the repeal of the Union, which he blamed in his Monster-Meeting address for enforcing emigration, by 1847 he was implicitly viewing emigration as a means of saving the lives of the destitute. Notwithstanding this, a sense of hopelessness pervades his return: gratuitous relief was too 'scanty', employment opportunities were lacking, emigration opportunities were contracting, and land was being left untilled, leaving more and more facing a precarious future.

Return of Revd Timothy Breen, P.P. of Kilchrist and Clondagad:

Number of deaths from the 1st October 1846 to 1st April 1847? 352.
Number of same who died destitute of any kind of food? 20.
Number who have died of insufficiency of food, fever, dysentery, &c. arising from same? 176.
Number of deaths from 1st October 1845 to 1st of April, 1846? 65.

Rev. Mr Hannon attended a poor man, who lay sick in his bed for over two months, living on water merely whitened with a little meal. The scanty support derived to the family from the wages of one female, his substitute in the [Public Works] employment, allowing him no better nourishment. Another poor man, who, induced by our earnest advice in public, left the works for the purpose of tilling his land, on finding after a few days that by the reduction of labourers on the works his name was struck off the lists by the returning officer, and seeing that all his resources were then exhausted, took to his bed in despair, and got

164. *Freeman's Journal*, 8 July 1841.
165. 1833 (634) *Abstract of Population Returns for Ireland, 1831*, BPP, 128, 130; 1843 (504) *Report of the Commissioners appointed to take the census of Ireland, for the year 1841*, BPP, 156, 158.
166. *First report of the Commissioners of public instruction*, 220c, 224c.

out of his mind, so that when Mr. Hannon was called to prepare him [for death], his only replies to him were blasphemies and curses. This poor man still lingers in the same deplorable condition. In fact, instances of a similar nature to these are numerous.

The new relief act for the gratuitous distribution of food [Soup Kitchen Act] is brought into operation in these parishes for the last three weeks; but the support is so scanty, and the unwillingness of the committee to extend its operation to many through fear of increasing taxation is so great – the strict vigilance of the finance committee is so scrutinising – that very many are only trying to protract a miserable existence on one meal a day. Add to this the delays accompanying the compliance with prescribed forms, especially when there are no funds of any kind arising from either subscriptions or donations.

With the exception of two small proprietors, who employ, perhaps, an aggregate of about sixty persons, all the others are absentees! And of these some are embarrassed, other minors, so that subscriptions were in vain sought for; and as the great mass of the people are all of the one class, there is not the least chance of casual employment among the farmers. Judge, then, of the grievance of collecting the whole of these famished wretches every day round the food depot for the purpose of receiving each his miserable pound of meal. Many have entreated to be left at home in order that by remaining in bed they may be enabled the better to endure the hunger.

One instance will suffice to show the wretched poverty of the people. The houses of worship of both parishes are two wretched thatched hovels, which were almost entirely stripped by the storms of last December and January. A subscription was attempted to be raised in both parishes for the purpose of repairing the ravages of the storm, and although the poor people are naturally religious, yet after every possible exertion the sum total received for the purpose up to the present moment is only 3*l.* 4*s.* This sum only partially repaired one chapel, the other still remains a wreck. The poverty of the people, on whom the priest depends for his support, has left him unable to ward off the rains of heaven from his poor flock, while they prostrate themselves in prayer during the celebration of the most tremendous mysteries.

In compliance with our earnest exhortations and advice, the poor people tilled almost all the land fitted for wheat, before the 1st of January, and as four fifths and more of the soil of the parish is not suited to the production of wheat they were vigorously proceeding with the culture of oats, barley &c., up to the beginning of April, when the vast numbers thrown out of employment by the reduction of the labourers on the [Public] works entirely paralyzed their energies by throwing them on their own resources. Many were afterwards obliged to consume the seed they had reserved, so that now taking the mountain districts of the parishes, more than a third of the available soil will remain untilled, or in other words, about a fourth of the soil of the entire parishes. Stafford O'Brien, Esq. and

Mr. Stackpoole, of Cragbrein, have taken care that not a perch of land on their properties shall remain untilled. Other proprietors have offered seed, but on such security that their offer is generally unavailing. Colonel Windham's property in his own immediate possession is unhappily very limited here – it is confined to Deer Island [Inishmore], but no part of Deer Island is suffered to remain a waste.

The last named gentleman has fitted out a ship in the Shannon, and is prepared to enable any of his tenantry to emigrate entirely at his own expense. Two numerous families of Deer Island are availing themselves of his bounty. All the other tenants are too comfortable to require voluntary exile. Through the rest of the parishes at least a fourth of the small cottiers would be anxious to emigrate, but they have not the means. Only those who have some interest in their farms and a share of stock can muster the necessary supplies by the sale of all their effects.

And even that interest is daily diminishing in value, from the number of small holdings offered for sale, and the decreasing anxiety for the purchase of land. In fact, numbers are now entreating their landlords to take their lands off their hands, in order that they may be entitled to rations which are withheld because they possess some land, with no other resources. Something about thirty families are either gone, or are preparing to go, from these parishes; but 'tis melancholy to have to add, that these generally are the most industrious and most healthy, often the most comfortable, and the best conducted among their neighbours! What will become of the mass of destitution and infirmity they leave behind?

Source: *The Pilot*, 28 April 1847, 4.

Kildysart, Killaloe Diocese

Commentary

The Catholic parish of Kildysart is located on the Shannon estuary, in the barony of Clonderlaw in south County Clare. It is coextensive with the civil parish of Killadysert. The return for the parish was compiled by the curate, Revd Patrick Horan, recently arrived in the parish.[167] The population of Kildysart parish was growing rapidly during the 1830s, rising from the 4,501 recorded in the 1831 census to 5,130 enumerated in 1841.[168] In 1841, 48 per cent of the housing was classified as fourth class and the female illiteracy rate was 70 per cent. The Protestant population of Kildysart was tiny; the Public Instruction Commissioners identified only 30 Protestants in the 1831 census listing.[169] The parish did not maintain a burial register, so Horan's figures for deaths are mere approximations. We estimate the Catholic population in mid-1847 at about 4,600,

167. *The Pilot*, 8 April 1846; *Tipperary Vindicator*, 24 October 1846.
168. *Abstract of Population Returns for Ireland, 1831*, BPP (1833), 634, 128; *Report of the Commissioners appointed to take the census of Ireland, for the year 1841*, BPP (1843), 504, 156.
169. *First report of the Commissioners of public instruction*, 45, 224c.

which would typically see between about 52 to 78 deaths occurring during a normal six-month period (October to March). Thus, the 150 deaths that Horan reported for the October 1846–March 1847 period was well above the expected upper bound for normal mortality.

A factor complicating any consideration of mortality rates from Horan's report, however, is that there is some doubt over the area covered by his return. Kildysart parish and neighbouring Kilfiddane parish were united before 1868,[170] and if Horan's mortality figures cover the two parishes of Kilfiddane and Kildysart instead of Kildysart alone then expected deaths in a normal six-month period would be doubled, and Horan's 150 deaths for the October 1846–March 1847 period would not appear particularly out of line.

Return of Revd Patrick Horan, curate of Kildysart:

After the receipt of your letter I made every inquiry to ascertain the exact number of deaths occasioned by famine during the time specified, and from the information so acquired, together with my own knowledge of facts I can say, not however with certainty, for we do not register the deaths, that about 150 died during that period (1st October, 1846, to 1st March, 1847), and about eighty from want or the common necessaries of life.

To mention particular cases that came under my own observations would, indeed, be too tedious – 'Ex uno disce omnes' [*From one, learn all people*]. I was called myself to prepare one of these victims, and he had nothing to allay his thirst, or probably to support life, but a drink of warm water; he was an able-bodied man, who was fasting. They told me three days before he got employment on the public works, but died immediately after from the effects of hunger. Indeed, it may be said of all the labourers who died on the public works – and they are many – that they died from hunger! About a fortnight ago a child died in this parish from hunger, there being eleven in family, and only the hire of one [i.e. one Public Works wage] to support them. About a fortnight ago, alas, there died a man here who was on the works the day before – the cause is evident. But why mention particular cases? Famine is the cause of almost all the deaths.

I am told by one of the overseers of the Board of Works, that the poor creatures under his superintendence, during the works, used to retire to a ditch at twelve o'clock to take their one scanty meal per day, and that a morsel of dry bread. And furthermore, he says their pale, emaciated, faces would frighten you.

Shame on the English government or on any government – for they could have prevented it in a great measure – to tolerate such a state of things even amidst her serfs, but especially in a country which has been her defence and safeguard – nay her right arm in time of danger.

170. https://registers.nli.ie/registers/vtls000634722#page/220/mode/1up.

If they wish, then, to preserve thousands of our fellow countrymen from starvation, they will give at least 2lb of meal per day to every one who has not the means of subsistence, or commence the works such as they were before.

Should they not do one or the other, the consequence will be frightful.

Pardon me now, dear Mr Ray, if I have trespassed too far on your valuable time, but compassion for the daily dying famine stricken poor would not allow me to say less. Seeing, then, the frightful state of things in Ireland, will any one be found so cold-hearted, so anti-Irish, as not to cry out for Repeal?[171]

With many thanks for your invaluable services in the cause of Old Ireland, in unison with our illustrious Liberator, whose life may God preserve until he sees his country happy and free, and a parliament in College Green.

I remain yours sincerely,

Pat Horan, C.C.

Source: *The Pilot*, 19 May 1847, 2.

Kilfenora, Kilfenora Diocese

Commentary

The Catholic parish of Kilfenora was coterminous with the two civil parishes of Kilfenora and Kiltoraght, in Corcomroe barony, in west County Clare. The return for the parish was signed by Revd Andrew Quinn, parish priest of Kilfenora since 1834.[172] Quinn was a supporter of O'Connell. He had rallied to O'Connell's side during the Catholic Emancipation election in 1828, and had collected for the O'Connell Compensation Fund in the 1830s, although his name was one of hundreds to be published in the press in October 1837 for being remiss in failing to contribute to the Tribute during 1836 and 1837.[173]

He was a supporter of Repeal too, joining the Association in June 1841, alongside his curate, and he was active in advertising the aims of Repeal amongst his parishioners. A letter of his was read to an Association meeting that month, which reported positively on the growth of the movement in his parish, which news received the hearty approval of O'Connell, and the meeting.

Kilfenora, County Clare.

In compliance with your suggestions I submitted the views of the Repeal Association to one of my parishes on this day. I by no means anticipated the enthusiasm manifested on the occasion. No other question but Repeal alone could produce such feeling. The organization of this parish commenced to-day; the difficulty is not to get [Repeal] wardens, but to make a selection from amongst the number who are most anxious and determined to undertake the duties of that office. I do not expect there will be a man found

171. Mr Ray was the secretary of the Repeal Association.
172. *First report of the Commissioners of public instruction*, appendix, 60.
173. *Dublin Weekly Register*, 21 October 1837, 5; 28 October 1837, 5.

in these parishes, after one month, who will not be a stanch Repealer. Clare will maintain its character – Clare will and must have its proud position in the repeal of the accursed Union as well as in the emancipation of Ireland. The wardens I recommend, today, are – Messrs Thomas Callaghan, jun., Kilfenora; William Curtin, Kilfenora; Morty Kerin, Lisdooney; John O'Brien, Ballagh. Any commands for them, directed to Kilfenora, shall be punctually attended to. On next Sunday, please God, my second parish will be equally organized. The names and subscriptions shall be forwarded regularly from this week; and no energy of head or heart shall be for an hour relaxed until we are once more ranked amongst the nations of Europe.

I regret that that excellent patriot, Mr. Reynolds, did not make a longer stay amongst us. May I request to be admitted a member of the Association, with my assistant, the Rev. Mr. Skelly? The Liberator himself would, I am satisfied, have no objection to propose me, an old Clare agitator of '28, as a Repeal member.

Andrew Quinn, P.P.

Mr. O'Connell – I have the greatest pleasure and gratification in proposing my old and esteemed friend the Rev. Mr. Quinn, as a member of the Association. He is one of the truest patriots I ever knew; he was one of the patriots of '28, and is now one of the patriots of '41. I move that that letter be inserted on the minutes, and that the thanks of the Association be given to the old and respected patriot of '28 (cheers).

The resolutions were seconded and passed unanimously.[174]

The population of the Catholic parish of Kilfenora was of 3,897 in 1831 and 4,360 by 1841.[175] In 1841, 54 per cent of the housing was classified as fourth class and the female illiteracy rate was 75 per cent. The inhabitants were overwhelmingly Catholic; the Public Instruction Commissioners found only 46 Protestants in the parish in 1831.[176] Quinn's figures for deaths seem likely to be only a partial count. The parish's Catholic population was about 4,500 in 1845, which would imply between 51 and 77 deaths in a normal October – March period. Quinn's figures for the October 1845–March 1846 period (between 8 and 10) do not come close to that range, and even his figure for the Famine six-month period barely scrapes into the lower end of the anticipated range. At the conclusion of Black '47 Quinn published the following brief account of life in Kilfenora:

Mr. Andrew Quinn, writing from Kilfenora on the unparalleled sufferings of the poor concludes a pathetic appeal in the followings words – "Scarcely half a dozen families in those parishes will have sufficient food until harvest. No employment whatever, though there are thousands of acres waste, and thousands of human beings perishing, who, had there been a little energy amongst the landlords, would thereby support themselves, and enrich the owners of those dreary and cheerless wastes. Instead of being thus employed, the poor people are perishing in the ditches. Scarcely an hour has elapsed, since I visited a whole family, seven in number, all in fever, a few sticks and scraws laid over a turf bank,

174. *Dublin Morning Register*, 16 June 1841.

175. *Abstract of Population Returns for Ireland, 1831*, BPP (1833), 634, 130; *Report of the Commissioners appointed to take the census of Ireland, for the year 1841*, BPP (1843), 504, 158.

176. *First report of the Commissioners of public instruction*, 45, 242.

> their only shelter against the torrents of rain, the sleet and storms that prevailed for the last few weeks with unusual violence. Out of the entire number not one was able to reach a drop of water to cool the parched lips of a dying mother. This is no solitary case, no unusual circumstance; and so terrified are the people, that it is not without difficulty, on many occasions, the priests can prevail upon a guide to accompany him to the door of the doomed and infected cabin.[177]

In spite of the suffering, Quinn would not be diverted from the cause of Repeal, supporting the unification of the Repeal strands in June 1848, without which there was 'no hope for our country'. In light of his desperate letter of December 1847 (above) he, surprisingly perhaps, maintains that Repeal remained a topic of interest amongst his parishioners. He stated:

> I have long since made up mind, in common with every Repealer, *i.e.*, every man in my parish, that there is no hope for our country save and except in a speedy and thorough amalgamation of the two classes of Repealers whose wretched dissensions have crushed the hearts and hopes of all of us. I fondly hope that nothing will divert the Association from this most desirable union. I am, and was, an humble follower of our beloved Liberator; so are all my parishioners. And in the name of all my parishioners, I give most willing adhesion to the terms of the re-union, and most fervently pray that nothing may interrupt this contemplated and most desirable object.[178]

Return of Revd Andrew Quinn, P.P. of Kilfenora:

Number of deaths from 1st October 1846 to 1st April 1847? 59.
Number of same known to be caused by famine? 40.
Number of deaths during the same period last year? 8 or 10.

Nine out of every ten living on insufficiency of food, a great majority of that number walking skeletons, barely existing, and falling victims to the slightest attack of sickness. The outdoor relief just commencing, but looked upon by every class as totally unsuited to this rural district, and the quantity of food prescribed by law altogether incapable to support life. There is about a third of the soil left untilled for want of seed and will remain so. The landlords of this parish gave no seed that I am aware of. Few have emigrated; there would not be fifty families in those two parishes [Kilfenora and Kiltoraght] in a month's time, had they means to emigrate; about forty have gone and many more are preparing if they can, our prospects for the coming year gloomy in the extreme from the scanty amount of land tilled and under corn; no potatoes sown here.

Source: *The Pilot*, 7 May 1847, 1.

177. *The Pilot*, 22 December 1847.
178. *Dublin Weekly Nation*, 24 June 1848.

County Cork

Ballinhassig, Cork Diocese

Commentary

The Catholic parish of Ballinhassig, in the diocese of Cork, is located to the south-west of Cork city. In 1841, 44 per cent of the housing in the *civil* parish of Ballinaboy (not coterminous with the Catholic parish of Ballinhassig) was classified as fourth class and the female illiteracy rate was 78 per cent. The parish priest at the time was Revd John Halanan, and it was he who submitted the mortality report. Halanan had been parish priest for more than two decades by that time, and he was well known and well regarded within his community. The earliest surviving Catholic parish register for Ballinhassig commences in 1821, and its opening page contains the following brief biography of Halanan.

Rev John Halanan was born on the 13 December [?] in the parish of Ballymoodan, Bandon. Entered College on 20 September 1815 (Doctor Murphy [ordained?] Bishop of Cork the May previous.) Was ordained [subdeacon?] at Carey's Lane Chapel on 17 September 1820, Doctor Murphy and Doctor England having been [considered?] for an American Mission the day following; the other orders, Deaconship and Priesthood, were conferred by him, Doctor England, the two successive days [after?] his consecration. Revd Mr Halanan got his first mission to Enniskean on 20 October following, from whence he was translated to be administrator of Ballinhassig parishes on 20 March [1821] (Revd Dennis O'Sullivan, P.P. being incapacitated by illness). In the May following Mr Halanan commenced his North Chapel, commonly called the Mountain one, and had it finish'd against the ensuing Christmas. He undertook the Ballyheady chapel in the summer of 1823 and had it finished that year. Halanan wrote:

> Distress was very great in those years, so much so that the people of England had sent money and food to relieve the wants of thousands who were perishing in this country. Revd Mr O'Sullivan, P.P. died on the 25th of April 1824 and Revd John Halanan was appointed his successor the day of his funeral, which was on the 27th in the Ballyheady Chapel, where he, Mr O'Sullivan, is buried - *Requiescat in pace.*
>
> Jeremiah Halanan Senr died in January 1820, and Mary Butler, wife, of the above Jeremiah died (my parents) in January 1823. May God have mercy on their souls.[179]

Halanan was an active member of the local Famine relief committees, a supporter of O'Connell's Repeal drive,[180] and a zealous campaigner for his suffering parishioners during the Famine. A letter published in the *Cork Examiner*, 25 June 1847 somewhat surprisingly, held out positive hope for the upcoming harvest, while cautioning that disease was rampant in the area:

179. https://registers.nli.ie/registers/vtls000631893#page/6/mode/1up.

180. *Cork Examiner*, 23 June 1847; *Freeman's Journal*, 3 January 1844.

Sir, I have much pleasure in stating that potatoes and corn are promising to be most abundant. The former for the quantity planted, *not inconsiderable,* is by many degrees superior to what we have had, at this season any year for the last ten. Amongst them there is not the least appearance of disease.

In this opinion I am confirmed by the testimony of members of Relief Committees and farmers from Kinsale to Ballincollig.

I am sorry I cannot say that disease does not exist amongst the human beings. Fever is almost in every house in the villages of Ballinhassig and the half way to Bandon. Every cabin in the Mountain part of Inniskinny Electoral District is infected – and not one particle of food or medicine is given to relieve those destitute people by the Relief Committee. I attended this committee meeting today, and although their wants were admitted by every member, nothing was done save to request the Commissioners of relief to send us some Medical Inspectors. I suggested to have the houses and habitations of the poor washed with lime and otherwise purified; but this was considered by one of our leading members a matter very difficult to be done. So then the poor sick people are now, all hands idle from public works, to live or die without medical aid. It has been stated also that as sufficient accommodation is in the Union Workhouse for all old and helpless people, there, and there alone, are they to be supported, that any rations given them at the long-withheld food depots would render the accounts and expenditure of such depot incapable of being passed by the Cork Finance Committee.

I am satisfied that such is not the law and I am sure the gentlemen acting on that Finance Committee, whose names our former chairman mentioned, are incapable of doing the poor such injustice.

I am, Mr. Editor, yours truly,
John Halanan, P.P. Ballinhassig.

However, in October, he was begging 'a gentleman in Dublin' for aid, which letter again found its way into the national press, prompting some support.

Extract [of] letter from Rev. John Halahan [Halanan], P.P., Baslinhassig, County Cork, dated 9 October, 1847, to a gentleman in Dublin, requesting him to procure some assistance from the General Central Relief Committee for Ireland:

Could I again presume to solicit assistance for my afflicted people? I assure you, on the word of a priest of the living God, they are in dire want of it. Numbers have not food; sickness is still amongst them; the cold, oh, the cold winter is setting in on them, without day or night covering for their emaciated bodies. For charity sake, implore, I pray you, some timely aid for me even to alleviate those sufferings. I could do a great deal with thirty or forty pounds. I would buy some coarse cloths, and gather the daughters of farmers in the school houses, and fit up those for the naked, cold, and suffering poor. Oh, my dear Sir, imagine the prayers of those creatures ascending to Heaven in behalf of the benefactors; those cloths, with a few tons of meal, would cheer us on to meet the inevitable enemy, death, unless speedy assistance be given.[181]

Halanan's report is one of the few to provide, not only mortality statistics, but also the names and addresses of the dead in his parish. Children less than seven years

181. *Freeman's Journal*, 15 October 1847.

of age were buried without Halanan's prayers, so he was unable to account for them. It may be an indication of his deep involvement with his community and his commitment to his parishioners that he left the mortality roll for the October 1846–March 1847 period for public memory. Halanan's death was announced in February 1849:

> We have much regret in announcing the death of the respected and hospitable Parish Priest of Ballinhassig, the Rev. John [Halahan]. The Rev. gentleman died at his residence, at 6 o'clock on Friday evening, after a very short illness. He was much loved by his parishioners over whose spiritual welfare he watched for many years; and but few of his class exerted themselves more strenuously to sustain the poor of their flocks during the late famine period than did he. His remains were to have been removed, on this morning to the "mountain" or "northern" chapel, in the parish of Ballinhassig, where, after the conclusion of the "office for the dead," and the recital of the funeral service they will be interred.[182]

Return of Revd John Halanan, P.P. of Ballinhassig:

Number of deaths from 1st October, 1846, to 1st April, 1847? 62, the whole of them occasioned by famine, namely: - Joseph Woods, Ballinhassig; Patrick Murphy, Curran; Thomas Jordan's wife, do.; Timothy Kehely, Cullaheder; Daniel Magrath, do.; Jeremiah Leary, Corrin; Benjamin Walters, do.; John Gillis, ditto; Patrick Ford, do.; Jeremiah Long, do; his wife, do.; a woman from Innishannon; John Sweeney, Gurtnalough; Margaret Farrell, Ballyhulin; Timothy Carthy, ditto; John Goldspring, do; his son, do; his daughter, do; Catherine Wise, do; Widow Murphy, do; Widow Breen, ditto; John Gliseane, Gogginshill; Widow Hislehy, do; J. Croly, do; Ellen Allen, do; Michael Sullivan, do; John Mahony's wife, do; Daniel Sherin, Reasore; Matthew White, do; Michael Donohoe, Barrett's Hill; a stranger at Ballinhassig; M. Barry's wife, Old Abbey; Ellen Murphy, do; John Sullivan, Lisgilea [Liskilea]; his sister and her child, do; John Goolden, do; Patrick Sheehan, Old-abbey; Ellen Murphy, do; Mary Whelton, Lisgilea; Owen Sullivan, Ballinabearney; a woman at Ballyheady roadside; Jeremy Murnane, Ballyheady; Florence Whelton, ditto; Patrick Ahern, do; Jeremiah Carthy's sister, Rygsdeale; Mary Bryan, Ballinpardsley; Patrick Cross, Killommogue; Timothy Reardon, do upper; Owen Carthy, do; Patrick Reardon, Rysdeal; Timothy Woods, Gogginshill; Widow Murphy, Old Abbey; Daniel Murphy, Gurtnalock; James Deleigh, Ballinagumleigh; Widow Murphy, Cooleskin; Dennis Denehy, Conlatudor; John Waters, Corran; John Collins, Shehanagh; Widow Murray, Corrin, and many young children up to seven years old died, the account of whom I did not receive, as they were so young and not requiring my personal attendance.

Source: *The Pilot*, 7 May 1847, 1.

182. *Cork Examiner*, 26 February 1849.

Castletownroche, United Dioceses of Cloyne and Ross Diocese

Commentary

Castletownroche is located in north-east County Cork, in the barony of Fermoy. In 1841, 41 per cent of the housing was classified as fourth class and the female illiteracy rate was 72 per cent. The return for the parish was compiled by Revd James Fitzpatrick. Fitzpatrick had been stationed in the parish since at least the early 1830s, and was very active within his parish community.[183] In 1833 he can be seen collecting the O'Connell National Annuity in Castletownroche, and in the same year he received public praise from O'Connell for radically organising local arbitration committees to resolve local disputes.[184]

> In Castletownroach the enemies of the country have not succeeded in exciting illegal outrages. The spirit of the Volunteers [i.e. the Society of Irish Volunteers for Repeal of the Union] prevails at Castletownroche. The people there were not satisfied with the conduct of their magistrates, and they determined to do without them. The parish priest, my friend, the Rev. Mr. Fitzpatrick, has formed there a tribunal of arbitrators, who decide upon the quarrels of the people. One day of the week is allocated to the decision of their disputes. There have been summonses to come before that tribunal printed by one the shopkeepers, and the tribunal has been found effective in settling amicably all disputes. They get together a body of Volunteers on a jury panel; I have them here, and shall now read them for you. [Mr. O'Connell here read the resolutions adopted by this body, forming themselves into Irish Volunteers. The resolutions were received with cheers.] Mr. O'C. continued by saying, I have here a list of 100 of them, who have formed themselves into an arbitration jury, six of which sit each Saturday by rotation, in order that too much time may not be given by each individual to his duty. Mr. Fitzpatrick sits constantly, and sometimes two hundred cases are on his paper, [hear, and laughter]. There is not a single instance in which people have been fined by this tribunal that they have not paid the money, and discharged it too, much more quickly than if ordered to do so by a magistrate. See what an admirable and practicable thing this would be for the Volunteers to spread throughout the country. By this means they get rid of all favouritism in their decisions, for every man knows when he is decided against, that the decision is dictated by honesty, fairness and justice. Every difficult point that occurs Mr Fitzpatrick calls on the six arbitrators to aid him. The consequence ofholding this tribunal is, that the magistrates are perfectly idle in that part of the country – not a single summons was issued by them, and instead of holding their sessions at Castletownroche, they are going to Killwellan [the church with the mill near it,] to look for grist to their mill [hear and laughter) They are exceedingly mortified that they have no cases coming before them, and I am told that they have complained of this to the Conservatives. I entreat that the example may be followed in the other parts of the country, and that the Conservatives may have more occasion to grieve upon this account. By such a tribunal all these cases are decided for the people – justice is done to them, and magistrates are rendered as unnecessary, as they have been found useless, to say the best of them (loud cries of hear, hear). Two factions who

183. Fitzpatrick was, as parish priest, baptising children in the parish from at least as early as March 1832 (https://registers.nli.ie/registers/vtls000632864#page/141/mode/1up).

184. *Dublin Weekly Register*, 5 January 1833, 7.

> disturbed that part of the country quarrelled with each other, and were summoned before this tribunal; the principal delinquents were fined, and the sentence passed upon the others was, that they should meet at their chapels, and in the presence of their clergymen, promise that they would never quarrel more. They did so, and they have kept their words for many months. This is the way to work for Ireland (hear). The Irish people are lovers of justice. Sir John Davies said of them, "there was no people loved justice more, even when exercised against themselves, than the Irish nation". Here are in Castletownroche 100 Volunteers dispensing to the people that which they only seek for – justice (hear).[185]

Revd Fitzpatrick estimated the parish's population at about 9,000. He provided a rough estimate of the deaths occurring in the period between October 1846 and March 1847, but notes that this covered only part of the parish. His curate was responsible for the remainder of the parish, but was too overwhelmed with work to respond to the Death Census. Fitzpatrick provided a list of names of those succumbing but these were not published.

Return of Revd James Fitzpatrick, P.P. of Castletownroche:

Number of deaths in this parish from 1 October 1846 to 1 April 1847? 116.
Number of same known to be caused by famine? 99.

I could not ascertain accurately the number of deaths the preceding year. At all events there was not one from starvation.

The Catholic union of this parish includes four electoral divisions, having the same number of relief committees, which I have to attend in addition to my other duties. Rations of meal are given out every day, but these are not sufficient to support life [for] long. There is no allowance made for cooking. The people would rather work; they say they have pains in their bones from being idle. All the [Public] works here, with a single exception, were discontinued, leaving the poor people in a very miserable state. We read of certain ascetics [hermits] who kept three Lents in the year, but Lord John [Russell] has outdone all orders of the monastic institute as he will compel the poor Irish to make the whole year round one Lent!! It would be well if the poor people had the merit of fasting, but it is to be feared they have not, for they are too frequently tempted to curse their rulers, and the authors of their miseries. I have given only the census of one electoral division and part of another, viz, Castletownroche and part of Kilcummer and Bridgetown, north of the river Blackwater. My curate has so much to do in attending sick calls, stations, and the select committee of Ballyhooly, that he cannot spare time to make out the mortality census. The population of my parish is about 9,000, and more than half of these are on the relief list! We had 900 on the public works. [It is then noted that the return included a list of names and residences of the persons having died of famine, but these were not published in the newspapers].

Source: *The Pilot*, 19 May 1847, 2.

185. *Southern Reporter and Cork Commercial Courier*, 24 January 1833.

Kilmeen, Cloyne and Ross Diocese

Commentary

The return for Kilmeen parish, in west County Cork, near Skibbereen, was compiled by Revd Patrick Hartnett. Hartnett had been curate in nearby Skibbereen parish,[186] but by 1843 had moved to Kilmeen as parish priest, where he was active, alongside other priests in the diocese, in drumming up support for a petition to parliament in favour of Repeal.[187] A Repeal Movement meeting in west Cork on 22 June 1843 – reported as a 'magnificent demonstration in the Carberies – congregation of five hundred thousand persons' was attended by 'the men of Kilmeen' headed by the Rev. P. Hartnett, P.P., and the Ref. John M'Carthy, C.C.[188] The 1841 census enumerated the population of the entire county, excluding the city, at 773,000.[189] Hartnett, a Repealer, organised the collection of the Repeal Rent in his parish, and was involved in the planning of public relief works in the area during 1846.[190]

Hartnett's parish of Kilmeen was coextensive with the civil parishes of Castleventry and Kilmean.[191] In 1841, 52 per cent of the housing was classified as fourth class and the female illiteracy rate was 80 per cent. The 1841 census enumerated 4,570 people in the two parishes, close enough to Hartnett's population estimate of *c.* 4,000 in May 1847, given the inevitable dislocation of populations caused by the crisis. If Hartnett's population estimate is reasonably accurate then his estimate of the number of deaths in the period October 1845–March 1846, amounting to about 70 in a full year, implies a mortality rate of about 18 per 1,000 people, slightly below the lower-bound expected figure (20 per 1,000 – although the 1846 population of the parish was likely closer to 5,000). The 156 deaths that he observed for the October 1846–March 1847 period – about 300 deaths in a full calendar year – points to a mortality rate of about 75 per 1,000.

Return of Revd P. Hartnett, P.P. of Kilmeen:

Population of the parish about 4,000 and the deaths from the 1st October 1846 to 1st April 1847 is on an average six per week. Total 156.
Number of same known to be caused by famine? (fully two thirds of the above), 104.
Number of deaths during the same period last year? About one to two per week, 40

The present state of the parish is beyond all description – *viz.* starvation, fever, dysentery, swelling, and all such direful diseases in every house. The very appearance of the people is altogether altered. The arrangements on foot quite inadequate to stay the famine – not one fourth of the land as compared with former

186. *The Pilot*, 30 December 1836; *Catholic directory and annual register for 1838*, 136.
187. *Southern Reporter and Cork Commercial Courier*, 10 June 1843.
188. *Cork Examiner*, 23 June 1843.
189. *Report of the Commissioners appointed to take the census of Ireland, for the year 1841*, BPP (1843), 504, 190.
190. *Cork Examiner*, 10 January 1844; *Cork Examiner*, 25 September 1846.
191. *Thom's Irish Almanac, 1850*, 340.

years cultivated – the prospects for the ensuing year cheerless in the extreme – emigration on the most extensive system – all, or greater part of those having means flying off from the scenes of horror – farmers in the worst possible spirits – the landlords more extracting than ever – the driver each day travelling through the parish.

Source: *The Pilot*, 12 May 1847, 4.

County Kerry

Ardfert and Kilmoyley, Kerry Diocese

Commentary

The Catholic union of Ardfert and Kilmoyley was located on Tralee Bay, north of Tralee town. It was coextensive with the two civil parishes of Ardfert and Kilmoyley. The return for the parish was compiled by Revd Jeremiah O'Sullivan, parish priest of the parish since at least 1822, when his house was 'entered from the window [...] and plundered of two watches'.[192] O'Sullivan was an agitator for the rights of Catholics, and was alive to the dangers of creeping Protestantism.

> The following document accompanied by a sharp letter from the pen of the Rev. Mr. M'Crea, has appeared in the Kerry Papers:
>
> Persecution against Thomas D'Stack, Teacher of the Ardfert School, and the Parents of the Roman Catholic children who attended said School, commencing July 1, 1826, by the Rev. Jeremiah O'Sullivan, P. P. of Ardfert and his Coadjutor, the Rev. Michael Walsh. The said Mr. J. O'Sullivan, from the altar repeatedly expressed at Mass on several Sundays, that the said teacher was an arch heretic, a man of contaminated principles and character, a public notoriety, that he was surprised why the neighbours should allow him among them, or associate with him. That the parents who sent their children to that school were cursed heretics, the scum of, and the most degraded people in the parish, that they were excluded from all the rules of the Catholic Church, nor had they any benefit from hearing Mass, naming and calling every one of their names in particular from the altar.
>
> The Rev. Mr. Walsh, in his turn was rather more sanguine in his attack, saying the Devil had the Teacher and the Parents of the children bound in hellish chains, and particularly those who went to hear to the preaching of the Rev. J. B. M'Crea, that they were under an excommunication, and that Mr. M'Crea was a dangerous *incendiary*. That Mr. Walsh on Sunday last, spoke beyond all bounds of the School, and of the Teacher, said, that he conveyed some of his scholars into Ardfert Church. That he was a heretical Devil on the week days, and wished to be a Catholic on Sunday, and imperatively required of the flock to turn the Devil out of the Chapel. Although the said teacher never spoke against any of the Priests, but attended his business in a regular, humble and attentive manner, (as was his duty). That the two Priests are unanimous in speaking after this unchristian, tyrannical manner, of the school and teacher, and of the said Rev. M'Crea. The said

192. *Belfast Commercial Chronicle*, 4 March 1822.

> Thomas D'Stack, humbly defers his persecution to the wisdom of the Hibernian Society, and their Agents, as he dreads that he and family may be personally materially injured by either of these Priests or their satylites [.e. satellites].
>
> Walsh on last Sunday exhorted the people in like manner not to associate with the said teacher, Thomas D'Stack, nor with the parents of his pupils, nor with the pupils, that they were excommunicated by the Church.[193]

Needless to say, his fiery language against Protestant missionary activity in the town did not always win friends, as John Dineen showed:

> To the Rev. Jeremiah O'Sullivan, P.P. Artfert.
> Rev. Sir, I beg to inform you that, on account of your threatening and opprobrious language from the altar against me for sending my children to the Ardfert school, I am no longer a member of the Church of Rome, as I am sure that a Church such as yours, that requires to be supported by unchristian and uncharitable language, cannot be right. Therefore, should you further continue to make use of my name, I shall be under the necessity of taking such proceedings against you as the law directs. It is astonishing that you, professing to be a member of the true Church, who was foremost in establishing a school at Barrow, similar to the one you now oppose, should be so inconsistent, as you sent your nieces and nephews to the said school at Barrow, and directed others also to go there, whereas now you make use of the most opprobrious language against those who send their children to the Ardfert, school. For my part, I thought that God was the same yesterday, to-day, and for ever.
> I am, &c. &c.
> John Dinneen.[194]

O'Sullivan was aligned with O'Connell for two decades. He contributed financially to the Catholic Rent in the 1820s,[195] and the various O'Connell tributes, collections and events in the 1830s and 1840s.[196] An Ardfert Repeal meeting in June 1843 was attended by 'twenty thousand', after which in the evening 'the Rev. Jeremiah O'Sullivan, P.P., with his proverbial hospitality, entertained to a splendid dinner the gentlemen who attended at the meeting'.[197] 'After dinner the Ardfert Temperance band played many national airs in the pleasure grounds attached to the Rev. Mr O'Sullivan's hospitable mansion'.[198] In June 1844 O'Sullivan chaired the Ardfert meeting calling for O'Connell's release from prison.[199]

The pre-Famine national censuses reported a population advancing very rapidly in the Ardfert region during the 1830s; increasing from 7,110 inhabitants in 1831 to 9,793 in 1841 (3.3 per cent per year). We are wary of population increases of this order.

193. *Cork Constitution*, 14 October 1826, 4.
194. *Limerick Chronicle*, 26 September 1835, 3, col a. See, also, *Kerry Evening Post*, 7 October 1835, 3, col a.
195. *Dublin Weekly Register*, 2 August 1828, 8.
196. *Freeman's Journal*, 27 March 1838.
197. *Cork Examiner*, 21 June 1843.
198. *Tralee Chronicle*, 24 June 1843, 2.
199. *Kerry Examiner and Munster General Observer*, 28 June 1844.3.

The 1821 census had recorded only 4,178 people in the two parishes, in 766 houses, but an earlier survey, conducted by the parish priest about 1805, had reported 960 Catholic families there.[200] It is possible that resistance to state census surveys was distorting the population counts, particularly in the 1821 and 1831 surveys. What is certain is that the union was overwhelmingly Catholic; the Public Instruction Commissioners could only identify 120 Protestants (1.7 per cent) in the 1831 census list.[201] In 1841, 54 per cent of the housing was classified as fourth class and the female illiteracy rate was 79 per cent.

If we accept the 1831 and 1841 census figures at face value, then we would estimate a Catholic population of about 10,000 in mid-1845, falling back by almost 2,000 two years later. In a population of this size, we would expect to witness between 114 and 171 deaths during a normal six-month period. O'Sullivan's estimate for deaths during the period October 1845–March 1846 is slightly above the upper bound limit. According to his figures the mortality rate in the six-month Famine period was more than four times the 'normal' rate.

Return of Revd Jeremiah O'Sullivan, P.P. of Ardfert and Kilmoyly:[202]

Number of deaths from 1st October 1846 to 1st of April 1847? About 15 each week in Ardfert and 20 each week in Kilmoily; total, 910.
Number of same known to be caused by famine? Nearly nine a week in Ardfert and seven each week in Kilmoily; total, 416.
Number of deaths during the same period last year? About three each week in Ardfert and five each week in Kilmoily; total, 208.

My curate, the Rev. Mr. Moore, and I have been obliged to give the last rites of the church sometimes to persons on the public roads. It is my opinion that half the poor of my parishes will not survive the present year, as there are only a few now employed on the public works, and no outdoor relief is given at present.

Source: *The Pilot*, 12 May 1847, 4.

Ballylongford and Tarbert, Kerry Diocese

Commentary

The Catholic union of Ballylongford and Tarbert was located on the south-west coast, in north Kerry, in the barony of Iraghticonnor. Ballylongford Catholic parish was coextensive with Aghavallen civil parish and Tarbert Catholic parish, with

200. *Abstract of answers and returns*, BPP (1824), 577, 176; *Abstract of Population Returns for Ireland, 1831*, BPP (1833), 634, 162; *Report of the Commissioners appointed to take the census of Ireland, for the year 1841*, BPP (1843), 504, 96, 200; Newenham, *A View of the Natural, Political and Commercial Circumstances of Ireland*, 30.
201. *First report of the Commissioners of public instruction*, 45, 160c.
202. His spelling of Kilmoyley.

Kilnaughtin civil parish. The 1831 census reported parish populations of 5,698 (Ballylongford/Aghavallen) and 4,371 (Tarbert/Kilnaughtin) respectively.[203] In 1841, 41 per cent of the housing was classified as fourth class and the female illiteracy rate was 74 per cent.

The population of the Union was overwhelmingly Catholic. The Public Instruction Commissioners identified 93 per cent of the 1831 population as Catholic, but the Protestant numbers were artificially boosted by the presence of military fortifications, a customs office and a lighthouse on Tarbert Island.[204] It was because of these facilities that Protestants comprised an untypically large 12 per cent of the population in Tarbert parish, compared with below two per cent in neighbouring Ballylongford. By 1841 the population in the two parishes had advanced significantly, to 11,708.[205]

The return from the Union was the work of Revd Daniel McCarthy, parish priest of the Union since at least 1834/5.[206] McCarthy was a supporter of O'Connell. In the 1841 general election in County Kerry a rally in favour of the two anti-Tory election candidates was arranged for the strand at Ballyeagh, Ballybunion. With typical bombast, the *Kerry Examiner* pronounced that 'never within the memory of the oldest inhabitant of Kerry was so stupendous an assemblage presented to the view of any one locality in Munster as the beautiful Strand of Ballyeagh exhibited on last Thursday.'[207]

Four candidates were standing for election, the two sitting M.P.s, O'Connell and the Tory, Arthur Blennerhassett, Mahony, a second Conservative candidate, and Honourable William Browne, a Liberal. *En route* to the rally:

> The carriages of the Hon. Mr. Browne and John O'Connell, Esq., were met at the cross of Liselton by the Ballylongford, Ardee, and Tarbert Societies, headed by their truly amiable and patriotic pastor, the Rev. Daniel M'Carthy, and by his excellent curate, the Rev. William Stack M'Carthy.
>
> Were I to describe the marching order of the other Societies … my space would not be sufficient. I must, therefore, reluctantly be brief and simply state, that the Ballydonohue Society, the Ballybunnion Society, the Kilconly Society, the Benmore Society, the Ballyheigue Society, the Causeway Society, and several other Societies whose locality I could not obtain, now marched past in quick succession for the Strand, making the air ring with reverberating shouts for 'BROWNE AND O'CONNELL FOR EVER'.
>
> As the immense multitude was entering the strand, an envious conservative cloud wept a few natural tears for the fall of the Tories. But the sun who was always an *enlightened* Liberal, a Radical, and a Catholic to boot soon illuminated the scene, and dissipated the cloud.

---

203. *Abstract of Population Returns for Ireland, 1831*, 164.
204. *Public Instruction Commissioners, first report*, 160c, 176c; Lewis, *Topographical. Dictionary*, ii, 597.
205. 1843 (504) *Report of the Commissioners appointed to take the census of Ireland, for the year 1841*, BPP, 198.
206. *First report of the Commissioners of public instruction*, appendix II, 58.
207. *Kerry Examiner and Munster General Observer*, 29 June 1841.

> It was computed that there could not have been less than one hundred and twenty thousand souls – from which deduct half for females, children, and the aged men, the result would show an array of SIXTY THOUSAND ABLE-BODIED MEN, peaceably assembled to fight constitutionally for their religion – their clergy – their country – and their rights.[208]

In spite of the emerging crisis in 1846, normal life had to continue in the area, and McCarthy could find the time to attend a party at Tarbert House to celebrate Robert Leslie's attainment of his majority in April. There, 'the most substantial and abundant dinner which we have ever seen on a public occasion' was served, with

> the Rev. D.M'Carthy, the Rev. Richard Fitzgerald, the respected Protestant rector of Tarbert, Mr. Patterson, Mr Wm Sandes, and Mr P. Leslie severally presided at the different tables, the centre being occupied by the worthy parish priest, who on this occasion, as well as throughout the whole course of his ministry in those parishes, has given so many evidences of his anxiety not alone to cultivate, in his own person, a mutuality of good feeling with the Protestant gentry of his district, but to inculcate on the minds of his people the same hearty good will [...]
>
> And now we betake ourselves to the interior of Tarbert House, where a costly and elegant collation is prepared for the ladies and gentlemen invited to witness the delightful festivities of the day. In either room, as you enter from the capacious and lofty hall, were spread in profusion the choicest viands of every description, while wines of the purest vintage sparkled around.[209]

As the event was concluding McCarthy was honoured at the event with a toast – 'A better man does not stand on British ground', though he had withdrawn by that time.[210]

McCarthy's return is brief, considering the gravity of his account, reporting nearly 800 deaths in the six-month period after October 1846, about three times larger than the number of deaths that had occurred 12 months previously. We estimate the union's Catholic population in mid-1845 at about 11,450, from which between about 130 and 195 deaths could be expected in a normal October – March six-month period. McCarthy's 780 deaths in the six-month period during the Famine amount to a yearly total of nearly 1,400. By this time the parish's population had dropped to perhaps about 10,500, which implies a catastrophic mortality rate of about 130 per 1,000 people. According to McCarthy, some of the 780 bodies mentioned by him had been buried without coffins.

---

208. *Kerry Examiner and Munster General Observer*, 29 June 1841.
209. *Ibid.*
210. *Ibid.*

Return of Revd D. McCarthy, P.P. of Ballylongford and Tarbert:

Number of deaths from 1st October, 1846 to 1st April 1847? 780.
Number of same known to be caused by famine? Over one-half.
Number of deaths during same period last year? 10 a week [i.e. about 260].

Several of my parishioners have been buried without coffins – the greater portion of them actually starving. Giving them seed gratis, and paying them daily hire for the fortnight they may be engaged in cultivating the land is, in my opinion, the only way of staying the famine.

One twentieth of the usual tillage land in my parishes is not, and will not, be cultivated this year for want of seeds. No emigration for want of means.

Source: *The Pilot*, 28 April 1847, 3.

Ballybunion, Kerry Diocese

Commentary

This return is stated as being from 'Liselton, Listowel, County Kerry'. It might be presumed that this points towards Listowel Catholic parish, but Lisselton civil parish, to the west of Listowel civil parish, was part of the Catholic union of Ballybunion. Revd James Walsh, parish priest of Liselton, must have been newly arrived there at the time of the Death Census, as Revd Michael O'Sullivan was parish priest there as late as May 1846.[211]

The return for Liselton, or Ballybunion, was signed by Walsh. Ballybunion Catholic parish covered the civil parishes of Kilconly, Killehenny and Liselton. The 1831 population of the union was 6,117, rising to 7,481 ten years later.[212] In 1841, 49 per cent of the housing was classified as fourth class and the female illiteracy rate was 84 per cent. The Catholic population of the union would have been about 7,750 in mid-1845 and about 6,780 two years later.[213] A population of 7,750 would typically witness at least 88 deaths in the period from October to March in normal times, so Walsh's count of 25 deaths between October 1845 and March 1846 is clearly an underestimate. He suggests that deaths in the Famine six-month period were about five times the normal number.

211. *Cork Examiner*, 13 May 1846.
212. *Abstract of Population Returns for Ireland, 1831*, BPP (1833), 634, 164; *Report of the Commissioners appointed to take the census of Ireland, for the year 1841*, BPP (1843), 504, 198.
213. There is a discrepancy of 173 between the 1831 census figures and the aggregate populations given in the Public Instruction Commissioners' report; we have boosted the Catholic population in 1831 by this figure, to 6,075.

Return of Revd James Walsh, P.P. of Ballybunion:

Number of deaths from 1st of October 1846, to 1st of April, 1847? 120.
Number of same known to be caused by famine? Would say 80.
Total number of deaths during the same period last year? 25.

On the day before yesterday we had three bodies interred without coffins; all died of perfect starvation. There are about 74 acres of land at present tilled, some more in progress, and a great portion left idle for want of seed.

Source: *The Pilot*, 28 April 1847, 4.

Castlemaine (Keel), Kerry Diocese

Commentary

The Catholic parish of Castlemaine was broadly coextensive with the civil parishes of Kilgarrylander, Kilcolman and Kiltallagh. The statutory censuses report a fluctuating population. The 1821 survey reported 6,923 people in the three civil parishes (likely an underestimate). In 1831 the population was recorded as 9,469. According to the 1841 census it subsequently declined to 8,937.[214] In 1841 66 per cent of the housing in the *civil* parishes of Kilgarrylander, Kiltallagh and Kilcolman (not coterminous with the Catholic parish of Castlemaine) was classified as fourth class and the female illiteracy rate was 81 per cent. The population was strongly Catholic but it had a small Protestant community; the Public Instruction Commissioners reported a Protestant population of 645 (6.7 per cent) in 1831 as compared with 8,920 Catholics (93.3 per cent).[215]

The report for Castlemaine was compiled by Revd Thomas Carmody, parish priest. Carmody was a recent arrival at Castlemaine, replacing, in 1845, the suspended Revd David O'Connor, who had been in charge of the parish for nearly three decades.[216] Carmody's arrival in Castlemaine had not been without controversy, and many newspapers carried reports during May 1845 of the unseemly events unfolding in the parish, following the locking of the chapel doors against Carmody:

> For the last three months the Roman Catholic Chapels of Keelgarrylander and Castlemain, Kerry, has [*sic.*] been closed against the Rev. Mr. Carmody, deputed by Bishop Egan to take charge in place of the old priest, Rev. David O'Connor, suspended. Rev. Mr. Carmody attempted, about three weeks since, to take forcible possession of them against the wish of the people who resisted the attempt, and succeeded in recovering possession of their

214. *Abstract of answers and returns, pursuant to act 55 Geo. 3, for taking an account of the population of Ireland in 1821*, BPP (1824) (577), vol.22, xxii.411, 182; *Abstract of Population Returns for Ireland, 1831*, BPP (1833), 634, 166; *Report of the Commissioners appointed to take the census of Ireland, for the year 1841*, BPP (1843), 504, 198, 200. It is possible that the 1821 figure given does not include part of Kilcolman parish.
215. *First report of the Commissioners of public instruction*, 45, 172c, 178c.
216. *Limerick Chronicle*, 17 May 1845, 2.

> Chapel, after a sharp struggle. This led to a summons against nine persons at the suit of the Rev. Mr. Carmody, which came on for hearing at the Miltown Petty Sessions before a full bench of magistrates. Rev. Mr. Carmody and other witnesses were examined by Mr. Dowling for the prosecution, who proved the opposition offered and the riot in the Chapel. Mr. Morphy, in reply, argued that the Chapel was the property of the parish, and that as such Mr. Carmody and his friends were trespassers in [it]; he further contended that the parties prosecuting [Revd Carmody] were the real rioters, and said that his clients intended to summon them for breaking the Chapel. The Bench deprecated this unseemly quarrel between the people and their appointed Pastor, and granted informations against six of the parties charged, who will be tried at the quarter sessions.[217]

The *Banner of Ulster*, hardly an unbiased vehicle for commentary on the matter, spoke vigorously of the parishioners 'direct and determined [...] opposition to the hierarchical and priestly authority' that was evinced by the dispute. O'Connor had accepted, following the riot, that his suspension could not be overturned, but the *Banner* found that waning opposition to Carmody had been stymied by the riotous incident, and 'the parishioners now declare their fixed determination never to yield, or receive Mr Carmody as their parish priest'.[218]

In spite of the opposition to Carmody, before the year was out some, at least, had rallied to his cause, when he led 'the men of Castlemaine' to a Killarney rally in favour of O'Connell and Repeal,[219] and by 1847 he was involved in inter-denominational relief efforts in the area, which included the opening of a soup kitchen in the town.[220] His Death Census report is untypical, as it contained no mortality figures. This may be indicative of the conflict which had greeted his appointment in the parish. New parish register books were opened soon after his arrival, and for a brief period O'Connor and Carmody were simultaneously conducting services there, O'Connor recording in the old books, and Carmody in the new ones. It is possible, therefore, that he was denied access to records compiled before his arrival.

Return of Rev Carmody, P.P. of Castlemaine:

My calls are so numerous that it is not possible for me to ascertain the number of deaths which have occurred in this parish by famine from the 1st October, 1846, to the 1st April, 1847. My curate and I are kept going, day and night, preparing the unfortunate people for death; the state of the parish is deplorable, many dying on the roads, so exposed for days, at length buried without coffins and in the fields. Very few are able to till, and any able are not inclined or in spirits to do so. The greatest rage prevails to emigrate, but thousands willing have not the means. The landlords, with few exceptions, were never so urgent, never so inexorable [in collecting rent].

217. *Limerick Chronicle*, 17 May 1845.
218. *Banner of Ulster*, 3 June 1845.
219. *Cork Examiner*, 6 October 1845.
220. *Cork Examiner*, 12 March 1847.

'*Ex uno disce [omnes]*'.[221] A certain landlord was so cruel as to tell a tenant, able to stand his ground and pay the rent if he got fair play, 'that he should pay each gale [day] the very moment it would fall due, while he had a hen in the world.'

'Shame where is thy blush?'

I could mention other acts more revolting.

Source: *The Pilot*, 7 May 1847, 1.

Moyvane (Newtownsandes), Kerry Diocese

Commentary

Moyvane parish, also called Newtownsandes, is located in north-east Kerry, to the east of Listowel parish. Revd John Long, of Murheer Lodge, had been parish priest of Moyvane since at least 1834/5.[222] The parish is called 'Menheer' in the printed return, but this is probably a misprint for the name Murher, as the Catholic parish was coterminous with the civil parishes of Murher and Knockanure. In 1841, 49 per cent of the housing was classified as fourth class and the female illiteracy rate was 78 per cent.

The return for Moyvane was compiled by Long. Long had been a staunch supporter of O'Connell's politics for a prolonged period, collecting money for his cause during the 1830s and 1840s.[223] In 1841 Long made his pitch to the Repeal Association for Volunteer status, on the basis of the funds he had secured for the cause:

> The Rev. John Long, C.R, Murheer – 'I send you [Repeal Association] a bank post bill of £6, with list of the subscribers, being the first instalment towards the Repeal rent from the parish of Murheer. You may calculate on another remittance from me without much delay. I lately sent £7, through the Repeal Wardens, Mr O'Sullivan and Mr Moore, from Knocanure, another small parish united to this, making in all £13. This, with my own subscription of £1, would, I think, entitle the union to a weekly paper, and me to the high honour of being enrolled a Volunteer, with moral arms. Please send cards for those 120 persons, whose names I send, and depend on it that no exertion on my part will be wanting to forward the only measure calculated to raise Ireland from her present prostrate condition.[224]

A Monster Meeting in Listowel in June 1843, attended by 'the gallant men of the baronies of Irraghticonnor and Clanmaurice in large bodies [who] entered the town headed by their excellent bands, playing national, soul-stirring airs'

221. Horan (Kildysart) used a similar Latin term.
222. *First report of the Commissioners of public instruction*, appendix II, 45, 58 (Murhar and Knuckanure parishes). For the name of Long's house see *Dublin Weekly Register*, 24 March 1838.
223. *Freeman's Journal*, 14 April 1831 (£14 11*s*.); *Dublin Weekly Register*, 25 January 1834; *Saunders News-Letter*, 15 March 1837; *Dublin Weekly Nation*, 9 December 1843.
224. *Freeman's Journal*, 25 September 1841.

was attended by Long, with 5,000 men from his parish, and its surrounds.[225] The following month a convoy from Listowel heading for a meeting in Glin, in west Limerick, was 'met by the Newtownsands Repealers, headed by the Rev. John Long, P.P., and sixty horsemen'.[226]

The statutory censuses had reported combined populations of 4,224 in 1831 and 4,651 in 1841 for the parishes of Murher and Knockanure.[227] The population was almost exclusively Catholic; only 6 of the 1831 population were identified as Protestants by the Public Instruction Commissioners.[228] We estimate the Catholic population at about 4,800 in mid-1845, well above Long's estimate of 2,500. Long's figures for deaths are, he states, exclusive of children, although he provides tentative figures for those for the Famine period. The number of adult deaths in the period October 1846–March 1847 was more than four times that of the previous year. A parish of this size should have been experiencing between about 55 and 82 deaths in the six months from October in normal times.

Return of Revd John Long, P.P. of Moyvane:

Number of deaths from 1st October 1846 to 1st April 1847? – 180, exclusive of children, of whose deaths there was no return kept, but I would venture to say there could not be less than 40.
Number of same known to be caused by famine? 106 adults, exclusive of children, and I would say from their tender age that a higher proportion of them died by famine.
Number of deaths during the same period last year? – 40 adults, besides children. I mean by adults all those who receive the rites of the church in the last sickness.

Of the number who died by the famine a whole family, consisting of eight, died almost unknown to the people, as they lived in a remote part of the parish. Eight died by the ditches, and four of them were buried without coffins – three in one day. The present state of the parish is awful, and it is my firm conviction the arrangements now on foot will rather aggravate than stay the famine, inasmuch as that twenty per cent of the limited number on the public works are it is said, to be knocked off on the 24th instant, and the entire on the first of May; and I am afraid – nay I am certain, from passing events – that even the more destitute will not get any relief adequate to that which (though miserably poor and scanty) they could purchase for their hire were they continued on the public works – while by the outdoor relief bill many cottiers having small plots of ground and many small farmers equally destitute, will be precluded from any relief under the new arrangements, so that there is no prospect

225. *Londonderry Journal*, 7 June 1843.
226. *Tralee Chronicle*, 5 August 1843.
227. 1824 (577) *Abstract of answers and returns*, BPP, 178; 1833 (634) *Abstract of Population Returns for Ireland, 1831*, BPP, 164; 1843 (504) *Report of the Commissioners appointed to take the census of Ireland, for the year 1841*, BPP, 198.
228. *First report of the Commissioners of public instruction*, 174c, 176c.

before them but irremediable despair. As to the extent of land tilled and being tilled, those famers who were able to keep their seed corn have already tilled, and are tilling more corn than ever they did before; but the cottiers and small farmers have neither seed nor provisions, and consequently their lands will remain untilled. There are none as yet emigrated from this parish, but numbers of the small farmers have given up their holdings either to their landlords or others for some pecuniary assistance to take them out of the country, and are preparing themselves. I should mention, of the number who died of hunger I administered the last rites to eight of them in my own house, seven of whom died shortly after. Perhaps I ought also acquaint you that before the famine my parishioners were honest, exemplary and religious. I am sorry to say now that theft and robbery, and nightly burglary are commencing to appear among them, and of course the dismissal of the poor from the public works will increase these dreadful crimes. The out-door relief cannot be in operation in this parish for five weeks.

Source: *The Pilot*, 28 April 1847, 3–4.

County Limerick

Ballybricken (Location Uncertain, Though Probably County Limerick Rather Than County Cork)

A return was received from Ballybricken parish, which was noted as being located in County Cork, but there is no parish of that name in Cork. In addition, the name of the priest is usually given in the returns; but none is recorded against this return, frustrating attempts to identify it. A townland called Ballybricken is located in Barnanhely civil parish, south of Cork city, on the western shore of Cork harbour (corresponding to Monkstown Catholic parish), but we do not believe the return originated from there. There are two Catholic parishes called Ballybricken located elsewhere; one in Waterford city, the other in east County Limerick. It is our view that the parish has been incorrectly noted as being in County Cork, and is actually a return for Ballybricken parish, in the diocese of Cashel and Emly, and County Limerick, possibly compiled by Revd John Fennelly, the curate, or Revd Nunan, the parish priest.

We argue this for two reasons. First, three other returns were received from County Limerick, two of which – Pallasgreen and Knockany – are also located in Cashel and Emly diocese, and are neighbouring parishes to the County Limerick parish. Second, although Great Repeal Meetings were held on the Hill of Ballybricken, County Waterford, in 1840, when 'there could not have been less than 100,000 persons present, whilst all the surrounding roads still presented an uninterrupted mass of human beings, all advancing to the place of meeting', and at other times during the opening years of the 1840s, it was the County Limerick parish which featured most prominently in the Repeal campaign.[229]

229. *Freeman's Journal*, 30 October 1840, 3–4; *Freeman's Journal*, 2 August 1841, 3–4; *Freeman's Journal*, 7 July 1843.

Revd John Fennelly, a firm Repealer, was appointed curate of Ballybricken, County Limerick, in 1841, assisting the parish priest, Revd Philip Cleary, also a Repeal supporter. Fennelly quickly became prominent in organising the political campaign in the parish.[230] He collected the Repeal Rent in the parish, from where a petition calling for Repeal was issued in 1841, signed by 750 people.[231] Both Cleary and Fennelly were members of the Repeal Association, paying their £1 annual subscription in 1845.[232] We can be certain that the author of the Census was not Cleary, as he 'died suddenly [...] while conversing in the most sprightly and familiar manner with Revd. Mr Raleigh, and others' in Sexton Street, Limerick, in January 1846, to be replaced by Revd Nunan.[233]

Although most of the evidence, circumstantial rather than definitive, points to this being a return for the Limerick parish rather than the Waterford one, the location of Ballybricken is perhaps a moot point, as the return for the parish is sparse and relatively uninformative. Deaths had increased by a factor of three since the October 1845–March 1846 period, and bodies were going unburied. The people of the area were in 'a threatening attitude', and emigration was rife. In 1841, 63 per cent of the housing in the *civil* parish of Caherelly (not coterminous with the Catholic parish of Ballybricken) was classified as fourth class and the female illiteracy rate was 64 per cent.

REPEAL OF THE UNION – MR O'CONNELL IN MURROE

> The honourable and learned gentleman (the Liberator) accompanied by honest Tom Steele, arrived in this city on Monday evening about six o'clock in his travelling carriage and four horses, and having stopped at Cruise's Hotel, was waited on shortly after by many of the most respectable of our citizens who were anxious to pay their respects to him. He left Limerick this morning for Murroe shortly after eleven o'clock, accompanied by the Very Rev. Dr Costelloe and Mr. Steele, and had not proceeded far on the way when he was met by hundreds and thousands of his admiring countrymen. The day was calm and beautiful. The people from the remotest districts in the county were astir as the morning dawned; women mixed in the gay throng, and boys and girls forgot the fatigue of a long journey in their anxiety to reach Murroe before the Liberator's arrival. Croom, Abington, Newport, Caherconlish, Boher, Barrington's Bridge, Castleconnell, Ahane, Pallasgreen, Ulla, Ballybricken, and other villages and districts, poured forth their tributary streams of human beings, and headed by their temperance bands.[234]

230. *Freeman's Journal*, 2 September 1841.
231. *Freeman's Journal*, 23 June 1843; *Freeman's Journal*, 1 December 1843; *Freeman's Journal*, 29 February 1841.
232. *Freeman's Journal*, 18 March 1845; *Freeman's Journal*, 14 August 1846.
233. *Limerick Chronicle*, 31 January 1846; *Limerick Chronicle*, 11 February 1846.
234. *Freeman's Journal*, 16 June 1843.

The name of the author was not included on the return:

Number of deaths from 1st October 1846 to 1st April 1847? 45.
Number of same known to be caused by famine? 19.
Number of deaths during the same period last year? 15.

Four persons remained unburied for four days for want of means: one woman dropped dead on the field through exhaustion.

The majority of the people in a famishing state, and in a threatening attitude, and the present committee arrangements inadequate to arrest the progress of the famine.

At least one fifth of the tillage ground remains unsown.

The small farmers are emigrating in great numbers.

No resident proprietor to employ the poor, or to aid them by subscriptions.

Source: *The Pilot,* 12 May 1846, 4.

Killeedy, Limerick Diocese

Commentary

The Catholic parish of Killeedy is located in south-west Limerick; it is not coterminous with any combination of civil parishes. In 1841, 65 per cent of the housing in the *civil* parish of Killeedy (not coterminous with the Catholic parish of Killeedy) was classified as fourth class and the female illiteracy rate was 74 per cent. The parish priest of Killeedy at the time of the Death Census was Revd Henry Fitzgibbon. In the 1838 *Catholic Directory*, Fitzgibbon is recorded as one of the curates of St Mary's parish, in Limerick City. Revd John Nolan was the other curate. Fitzgibbon compiled the report for his parish, and a few years later, in June 1850, he emigrated to North America, following in the footsteps of Nolan, who had also emigrated there.[235] Unfortunately, Fitzgibbon felt unable to provide information on the number of deaths as he kept no register. Nonetheless, he recognised that famine had caused a significant increase in the number of deaths in his parish.

Return of Revd Henry Fitzgibbon, P.P. of Killeedy:

Sir – I have kept no registry of the deaths in my parish. It is, therefore, altogether impossible that I could furnish the information required. I have at the same time to say that the number of deaths has been very much increased this year, not so much arising from the want of the usual food, but from the want of means to purchase food according to the demand for it. As the new system of relief [soup kitchens] is likely to be in operation in about ten days, we cannot expect an addition to the average mortality of past weeks. The small farmers are not tilling the land save in few instances, having no capital for seed or support while tilling it, and consequently all that can provide the means by selling out their small holdings are emigrating to America.

Source: *The Pilot*, 28 April 1847, 4.

235. *Freeman's Journal*, 12 July 1850; *Catholic Directory and Annual register for 1838,* 125.

Knockany, Cashel and Emly Diocese

Commentary

Knockany Catholic parish, in Small County barony, east Limerick, was coextensive with the civil parish of Knockainy. The parish priest at the time of the Death Census was Revd John Ryan. Ryan was a Repeal supporter, subscribing his £1 membership fee in 1846 ('verbal assurances of friendship and confidence are often worth very little, but pecuniary remittances – particularly in such times as the present – may be deemed incontestable proofs of sincerity') and signing, in communion with all 114 clergy of Cashel and Emly diocese, a futile Repeal address to the Queen in 1848 calling for the creation of a parliament in Dublin.[236]

CASHEL AND EMLY – REPEAL

The subjoined truly admirable address from the Archdiocese to the Queen, praying her Majesty to assemble her Parliament in Dublin, has been transmitted to Sir George Grey, by the Rev. John Mackey, P P, Clonoulty, who acted as Secretary to the meeting at which it was adopted. The address is signed by the Archbishop, and all the clergy of Cashel and Emly, one hundred and fourteen in number. It is a significant proof that the feelings of the venerable body from which it emanates beat in unison with those of the people, to whose temporal as well as spiritual requirements they sedulously minister; and that state craft, no matter how disguised, can never sever those legatures of affection and love which mutually bind the pastor to the flock, and the flock to the pastor in Ireland:

TO HER MOST GRACIOUS MAJESTY THE QUEEN.
The Address of the Archbishop and Roman Catholic Clergy of the Dioceses of Cashel and Emly.

May it please your Majesty – We, the under signed Archbishop and Roman Catholic clergy of the dioceses of Cashel and Emly, beg leave to approach your Majesty with sentiments of dutiful allegiance to your throne, and of cordial attachment to your Majesty's gracious person.

We are the pastors of thousands of your Majesty's Roman Catholic subjects in Ireland, and have always been the advocates and supporters of peace and social order. We have unceasingly inculcated on our respective flocks allegiance to the Sovereign and respect to the constituted authorities of the Empire. We have always taught them to fear God, to honour the Queen that reigns over them, and to be obedient to the laws.

From sad experience, however, we know that the social condition of this country is greviously [*sic.*] deranged, whence the great body of our people have many grievances to complain of, and many privations to endure. To us they have recourse in their difficulties – to us they utter their complaints – and from us they expect consolation and advice. They repose an unlimited confidence in us, and we are therefore the depositories of all their sufferings, their wants, and their woes. To us they naturally look for sympathy, and if we refuse it to them we should cease to be men.

236. *The Pilot*, 19 August 1846; *The Pilot*, 19 May 1848.

> Your Majesty is, no doubt, well aware that we possess a very powerful influence over our people – an influence that has always been exercised by us for the public weal, notwithstanding the calumnies by which we have been recently assailed; nevertheless we shall not conceal from your Majesty our unanimous and decided opinion that this very influence has its limits, and that there is a certain point beyond which it cannot be expected to prevail; neither can conscientiously conceal from your Majesty the important fact, that there exists at present in Ireland a deep and general feeling of discontent, and a daily increasing conviction among all classes that an English legislature is utterly incompetent to remedy the evils of our social condition.
>
> As Christian ministers, therefore, as the friends of peace and social order, and as loyal subjects, we have ventured to interpose as mediators between the Sovereign and her people, and we most humbly but earnestly pray your Majesty will be graciously pleased to summon your Irish Parliament of Lords and Common in Dublin, and thereby allay the discontent of your people, give additional security to your throne, and increase the prosperity of your Empire.[237]

The population of Ryan's parish was advancing steadily in the run-up to the Famine. The statutory censuses reported 4,531 inhabitants in 1831, and 4,939 by 1841, suggesting a yearly rate of growth of about 0.9 per cent during the 1830s.[238] Ryan's mention of 800 families in the parish in his return is probably reasonably accurate; the 1841 census had counted 791 households a few years earlier.[239] In 1841 49 per cent of the housing was classified as fourth class and the female illiteracy rate was 67 per cent. The population was overwhelmingly Catholic; the Public Instruction Commissioners identified only 44 Protestants (1.0 per cent) out of the inhabitants enumerated in 1831.[240]

We estimate that the Catholic population would have been about 5,100 by mid-1845, falling back to about 4,350 two years later.[241] A population of this size would have produced between 58 and 87 deaths in the period from October 1845 to March 1846, well above Ryan's figure of 22. Although Ryan does note that his totals counted adults only (15 years old, and older), he may not even have included all adults. His figures suggest a tripling of the death rate between October 1845–March 1846 and the same period a year later.

237. *The Pilot*, 19 May 1848, 3. Dozens of priests put their names to this.

238. *Abstract of answers and returns*, BPP (1824), 577,, 194; *Abstract of Population Returns for Ireland, 1831*, BPP (1833), 634, 182; *Report of the Commissioners appointed to take the census of Ireland, for the year 1841*, BPP (1843), 504, 218.

239. *Report of the Commissioners appointed to take the census of Ireland, for the year 1841*, BPP (1843), 504, 218.

240. *First report of the Commissioners of public instruction, Ireland*, 68c.

241. Note that the Public Instruction Commission population figures exceed the 1831 census figures by 11; we adjust the Catholic population for 1831 downwards by these extra 11 people.

Return by Revd John Ryan, P.P. of Knockany:

Number of deaths from 1st October 1846, to 1st April 1847? 66 of the age 15 and upwards.
Number of same known to be caused by famine? There is no doubt that the excess above the previous year is owing to diseases brought on from want of sufficient food, and the cold and suffering the poor had to bear on the public works.
Number of deaths during the same period last year? 22 of the age of 15 and upwards.

The contributions for the relief of the poor during this and the last year came principally from the resident gentry, clergy and farmers; very little in proportion to their rents from the proprietors.

The present state of the parish is truly alarming; out of 800 families, 600 are in want of relief. I don't think, under such circumstances, that taxes, under the present relief bill, adequate to the wants of this immense number of paupers, can be collected.

The tillage of the land is only as usual, all now at an end – and no further employment for the people, unless public works may be resumed, for the landlords are not inclined to proceed with drainage.

Great numbers are emigrating, in fact, every poor person who can make out the means; many more would be gone, if the small farmers could get any sum for their holdings.

I am quite sure that the number of deaths above stated, together with those who have died under the age of fifteen, is three times the number of births in the same period.

Source: *The Pilot*, 7 May 1847, 1.

Pallasgreen, Cashel and Emly Diocese

Commentary

The return for Pallasgreen parish was compiled by Revd Thomas Mahony. In 1841, 43 per cent of the housing was classified as fourth class and the female illiteracy rate was a lowish 58 per cent. Mahony had been parish priest since at least 1834, when he compiled a detailed religious census of the parish for submission to the Public Instruction Inquiry.[242] Mahony was a Repeal supporter. He signed, along with all other priests in his diocese, the 1848 address appealing for the opening of a parliament in Dublin (see report for Knockany), although he had the good sense to temper his enthusiasm for the cause when his parishioners were starving.

242. *First report of the Commissioners of public instruction*, appendix II, 54 (Nicker, Templebreaden); Fergus O'Ferrall, 'The population of a rural pre-Famine parish: Templebredin, Counties Limerick and Tipperary, in 1834' in *North Munster Antiquarian Journal*, xvii (1975), 91–101.

> No amount of eulogy which the Committee could bestow would at all indicate their gratitude to the rector of Pallasgreen, the Rev. Thomas Mahony. This reverend gentleman is known in his diocese as a hard working but retiring priest, and a generously devoted patriot. His present communication sustains both characters. He could not, he says "attempt a public collection" – but neither could he omit to record his estimation of the transcendent services of O'Connell; and therefore he "solicited from those who could he knew afford little or much" contributions towards this Fund [to erect a monument to O'Connell in Dublin]. The result has been the present remittance of £6 0*s.* 6*d.*, of which the Rev. Gentleman has contributed himself £2, and the Rev. John Murphy, his patriotic curate, and Thomas Ryan Esq., a no less patriotic lay parishioner, subscribed £1 each.[243]

Mahony's report was brief, and, regrettably, gave no numbers for deaths in the area. It is notable, however, that he implies that the death rate at the time of writing was lower than it had been during the 'previous cold weather' (i.e., the winter of 1846–7). A similar point is expressed in Ryan's return for Knockany.

Return of Revd Thomas Mahony, P.P. of Pallasgreen:

The deaths from dysentery and destitution were more numerous during the previous cold weather than at present.

There are many small portions of land untilled, owing to the want of seed by the occupants, or provision for themselves or families while tilling it.

The prospects for the coming year are, in my mind, awful to contemplate, as the labourers in the country have no land or a prospect of employment that would enable them to purchase food for their families.

The holders of land from about twenty acres downwards are, in many instances, when practicable, disposing of it, together with their other effects, and going to America.

Lastly, I am sorry to inform you that fever is rapidly on the increase.

Source: *The Pilot*, 7 May 1847, 1.

County Tipperary

Ballinahinch and Killoscully, Cashel and Emly Diocese

Commentary

The Catholic parish of Ballinahinch and Killoskully parish is located in west Tipperary, close to the border with County Limerick. It is coextensive with the civil parish of Killoscully. The parish priest at the time of the Death Census was Revd Raymond Burke, with Revd John M'Craith serving as curate.[244] It was M'Craith who prepared

243. *The* Pilot, 20 December 1847, 3.

244. https://registers.nli.ie/registers/vtls000632639#page/5/mode/1up.

the parish's submission. M'Craith was a recent arrival in the parish as he was curate of nearby Monasea at the beginning of 1845; Burke had been appointed in March 1844.[245]

The statutory censuses recorded the population of the parish as 2,993 in 1831, rising marginally to 3,099 in 1841.[246] In 1841, 40 per cent of the housing was classified as fourth class and the female illiteracy rate was 57 per cent. Most of the parishioners were Catholics; the Public Instruction Commissioners noted a denominational breakdown of 109 Protestants and 2,884 Catholics in the parish in 1831. We estimate the Catholic population at about 3,112 by mid-1845, which would lead us to expect about 35 to 53 deaths in a normal six-month period spanning October to March. M'Craith's total of 30 deaths between October 1845 and March 1846 is not far below the lower bound of the range, although those are adult deaths only. His figure for the number of deaths for the later six-month period is 104, although he noted that 36 more had died between 1st April and 7th May. According to M'Craith, mortality was about three times greater in the six months from October 1846 to March 1847 compared to the same period the year previously.

Return of Revd John M'Craith, curate of Ballinahinch:

Number of deaths from 1st October 1846 to 7th May 1847? – all adults – having kept no register of younger deaths – 36, of whom died since the 1st of April, last – 140.
Number of the same known to be caused by famine? 40. And not less than fifty of the remainder, although not having died of famine, died after a lingering illness of its effects.
Number of deaths during the same period last year? 30.

There has been no remarkable mortality here for the last three years.

The arrangements on foot [i.e. provision of gratuitous food under the Soup Kitchen Act], it is to be feared (though they may be calculated to keep body and soul together) will be found very inadequate as a check on gradual starvation. The rations distributed by relief committees are too small – what is a pound of Indian meal per diem to an able bodied man, who may have to walk three miles and more to get even that much to keep him alive?

There is at least one third of the land which ought to be tilled now lying waste, the owners of it being unable to procure seed, and besides, unwilling to forfeit the pay which many here still receive, and which, though little it may be, is the chief support of themselves and their families.

The inquiry we have made warrants me in stating that about fifty families, or in the aggregate about 250 persons, would be under the number of emigrants from these parishes since the beginning of the year. They consisted of a class of

245. *Dublin Evening Post,* 23 January 1845; https://registers.nli.ie/registers/vtls000632639#page/5/mode/1up.

246. 1833 (634) *Abstract of Population Returns for Ireland, 1831*, BPP, 196; 1843 (504) *Report of the Commissioners appointed to take the census of Ireland, for the year 1841*, BPP, 232.

holders of from five to ten acres or more of land, which they gladly sold to enable them to emigrate. Many others of the same class would follow them if they only could do so; but they cannot sell their small farms and most reluctantly remain. So also must remain a population of at least 2,000 without land! without food! whose whole earthly reliance is on the continuance of work to employ them; or on the provisions of the new poor relief bill to feed them.

Source: *The Pilot*, 14 May 1847, p. 4.

Ballingarry (Slievardagh Barony), Cashel and Emly Diocese

Commentary

There are two parishes named Ballingarry in County Tipperary, one in Cashel and Emly diocese, the other, also known as Shinrone, in Killaloe diocese. Returns were received from both parishes (see Shinrone and Ballingarry, King's County). Bordering County Kilkenny, the Cashel and Emly parish covered the four civil parishes of Ballingarry, Crohane, Lismalin and Mowney. In 1841, 33 per cent of the housing was classified as fourth class and the female illiteracy rate was 57 per cent. The parish priest was Revd Edward Prendergast, stationed in the parish since at least 1834/5.[247] One of his two curates was Philip Fitzgerald, there in 1841, and it was Fitzgerald who submitted the report for the parish. Both Prendergast and Fitzgerald were committed Repealers – members of the Association, and recruiters for the cause. At the end of 1841 they enrolled 407 of their parishioners in the Association; in 1844 Prendergast contributed £3 and Fitzgerald £1 to the O'Connell Tribute.[248]

The statutory censuses reported a steadily growing population in the parish, climbing from 9,559 in 1831 to 10,724 by 1841.[249] The area was overwhelmingly Catholic; the Public Instruction Commissioners identified only 276 Protestants (2.9 per cent) in the 1831 census returns.[250] We estimate the Catholic population at about 10,858 by mid-1845, falling to 9,613 two years later. In a population of 10,850 we would typically expect to see between about 123 and 185 deaths in the October 1845–March 1846 period, more than double the number of deaths reported by Fitzgerald. In fact, his figure of 170 deaths in the Famine six-month period also lies within the expected range during non-crisis times, and is clearly below the true figure. It seems that Fitzgerald was counting adult deaths only. His picture of conditions in Ballingarry during the Famine is harrowing. He notes that adult deaths averaged ten per month in normal times, but began to climb upwards from October 1846 and particularly after February 1847. They averaged almost 30 per month over the course of the Famine six month period.

247. *First report of the Commissioners of public instruction*, 45, 54.

248. *Freeman's Journal*, 23 December 1841; *Tipperary Free* Press, 21 December 1844.

249. *Abstract of answers and returns*, BPP (1824), 577, 212; *Abstract of Population Returns for Ireland, 1831*, BPP (1833), 634, 196; *Report of the Commissioners appointed to take the census of Ireland, for the year 1841*, BPP (1843), 504, 234.

250. *First report of the Commissioners of public instruction, Ireland*, 45, 40c.

Return of Revd Philip Fitzgerald, curate of Ballingarry:

Number of deaths from 1st October 1846, to 1st April 1847? 170.
Number of same known to be caused by famine? 80.
Number of deaths during the same period last year? 60.

The present state of the country is truly awful, but to look back into the past and reflect on the multitudes who have gone prematurely to their graves within the present year, is heart sickening indeed. If anything could add to their extreme misery, it is the cruel disappointments to which they are doomed when brought every day of meeting about the committee excepting relief, and compelled to return home in the evening with the same sad prospect with which they have been constantly deluded since February last, that before the next committee day there would be funds at our disposal for them; for which reason many have despaired of ever seeing it, and now look only to death for relief. And that many of them have been so relieved already, you will see by the following number which, without pretending to entire accuracy, may be considered a sufficiently correct estimate of the whole. Speaking of adults, the deaths at ordinary times would average ten each month, though since last October the increase was constant; it was comparatively slow until February, when they amounted to about twice the number. After this, when most of those on the public works were attacked with dysentery – the effects of cold and want – the mortality amongst them became much greater. But, at the present time, that to this wasting and widespread disease, fever, unusually malignant and fatal, is superadded, the deaths far exceed anything remembered by the oldest persons living. If anyone entertains a doubt of what I have stated, the scenes of wretchedness and desolation which everywhere meet his eye, will soon convince him of the truth – funerals passing and repassing in every direction – the congregations on Sunday reduced by half – the church yards like fields lately tilled, without a green spot, constantly visited by processions of a few gaunt figures, carrying with difficulty the remains of some more fortunate relative or friend, themselves not less pale and ghastly, and scarce sufficient in strength and numbers to make the grave.

During the last three months I have often attended whole families of whom some were dead and others dying, stretched on the damp ground, with hardly as much straw as covered where they lay, having neither food or drink besides cold water to allay the burning heat of sickness longer – they are pest houses of contagion and famine, and more receptacles of the dead than dwelling places of the living. That such persons could at all think of cultivation is what no reasonable being could expect. Their holdings indeed are very small, but in them there is not sown even a cabbage plant, nor is there amongst them the smallest preparation making for the next year to prevent recurrence of a similar calamity.

I cannot conclude without expressing my sincere regret for the loss our committee have sustained by the death of one of its most efficient members, the Rev James Mansergh, the Protestant curate of those electoral divisions, whose remains were removed from the Rock of Cashel on yesterday. For some time past he showed symptoms of decline; neither the weakness of his constitution, nor his delicate state of health prevented his attendance at our committee, where he laboured with ability, disinterestedness and zeal, to give effect to every new measure of relief. He felt intensely for the afflictions of the poor, and his solicitude to alleviate their infirmities made him forget his own. Affable and kind in manner, and ever ready to oblige all, he possessed their esteem and regard whilst living and has carried with him to his grave their deep sympathy for his young and tender family, and poignant sorrow for the loss they have sustained by his death.

Source: *The Pilot*, 5 May 1847, 4.

Ballyneale, Waterford and Lismore Diocese

Commentary

Ballyneale Catholic parish is located in south-east Tipperary, bordering County Waterford, and close to Carrick-on-Suir. The parish priest of Ballyneale at the time was Revd Patrick Morrissey, appointed to the post in 'the early part of 1824'.[251] He was assisted by Revd P. Power, his curate, recently graduated from the diocesan college in Waterford, and, like Morrissey, a supporter of Repeal and O'Connell.[252]

It was Power who prepared the submission for Ballyneale, which was coextensive with the four civil parishes of Garrangibbon, Grangemockler, Kilmurry and Templemichael. The population of the four parishes was reported by the population censuses at 5,270 in 1831 and 5,573 in 1841.[253] In 1841, 31 per cent of the housing was classified as fourth class and the female illiteracy rate was 73 per cent. Catholics comprised the overwhelming majority of the population, and the Public Instruction Commissioners identified only eight non-Catholics in the parish in 1831.[254] We estimate the Catholic population of Ballyneale at about 5,800 by mid-1845, falling to about 5,225 by mid-1847. A population of that order would typically experience between 66 and 99 deaths in a normal October - March six-month period, well above the 16 deaths reported by Power for the pre-Famine period. Power was clearly not reporting all deaths in the parish. Nonetheless, his report indicates that the area was being devastated by famine. In February 1847 the *Dublin Evening Post* reported:

251. https://registers.nli.ie/registers/vtls000632126#page/3/mode/1up.

252. *Waterford Chronicle*, 2 July 1842; *Dublin Weekly Nation*, 14 February 1846; *Freeman's Journal*, 17 November 1846.

253. *Abstract of Population Returns for Ireland, 1831* BPP (1833), 634, 190, 196 (using Mowney population for Templemichael).

254. *First report of the Commissioners of public instruction*, 45, 20c, 24c, 36c. The 1831 census figures exceed the Public Instruction Commissioners' population figures by 120; thus, we increase the 1831 Catholic population figure by 120.

> In the rural parish of Ballyneale, £318 have been subscribed for the relief of distress. £68 have been received from the proprietors connected with that parish and union, Grangemockler, including £10 each from Lord Clonmel, Sir Thomas Esmonde, Sir John Power, Bart; W. Moore, esq., and James Power, esq., D.L. The tenantry have contributed £230, their respective subscriptions varying from £7 to £1. Rev. P. Morrissy, P.P., has subscribed £10; and £5 each received from the Rev. R. Comerford, C.C., and Rev. P. Power, C.C.[255]

According to Power's submission to the Association mortality was significantly above the normal level in the October 1846–March 1847 period, and he noted that 43 deaths had occurred in the previous month. Veiled hints at violence from a population that was no longer listening to the measured advice of their clerics permeate Power's report.

Return by Revd S. [sic. P.] Power, curate of Ballyneale:

Number of deaths from 1st October 1846 to 1st April 1847? 152.
Number of same known to be caused by famine? 3.
Number of same occasioned from cold and want of necessary subsistence? 122.
Number of deaths during the same period last year? 16.

From the marked difference in the number of deaths between both periods, it will be seen that famine and its accompaniment, pestilence, are doing their fearful work even here in the sunny south. Mortality is alarmingly on the increase. Though the cases of deaths occasioned directly by famine are few, yet the want of nourishing food for the people while labouring under attacks of fever and dysentery, has occasioned the greater number. During the last month there occurred forty-three cases of death, and that in a parish not containing 6,000 people. The deaths are in proportion to the births as five to one. A few years ago and three months would elapse without a single case of mortality, and five weeks would pass over without a sick call. This parish was then considered the most healthy in the diocese of Waterford – but now what a sad and melancholy change!

The temporary relief act becomes here a fatal oppressive act, and, so far from checking pestilence and deaths, only aggravates the miserable position of the people.

The hardships endured in the winter have left in their frames the seeds of disease and death. Their constitutions are enfeebled, and a weary journey every day of eight miles, the distance to and from Carrick-on-Suir, where the meal is distributed, they are unequal to. So exhausted are they on their return in the evening, that the scanty pittance allowed them they are scarcely able to partake of.

P.S. – On last night some heads of cattle were taken from the farmers of this locality and slaughtered by the famishing people. The grievance to which they are subjected by walking a distance of four miles for their rations, and then not receiving half the quantity to which they are entitled, by some mismanagement

255. *Dublin Evening Post*, 27 February 1847.

of the 'relief committee,' have thrown them into a state of wild excitement. They are all unemployed as the 'public works' were discontinued a fortnight ago. The influence which their priests hitherto possessed over them I hear is at an end. Employment, and only that, will remove the discontent. Let them be unemployed for another fortnight and the consequence will be .. Rulers of Ireland look to it!

Source: *The Pilot*, 21 May 1847, 4.

Boherlahan and Dualla, Cashel and Emly Diocese

Commentary

The Catholic parish of Boherlahan and Dualla was located in the barony of Middlethird, in mid-Tipperary. In 1841, 42 per cent of the housing was classified as fourth class and the female illiteracy rate was 57 per cent. The parish priest was Revd William Kirwan, who had been based in the parish since at least 1829.[256] Kirwan was an O'Connellite from the days of the struggle for Catholic Emancipation, chairing a meeting in his parish in February 1829 which stood in favour of 'unconditional' access to the House of Commons for Catholic M.P.s.

> At a numerous Meeting of the Roman Catholic parishioners of Boherlahan, held in the Parish Chapel on Sunday, the first instance [1 February 1829], The Rev. Wm Kirwan, P.P. in the Chair, the following Resolutions were unanimously agreed to:
>
> Resolved – that tremblingly alive to the unjust, because unmerited degradation which has been cast upon us by an anomalous code of laws, and exclusive and capricious system of administration, we shall never cease to proclaim our wrongs, in both Houses of Parliament, firmly, but temperately, until importunity shall have extorted what passive acquiescence never could – full, unqualified, and unconditional Emancipation.
>
> Resolved – That the Petition now read be adopted as the Petition of this Parish – that the Marquis of Anglesey be requested to present it in the House Lords, and that in the House of Commons it be confided to Daniel O'Connell, Esq. Member for Clare, who is eminently entitled to our admiration, gratitude, and respect, for his unceasing exertions in the cause of our country, and particularly in the pacification of this County.
>
> Resolved – That preferring the Penal Code, with all its blood-stained enactments, to any infringement on the independence of our Church, or the purity of her doctrine, we shall never willingly accept of any political power, through the medium of any interference, direct or indirect, on the part of the Crown in the nomination of our Bishops, or the pensioning of our Clergy. That we deem it not less abhorrent to our feelings as Christians and Citizens, to barter the just rights of the Forty Shilling Freeholders, by consenting to any Bill of Relief, purporting to abolish or curtail their elective franchise, by the enthusiastic and heroic exercise of which so much has been achieved for the country at large, and particularly for the Counties of Waterford and Clare, in the annihilation of the Beresford faction, and the signal discomfiture of the hollow friend, the minion of ascendancy, the pliant tool of faction, and the consequent triumph of the Man the People, Daniel O'Connell, Esq. M.P.

256. *Tipperary Free Press*, 7 February 1829.

Resolved – that we view with mingled feelings of affliction, alarm, and horror, the removal of the Marquis of Anglesey from the Government of Ireland, because calculated to depress the well-founded hopes of the many, and to stimulate the rapacious, sanguinary and desolating passions of the favoured few – a Nobleman under whose kind and paternal administration, the balmy influence of even-handed-justice and strict impartiality began to be very generally felt throughout the Land, and won the cordial affections of a long-suffering people.

Resolved – That in the present eventful period of Catholic affairs, we deem it a paramount duty to resume with renovated energy and zeal the collection of the Catholic Rent in this Parish.

Resolved – That these our Resolutions be published in that truly independent and patriotic paper, *The Tipperary Free Press.* Wm Kirwan, P.P. Chairman, John Dwyer, Secretary.[257]

Kirwan was generous in his financial support of O'Connell, organising numerous collections in his parish, to which he contributed liberally, and regularly.[258] When the local relief committee was established in the summer of 1846 Kirwan's personal contribution was substantial, giving £30 for the relief of the destitute in Boherlahan, another £30 for relief in Dualla, and 80 barrels of potatoes 'to meet the pressing wants of his parishioners'. Charles Bianconi, mayor of Clonmel, and innovator in transport, contributed £20.[259] In spite of Kirwan's efforts, and those of the Boherlahan relief committee, the area was severely affected by the Famine. According to Kirwan, the mortality level, in the six-month period between October 1846 and March 1847, was running at around four times the normal level. He held little hope of improvement in the immediate future, in spite of the enthusiastic efforts of locals.

Return of Revd William Kirwan, P.P. of Boherlahan and Dualla:

Number of deaths from 1st October, 1847 [*sic.* 1846], to 1st April, 1847? 200.
Number of same known to be occasioned by famine? 150.
Number of deaths for the same period during the prior year? 50.

The land of the destitute (say the occupiers from one to five acres) a complete waste; no attempt at cultivation from the necessity of self protection on the public works. We apprehend the most awful consequences from a third reduction of labourers on the public works, turning out the old, the young, and only retaining the able bodied to finish the works.

The occupiers of larger farms have made a very great effort, but still a practically ineffectual one, to sow their farms for their support during the next year. Emigration to a most alarming extent, has and will take place in this union. The grave alone will put a period to our most unheard of sufferings.

Source: *The Pilot*, 14 May 1847, 4.

257. *Tipperary Free Press*, 7 February 1829.
258. *Freeman's Journal*, 28 November 1837; *Freeman's Journal*, 27 January 1840; *Dublin Weekly Register*, 2 December 1843.
259. *Tipperary Vindicator*, 23 May 1846.

Borrisoleigh (Glenkeen), Cashel and Emly Diocese

Commentary

The Catholic parish of Borrisoleigh, in Kilnamanagh barony, was coterminous with the civil parish of Glenkeen. The parish is named 'Clankeen' in the return. In 1841, 41 per cent of the housing was classified as fourth class and the female illiteracy rate was as low as 47 per cent. The parish priest of Borrisoleigh was Revd William Morris. Morris had been stationed in the parish since the late 1820s at least, becoming parish priest in 1833, when Michael Slattery, the previous incumbent, was appointed Archbishop of Cashel and Emly on the death of Archbishop Robert Laffan.[260] Morris was a moderate nationalist, committed to non-violent methods, who stood against agrarian disturbances in his county. An April 1836 meeting held in Thurles to consider 'agrarian outrages' resulted in the formation of The Tipperary Society – 'for the suppression of outrage, and the maintenance of peace in this County' – with Morris one of its committee members. Branch Associations were formed in each parish, and it was made the duty of the members of such Associations, to use every means in their power to root out and expose the violence and outrage in their respective districts.[261]

A Repealer, 'who occupies a high place amongst the adherents of O'Connell, as may be seen by his liberal personal example [£3] in connection with this manifestation [O'Connell's annuity for 1842] from his spirited parish', he chaired the 'numerous and highly respectable meeting' held in Borrisoleigh in June 1844 which protested the imprisonment of O'Connell and the other 'Repeal Martyrs'.[262] Thanks to Morris's diligent support of O'Connell, the Association could note that 'Borrisoleigh, County Tipperary, merits high and continuous compliment for the spirit and efficacy which characterises its support [...] per Rev. William Morris, CR, to whom the measure [O'Connell Tribute] is indebted for countenance and precept, enforced by generous personal sustainment'.[263]

Towards the end of 1844 Morris was involved in discussions to ensure that a suitable candidate contested the by-election caused by the death of Robert Otway Cave, one of the county's Liberal MPs.[264] The following year, in September, he attended the vast demonstration in Thurles in favour of Repeal. He was present on the platform that day, supporting resolutions in favour of the restoration of a parliament in Dublin. The second resolution was moved by Robert Keating, esq.: 'that the Irish Legislature being constituted for the purpose, and with the power only of exacting laws for the country, in agreeing to the Union, and thereby abrogating the constitution of the kingdom, abused its trust, and exceeded its power; and that, therefore, its compact was not the compact of the Irish people, and is not, and ought not, to be binding upon their

260. *Dublin Evening Post*, 7 February 1829.

261. *Tipperary Free Press*, 20 April 1836; *Dublin Weekly Register*, 16 April 1836.

262. *Weekly Freeman's Journal*, 7 January 1843; *Tipperary Vindicator*, 15 June 1844.

263. *The Pilot*, 3 December 1845.

264. *Tipperary Vindicator*, 21 December 1844.

consciences.'[265] The resolution was seconded by Rev. William Morris, P.P., Borrisoleigh, and passed unanimously.

By the following year, however, his focus was on other matters. In April 1846 a meeting, jointly chaired by Morris and the Church of Ireland rector, Alexander Hoops, agreed that a quarter of the inhabitants of the parish were 'in a state of extreme destitution', and issued a call to the landed proprietors for assistance.[266] Relations between Morris and Hoops appear to have been cordial, as meetings of the local relief committee were typically jointly chaired by the two clergymen.[267]

The pre-Famine statutory censuses reported the population of Borrisoleigh (Glenkeen) parish at 6,585 in 1831, rising rapidly to 7,481 by 1841, representing an increase of 1.3 per cent per year throughout the decade.[268] The population was strongly Catholic; only 118 of the 6,585 parishioners in 1831 were identified as Protestants by the Public Instruction Commissioners.[269] By mid-1845 the Catholic population may have reached as high as 7,650, which would lead us to anticipate between 87 and 131 deaths in the six months between October 1845 and March 1846. Although Morris admits that his enumeration excludes child deaths, we also suspect that his return only dealt with part of his parish. Borrisoleigh was served by a curate, William Mullally, and there was a chapel located at Ileigh, in the centre of the parish; it is likely that Morris's data did not include burials in the Ileigh graveyard. As the figures stand, Morris's suggestion of 25 deaths between October 1845 and March 1846 are far below our proposed lower-bound figure. Mortality during the six-month Famine period had, according to Morris's return, increased fourfold over the previous year.

Return by Revd William Morris, P.P. of Borrisoleigh:

Number of deaths from October 1st 1846 to 1st of April, 1847? 100. I keep no registry of children.
Number of the same known to be caused by famine? I cannot say how many died of actual famine. I would be inclined to say not one; but I am quite certain diseases which led to death had, in most cases, their origin in insufficient and unwholesome food, and exposure to the cold and rain during the winter on the public works.
Number of deaths during the same period last year? 25.

The reverend gentleman observes – Fever and dysentery are on the increase with us. The people wretchedly poor, and from the necessity that exists of converting all that can be earned into food, all the other comforts of families are neglected. People not able to come to chapel on Sunday, in consequence of their

265. *Dublin Weekly Register*, 27 September 1845; *Limerick Reporter*, 26 September 1845.
266. *Tipperary Vindicator*, 25 April 1846.
267. *Tipperary Vindicator*, 16 May 1846; *Tipperary Vindicator*, 27 June 1846.
268. 1833 (634) *Abstract of Population Returns for Ireland, 1831*, BPP, 192; 1843 (504) *Report of the Commissioners appointed to take the census of Ireland, for the year 1841*, BPP, 230.
269. *First report of the Commissioners of public instruction*, 50c.

clothes being worn out and no means of renewing them. Under the labour [Public Works] act and the temporary relief [Soup Kitchen] act the people will be saved from starvation during the summer, but there are a great many requisites necessary for the poor besides food. The land in general is cultivated in this parish. A good deal of corn put down. Very little potato planting. A greater number leaving for America than has been remembered for many years.

Source: *The Pilot*, 28 April 1847, 4.

Cahir, Lismore Diocese

Commentary

Cahir Catholic parish, in south Tipperary, was coextensive with the large civil parish of Caher. It lies primarily in the barony of Iffa and Offa West. The report for the parish was compiled by its parish priest, Revd Michael Tobin, who had been located there since at least 1830, where he involved himself in political campaigns.[270] During the 1832 general election he, alongside his curates Stephen Lonergan and Gerald Long, pushed for the county's electors 'to petition the Legislature on the subject of tithes, of the jury laws, of the Repeal of the Union, and such other measures as may be calculated to advance the interests of Ireland'. At a 'numerous and highly respectable meeting of the parishioners of Caher' held on St Patrick's Day 1833, and chaired by Tobin, the Union was deemed as 'desolating and destructive to our interests in every respect', and O'Connell, 'that uncompromising patriot' was judiciously praised. The chapel gate collection in support of O'Connell raised £34 1*s*. ('exactly one pound over last year's collection'), ably helped by Tobin's contribution of £3.[271]

Tobin was actively involved in his community's affairs and was respected within the diocese. Distress in the area in the summer of 1834 prompted his swift response.

> In consequence of the extreme distress in Caher, the Rev. Michael Tobin has applied last Sunday's chapel collection (£15) towards purchasing oatmeal, which he is now distributing to the poor of Caher at half price, and intends doing so during this distressed season. It is expected that next Sunday's collection will treble the last, when a subscription list will be opened for that laudable purpose and published in due time.[272]

270. Baptism of Aliciam Heany, 28 October 1830 (https://registers.nli.ie/registers/vtls000632134#page/113/mode/1up). Power incorrectly dates his translation to Cahir to 1836 (Patrick Power, *Waterford and Lismore, A Compendious History of the United Dioceses* (Cork, 1937), 75).
271. *Tipperary Free Press*, 24 November 1832; *Tipperary Free Press*, 30 March 1833; *Tipperary Free Press*, 16 November 1833.
272. *Tipperary Free Press*, 19 July 1834.

He was a member of the Repeal Association, and petitioned for the Repealer, Nicholas Maher, in the 1844 by-election in the county.[273] In 1841, on the departure of Morpeth from the Chief Secretary's Office, he delivered 600 signatures from Cahir for the petition.[274] When the bishopric fell vacant in 1837, on the death of William Abraham, Tobin's was one of three names proposed by the parish priests of the diocese to Rome for consideration.[275] There can be little doubt that he was eminently qualified to provide the Repeal Association with the answers it sought through its Death Census.

The population of Caher civil parish was reported at 8,594 in the 1831 census, rising to 8,801 in 1841.[276] In 1841, 22 per cent of the housing was classified as fourth class and the female illiteracy rate was 61 per cent. Its Protestant community was small; the Public Instruction Commissioners identified just 276 Protestants in the 1831 census return.[277] We estimate the Catholic population at about 8,880 by mid-1845, and about 8,200 by mid-1847. A population of near 9,000 suggests a mortality range of between 101 and 151 in the October 1845–March 1846 period, double the number reported. Revd Tobin notes that deaths in the later six-month period had more than tripled over the same period a year earlier, and that mortality was continuing to escalate rapidly. In the month prior to preparing his return, Tobin stated that 52 deaths had occurred.

Return of Revd Michael Tobin, P.P. of Cahir:

Number of deaths from 1st October 1846 to 1st April 1847? 160. In this number no child under twelve years is included. Within the last month we had fifty-two deaths, being one more than the number of deaths in six months last year. Fever and dysentery are on the increase.
Number of deaths known to be caused by famine? 80. Very few of those died of actual starvation, but about half had died slowly from want of sufficient food.
Total number of deaths during the same period last year? 50.

Destitution is very general. Relief under the [Temporary Relief] act is now in operation, and this fortnight back the ration allowed is just above half of what it should be, and of course is not calculated to stay the famine. Land is tolerably well prepared and tilled, but there are numbers holding from one to ten acres who have no means to procure seed barley, the stubble still remains undug, unploughed; they can be, however, available still for turnips. They are allowed to stop at home to prepare those bits of land. A fortnight is generally allowed, but if more time be necessary they get it; one of the family brings home

273. *Freeman's Journal*, 14 April 1841; *Freeman's Journal*, 28 September 1841; *Tipperary Free Press*, 27 January 1844; *Freeman's Journal*, 11 June 1844.
274. *Cork Examiner*, 10 September 1841.
275. *Freeman's Journal*, 24 February 1837.
276. *Abstract of Population Returns for Ireland, 1831*, BPP (1833), 634, 190; 1843 (504) *Report of the Commissioners appointed to take the census of Ireland, for the year 1841*, BPP, 228.
277. *First report of the Commissioners of public instruction*, 45, 14c. The Public Instruction Commissioners were unable to ascertain the religion of 132 people; we have assigned all of these to the Catholics total.

the rations. The crops are beginning to look well. Emigration is very considerable; some of our best, most comfortable farmers have sold out, and carried with their families some 50*l.* – some 100*l.* and as high as 300*l.* Many of whom are preparing to be off as soon as possible and hundreds remain from the want of means.

Source: *The Pilot*, 14 May 1847, 4.

Clerihan, Cashel and Emly Diocese

Commentary

Clerihan parish, located near Clonmel, in south Tipperary was, according to Revd William Heffernan, the author of its report, the 'smallest parish in the county as far as regards population', containing about 350 households or 2,000 people. In 1841 52 per cent of the housing in the *civil* parish of Colman (not coterminous with the Catholic parish of Clerihan) was classified as fourth class and the female illiteracy rate was 54 per cent. Heffernan had been parish priest for seven years by the time of the Death Census, arriving there from the curacy of Templemore parish.[278] In January 1845, however, he found himself in Clonmel gaol, on charges that 'he took from the late Mr Thompson [died in 1838], of Templemore, a Protestant, on his death-bed, from £600 to £700', which he claimed had been given to him by Thompson for 'charitable purposes', though within a few weeks he was a free man, attending 'a numerous and highly respectable meeting of the inhabitants of Cashel'.[279] A supporter of O'Connell, Heffernan facilitated the collection of the Repeal Rent in his parish, prompting an acknowledgement that 'the fund possesses not a more respected or unswerving supporter'.[280] In 1845 he was one of more than 350 'clergymen and electors, and other inhabitants of the County of Tipperary', which list included a mayor, aldermen and town commissioners, parish priests, curates, vicars-general and archdeacons, and businessmen petitioning for Repeal.[281]

Research on Clerihan is compromised by the loss of its earliest Catholic parish registers which 'were accidentally burned about that date [1852] & during the incumbency of the Revd Wm Heffernan P.P.'.[282] Furthermore, its boundaries did not coincide with any civil parishes, so we cannot check Heffernan's population estimate against the statutory censuses. Nonetheless, if we assume a mean household size of 5.5 in the parish (population 1,925) we would expect to see more than 20 deaths during a normal October – March six-month period, above the 13 deaths that were reported for the pre-Famine period. The picture Heffernan presented in the return for October 1846–March 1847 is one of

278. Heffernan had been curate in Templemore in 1839, but was in Clerihan by October 1840: *Catholic directory and annual register for 1839,* 131; *Dublin Morning Register*, 17 October 1840
279. *Limerick Chronicle*, 29 January 1845; *Freeman's Journal*, 27 January 1845; *Dublin Evening Post*, 29 March 1845.
280. *Dublin Weekly Register*, 26 November 1842; *The Nation*, 9 March 1844; *The Pilot*, 1 October 1845.
281. *Tipperary Vindicator*, 24 September 1845.
282. https://registers.nli.ie/registers/vtls000632685#page/5/mode/1up.

severe misery and social dislocation, with 'prospects [...] most gloomy'. In keeping with his long-held political position, he concluded his report with a call for an Irish parliament.

Return of Revd William Heffernan, P.P. of Clerihan:

Number of deaths from the 1st October, 1846 to 1st April 1847? 30.
Number of same known to be caused by famine? 12.
Number of deaths in same period last year? 13.

N.B. – This is the smallest parish in the county as far as regards population, containing only 350 families.

The farmers are next to bankrupts; enormous taxation equal to the rent; inexorable landlords; the occupiers of small farms not able to buy seed for a spring crop, and the land [left] idle; the labourers all discharged from the public works, and trying to live on the government rations; no fuel, no clothing, and bearing all with great patience; multitudes emigrating to America, and bringing the gold out of the country with them; altogether, the prospects are most gloomy. We are a nation of beggars, and will remain so until we have our own Parliament.

Source: *The Pilot*, 5 May 1847, 4.

Donohill and Kilpatrick (Anacarty), Cashel and Emly Diocese

Commentary

The return for the Catholic Union of Donohill and Kilpatrick (Annacarty) was compiled by Revd William Mullally, who was appointed parish priest in March 1845, arriving there from Borrisoleigh, where he had been curate.[283] His departure from Borrisoleigh provoked a public meeting where the following resolutions were passed:

> That the exemplary piety, zeal, and philanthropy of the Rev. Mr Mullally, late a Catholic curate of this parish demand a public expression of our unanimous sense of the many virtues combined in the person of this truly pious Divine.
>
> That rejoiced as we are at his elevation to a Benefice, we can with difficulty repress an envious feeling towards those who are to enjoy his presence, whilst we sustain an almost irreparable loss by his removal, for we can scarcely hope to be blessed with "his like again".
>
> That we deem simple words a very inadequate tribute to such exalted merit, and therefore resolve to commence a subscription, with the view to accompany the expression of our grateful sentiments with some respectable and lasting memorial of our sincere esteem, and veneration of his great worth.
>
> That Messrs John Cooke, of Rathmoyne; George Bourke, Daniel Fogarty, and Dr Pinchin, of Borrisoleigh, Nichols Bourke of Curraghbaha, Richard Chadwick, Stephen Ryan, Theobald Gilmartin, Michael Chadwick, Michael D. Ryan, and Patrick Ryan, of Borrisoleigh, be appointed a Committee, with power to add to their number (six to form a quorum) to carry our object into effect, and therefore are hereby entrusted with the preparation of an Address in accordance with these our resolutions, to be signed by our

283. *The Pilot*, 14 March 1845.

> Chairman on our behalf, and who are also authorised to purchase out of the fund to be collected, such testimonial as they shall deem sufficiently respectable, and suited to the high sense we entertain of his inestimable qualities.[284]

Mullally was not averse to involving himself in political affairs, and prominently supported O'Connell's various campaigns. The appointment of the county's MP, Richard Lalor Sheil to the vice presidency of the Board of Trade in 1839 prompted a meeting of the Borrisoleigh electors, chaired by Mullally, which affirmed their support for Sheil in the by-election.[285] Unsurprisingly, he supported O'Connell's political campaigns, contributing financially to his funding drives.[286] In 1833 he collected £21 13*s*. 'for the benefit of those who have undergone prosecution on the score of tithes'.[287]

Mullally's parish of Donohill and Kilpatrick is coextensive with the civil parishes of Donohill, Kilpatrick and Aghacrew, which had combined populations of 6,215 in 1831 and 6,977 in 1841.[288] In 1841, 36 per cent of the housing was classified as fourth class and the female illiteracy rate was 55 per cent. The area was overwhelmingly Catholic; the Public Instruction Commissioners reported the Protestant population at a mere 87. We estimate the Catholic population by mid-1845 at about 7,172, which would mean between about 81 and 122 deaths in a typical six-month period from October to March; well above the 22 that Mullally reported for the period between October 1845 and March 1846.[289] Mullally's return is one of only two which provides a breakdown of the number of deaths occurring per month (the other parish reporting monthly data was Clonmellon, County Westmeath). The rise in the number of monthly deaths is dramatic, jumping from seven deaths during October and November 1846, to one per day in April 1847.

Return of Revd W. F. Mullally, P.P. of Donohill:

Number of deaths from the 1 October 1846, to 1 April 1847	1846	October	2
		November	5
		December	10
	1847	January	13
		February	15
		March	26
Total			71

284. *Tipperary Free Press*, 12 March 1845.

285. *Tipperary Free Press*, 11 September 1839; B. M. Walker (ed.), *Parliamentary elections in Ireland, 1801–1922* (Dublin, 1978), 313; *Dublin Weekly Register*, 15 May 1830.

286. *The Pilot*, 23 August 1837.

287. *Tipperary Free Press*, 20 March 1833.

288. 1833 (634) *Abstract of Population Returns for Ireland, 1831*, BPP, 188, 192; 1843 (504) *Report of the Commissioners appointed to take the census of Ireland, for the year 1841*, BPP, 226, 230.

289. *First report of the Commissioners of public instruction, Ireland*, 45, 40c, 44c, 56c. The 1831 census figure is 34 greater than the Public Instruction Commissioners' count; accordingly we increased the Catholic population estimate for 1831 by 34, to 6,128.

In April, the current month, the deaths are 29 up to the 29th, showing a progressive increase of deaths.

Number of same known to be occasioned by famine	1847	January	2
		February	8
		March	8
Total...			18

In April, the current month, the number of deaths occasioned by famine is proportionably greater. The greater proportion of deaths may be ascribed to famine indirectly, being consequent on a subtraction of the usual quantity of food.

Number of deaths during the same period last year? 22. No deaths occurred in this parish during that period (*viz*. 1st October '45 to 1st April '46) from famine.

Source: *The Pilot*, 5 May 1847, 4.

Fethard, Cashel and Emly Diocese

Commentary

Michael Laffan was appointed parish priest of Fethard in the early 1820s and was promoted to archdeacon in 1832.[290] Laffan's commitment to the O'Connellite cause could not be doubted, contributing financially and morally to the many campaigns from a period before Catholic Emancipation had been secured, through to the struggle for Repeal.[291] Unable to attend a Repeal Banquet in Lismore in September 1843, attended by O'Connell, he was careful to send a letter of support, to be read before the meal.[292] The following year he attended 'The Great Munster Banquet to the Liberator', one of hundreds to do so.[293] In 1843 he secured election to Fethard Town Commission, becoming its Chairman.[294] O'Connell's imprisonment in May 1844 gave Laffan's political crusade a new focus. As Chairman of the Town Commission, he attended a mass rally of mayors and local-government members in Dublin in June 1844 demanding the release of O'Connell, and later that month in Tipperary 'the ever-vigilant patriot' was addressing meetings with the same aim, and organising 'a great collection [...] in sustainment of the national treasury [Repeal Association's funds]'.[295] Following the death of Valentine Maher, Liberal MP for Tipperary, Laffan was prominent in local attempts 'to select a representative who is a tried Repealer, and who is ready to vindicate in Parliament and elsewhere the unqualified legislative independence of Ireland',

290. *Dublin Observer*, 19 February 1832, 3, col a.
291. *Dublin Morning* Register, 25 May 1825; Dublin *Morning Register*, 4 December 1826; *Limerick Evening Post*, 15 August 1828; *Dublin Weekly Register*, 10 August 1844.
292. *Dublin Evening Packet and Correspondent*, 28 September 1843.
293. *Freeman's Journal*, 11 April 1844.
294. *Tipperary Free Press*, 5 July 1843; *Cork Examiner*, 17 June 1844.
295. *Dublin Evening Post*, 6 June 1844

and in 1846 he was instrumental in drawing the clergy of Cashel and Emly 'to come forward and place on record our unbounded and unalterable confidence in the wisdom, the prudence, experience, and long-tried integrity of the LIBERATOR'.[296]

Laffan's parish is located in south County Tipperary, near Clonmel. In 1841, 26 per cent of the housing was classified as fourth class and the female illiteracy rate was 58 per cent. Named as Fethard and Kilusty in Laffan's brief return, the area was severely impacted by the Famine. Given Laffan's firm commitment to O'Connell, it is perhaps surprising that his return contained so little detail. According to it, deaths during the period between October 1846 and March 1847 were running at six times higher than they had been in the same period twelve months earlier. In spite of this increase, however, Laffan claimed that, although 'extreme destitution' was common, the area had not been as badly affected as surrounding areas because of the efforts of the local clergy.

Return of Very Revd Archdeacon Laffan of Fethard:

Number of deaths from 1st October 1846 to 1st April 1847? 185.
Number of same known to be caused by the famine? 120.
Number of deaths during the same period prior year? About 30.

There have been many cases amongst these deaths of extreme destitution. The present condition of the people is much better than in many of the surrounding districts, owing to the increasing exertions of the clergymen of all creeds, and the landed proprietors. But there is a fearful prospect before us. May the great God look down upon us with mercy.

The land is in general in a state of tillage, and the crops are very promising. The extent of emigration has exceeded anything known or remembered by the oldest man here.

Source: *The Pilot*, 21 May 1847, 4.

Lorrha and Dorrha, Killaloe Diocese

Commentary

The Catholic union of Lorrha and Dorrha, in north Tipperary, was coterminous with the two civil parishes of Dorrha and Lorrha, in the barony of Lower Ormond, in north Tipperary. The parish priest of the Union was Revd Cornelius O'Brien, who was appointed to the parish in 1838, replacing Revd John Spain, who was translated to Birr.[297] Heavily involved in the life of his parish, he was commended in the press for his vigilance in keeping his parish free of agrarian disturbances:

> Even the enemy are obliged to admit the zeal and efficiency of the Catholic Clergy, throughout the disturbed districts in Ireland, in tranquillising the People. We take the following extracts from the *Limerick Chronicle* (a Tory print) – they will speak for themselves:

296. *Tipperary Vindicator*, 1 January 1845; *Tipperary Vindicator*, 8 August 1846.
297. *Tipperary Free Press*, 16 May 1838.

> The peaceable conduct of the parishes of Lorrha and Dorrha. in the northern part of Tipperary, and a large portion adjoining the Shannon, contrasted strongly with the disorganised state of several parts of Tipperary, may, in great measure, be attributed to the persevering exertions of the respected parish priest, the Rev. Cornelius O'Brien, who is continually inculcating obedience and submission to the law, and warning them, in particular, to hold no intercourse with strangers of doubtful character. The result is that not a single outrage has occurred in those parishes for a long period.[298]

Given O'Brien's commitment to peace and legal pursuits, it is unsurprising to see him as a member of the Repeal Association, and a supporter of O'Connell. He was prominent in relief efforts in his locality.[299] Hi thoughts were recorded in the local press:

> The crops in this neighbourhood look very well [July 1846], the late rain has much improved them. The wheat is most abundant, and will exceed any for several years past; should be have a continuance of fine weather for a few days the greater portion of it will be fit for the sickle. The oat crop also promises well, and will make up for the loss in the potato crop, which I regret to say, in many places, does not present a very healthy appearance.
>
> Relief of the poor – Public works are varying on in this and the adjoining parish [unnamed, perhaps Birr], and very few of the labouring classes are unemployed. Indian meal is sold here twice a week by Archdeacon Knox, Rev. Cornelius O'Brien, P.P., Col. Dwyer, J.P., Ballyquirke Castle, Doctor James Walsh, and Mr John Coughlan, at 1*s.* per stone to the labourers, and at 1*s.* and 9 *d.* per do, to the farmers. The people purchase the meal with eagerness and relish it very much. I regret to say that we have several cases of fever, but of a mild character.[300]

Notwithstanding these efforts, his parish was badly impacted by the Famine. The statutory censuses had reported populations of 7,382 in 1831 and 9,009 in 1841, representing a yearly growth rate of two per cent.[301] In 1841, 38 per cent of the housing was classified as fourth class and the female illiteracy rate was 55 per cent. According to the Public Instruction Commissioners only 181 (2.4 per cent) of the inhabitants were Protestants in 1831, and we estimate the Catholic population of the union at about 9,175 in mid-1845, and about 7,685 by mid-1847.[302] O'Brien's figures for deaths are simply too low. A population of 9,175 would typically experience between about 104 and 156 deaths in a normal October – March period, well beyond the 40 deaths he mentioned for October 1845–March 1846.

298. *Dublin Monitor*, 3 June 1842.
299. *Tipperary Vindicator*, 6 February 1847.
300. *King's County Chronicle*, 22 July 1846.
301. *Abstract of Population Returns for Ireland, 1831* (1833), 634,194; 1843 (504) *Report of the Commissioners appointed to take the census of Ireland, for the year 1841*, 232.
302. *First report of the Commissioners of public instruction*, 230c. The Public Instruction Commissioners' figures for 1831 exceed the 1831 census population by 10; we have ignored this minor discrepancy.

His report is very brief, and provided information of a broad, general character. He wrote it 'in great haste'. Nontheless, he expressed a willingness to provide monthly statistics to the Association.

Return by Revd Cornelius O'Brien, P.P. of Lorrah and Dorrah:

Number of deaths from 1st October, 1846 to 1st April 1847? 143.
Number of same known to be caused by famine? 100.
Number of deaths during the same period last year? About 40.

On yesterday, my assistant, Rev. Mr Cleary, on visiting a townland, and hearing of a man being ill, and having been shown the house, he called at the door, and a little child, after some time, opened the door. He then asked where the father was? 'He is sick, sir'. He asked 'Where is your mother?' 'She is sick, sir.' 'Where are your brothers?' 'They are all dead, sir, and one is now dead in the corner.' This unhappy family consisted of seven on last week; now they are only three; and at the same time I write, perhaps not two. The land is partially tilled. If the public works be stopped the 1st May, the parish will be another Skibbereen. A great number have emigrated. It has been said Lord John Russell is no friend to emigration; but we can deny that, since his legislation is causing them hourly to emigrate to a land from whose boundaries no traveller has yet returned.

Lorha, Sunday morning, April 25.

Sir – I will feel most happy in supplying the Association with the information required monthly.

Excuse this, as I write in great haste, yours, &c.

C. O'Brien.

Source: *The Pilot*, 28 April 1847, 4.

Mullinahone, Cashel and Emly Diocese

Commentary

Mullinahone parish, in south-east Tipperary, near Callan, was coextensive with the civil parishes of Kilvemnon, Isertkieran and Modeshil.[303] Its parish priest was Revd Daniel Corcoran, appointed there, from Cappawhite, following the January 1846 death of the parish priest of long-standing, William O'Flanagan.[304] A supporter of O'Connell's

303. Lewis, *Topographical dictionary of Ireland*, ii, 218. It may also have covered Modeshil parish.
304. *The Pilot*, 21 January 1846.

campaign for Repeal,[305] it is, perhaps, a measure of how Corcoran was viewed by his Cappawhite congregation, that some of its parishioners publicly addressed him in this fashion:

> Sir, We the undersigned Protestant and Roman Catholic inhabitants of Cappawhite and its vicinity, beg leave to express our most unfeigned feelings of sorrow and regret at your removal from among us, and consequently the resignation of the clerical and other duties of this Parish, so faithfully performed by you during the last eleven years – duties arduous in every point of view – whether considered as regards the local situation of the parish, or the strenuous exertions used for both the temporal and eternal welfare of your hearers. The Sunday and Holiday duties in your Chapel, though discharged with all that zeal and fervor so characteristic of the Christian Pastor, were outstripped by your efforts in organizing those preparatory duties throughout your flock at all times needfull – at all times beneficial. When divested of your robes and in the every day habiliments of life, you were always found at the bed of the sick and indigent, administering what of earthly comforts they stood in need of; or, by pious exhortation and admonition, smoothing their path to another and better world. Ever alive to the well being and interest of society, you always inculcated upon your flock the necessity of their cultivating charitable and friendly feelings towards all denominations of Christians. Suffice it to say, that no exertions have been spared – in nothing have you been found wanting. We cannot refrain from casting a retrospective glance at that period when you first came amongst us – when party factions reared their head and party feuds ran high; and when you, by well-timed and praiseworthy exertions, harmonized the jarring strife then existing, and turned the boisterous stream of contending factions into the placid channel of mutual forbearance and brotherly love.
>
> We, now, dear Friend, take our leave of you, by invoking a blessing on your continual endeavors to impress on the flock now entrusted to your care the same mutual forbearance and brotherly love, and that blessing on your own head, which you so oft have implored for the inhabitants of this district.
>
> Believe us, dear Sir, yours, respectfully and truly,
>
> [Here follows 31 names, including two justices of the peace, and one lieutenant of the Revenue Police.[306]

In 1846, with the Repeal Association sundering over the Peace Resolutions, Corcoran, along with most priests in his diocese, sided with O'Connell, and renewed his membership subscription.[307] The following year he supported the drive, successful, as it was, to secure the return of two Repealers in the county's election.[308] He was also central to relief efforts in the parish, and a conduit for information from

305. *Tipperary Vindicator*, 27 September 1845.
306. *Tipperary Free Press*, 18 February 1846
307. *Tipperary Vindicator*, 1 August 1846; *Freeman's Journal*, 18 August 1846.
308. *Tipperary Vindicator*, 23 June 1847.

the central authorities. When a parish relief committee was established in April 1846, to confront 'the awful calamity of an approaching scarcity of potatoes', Corcoran was a committee member, alongside his curate John Cooney, and the incumbent Revd Edward Labaite.[309]

Return of Revd Daniel Corcoran, P.P. of Mullinahone:

Number of deaths from the 1st October 1846 to the 1st April 1847? 40.
Number of same known to be caused by famine? 20.
Number of deaths during the same period last year? 20.

The people are weak from want of a sufficient supply of food. We have a soup kitchen in Mullinahone for the destitute. The committee are making arrangements for the small farmers, and the labouring classes who are to be removed from the works on the 1st of May.

A great proportion of the land in this parish remains untilled for the want of seed. No assistance in this way given by any landlord in the parish to their tenants; they are collecting their rents with the usual rigour. We have received no subscriptions from forty landlords who hold property here. Four generous persons have contributed according to their means to aid our funds, which were raised by the poor farmers and by local clergy.

Source: *The Pilot*, 5 May 1847, 4.

The pre-Famine statutory censuses had reported a steadily advancing population in Corcoran's parish, rising from 5,528 in 1831 to 6,357 by 1841.[310] In 1841, 32 per cent of the housing was classified as fourth class and the female illiteracy rate was 61 per cent. The population was almost uniformly Catholic. The Public Instruction Commissioners identified only 72 Protestant inhabitants in the parish in 1831.[311] We estimate the Catholic population at about 6,500 by mid-1845, which means that deaths of the order of 62–93 would have been experienced in a typical October – March period. The deaths reported by Corcoran lie well below the minimum number that could be expected for both periods, suggesting that they are only partial counts.

309. *Dublin Evening Packet and Correspondent*, 23 April 1846.

310. *Abstract of Population Returns for Ireland, 1831*, BPP, 196; 1843 (504) *Report of the Commissioners appointed to take the census of Ireland, for the year 1841*, BPP (1833), 634, 234.

311. *First report of the Commissioners of public instruction*, 45, 52c.

Thurles, Cashel and Emly Diocese

Commentary

Thurles Catholic parish was coextensive with the Church of Ireland union of Thurles, which incorporated the neighbouring vicarages of Athnid, Rahelty, Shyane.[312] In 1841, 39 per cent of the housing was classified as fourth class and the female illiteracy rate was 58 per cent. The Cathedral Church of the archdiocese was the Cathedral of the Assumption, in Thurles, and the parish's clergy included Archbishop Michael Slattery. Its return was compiled by the parish priest, and Administrator of the Diocese, Revd William Barron. Barron was curate of Thurles by 1838, translated there from nearby Boherlahan.[313]

Barron was a moderate Nationalist, and a vocal and financial supporter of Repeal and O'Connell.[314] At a 'large and influential meeting of the inhabitants of Thurles and neighbourhood' held in the town in June 1844, Barron proposed 'that we, in common with every true-hearted Irishman, deeply and intensely sympathise with the Father of our Country [O'Connell] upon his being thrown into prison, for no other crime save that of loving his country too well'.[315] Unsurprisingly, when the Association split in 1846 Barron remained with the mainstream O'Connell grouping, seconding a resolution at a meeting of the clergy of Cashel and Emly which expressed 'sincere regret [on] the secession of Mr Wm Smith O'Brien from the Repeal Association, and we do feel the deepest gratitude for the many important services rendered by him to the National Cause'.[316] He was widely involved in affairs in his parish. He contributed to the local poor-relief fund in Thurles, and to the parish's Temperance Movement, as well as the compensation fund for Theobald Mathew, to rescue him from his 'pecuniary embarrassments'.[317] In 1844, 'on the ever to be remembered 30th of May 1844', the day of O'Connell's conviction for 'conspiracy' he lodged £1 in the Thurles Repeal Fund.[318] At the Monster Meeting of the supposedly 'six hundred thousand men' at Knockroe, near Thurles, in 1845 Barron was prominent on the 'substantial platform of about one hundred and twenty feet long, by forty broad'.[319] In April 1846 he contributed the substantial sum of £10 to the newly established local Relief Committee, which immediately invested in wheat, to be sold 'at first cost'.[320]

312. Lewis, *Topographical dictionary*, ii, 623.
313. *Dublin Weekly Register*, 25 June 1836; *Catholic directory and annual register for 1838*, 116.
314. *Dublin Weekly Register*, 18 January 1840; *Dublin Weekly Register*, 12 December 1840; Tipperary *Vindicator*, 6 July 1844.
315. *Tipperary Vindicator*, 8 June 1844.
316. *The Pilot*, 10 August 1846.
317. *Tipperary Free Press*, 5 August 1840; *Dublin Morning Register*, 16 January 1841; *Tipperary Vindicator*, 4 January 1845.
318. *Tipperary Vindicator*, 6 July 1844.
319. *Tipperary Vindicator*, 27 September 1845; *Freeman's Journal*, 27 September 1845. These and other claims as to attendances at Repeal meetings should be taken with a large pinch of salt.
320. *Tipperary Vindicator*, 4 April 1846; *Tipperary Vindicator*, 29 April 1846.

Barron's was a large parish. The statutory censuses had reported populations there of 12,199 in 1831, rising to 12,701 in 1841.[321] Thurles was a large market town and its inhabitants were overwhelmingly Catholic. The Public Instruction Commissioners identified only 296 Protestants (2.5 per cent) in the 1831 census, but as the combined populations in the Public Instruction report fall 428 below the 1831 census figure, we can only roughly estimate the Catholic numbers for the parish for 1845.[322] However, if we assume that the Catholic population in 1845 was of the order of 12,500, Barron's figures for deaths between October 1845 and March 1846 are around half the total that might be expected. During the Famine six-month period deaths increased considerably, and mortality in the workhouse was running at catastrophic levels.

Barron's submission to the Association, more detailed than many of the more curt responses, spoke of a catastrophic situation in Thurles. Three hundred people had died between October 1846 and March 1847, not including hundreds of victims in the public institutions, and were it not for the efforts of the local Relief Committee, many hundreds more would have perished. Half the parish was destitute, a quarter more in 'great want'. Politics had frustrated relief, compelling a walk-out of the Catholic clergy from some of the local relief bodies, and 'every step taken during the last six months in the way of legislation [he complained] has been one of greater bungling and confusion', and utterly contradictory. The town's workhouse could offer little by way of additional relief, as 'our poorhouse was built to accommodate 700 – we had about three weeks ago [March 1847] 900 packed into it'.[323]

Return of Revd William Barron, R.C. Administrator, Thurles:

Number of deaths from 1st October, 1846 to 1st April 1847? Nearly 300; and in the three weeks of April passed nearly 100 more – a remarkable fact. The above numbers are exclusive of the deaths in our Fever Hospital and poorhouses, which I believe would, if added, make the total nearly 800!
Number of same known to be caused by famine? At least 300 have pined and died by the famine.
Number of deaths during same period last year? About 70.

We have had but few cases of persons dropping dead from absolute starvation, but hundreds have died and pined of hunger and pestilence brought on by famine, as also by the mode of relief. We have at the present moment thousands of walking

321. *Abstract of Population Returns for Ireland, 1831* (1833), 634, 188; *Report of the Commissioners appointed to take the census of Ireland, for the year 1841* (1843), 504, 226.

322. *First report of the Commissioners of public instruction*, 58c. The Public Instruction Commissioners' population count totalled only 11,771, 428 fewer than were enumerated in 1831.

323. *Weekly Vindicator*, 20 March 1847.

skeletons living deaths, and were it not for the unceasing watchfulness and extraordinary exertions of our relief committee thousands instead of hundreds would, I am satisfied, have perished.

The population of the parish was last September about 14,000; of these about 7,000 are in a state of great destitution, about 3,000 more in great want. There are between 30 and 40 noblemen and gentlemen holding property in the parish; three or four have subscribed liberally, some others, four or five of the principal and most wealthy have sent paltry subscriptions of 3*l.* 5*s.*, and 10*l.*, the rest nothing, neither this nor last year.

The new temporary relief (Soup Kitchen) act has not yet come into operation, this is owing in a great measure to the fact of the Catholic clergy having been forced to withdraw from the committees by the foul aspersions cast on their characters by a government official, who charged them with putting improper persons on the works, and that from base mercenary motives.

I believe not less than 1,000 poor famishing creatures have been dismissed from the works in this parish, without any substitute in the way of relief; this has caused vast suffering and certainly increased the number of deaths.

Upon the whole we have, alas! bitter reason to complain that every step taken during the last six months in the way of legislation has been one of greater bungling and confusion; nay, we have better reason to think that our rulers are absolutely demented. In the depth of dreary winter – in rain, and snow, and sleet, and storm – they forced our poor people out to work from morning until dark, standing in puddle or perched on heaps of cold stones which absorbed every spark of caloric in their shivering frames. In this state or in rags saturated with rain, they returned at night to their dreary cabins, without perhaps a spark of fire or morsel of food, or piece of blanket other than the dripping rags worn during the day. Now that the weather is mild, fit for out door work, they are to be relieved gratuitously – to be fed in idleness. Does not the thought force itself on the mind that those in whose hands the destinies of our unfortunate people are placed are literally demented!

Half the sum granted by the British Parliament to purchase liberty for the black slave – at all times better lodged, infinitely better fed, than millions of their own free born fellow subjects – properly managed in administering relief, would have saved the lives of the hundreds of thousands sacrificed through the narrow mindedness or heartlessness of our statesmen.

As to emigration I can state – that it is far and away beyond all precedent. The people generally in this parish are making great exertions to till and sow the land and without the assistance of the landlords.

Source: *The Pilot*, 5 May 1847, 4.

Toomevara, Killaloe Diocese

Commentary

The return for Toomevara was compiled by Revd John Meagher, parish priest there since at least October 1827, when he was a member of the Toomevara Dispensary Committee, which voted 'sincere thanks' to him for his 'firm and manly stand against Proselytism'.[324] A moderate nationalist, Meagher was a supporter of O'Connell from the days of the struggle for Catholic Emancipation, making his chapel available for collecting substantial funds for the Catholic cause.[325] He also involved himself in popular political causes, including the campaigns against tithes, and for the reform of municipal government, and stood firmly against agrarian disturbances in his parish, through 'incessant, disinterested exertions to prevent crime and preserve the peace of the country'.[326]

Meagher was especially exercised by the matter of Repeal, and he fulsomely supported, in his words, leaving 'England to *mismanage* her own affairs'.[327] He chaired 'a most numerous meeting of the parishioners of Toomevara' in June 1844 which strongly condemned 'Tory domination and bigotry' following the imprisonment of O'Connell and passed resolutions calling for the withdrawal of Liberal Irish MPs from the Commons.[328] The following Sunday

> Under the presidency of the Rev. Mr. Meagher, P.P., the men of Toomevara will assemble on Sunday to raise their indignant voice against, the unjust and tyrannical measures adopted by a Jacobinical and insane faction against the peace and prosperity of Ireland in the person of our beloved Liberator, and the state traversers. Toomevara will send forth a loud shout for freedom and independence, liberty and Young Ireland. Hurrah for Repeal is the cry – Ireland for the Irish is the watchword under the shadow of the Devil's Bit.[329]

Passing through Toomevara *en route* to Derrynane, following his release from incarceration, Meagher led 'enthusiastic crowds' and 'several of the active patriots of that important district' to welcome The Liberator.[330]

Given Meagher's deep involvement with his community and his commitment to O'Connell's campaigns it is, perhaps, surprising to find his report to be as brief as it is. According to his count, deaths in Toomevara in the period between October 1846 and March 1847 were 2.5 times the number reported for the same six-month period a year previously. Toomevara's Catholic parish was coextensive with the civil parishes of Aghnameadle, Ballymackey, Kilkeary and Templedowney, and may have also covered Ballygibbon. If only the former four parishes were spanned, we would expect to see

---

324. *Tipperary Free Press*, 21 November 1827.
325. *Tipperary Free Press*, 10 March 1830; *Dublin Morning Register*, 21 January 1831; *The Pilot*, 15 January 1834.
326. *Dublin Morning Register*, 31 May 1836; *Limerick Reporter*, 1 August 1843; *Tipperary Vindicator*, 6 April 1844.
327. *Tipperary Vindicator*, 29 June 1844.
328. *Dublin Evening Post*, 13 June 1844.
329. *Dublin Weekly Nation*, 15 June 1844.
330. *The Sun (London)*, 30 September 1844.

between 94 and 141 deaths reported from there for the pre-Famine six-month period, from a Catholic population which we estimate at about 8,280. If Ballygibbon civil parish was also within the bounds of the Catholic parish the range for expected mortality increases to between 109 and 164 deaths. Meagher's figures for deaths fall well below the lower end of the range for both periods, meaning that his numbers represent only a partial count of deaths. Looking at social indicators, in 1841 55 per cent of the housing in Toomevara was classified as fourth class and the female illiteracy rate was 59 per cent.

Return of Revd J. Meagher, P.P. of Toomevara:

Number of deaths from 1st October 1846 to 1st April 1847? 50.
Number of same known to be occasioned by the famine? 30.
Number of deaths during the same period last year? 20.

No resident landlords; no subscription from landlords; the people perishing since the public works ceased; cruel and murdering delay in putting the relief system into operation, in consequence of the inexplicable and cumbrous queries and crotchets with books to be filled up. This crisis, between the putting people off the works, and delaying the relief till finance committees and inspectors are satisfied, is the most alarming that has occurred yet; much land untilled for want of seed, no landlord assisting – emigration was great'.

Source: *The Pilot*, 28 April 1847, 3.

County Waterford

Aglish and Whitechurch, Waterford and Lismore Diocese

Commentary

The Catholic parish of Aglish and Whitechurch is located in west County Waterford, near Dungarvan. In 1841, 31 per cent of the housing in the *civil* parish of Aglish (not coterminous with the Catholic parish of Aglish and Whitechurch) was classified as fourth class and the female illiteracy rate was 82 per cent. The return for the parish was compiled by its parish priest, Revd John or Jeremiah O'Meara. O'Meara was 'an eminently respected supporter' of the Repeal Movement, a popular position in the parish, which was served by 45 Repeal Rent collectors and 4 Repeal Wardens.[331] When Waterford's Repealers gathered for a 'great demonstration on the hill of Ballybricken', near Waterford City, in July 1843, O'Meara was there, leading his parishioners. When O'Connell appeared 'he was greeted by a cheer such as was not heard in Ballybricken since the year 1826', when the Beresford interest was trumped.[332] O'Meara was steeped in the social life of his parish, even funding prizes for the annual Aglish Races, and was well-equipped to provide information to the Repeal Movement on distress in his parish.[333] In 1846

331. *Weekly Freeman's Journal*, 18 December 1841; *Dublin Morning Register*, 1 January 184; *Dublin Weekly Register*, 23 December 1843; *Weekly Freeman's Journal*, 14 December 1844.
332. *Dublin Evening Post*, 11 July 1834.
333. *Waterford Chronicle*, 15 October 1842.

he was involved in attempts to provide emergency relief in his district, where 'the potato crop was totally destroyed'.[334] The mortality figures provided by Revd O'Meara do not, as he mentioned, include children, who were buried without recourse to a priest. They are also no more than broad estimates, as no regular register of deaths was kept in the parish, but they do point to a threefold increase in the number of deaths during the Famine.

Return by Revd J. O'Meara, P.P. of Aglish and Whitechurch:

Number of deaths in this parish from 1st October 1846 to 1st April 1847? 360.
Number of deaths during the same period last year? 120.

We have no regular register of deaths in this parish, nor can we, as several of the children are buried without any notice given to the parochial clergy. I should think that in the period above required to be reported on fourteen deaths each week is a low average, so that for the whole time I may safely state the number of deaths in the parish amounts as above stated to at least three hundred and sixty.

Some few were found dead in the fields, and were supposed to have died of famine. The three-fourths of the mortality was produced by lingering starvation, added to the cold public works during the winter, with not more than half the usual rations to the poor, from the low wages allowed, and the exorbitant price of the cheapest food.

Five in the week is rather a high average. I think it is rather over the number when I say that within the corresponding period of the preceding year the deaths were 120.

It is remarkable that the poor people here are more pleased than afflicted when one of their family dies! I have known a poor man who buried two of his children, and thanked God that a third was dying. The poor fellow was a loving father and an excellent member of society – sober, industrious and religious, and appeared delighted that his child was taken away before he should witness the distress of such times. I know another virtuous poor fellow who said he was happy when his wife (whom he always treated with attention, and who deserved his affection) died because she was happy and he might escape starvation with his short earnings to support himself and the rest of his family.

The soup kitchens are at work, but the rations are too scanty, and are sufficient only to prolong life – to make it a sickly thing, miserable to the individual, and of no value for the purposes of society or the state. Tillage of large farms tolerable, but small ones altogether neglected for want of capital to prepare and sow them.

Every man who can make out as much money as will enable him to tear away himself and family from the endearments of his native land, is emigrating to America. This is a sad picture, but a true one!

Source: *The Pilot*, 21 May 1847, 4.

334. *Cork Examiner*, 26 August 1846.

PROVINCE OF ULSTER

Summary of the returns for Ulster

County	Parish	Deaths		
		Oct. 1845– Mar. 1846	**Oct. 1846– Mar. 1847**	**... from famine**
Antrim	Ahoghill	18	37	11
	Cushendall	15	43	6
Armagh	Kilmore	37	182	136
Cavan	Ballymachugh and Drumlumman South	19	76	50
	Killinagh	28	168	139
	Knockbride	24	109	35
	Mullahoran	42	225	164
Donegal	No return.			
Down	Rossglass	NA	NA	NA
Fermanagh	Galloon	80	200	140
	Killesher	13 Caths; 10 Prots	43 Caths; 17 Prots	20 Caths; Prots, unknown
Londonderry	Desertmartin and Kilcronaghan	40	84	35
	Faughanvale	NA	No increase	0
	Kilrea, Desertoghill and Tamlaght O'Crilly, pt of	No registry	62 adults; *c.* 30 children	0
Monaghan	Tyholland	10	50	3
Tyrone	Ardstraw East	No registry	113	20
	Cappagh	NA	656 + 388 in workhouse	22 + 49 in workhouse
	Donaghmore	26, age 10+; 10 aged below 10	30, aged 10+; 22 aged below 10	50% of deaths
	Termonamongan	NA	46	20

County Antrim

Ahoghill, Down and Connor Diocese

Commentary

The Catholic parish of Ahoghill is located in west County Antrim, near Lough Neagh and the river Bann. The return for the parish, one of only two returns received from County Antrim, was compiled by Revd John Lynch, parish priest there since 1834.[335] Lynch was a local, born in Portglenone in 1805, and his transfer from Cushendall to his home parish was effected to reduce tensions between Orangemen and Catholics.[336] The area, in west Antrim, near Ballymena Town, was a predominantly Presbyterian region. The Public Instruction Commissioners reported nearly 15,000 people in Ahoghill Church of Ireland parish (which was much larger than the Catholic parish), and Catholics accounted for only 1,840 (12.3 per cent) of the population. Presbyterians accounted for almost 90 per cent of the Protestant community.[337] In 1841 31 per cent of the housing in the *civil* parish of Ahoghill (not coterminous with the Catholic parish of Ahoghill) was classified as fourth class and the female illiteracy rate was only 22 per cent.

Lynch's report depicts an area where the Famine did not strike particularly badly, at least as compared with returns from the midlands, the south and west. Undoubtedly, much of the population was suffering, occasioned both by food shortages and economic difficulties. His reference to the state of the linen trade is interesting, though it is not clear if he was speaking of the spinning or the weaving side of the trade, and his number for deaths in the period between October 1846 and March 1847 is double that of the year previously.

Return by Revd John Lynch, P.P. of Ahoghill:

Number of deaths from 1st October 1846 to 1st April 1847? 37.
Number known to be caused by famine? 11.
Number of deaths for the same period last year? 18.

General approach of want, occasioned at this particular time by the almost total ruin of the linen trade and want of other employment.

Fever is already spreading in some districts. We have soup kitchens well managed, and most impartially, in Portglenone, Ahoghill, and Cullybarkey [Cullybackey], by which the lives of multitudes have been unquestionably saved.

We are considering the necessity and means of providing a small hospital at Portglenone. An address to the poor will be issued immediately from

335. *Belfast Commercial Chronicle*, 28 June 1837. O'Laverty gives Lynch translated to Ahoghill from Cushendall in 1832 (James O'Laverty, *Historical Account of Diocese of Down and Connor*, 4 vols, Dublin: J. Duffy, 1878–87, iii, 405.
336. O'Laverty, *Historical Account, Down and Connor*, iv, 560.
337. *First report of the Commissioners of public instruction, Ireland*, 212a.

Cullybarkey, calling on them to present themselves clean at the soup kitchen, and warning them to have their houses cleansed, and the dung pits at their dwellings filled with earth or bog within a fortnight, when a visit or inspection may be paid, on pain of forfeiting their rations.

I cannot say as yet more of our prospects for next year than that the land is, I think, entirely cropped by the landlords in some instances. By wealthier neighbours, who bought the potato ground from the poorer occupiers for this year, in others.

I lament to say that corn has been sown in land in many instances not suited for it, and thus partial failure so far is to be apprehended. Besides, the early sowed corn looks very sickly, and in a few instances corn sowed in good and suitable ground looks thin and unpromising: all, however, will depend on the potato, whose fate is yet in the hands of a merciful God. There are enough planted to work a restoration if they do well.

There is a considerably larger quantity of turnips, carrots, and parsnips sowed in this neighbourhood than we ever had before; what they will do for use we cannot estimate with any certainty, yet, I hope, I have answered your inquiries.

Source: *The Pilot*, 11 June 1847, 4.

Cushendall, Down and Connor Diocese

Commentary

Located on the north-east coast of County Antrim, Cushendall had a predominantly Catholic population. In 1841, 33 per cent of the housing in the *civil* parish of Layd (not coterminous with the Catholic parish of Cushendall) was classified as fourth class and the female illiteracy rate was 56 per cent. The return for the parish was compiled by Revd John Fitzsimons, a native of Lisburn, who had been translated to the parish from Saintfield, County Down, in September 1837.[338] In 1842–4 Fitzsimons found himself involved in a bitter and remarkable scandal in relation to Irish-language schools funded by the Presbyterian Home Mission in Irish-speaking areas of the Glens. These schools had been established by the Home Mission to proselytize children by teaching them through the medium of Irish, and many of the 'schools' were shown to be fictitious, with teachers drawing salaries, though not teaching. Fitzsimons and the parish priest of neighbouring Culfeightrin, Luke Walsh, publicly exposed the fraud by way of a published pamphlet – *The Home Mission Unmasked* – and by letters to the press, highlighting schools that were registered in places that did not exist, fictitious names of students on reputed schools' lists, and funding claims for schools located elsewhere in Ireland. 'There is no school, there are no scholars', observed Fitzsimons, noting that it was his duty to expose the fraud, 'both in justice to the Presbyterian public, and myself'.[339]

338. O'Laverty, *Historical account, Down and Connor*, iv, 561; *Freeman's Journal*, 7 November 1837.
339. *Dublin Weekly Register*, 23 December 1843.

> I, Francis Brennan, for eighteen years inspector of schools under the Irish Society, and, for the last seven years, in the employment of the Synod of Ulster, in the same capacity, being struck with remorse, and the accusations of conscience, for having, for such a length of time, in violation of its dictates, lent myself, and been instrumental in propagating a system hostile to the faith of the church in which I was bred, and one which is founded on fraud and deception, now feel it a duty which I owe to God, to society, and myself, and in order to make what reparation and satisfaction in my power, and to remove, as far as I can, the scandal I have given, to come forward and expose the system of delusion and deception employed by the agents of the Home Mission to pervert the Catholics, and deceive the people of their own communion. I, therefore, declare that the following class-rolls and fictitious schools were fabricated and manufactured by the nominal masters whose names they bear, with my approbation and connivance, for the purpose of obtaining money; and that the superintendent himself knew (as in the case of Hugh Sheals) that there were no such schools, but said it was necessary to admit them, till the persecution, as he called it, would blow by, in order to keep up the credit of the mission. The above declaration I make voluntarily, without either reward or the expectation of it, in order to repair, as far as I can, the injury I have done to society, and hoping God may forgive me.
> Given under my hand this 9th day of November, 1843.
> Francis Brennan, Late Inspector of Schools to the Synod of Ulster.
>
> Source: O'Laverty, *Historical account, Down and Connor*, iv, 509.

Fitzsimons was a supporter of the Repeal Association and O'Connell was particularly pleased to receive support from Ulster, offering the questionable observation that such contributions showed the popularity of the cause there. Cushendall's seven enrolled members and the 275 associates contributed a handsome £21-5s. The press reported, '[t]his contribution from the most Northern part of Ireland (the Glens of Antrim) may be taken as a slight proof that the desire of the people for a repeal of the odious Act of Union is anything but abated'.[340]

The seven full members included Fitzsimons and Revd John M'Graham, his curate.[341] Fitzsimons' submission described conditions in his parish as 'very bad', and his figures for deaths suggest a three-fold increase between October 1846 and March 1847 compared with the same period a year previously. Notwithstanding his claims, the area was not suffering distress to the degree that was being experienced elsewhere. The population of the area declined only modestly between 1841 and 1851, a sign that the famine impacted less in this area than in other locations. The population of the two civil parishes of Ardclinis and Layd declined by just eight per cent, from 6,464 in 1841 to 5,950 ten years later.[342]

340. *The Vindicator*, 5 March 1845.
341. *Dublin Weekly Nation*, 8 March 1845.
342. 1843 (504) *Report of the Commissioners appointed to take the census of Ireland, for the year 1841*, 268; 1856 (2134) *Census of Ireland 1851*, 382. The population data are for the two civil parishes and for the Grange of Inispollen and the Grange of Layd. The boundaries of these four administrative areas probably do not coincide with the boundaries of Cushendall Catholic parish.

A few weeks before his submission, Fitzsimons received £10 relief for clothing from the Belfast Ladies Association, which may have been hinted at, but was not specifically mentioned in his report.[343] He was Chairman of the Cushendall and Redbay Relief Committee, responsible for distributing gratuitous relief, which, in contrast to sentiments felt by priests elsewhere, noted, in September 1847, that

> Our duties as a Relief Committee being about to terminate, we cannot think of allowing this opportunity to pass by without expressing our earnest thanks, and deep sense of gratitude, to Government, for the efficient and timely assistance afforded by them to these Electoral Divisions, whereby very many of our fellow-beings have been rescued from falling untimely victims to famine and pestilence... That we beg also to express our satisfaction at the comparatively economical manner in which the Relief Act has been carried out in these Divisions, and to state as our candid opinion, that when willingly and fairly carried out, it was, notwithstanding all the abuse that has been unjustly lavished on it, exceedingly well calculated to attain all the ends for which it was passed, and to carry into effect the benevolent intentions of the Government.[344]

Return of Revd J. Fitzsimon, P.P. of Cushendall

Number of deaths from 1st October, 1846 to 1st April 1847? 43.
Number of same known to be caused by famine? 6.
Number of deaths during the same period last year? 15.

The present state of this parish is very bad; destitution increasing rapidly – most of the small farmers are now in want. The relief committee under the new act is affording great relief; it is working well, and is likely in a great measure to meet the existing distress.

The land is generally tilled, but the prospects of the coming year are not good. Some few farms are lying waste for want of seed – there is a great failure in the oaten crop.

Emigration to a great extent has taken place. In fact all who are able to raise the means are going to America, leaving behind a pauper and miserable population; land lords exacting rents.

Source: *The Pilot*, 11 June 1847, 4.

County Armagh

Kilmore, Armagh Diocese

Commentary

The Catholic parish of Kilmore, in north Armagh, was coextensive with the civil parish of the same name. Kilmore was a large, populous parish. Its parish priest was Patrick Quinn, located there since at least 1834/5.[345] Quinn was a fierce opponent of the Tories,

343. *Belfast Protestant Journal*, 8 May 1847.
344. *Dublin Evening Post*, 30 September 1847.
345. *First report of the Commissioners of public instruction*, Ireland, appendix II, 41.

his public stance evidenced by the passage of a series of forceful resolutions against the party, and in favour of Liberal interests, at a meeting of his parishioners, and chaired by him, held in Kilmore chapel in February 1840.[346] At the meeting 'the evils of Tory misrule' were pointed out by Quinn.[347]

> At a numerous meeting of the parishioners, held at the Parish Chapel [of Kilmore], the Rev. Patrick Quinn, P.P., having been called to the Chair, the following Resolutions were unanimously adopted:
>
> Proposed by Mr. John Kiegan, Jun., and seconded by Mr. Owen M'Neile.
> Resolved – that we yield to none in loyalty and attachment to our beloved Queen, and are determined to use every constitutional means in our power to assist in preventing the return of her enemies and the enemies of Ireland, the Tories, to power.
> Proposed by Mr Edward M'Donnell, and seconded by Mr Patrick M'Cann.
> Resolved – that we fling back with contempt the vile calumnies of the itinerant or slanderous defamers of our venerable Catholic Clergy and the faithful people of Ireland.
> Proposed by Mr Bernard O'Hagan, and seconded Mr John M'Grane.
> Resolved – that the Melbourne Administration is entitled to our best support for giving us such Viceroys as the great and good Marquis and his worthy successor, Lord Ebrington.
> Proposed by Mr Thomas Lennon, and seconded by Mr James Corrigan.
> Resolved – that we are determined not to relax in our exertions until we obtain these just rights and privileges for Ireland, or till Roman Catholics are placed on an equality with their Protestant and Dissenting fellow subjects.
> Proposed by Mr Peter Finnegan and seconded by Mr William Adams.
> Resolved – that an Address to the Queen, and a Petition to the House of Commons, grounded on the foregoing Resolutions, be drawn out and signed by this meeting.
> Proposed by Mr James Fearon, and seconded by Mr Arthur Tersney.
> Resolved – that the Address and Petition be forwarded to Lord Acheson for presentation.
> Proposed by Mr Francis O'Hanlon, and seconded by Mr. James Tersney.
> Resolved – that the foregoing Resolutions be published in *The Vindicator* and *Newry Examiner.*
> Patrick Quinn, P.P., Chairman. John Kiegan, Jun., Secretary.[348]

Repeal was a popular cause in Kilmore, with the *Dublin Weekly Register* in July 1844 listing the names of 166 parishioners, men and women, who invested in the cause, including Quinn, who donated £1 and Edward M'Gurk, his curate, who added 5*s*. Quinn's stance on the Repeal Question is unlikely to have aided the fostering of cordial interdenominational relations, which were strained.[349] In 1843 Quinn told the Association that his Church of Ireland counterpart, Revd James Jones, 'had dispossessed ten families from his property', prompting a rebuke from The Liberator. 'He [O'Connell] said if the reverend gentleman alluded to [Jones] were a pastor, he appeared to be better fitted for shearing his flock than for tending them in any other way'.[350]

346. *The Vindicator*, 5 February 1840.
347. Ibid.
348. *The Vindicator*, 5 February 1840.
349. *Dublin Weekly Register*, 27 July 1844, 7.
350. *Dublin Weekly Nation*, 29 April 1843, 12.

By spring of 1847, on the eve of the Death Census, a serious crisis was unfolding in the parish, prompting a desperate letter from Quinn to the editor of *The Vindicator* newspaper publicising the fact.

> Sir, It is painful to me to have to inform you, that destitution has been sorely felt for some months past, and is daily increasing, in this parish. Within the last twelve days I have attended thirty-two sick persons, and out of that number (most of whom have since died) twenty-seven were ill from want of human food. On yesterday evening, after attending two chapels, had to visit five persons, all under twenty-five years of age, and all suffering from the one only cause – want! want!! I have just come in this instant from visiting a boy whom I left speechless. Whilst I write he is surely dead. His disease and death were brought on solely from want of sustenance. There are hundreds of families in this locality, with four, six – aye, some ten acres of land, suffering the severest privations – privations unknown beyond their own threshold, except by a confidant. Their actual state of misery they keep secret – first, from a spirit of decency; and, secondly, seeing no immediate hopes of relief likely to arise from its being known. What blight! falling on as fertile soil and as moral and industrious a people as any to be found in all Ireland. True, we have three relief committees in this parish; but the funds are so small, that two-thirds, in want, can get none at all; and what is given is not, by any means, sufficient to support existence,
>
> I am, Sir, your obedient servant, Patrick Quinn, P.P. Kilmore, County Armagh, March 1, 1847.[351]

Quinn reported an even sorrier state. The pre-Famine statutory censuses had recorded 14,034 inhabitants in 1831, rising modestly to 14,256 by 1841. In 1841, 21 per cent of the housing was classified as fourth class and the female illiteracy rate was 38 per cent. Kilmore was one of the few parishes contributing to the Death Census which did not have a majority Catholic population.[352] The Public Instruction Commissioners noted 3,735 of those recorded in the 1831 census as Catholics (some 26.6% of the total). It is a challenge to reconcile that Catholic population estimate with Quinn's estimate of 450 Catholic families [households] in the parish (equivalent to *c.* 2,500 population), although rural industrial areas such as Kilmore may have had large numbers of Catholic servants living within Protestant households.[353]

We estimate the Catholic population by mid-1845 at about 3,950, falling to about 3,600 two years later. Based on this estimate for the pre-Famine period we would expect to see between 45 and 67 deaths, October 1845 to March 1846. Quinn's reported number of deaths (37) is slightly shy of the lower bound. His return suggests that mortality in the parish soared in the six-month period after October 1846.

---

351. *The Vindicator*, 6 March 1847.
352. *Abstract of Population Returns for Ireland, 1831*, BPP (1833), 634, 228, 230; *Report of the Commissioners appointed to take the census of Ireland, for the year 1841*, BPP (1843), 504, 278, 280.
353. *First report of the Commissioners of public instruction, Ireland*, 45, 148a, 168a. If all Catholics lived in Catholic households this would represent a mean household size of 8.3, which is too high. However, in an area with a strong Protestant community it is likely that some Catholics would have had employment in Protestant households.

Return of Revd Patrick Quinn, P.P. of Kilmore:

Out of the Catholic population of this parish in August last, consisting of 450 families, the number of deaths from 1st October 1846 to 1st April 1847 is 182.
Number of the same known to be caused by famine? At least three-fourths of the above number died from destitution, or 136.
Number of deaths for the same period prior year? 37.

This parish at present presents a horrid picture of famine, though one of the most fertile soils in all Ireland; with few exceptions the people are all beggars, receiving outdoor relief some four days, others every day in the week, from relief committees; all supported by various contributions. None of these four in all are under the new poor law act. The Richardson family, of Rich-hill, Castlehan, have come forward to the rescue most admirably. Most of the land is sown in grain.

Source: *The Pilot*, 28 May 1847, 4.

County Cavan

Ballymachugh and Drumlumman South, Ardagh Diocese

Commentary

The return for the parish of Ballymachugh and Drumlumman South was compiled by Revd Patrick Murray, parish priest since at least 1837.[354] In 1841, 43 per cent of the housing in the *civil* parish of Ballymachugh (not coterminous with the Catholic parish of Ballymachugh and Drumlumman South) was classified as fourth class and the female illiteracy rate was 67 per cent. Murray was a supporter of O'Connell, and, alongside many of the Catholic clergy of Ardagh, a loyal member of the Repeal Association.[355] In 1841 Murray responded to a call from the Association for parishes to organise local meetings against the Tories, by delivering a petition signed by 1,095 of his parishioners, and he facilitated the collection of the Repeal Rents and Tributes for O'Connell in his parish.[356]

The Catholic parish of Ballymachugh and Drumlumman South was not coterminous with any combination of civil parishes, so it is not possible to reconstruct the population of the parish from the statutory census figures. According to Murray the number of deaths in the period from October 1846 to March 1847 was about four times higher

354. https://registers.nli.ie/registers/vtls000632377#page/4/mode/1up.
355. *Freeman's Journal*, 2 February 1841.
356. *Freeman's Journal*, 12 June 1841; *Freeman's Journal*, 11 August 1843; *Freeman's Journal*, 21 June 1844; *Dublin Weekly Nation*, 3 January 1846.

than it had been during the equivalent period a year previously. Significantly, Murray states that he only included Catholic deaths in his statistics, and he speculated that the mortality among Protestants was likely lower, as their circumstances were generally better.

Murray appears to have been confused over dates when presenting his mortality statistics. He spoke of 15 deaths from starvation in the month of May 1847, but it seems likely that he meant April 1847, as his letter was published in *The Pilot* on 7 May. Also, he claims his figures for pre-Famine deaths are from 1 November to 1 May, but the stipulated period was 1 October to 1 April. The number of deaths he gives coincides with burials recorded in the parish register for the later period, which is reassuring.

Return of Revd P. Murray, P.P. of Ballymachugh and Drumlumman South:

Number of deaths from 1st October 1846 to 1st April 1847? 76; and in the month of May 15 more by starvation.
Number of same known to be caused by famine? 50.
Number of deaths for the same period last year? 19.

Two of the number died on their return from the public works. One of the others, fearing that he would not be able to 'bring round' his family, as they say, got into a gloomy state of mind and poisoned himself by taking arsenic. The wife of a small farmer named Denny had her throat cut by her husband, who got into a state of phrenzy from a similar cause.

The parish is at present in an awful state from fever and dysentery; the mortality is consequently not diminishing. Four hospitals in connexion with the workhouses of Cavan and Granard, with which this union is connected, are not prepared to receive patients. The public works were all closed in the middle of this week. There is little or no employment; no issue of food, cooked or otherwise, from the rates. In Ballymachugh there is a relief fund, from which the committee hope to supply limited rations for another week, after which time they expect that the relief from the rates will be available. In Drumlumman there is no relief fund; no supply of food of any sort. Private charity is taxed and exhausted. We hope for an issue of meal early next week. Disappointment in this respect, it is to be feared, may be followed by an outbreak and attack on property, or by numerous deaths by starvation, as the poor have not one hour's credit or a meal's provision. The rations allowed by the temporary relief (Soup Kitchen) act are ordered by finance committees to be reduced, in order that the rates may not be swamped! Thus attaching more value to property than to human life. The full rations allowed by law will hardly support human life; if curtailed, it must be totally inadequate for that purpose.

I am sorry to say that much of the holdings of the small cottier tenants remain untilled, and likely to continue so. The destitution is so general and deep that it has caused a prostration of energies and a hopelessness on the part of the occupiers likely to result in diminished supplies during the coming autumn. Many of the poor people had hoped, but in vain, that the government or the landlords would supply them with the seed, and in this expectation sold their grain to procure meal for their starving families. The breath of potatoes planted is not one tenth – perhaps I should say a fifteenth part of what it usually was in preceding seasons. The prospects of the ensuing year are therefore very gloomy.

Emigration has been on a large scale this spring, and it would have been still greater if the people had the means of going where, as they say, 'they would be sure to get plenty to eat and plenty to do, and fair play and liberty into the bargain.'

In the 'Death Census' I have not included any Protestants, not having any register of them, or any other accurate means of ascertaining their amount. In Ballymachugh and Drumlumman they probably are to the Catholics as one to seven, but being in more comfortable circumstances, the mortality among them may be less in proportion.

Source: *The Pilot*, 7 May 1847, 1.

Killinagh, Kilmore Diocese

Commentary

Killinagh parish is located in the north-west of County Cavan, bordering Fermanagh and Leitrim. The Catholic parish's boundaries were coextensive with the boundaries of the civil parish of the same name. In 1841, 54 per cent of the housing was classified as fourth class and the female illiteracy rate was 78 per cent. Revd Hugh De Lacy, born 1790, had been parish priest of Killinagh since 1839, moving there from Glenade parish, County Leitrim.[357] The return for the parish was compiled by De Lacy, a supporter of O'Connell, and a member of the Repeal Association, as were many other priests in Kilmore diocese.[358] Notwithstanding, De Lacy was on good terms with the Protestant clergyman, and both were in league to secure relief for those suffering in the parish, as evidenced in his letter published in the *Freeman's Journal*, weeks before his Death Census report appeared.

357. MacKiernan, *Diocese of Kilmore*, 94, 182.
358. *Freeman's Journal*, 18 August 1841.

Black Lion. May 26th, 1847,
Dear Sir, I regret to tell you that we are in an awful state in this parish – *blessed* with absenteeism having no resident landlord or magistrate to give employ to the poor, provide for the wants of the indigent, or feel for suffering humanity. My house is hourly surrounded, by groups of living spectres, whose cries and aspects are capable of moving the most callous hearts, and calling on me in the name of the Most High to get them some support ere they fall victims to death. My poor people are dying in dozens of dysentery and fever, occasioned by bad and unwholesome diet; and famine lending them a helping hand in decimating the quandom stalworth sons and lovely daughters of the Emerald Isle is *nobly* doing the work of death. My curate and self are hourly employed in attending the dying and burying the dead, and in many instances, ere we can reach the abodes of misery the inmates are *no more*, and frequently are found lifeless by the ditch sides, not having had the happiness of receiving the comforts of religion at the hands of their pastor, or having a friend to close their eyes when breathing their last.

We have no provision depots in this large parish, and are obliged to send either to Sligo or Enniskillen (the former 20, the latter 18 miles from part of this mountainous parish) for bread stuffs, which are very frequently taken that distance on the backs of donkeys, or shoulders of poor creatures, who are not able to buy more than a stone or half a stone of Indian meal, unless they satisfy the exorbitant and more than famine demands of country venders.

The public works are nearly suspended in this parish, no relief measures as yet in operation in it. Dockens and nettles are eagerly sought for by famine-smitten creatures; wakes not thought of in the abode of poverty; dead bodies unburied for six or more days for want of the *last coat*, or friends to take them to their long resting place. Where this awful and appalling state will terminate the Most High only knows.

The lands are not tilled in a part of this parish, owing to the poverty of the people, and the cruelty of the landlords, who would not give them seed.

To give you an idea of the *sympathy* and *feeling* of some of the absentee landlords, permit me to tell you that the Rev. Mr. Echlin, the Protestant incumbent of this parish, a kind and charitable gentleman, wrote some months past to an extensive absentee proprietor of this parish to get something to meet the wants of his standing tenantry. That *charitable man* replied to the Rev. Mr. Echlin as follows:- "Sir, I am in receipt of your letter, and am glad to hear that there is a good understarving [understanding?] between yourself and the Roman Catholic priest; but I think you both would be better employed in making the tenants pay me their rents." I give you only a portion of the *elegant* reply of that *feeling landlord* and *Christian* soul, and will not at present give his name, a second application being made to him for his subscription: but should he be *deaf* to the calls of suffering humanity, and not contribute to relieve his Lazarus tribe, it would be no more than justice that his name and pedigree should be wafted on the wings of the press, and the remainder of his humane and refined letter given at full length.
I have the honour to be, dear Sir, your ever devoted servant,
H. De Lacy, P.P. Killinagh.[359]

359. *Freeman's Journal*, 29 May 1847.

Despite De Lacy's efforts, it did not protect his own personal property from attack, much to the amusement of the *Fermanagh Reporter.* The Rev. Hugh Delacy, of Killinagh, County Cavan,

> a most estimable and respectable priest, had been addressing his congregation on the present dreadful visitation, and used some tropes and figures about the "people slaying and eating all before them". Be that as it may, or whether Dolan and his son understood him literally, on Wednesday week they broke into their priest's cowhouse, out of which they took a fine springer, to calve 5th April, worth £10, and killed her in his own field, leaving the calf, entrails, and hide, and taking the flesh. The Dolans were committed to Cavan gaol by the Earl of Enniskillen, whom it was difficult to persuade that they had so outraged the priest's premises and property.[360]

The statutory censuses reported populations of 5,383 in 1831 and 6,512 in 1841.[361] The Public Instruction Commissioners reported 601 Protestants (11.2 per cent) and 4,782 Catholics in the parish for 1831.[362] Based on these data we suggest that the Catholic population may have been about 6,030 in mid-1845, and perhaps about 5,500 two years later. This would lead us to expect between 69 and 103 deaths in a normal October to March period, well above the 28 deaths reported by De Lacy between 1 October 1845 and 1 April 1846.

Return of Revd H. De Lacy, P.P. of Killinagh:

Number of deaths from 1st October 1846 to 1st April, 1847? 168.
Number of same known to be caused by famine and pestilence caused by famine? 139.
Number of deaths during the same period last year? 28.

This parish is, I regret to say, in an awful state; its inhabitants dying by dozens of dysentery and fever, occasioned by bad and unwholesome diet, and famine, lending them a helping hand, is nobly doing the work of death.

The lands are in many instances not tilled, the public works nearly all suspended, no relief measures yet in operation. The cropped lands look well and promise well.

We have no provision depots in this parish, and are obliged to send to either Sligo or Enniskillen – the former twenty, the latter eighteen miles, for bread stuffs;

360. *London Evening Standard*, 8 March 1847.
361. 1833 (634) *Abstract of Population Returns for Ireland, 1831*, BPP, 240; 1843 (504) *Report of the Commissioners appointed to take the census of Ireland, for the year 1841*, BPP, 300.
362. *First report of the Commissioners of public instruction, Ireland*, 38a.

and the generality of the parishioners are obliged, when able to get a stone or half a stone of Indian meal, to give an exorbitant price to the few country provision merchants.

We have no resident landlord or magistrate in this parish to employ the people, provide for their wants, or feel for suffering humanity. Where this awful state will terminate God only knows.

My curate and myself are hourly employed in attending the dying, or burying the dead; and in many instances, ere we can reach the abodes of misery the inmates are dead, and frequently are found lifeless by the ditch sides, without having had the happiness of receiving the comforts of religion at the hands of their pastor! or having a friend to close their eyes when breathing their last!!

We had a great emigration two months past, but other poor creatures, anxious to leave this land of misery and go to the land of the brave and the free, have not the means of emigrating.

Source: *The Pilot*, 11 June 1847, 4.

Knockbride, Kilmore Diocese

Commentary

Knockbride parish is located in east County Cavan, in Clankee barony, bordering County Monaghan. The parish priest was Revd Patrick Brady (b. *c.* 1800), a recent arrival, being translated to Knockbride from a curateship in Carrigallen in May 1844.[363] Brady was a supporter of Repeal and a member of the Association, as was his curate, Revd James O'Reilly.[364]

Brady's parish of Knockbride was coextensive with the civil parish of the same name. He notes in his return that the parish's population was about 8,000, of which 6,500 were Catholics (*c.* 18.8 per cent Protestant), but the statutory censuses tell a different story. According to the pre-Famine national censuses, the parish's population was 9,746 in 1831, rising to 10,603 by 1841.[365] The Public Instruction Commissioners put a different slant on the religious breakdown within the parish, too, identifying 1,598 Anglicans and 1,468 Presbyterians (31.5 per cent), compared with 6,680 Catholics in the 1831 census list.[366] In 1841 33 per cent of the housing was classified as fourth class and the female illiteracy rate was 58 per cent. Brady's figure for deaths between October 1846 and March 1847, which only cover adult Catholics, was four times those occurring during the equivalent period a year previously.

363. MacKiernan, *Diocese of Kilmore*, 40, 112, 185.
364. *The Pilot*, 11 July 1845.
365. *Abstract of Population Returns for Ireland, 1831*, BPP (1833, 634, 238; *Report of the Commissioners appointed to take the census of Ireland, for the year 1841*, BPP (1843), 504, 298.
366. *First report of the Commissioners of public instruction*, 40a.

Return by Revd Patrick Brady, P.P. of Knockbride:

Number of deaths from 1st October, 1846 to 1st April 1847? 109.
Number of same known to be caused by famine? 35.
Number of deaths during the same period last year? 24.

In some instances deaths were very sudden – before they could be visited by a clergyman. There are about 1,100 receiving relief under the late [Temporary Relief] act, though the majority of the committee hitherto refused extending it to those holding more than one acre of land. There is a great number of small farmers who are in a most destitute state; the committee have rescinded their restriction to relief, and are now embracing into their list all most likely to perish which will swell the list of applicants for relief considerably.

If the public works were resumed it would be a great means of affording relief to the able-bodied small farmers. Cess-payers are in the greatest alarm at the enormous rate already struck, which in our electoral division of the parish amounts to 9*s.* 3*d.* in the pound, the poor rate included.

There is a greater breadth of land sown than in any former year; some few of the small farmers are not able to procure seed; about one tenth the proportion of potatoes set in former years.

A considerable number have emigrated to America, and many more would go if they could dispose of their property or had the means.

N.B. – The Catholic population of this parish is 6,500, that of Protestant and Dissenters about 1,500. The 'death census' I send is exclusively Catholic, not including children, or those who have died in the poorhouses of each electoral division, which were very considerable.

Fever is on the increase, and deaths in proportion to the preceding months. The people are peaceable, and bear their afflictions with great resignation to the Divine will.

Source: *The Pilot*, 11 June 1847, 4.

Mullahoran, Ardagh Diocese

Commentary

The report for Mullahoran was compiled by Revd Philip O'Reilly, parish priest since at least 1841. In 1841, 51 per cent of the housing in the *civil* parish of Drumlumman (not coterminous with the Catholic parish of Mullahoran) was classified as fourth class and the female illiteracy rate was 69 per cent. O'Reilly was a member of the Repeal Association, as were most Catholic clergymen in Ardagh diocese,[367] and in 1843 he, and his curate, Revd William [or Archibald] Conofry, were appointed Repeal Wardens for the parish.[368] Towards the end of 1846 O'Reilly, shocked by the deaths of seven of

367. *Dublin Morning Register*, 2 February 1841; *Freeman's Journal*, 3 September 1844.
368. *Freeman's Journal*, 31 May 1843.

his parishioners from starvation, was prompted to pen a letter to the press highlighting the worrisome situation which was unfolding in his parish:

> Dear Mr Barrett, Duty claims from me the melancholy task of reporting to the authorities, through your valuable journal, that three persons died of starvation in this parish within the past week!! Should the calamity end in this extensive district, with *seven* already on the list of mortality, happy would we feel. But hundreds are faintly burning the lights, which will flicker off shortly unless the government interpose, or some other channel of relief. Hundreds on the Public Works, and five times the number starving. *I witnessed the dying mother, and her child dead on her milkless breast!!*
>
> What is the government doing? Must the appearance of the hitherto brave and athletic men, virtuous and comely women, with their children – the dear objects of their love – must they sink to a premature grave without sympathy, and those moral and obedient to the laws as any other portion of her Majesty's subjects?
>
> I have the honour to remain, dear Sir, your obedient servant,
> Philip O'Reilly, P.P., Mullahoran, Granard. 12th December, 1846.[369]

Notably, O'Reilly had highlighted the importance of Public Works as a critical relief measure in the area, so it is unsurprising to see 500 labourers 'set loose by the cessation of the Public Works' storming into Cavan Town in protest, though 'at the suggestion of the parish priest, Mr O'Reilly […] they separated peaceably'.[370] If O'Reilly was shocked by the deaths of seven of his parishioners by mid-December 1846, one can only imagine how he felt by April 1847, when he was reporting 164 deaths from famine to the Repeal Association. According to O'Reilly, famine deaths accounted for about three quarters of all deaths occurring in his parish during the six months after 1 October 1846. Unfortunately, the Catholic parish of Mullahoran (or Drumlumman North) was not contiguous with any combination of civil parishes, so we are unable to estimate its Catholic population with any degree of confidence.

Return of Revd Philip O'Reilly, P.P. of Mullahoran:

Number of deaths from 1st October 1846 to 1st April, 1847? 225.
Number of same known to be caused by famine? 164.
Number of deaths during the same period last year? 42.

The reverend gentleman says – The husband, wife, and three children, all lying at the same time when I visited them, all dead; the mother in another case just breathing her last, and her child, about three months old, died while attempting to take nourishment from the breast of the mother; many cases equally revolting: the parish extensive, population dense, destitution commensurate, no local subscriptions, no gentry, the small farmers on the public works could not sow their lands; a total neglect on the part of the cottiers in cropping their gardens; their prospects for the ensuring year truly melancholy; few isolated cases of emigration.

Source: *The Pilot*, 28 April 1847, 4.

369. *The Pilot*, 16 December 1846.
370. *Morning Post*, 8 February 1847.

County Down

Rossglass, Down and Connor Diocese

Commentary

The parish priest of Rossglass – also known as Bright – parish, was Revd John M'Kenna (b. 1807), who was translated, from Cushendall, County Antrim, in September 1837. McKenna was a supporter of O'Connell and the Repeal Movement.[371] In 1843 he chaired a 'very numerous and respectable' meeting of the parishioners of Bright called in favour of Repeal, and the following year his chapel-yard was opened to the parishioners to protest the exclusion of Catholics from the Special Jury Panel, drawn up in advance of O'Connell's State Trial.[372]

M'Kenna's return for Bright is the only known return for a County Down parish, and it is one of the few returns that did not report terrible local suffering. Although his return was devoid of the numerical information sought by the Repeal Association, his descriptive account depicts a parish barely impacted by the Famine. M'Kenna's return prompted Maurice O'Connell to comment that 'this, I believe, is the only instance from the commencement of these returns of a clergyman stating that his parish was in such a state that there were only three or four cases of fever, and not one death from starvation'.[373] M'Kenna's commentary should be compared with other favourable reports, such as those for Faughanvale, County Londonderry, and Stamullen, County Meath.

We may note that in 1841 only 14 per cent of the housing in the *civil* parish of Bright (not coterminous with the Catholic parish of Rossglass) was classified as fourth class and the female illiteracy rate was 38 per cent.

Return of Revd John M'Kenna, P.P. of Bright:

The afflicting intelligence of the death of the Liberator prevented me from replying sooner to our circular regarding the census of deaths.

As neither the famine nor disease has occasioned any remarkable increase of mortality in this parish, I do not think it necessary for me to make a special return.

We have been very mercifully dealt with as regards disease in this parish; only three or four cases of fever; no death from starvation. We are under the 'temporary relief [Soup Kitchen] act,' and are about to adopt the voluntary system of assessment. We had done so for a considerable time before we went under the act.

Source: *The Pilot*, 16 June 1847, 2.

371. O'Laverty, *Historical account, Down and Connor*, i, 162.
372. *The Vindicator*, 1 April 1843; *The Vindicator*, 27 January 1844.
373. *The Pilot*, 16 June 1847.

County Fermanagh

Galloon (Drumelly), Clogher Diocese

Commentary

The Catholic parish of Galloon (Newtownbutler) in south Fermanagh, bordering County Monaghan, is broadly coextensive with the civil parish of the same name. The return for the parish was submitted by Revd James Clarke, its parish priest. Clarke was a Repealer, and a supporter of O'Connell, as were many other priests in Clogher diocese. Following the imprisonment of The Liberator in 1844 the priests of Clones District, one of whom was Clarke, issued the following resolution:

> On Tuesday last, 9th July, the following, being the united address of the six parishes of Clones district, was presented at Merrion Square by Dr M'Gennis, and John M'Mahon, esq:
>
> Illustrious Liberator and brave fellow-countrymen: We, the clergy and people of the six parishes of Clones district, feel it as a sacred duty of justice and religion to offer you, in your prison, our feelings of condolence in the unworthy punishment with which you have been visited, and to express our congratulation upon the triumphant position to which you have raised the great national cause of Repeal.
>
> We feel the indignities perpetrated on you as an insult to a father; we resent your imprisonment was a wrong against Ireland, and an outrage upon universal justice; and whilst we pledge ourselves to an eternal execration of Saxon injustice, we pray to assure you, at once, of our undying attachment to yourself, and of our unalterable determination to be guided by your counsels; and, come what may, to support you, as best we can, in all you may have yet to act or suffer in the cause of Ireland..[374]

The following year Clarke was praising O'Connell as 'the Defender of the Faith' when aligning himself with O'Connell and Archbishop MacHale in opposition to Archbishop Murray, and 'the anti-Catholic and subjugating tendency of the Bequests Act' whilst his curate, M'Nally, was of the view that an appeal to the 'Eternal City' was in order over the same matter.[375]

Clarke was a member of the Newtownbutler Relief Committee, which supported the construction and improvement of road and rail transport infrastructures, for the purpose of provision of relief. However, a meeting of the 'guardians, highest cess-payers, and principal acting clergymen of all denominations' held in Newtownbutler in March 1847, with Clarke in attendance, proved a curious affair. Chairing the meeting was the Earl of Erne, who 'strongly recommended political economy in every department. In illustration of his views he produced, to the no small amusement of the meeting, a small sample of bread composed of rice, Irish meal (it appears he is an Irishman), and barm'. The meeting called for the maintenance of funding for public road works, especially in Galloon parish, 'as the roads in many places are impassable', and Clarke called for the provision of gratuitous coffins for paupers. Yet, in spite of

374. *Freeman's Journal*, 13 July 1844. Signed by over a dozen clerics.
375. *Freeman's Journal*, 22 January 1845.

the evolving catastrophe, and in a snub to the chairman, it was moved by Mr G. Porter, and seconded by Rev. P. Maguire, P.P. of Maguires-Bridge, 'that nothing short of a federal Irish parliament could save Ireland from general bankruptcy'.[376]

According to Clarke, a registry of deaths was 'duly kept in this [Galloon] parish'. The population of the civil parish was reported by the statutory censuses at 10,507 in 1831, rising to 11,135 a decade later.[377] In 1841, 36 per cent of the housing was classified as fourth class and the female illiteracy rate was 51 per cent. The parish had a substantial Catholic majority – the Public Instruction Commissioners reported the Catholic population at 6,641 (63%) in 1831.[378] We believe the Catholic population may have reached about 7,300 by mid-1845, before dropping to perhaps about 6,250 two years later. A population of this order would typically see between about 83 and 125 deaths in the October 1845–March 1846 period. Clarke's count of deaths for this period, which he extracted from his 'duly kept' parish register, is close to the lower-bound figure, leading us to believe that his return represented an effort to report all deaths occurring in the parish. His data suggest that mortality more than doubled during the Famine period over the previous year.

Return of Revd James Clarke, P.P. of Galloon:

According to the registry of deaths which is duly kept in this parish, the number of deaths from the 1st October, 1846 to 1st April 1847 are 200.
Number of same known to be caused by famine? 140.
Number of deaths during the same period last year? 80.

The farmers, despairing a reduction in rack rent, are selling their farms and emigrating to the land of liberty. Small farmers, tradesmen, and labourers, being unable to procure employment publicly or privately, are going to England or elsewhere to avoid the horrors of famine, leaving their wives and families behind them in a state of starvation.

The relief committees of this parish, for so far, have done very little in order to arrest the progress of famine. Fever and dysentery are daily increasing, and mowing down the people to a most alarming extent. It is the general opinion that when the temporary relief [Soup Kitchen] act comes into operation in the different divisions it will bear no proportion to the magnitude of the distress; therefore it will be necessary for the government to grant some other measures which will effectually save the lives of the people.

The prospects of the coming year are far from being cheering. A considerable portion of the parish lies uncultivated, the tenants could not provide the seed, and were in many instances obliged to sell some of their stock in order to purchase provisions for themselves and their families.

Source: *The Pilot*, 11 June 1847, 4.

376. *Newry Telegraph*, 29 September 1846; *Newry Examiner and Louth Advertiser*, 3 April 1847.
377. 1833 (634) *Abstract of Population Returns for Ireland, 1831*, BPP, 262; 1843 (504) *Report of the Commissioners appointed to take the census of Ireland, for the year 1841*, BPP, 328, note.
378. *First report of the Commissioners of public instruction, Ireland*, 18a.

Killesher, Kilmore Diocese

Commentary

The Catholic parish of Killesher, in Clanawley barony, south Fermanagh, was coextensive with the civil parish of the same name. In 1841, 39 per cent of the housing was classified as fourth class and the female illiteracy rate was 59 per cent. The return for Killesher was compiled by Revd Francis Mason. Mason, curate of Kinlough parish in 1831, Newbridge, in 1835, and Shercock in 1836, became parish priest of Killesher in 1843.[379] A member of the Repeal Association,[380] Mason's report described a population experiencing extreme distress, with bodies swollen by malnutrition, and 'gaunt famine and pinching hunger' abounding. Gratuitous relief helped but was insufficient. The area was relatively thinly populated; the statutory censuses reported a population of 5,114 in 1831 and 5,225 in 1841.[381] This suggests a yearly growth rate of about 0.2 per cent. The Public Instruction Commissioners reported the parish's population to be roughly evenly split between Protestants (2,520, all Established Church) and Catholics (2,594). By mid-1845 the Catholic population may have reached about 2,750, which would indicate between 31 and 47 deaths of Catholics in the six months following 1 October 1845. Mason's numbers for this period fall well below this range, implying that not all deaths were being reported.

Although Mason's figures were only partial counts, they are especially important, as they facilitate a comparison between Catholic and Protestant famine mortality rates. For the pre-Famine six-month period deaths in the two broadly similarly sized communities were roughly the same (13 Catholics and 10 Protestants). But in the Famine six-month period a substantially higher mortality rate was reported for Catholics; 43 Catholics against 17 Protestants. The number of Catholic deaths – likely adults only counted – was more than three times higher in the October 1846–March 1847 period than it had been during the equivalent period 12 months previously.

Return of Revd Francis Mason, P.P. of Killesher:

Number of deaths from 1st October 1846 to 1st April 1847? 43 – all Catholics; and I understand from the Protestant curate that their number for same period, is about 17.
Number of above Catholics, who died in consequence of disease brought on from want of sufficiency of food? about 20.
Number of deaths during the same period last year? 13 – all Catholics; corresponding number of Protestants, same year, 10.

Some of the persons in the first column, after their entire day on the public works, returned with their limbs, heads, and bodies, greatly swollen, and did not live to the following morning. None of them remained unburied for any

379. MacKiernan, *Diocese of Kilmore*, 188.
380. *Dublin Weekly Nation*, 24 January 1846.
381. 1833 (634) *Abstract of Population Returns for Ireland, 1831*, BPP, 262; 1843 (504) *Report of the Commissioners appointed to take the census of Ireland, for the year 1841*, BPP, 278, 280.

serious length of time, owing, in a great measure, to the kindness of the Earl of Enniskillen, who has frequently supplied them with coffins gratuitously.

The state of the parish is at present alarming: gaunt famine and pinching hunger to be seen and met with in all quarters.

We have one large boiler, supported by local subscriptions and an equivalent government grant, at which about 600 destitute are moderately, but not sufficiently, helped three days in the week.

The class of small farmers who do not come within the provisions of the law are now the worst off, as they are receiving no relief, and generally have not been able to till their little holdings.

Emigration has been carried on to a great extent in this small parish, and is still going on. I believe about 50 entire families have gone this year to America, out of a Catholic population not amounting to 400 families.

Source: *The Pilot*, 28 May 1847, 4.

County Londonderry

Desertmartin and Kilcronaghan, Derry Diocese

Commentary

The united parishes of Desertmartin and Kilcronaghan are in south County Londonderry, in Loughinsholin barony, near the border with County Tyrone. The return for the united parishes was compiled by Revd James Collins, curate there since at least 1843, when he collected subscriptions for the Repeal Association, and subscribed £1 1*s*. to cover his membership fee.[382] Collins, 'the estimable coadjutor', was a vigorous supporter of the Association, regularly submitting small sums that he had collected from his parishioners.[383] The Catholic Union of Desertmartin and Kilcronaghan was coterminous with the two civil parishes of the same names. The Union's population was reported in the statutory censuses at 9,120 in 1831 and 9,368 in 1841.[384] In 1841, 38 per cent of the housing was classified as fourth class and the female illiteracy rate was 37 per cent. The Public Instruction Commissioners reported the religious breakdown in 1831 as evenly split; 4,541 Protestants and 4,579 Catholics. We estimate that the Catholic population may have reached about 4,900 by mid-1845, which would produce between 56 and 84 deaths in normal times (October to March). Collins' report of 40 deaths between October 1845 and March 1846 lies below the lower-bound limit, suggesting that not all deaths were included in his figures. He reports a doubling of the death-count in the six months after 1 October 1846 compared with the previous half-year's total. 'Great numbers' were emigrating, which must have helped save many lives.

382. *Freeman's Journal*, 5 December 1843.

383. *Dublin Weekly Register*, 9 November 1844; *Dublin Weekly Register*, 4 January 1845.

384. *Abstract of Population Returns for Ireland, 1831*, BPP (1833), 634, 270; *Report of the Commissioners appointed to take the census of Ireland, for the year 1841*, BPP, (1843), 504, 336.

Return by Revd James Collins, curate of Desertmartin:

Number of deaths from 1st October, 1846 to 1st April 1847? 84.
Number of same known to be caused by famine? 35.
Number of deaths during the same period last year? 40.

Typhus fever and dysentery prevailed to an alarming extent in these parishes since the month of February last, a great many fell victims to fever, and a still greater number died of dysentery.

The system of outdoor relief, since it came into operation here, is calculated to *increase rather than alleviate* the horrors of famine – the food which these poor famine-stricken victims receive at these relief depots is neither in quantity or quality sufficient to sustain nature.

Each family on an average does not receive more than a quarter pound per day of 'very unwholesome food' for every member of the family, and many of these families are distant six or seven miles from the depots from which they receive this *sham relief.*

The land in this locality (particularly of small farms) is only partially cultivated, and that, too, at an unusually late season.

There are vast numbers of the population of those parishes emigrating to America and other countries – not less than 150 of our people have left for America alone, not taking into account the great numbers that are emigrating to England and other parts.

Source: *The Pilot*, 28 May 1847, 4.

Faughanvale, Derry Diocese

Commentary

Faughanvale parish is located in north-west County Londonderry, on the southern shore of Lough Foyle, in Tirkeeran barony, close to Londonderry city. In 1841, 42 per cent of the housing was classified as fourth class and the female illiteracy rate was 34 per cent. The return for the parish was compiled by Revd Michael Hughes, a supporter of O'Connell, and his campaign for Repeal. In 1844 Hughes was praised in the press for his support of the O'Connell Tribute: 'Faughanvale, county of Derry, has spiritedly supplied the handsome sum of £12 to the Fund, and we need not say that such manifestations from Ulster possess vast value'. Hughes personally contributed £1 10*s*, while three others sent £1 each.[385]

Described as a 'a faithful and unceasing patriot',[386] Hughes collected £7 7*s* 6*d*. from his district in early 1845, an amount deemed an 'acceptable sum' by the Repeal Association.[387] According to Hughes, the Famine had barely touched the parish

385. *Dublin Weekly Register*, 6 January 1884.
386. *Freeman's Journal*, 10 March 1846.
387. *Dublin Weekly Register*, 5 October 1844; *The Pilot*, 14 February 1845.

at the time his report was compiled. He failed to report mortality figures but observed that the numbers dying and emigrating were no more than normal, and the Temporary Relief [Soup Kitchen] Act was providing food to the destitute poor, replacing the public-works relief that had been in place during the winter. Significantly, although the potato crop was small – less than half the normal crop – the famine was not impacting greatly on the parish, evidence of the lesser dependence of areas of Ulster on the potato. Hughes' commentary should be compared with other favourable reports, such as those for Rossglass, County Down, and Stamullen, County Meath.

Return by Revd Michael Hughes, P.P. of Faughanvale:

Number of deaths not known; but they are not more than other years.
No deaths by famine.
Number of deaths in former years not known.

Each electoral division has its [relief] committee, and the whole parish is under the [temporary] relief act. During the winter the destitute poor were supported by charitable subscriptions and work [i.e. public works]. Land is tilled as usual. Potatoes more than one half less than former years. Emigration, at their own expense, not more than in other years.

Source: *The Pilot*, 28 May 1847, 4.

Kilrea, Desertoghill and Part of Tamlaght O'Crilly, Derry Diocese

Commentary

Located in east County Londonderry, the Catholic union of Kilrea, Desertoghill and part of Tamlaght O'Crilly had experienced some of the ill effects of famine by the time Revd Samuel Otterson sat down to complete his return, though circumstances were not as bad as elsewhere in the country. Otterson had been parish priest of Kilrea since the close of the 1830s, having been curate there before his promotion.[388] In 1841, 31 per cent of the housing in the *civil* parish of Kilrea (not coterminous with the Catholic parish of Kilrea, Desertoghill and part of Tamlaght O'Crilly) was classified as fourth class and the female illiteracy rate was 28 per cent. Otterson was not shy about batting for his own area, as shown by his contention that Kilrea should be chosen over Ballymoney as the centre of the Poor Law Union. At the public meeting called to decide the matter Otterson, with others, spoke in favour of Kilrea, although he acknowledged, correctly as it turned out, the pointlessness of the discussion since 'the affair had already been disposed of'.

A supporter of O'Connell, Otterson was a member of the Repeal Association, in keeping with most Catholic clerics in the diocese of Derry.[389] In spite of his politics, however, he does not appear to have exaggerated the scale of the crisis for

388. *Catholic directory and annual register for 1838*, 93, *Catholic directory and annual register for 1839*, 114.
389. *Freeman's Journal*, 28 June 1844.

advantage, although a veiled criticism of the administration can be seen in his comment regarding the export of locally grown foods. He did not consider famine to be a direct cause of any deaths in his parish, although he recognised that it might have indirectly caused one-third of them. Otterson estimated the number of deaths in his parish in the six months after 1 October 1846 at about 92, including children, although he does not provide comparative figures for the earlier six-month period.

Return by Revd Samuel Otterson, P.P. for Kilrea:

Number of deaths in this parish from 1st October 1846 to 1st April, 1847? Adults 62. Children not registered – not being able to obtain an account of their deaths, we may say with tolerable accuracy, 30.Number of same known to be caused by famine? None can be exactly stated as having died of famine, but famine has been the distant cause of at least one-third of each of the two numbers mentioned. Number of deaths during the same period last year? There was no registry [of deaths] kept before the year 1846.

No case very remarkable. Present state disheartening. The soup establishment will serve the low class, but the class of what we may call the second rate farmers will be very badly off. Land is tolerably tilled. The prospects of support for the ensuing year are sufficiently good, if the crops get leave to stay in the country; but if grain be shipped off, as in former years, there will be a deficiency at least to the amount exported.

The quantity of potatoes planted here is so trifling, that they will not serve much even if they should turn out good in quality. Emigration is about treble that of other years. Numbers are going off.

Source: *The Pilot*, 28 May 1847, 4.

County Monaghan

Tyholland, Clogher Diocese

Commentary

The return for Tyholland parish, in north County Monaghan, on the border with Armagh, was compiled by Revd Peter McMahon, parish priest there since at least 1834/5.[390] McMahon was an active Repeal supporter, and his parish was described by the Association as 'one of the most zealous and active parishes [for Repeal] in Ulster'.[391] He was in attendance at the 'magnificent demonstration at Clontibret' in favour of Repeal, held in 1843, humorously reported on by the *Newry Telegraph* as attended by 'three hundred thousand (nearly one-third of a million!) peaceful,

390. *First report of the Commissioners of public instruction*, appendix II, 42.

391. *Belfast Commercial Chronicle*, 12 September 1835; *Dublin Morning Register*, 22 March 1842; *Dublin Weekly Register*, 18 March 1843.

resolute, but determined men!!! We have no record of the numbers of women and children in attendance.'[392] Notwithstanding McMahon's political views, however, he could work effectively with clergymen of other persuasions. In 1840 Mr. Walker, an agent of the Irish Temperance Union visited the parish, and spoke in the Catholic chapel at a meeting attended by, and addressed by, Revd Mr Bleakley, the Presbyterian Minister.[393]

McMahon's return for Tyholland parish is the only submission available from County Monaghan. McMahon's parish was coextensive with the civil parish of Tehallan. Its population was recorded as 4,846 in the 1831 census, but fell back to 4,630 in 1841.[394] In 1841, 43 per cent of the housing was classified as fourth class and the female illiteracy rate was 54 per cent. The inhabitants were predominantly Catholic, but there was a small Protestant community as well. The Public Instruction Commissioners counted 791 Protestants (16.3 per cent) in the 1831 census list.[395] We estimate the Catholic population at slightly above 4,000 by mid-1845, from which we would expect about 46 to 69 deaths in a normal October to March period; so McMahon's 10 deaths between 1 October 1845 and 1 April 1846 cannot include all deaths in the parish. He reported the numbers dying in the parish between October 1846 and March 1847 to have been five times greater than his figure for the earlier period. McMahon attributed a mere three deaths to starvation, compared with ten times that amount occurring from disease, a by-product of famine.

Return of Revd P. McMahon:

Number of deaths from 1st October, 1846 to 1st April 1847? 50.
Number of deaths from starvation, 3, and by dysentery and dropsy, brought on by bad diet, 32–35.
Number of deaths during the same period last year? 10.

The landlords are obliging their tenants to banish all the cottiers and pull down the houses, in order to get rid of the surplus population. A great number are getting help, but not sufficient in quantity or quality to keep them alive any time. The land in this parish is almost all tilled, and the crops look well. About ten families have gone to America, and many more would go if they could. The most of the labourers in this parish have gone to Scotland and England, having no employment at home.

Source: *The Pilot*, 28 May 1847, 4.

392. *Newry Telegraph*, 22 August 1843.
393. *Dublin Weekly Herald*, 25 April 1840.
394. *Abstract of Population Returns for Ireland, 1831*, BPP, (1833), 634, 274; *Report of the Commissioners appointed to take the census of Ireland, for the year 1841*, BPP (1843), 504, 344.
395. *First report of the Commissioners of public instruction,* 26a.

County Tyrone

Ardstraw East, Derry Diocese

Commentary

Named as 'Ardstrane East' in *The Pilot*, this is the return for Ardstraw East parish, or Newtownstewart, in west County Tyrone. In 1841, 39 per cent of the housing in the *civil* parish of Ardstraw (not coterminous with the Catholic parish of Ardstraw East) was classified as fourth class and the female illiteracy rate was 45 per cent. The report for the parish was compiled by Revd A. O'Doherty, parish priest. O'Doherty's report is brief. According to it, 20 of his parishioners had died as a result of famine in the six months after 1 October 1846; in the same period for the preceding year none had died of such a cause. Soup relief was greatly aiding the situation in the parish, and was clearly saving lives there.

Return of Revd A. O'Doherty, P.P. of Ardstraw:

Number of deaths from 1st October 1846 to 1st April 1847? 113.
Number of same known to be caused by famine? 20.
Number of deaths during the same period last year? No registry kept in the preceding year, but not one from starvation.

The distress of the parish is awful at present, owing to the immense number of cottiers; however, the support that the destitute poor are getting from the temporary relief [Soup Kitchen] committee avails not a little to stay the present famine. Were it not for that, the deaths would be really alarming.

The land in general is in a state of tillage, and the crops are very promising. The extent of emigration has exceeded anything known or remembered by the oldest man here.

Source: *The Pilot*, 16 June 1847, 4.

Cappagh, Derry Diocese

Commentary

The Catholic parish of Cappagh is coextensive with the civil parish of the same name. The return for the parish was compiled by Revd Daniel O'Doherty, appointed parish priest on 4 July 1843. His curates were Revd William Coneglan and Revd Michael Conway. On his transfer there, O'Doherty commenced the parish's first register of vital events.[396] O'Doherty, and his two curates, were supporters of O'Connell's Repeal

396. https://registers.nli.ie/registers/vtls000632976#page/5/mode/1up.

campaign – O'Doherty was, in fact, a member of the Repeal Association Committee – and he was instrumental in delivering an impressive £77 to the Association by October 1844.[397] Little wonder that the Association could refer to him and his parish in the following fashion:

> Cappagh, county Tyrone – Here too the vividly patriotic and unflinching admirers of O'Connell have acquitted themselves most creditably by furnishing to the popular fund [O'Connell Tribute] their gift of gratitude and justice, amount £15 3*s.*, per Rev Daniel O'Doherty, Catholic Rector of Cappagh, whose love of Ireland and her champion befits the respected bearer of his high Milesian name, also of so many historical reminiscences. We willingly make room for the array of valued contributors associated with this demonstration of honest feeling: [there follows a long list of contributors from Cappagh parish, headed by O'Doherty, £1 1*s.*; Revd Michael Conway, curate, £1 and Revd William Coneglan, curate, 10*s.*][398]

The statutory censuses put the population of Cappagh at 13,589 in 1831, and the 1841 enumeration reported a slightly lower population of 13,330.[399] In 1841, 42 per cent of the housing was classified as fourth class and the female illiteracy rate was 55 per cent. The parish was roughly evenly split between Protestants and Catholics in 1831; the Public Instruction Commissioners put the numbers at 6,795 Protestants and 6,669 Catholics.[400] While we are unsure if the figures in O'Doherty's report include Protestants, he provides numerical evidence on a range of issues including death and emigration. O'Doherty claimed that total population loss in his parish during the six months from October 1846 was 1,354, or about 10 per cent of the 1841 count.

Return by Revd D. O'Doherty, P.P. of Cappagh:

Total number of deaths from 1st October 1846 to 1st April 1847? 656.
Number of same know to be caused by famine? 22.
Died in the workhouse of famine? 49. Total deaths in the workhouse same time as above? 388.
Emigrated to America? 464.
Ditto to England and Scotland? 144.

397. *Weekly Freeman's Journal*, 29 June 1844; *Dublin Weekly Nation*, 5 October 1844. For O'Doherty's committee membership, see *Freeman's Journal*, 10 August 1847.
398. *The Pilot*, 9 May 1845.
399. 1833 (634) *Abstract of Population Returns for Ireland, 1831*, BPP, 280, 282; 1843 (504) *Report of the Commissioners appointed to take the census of Ireland, for the year 1841*, BPP, 350, 352.
400. *First report of the Commissioners of public instruction,* 244a, 264a. The Public Instruction Commissioners were unable to identify the religion of 26 people, and there is a discrepancy of 99 between their figures and the 1831 census figures.

Persons gone into the workhouse, or gave up their places? 90.
Decrease in the [population of the] parish in six months? 1,354.

The above are the statistics of mortality, emigration, &c., in the parish of Cappagh, County Tyrone, and diocese of Derry, for six months, commencing October 1846, and ending April 1847.

The extraordinary and still continued press of parochial business prevented me from forwarding the census until the present.

Source: *The Pilot*, 28 July 1847, 2.

Donaghmore, Armagh Diocese

Commentary

Donaghmore parish is in south-east Tyrone, near the border with counties Armagh and Monaghan. Its parish priest at the time of the Death Census was Francis Devlin, who succeeding to the parish on 3 August 1845, from Tullyallen parish, following the death of Revd Neal M'Guckin, from fever.[401] Devlin was active in providing relief to the destitute during the Famine, contributing £10 of a total of £135 acknowledged in the press in December 1846 'in aid of the numerous and destitute poor' of the parish, and receiving contributions for distribution. The *Dublin Weekly Register* carried the following article in March 1847:[402]

> We have very great pleasure in recording, at the instance of the respected Catholic Rector of Donaghmore, Dungannon, the Rev. F. Devlin, an instance of the great benevolence of disposition which characterises Master Litton as a landlord. The Rev. Mr Devlin received on yesterday an order from the Master, on his agent, for the sum of twenty guineas, to be distributed by the reverend gentleman among the poor of the parish of Donaghmore; and we have great pleasure in conveying the reverend gentleman's grateful thanks for the benevolence.[403]

Although Litton's charitable contribution was substantial enough to merit, at Devlin's insistence, advertisement in the newspaper, when Devlin's report was compiled, about eight weeks later, the only mention of landlords in his submission was that some were 'starving their poor tenants out of their holdings, and tumbling down their cottages'.

401. https://registers.nli.ie/registers/vtls000632551#page/3/mode/1up; *Dublin Weekly Register*, 9 August 1845; *Galway Mercury and Connaught Weekly Advertiser*, 16 August 1845.
402. *Newry Telegraph*, 29 December 1846.
403. *Dublin Weekly Register*, 6 March 1847.

Devlin's parish of Donaghmore was coterminous with the civil parish of the same name. The 1831 statutory census reported a population of 12,142, which had barely changed at 12,333 by 1841.[404] In 1841, 20 per cent of the housing was classified as fourth class and the female illiteracy rate was 49 per cent. Catholics comprised the majority of the parish's population – the Public Instruction Commissioners reported 4,570 Protestants and 7,582 Catholics in the parish in 1831.[405] We estimate the Catholic population of the parish at about 8,000 by mid-1845, falling to about 7,150 two years later. Since a population of about 8,000 would normally experience between 91 and 137 deaths in a typical October – March period, well beyond the number of deaths reported by Devlin for both periods, it is clear that Devlin's mortality numbers did not include all of the deaths in his parish.

Return by Revd F. Devlin, P.P. of Donaghmore:

Number of deaths from 1st of October, 1846, to 1st of April, 1847? Above ten years [old], 30; under do., 22; total 55 [*sic.* 52].
Number of same known to be caused by famine? About one-half.
Number of deaths during the same period last year? Above ten years, 26; under do., 10; total 36.

The mortality in this parish very likely would have been much more appalling, were it not for the sources of private benevolence opened to us on the 27th of last October, by which we were enabled to sell meal at 1*d.* per lb to the industrious middle poor class, and *gratis* to the very poor; but 300 families then purchasing at this rate up to the opening of the relief committee as by law could not now purchase any – they, with 500 more families, are exhausted, have no money, or any possible means of procuring it. Our state then is getting much worse; and, far more alarming, fever and dysentery in every third house, and on the increase daily, the rations given being little, in general, more than one half of the government standard. The deaths have increased the last 40 days 30 per cent. Some landlords and middlemen are starving their poor tenants out of their holdings, and tumbling down their cottages. The fields are cropped in general – about one tenth of the usual quantity of potato. Unless some stringent law be quickly passed to stay the desolating angel bearing off the poor people, I cannot see where [this] woe shall end.

Source: *The Pilot*, 21 May 1847, 4.

404. *Abstract of Population Returns for Ireland, 1831*, BPP (1833), 634, 280, 282; *Report of the Commissioners appointed to take the census of Ireland, for the year 1841*, BPP (1843), 504, 350, 352.

405. *First report of the Commissioners of public instruction,* 140a, 154a. The Public Instruction Commissioners' population figure was 10 above the 1831 census figure.

Termonamongan, Derry Diocese

Commentary

The parish priest of Termonamongan parish, in west Tyrone, bordering County Donegal, was Revd John McCullagh, who had been based there since at least 1834/5.[406] McCullagh was a Repeal supporter, and, along with his near-neighbour, Revd Daniel O'Doherty, of Cappagh, a member of the Repeal Association's committee.[407] Given his political leanings, however, McCullagh's report is surprisingly brief, and his parish does not appear to have been suffering too badly from the stresses of fever and famine. The cultivation of oats on a considerable scale may have helped insure against the worst effects of poor potato harvests.

The Catholic parish of Termonamongan was coterminous with the civil parish of the same name. The population in 1831 was 7,253, and it had risen to 7,561 by 1841, indicating a modest yearly rate of growth of about 0.4 per cent. In 1841, 45 per cent of the housing was classified as fourth class and the female illiteracy rate was 67 per cent. The Public Instruction Commissioners found 2,333 of the 1831 population to be Protestant (32.2 per cent) and 4,920 Catholics (67.8 per cent). We estimate the Catholic population at about 5,350 by mid-1845, falling to about 5,100 by mid-1847. That size of population would deliver between 58 and 87 deaths in a normal October to March period. Revd McCullagh's return of deaths for the Famine six-month period fails to reach the lower-bound limit, which suggests that his mortality count was only a partial return.

Return by Revd John McCullagh, P.P. of Termonamogan:

Number of deaths from 1st October 1846 to 1st April 1847? 46.
Number of same known to be caused by famine? 20.
Number of deaths for the same period last year? Not known, the registry being lost, but the number was far below the present.

There are in the parish three relief stations, but the quantity of food is quite insufficient to support life. The land is generally well cropped with oats, and a considerable quantity of potatoes. A considerable number here left for America, although not so large as was thought it would be in the beginning of the year.

Source: *The Pilot*, 28 May 1847, 4

406. *First report of the Commissioners of public instruction*, appendix II, 43.
407. *Freeman's Journal*, 16 July 1844; *Dublin Weekly Nation*, 2 November 1844; *Freeman's Journal*, 10 August 1847.

PROVINCE OF LEINSTER

Summary of the returns for Leinster

County	Parish	Deaths		
		Oct. 1845–Mar. 1846	Oct. 1846–Mar. 1847	from famine
Carlow	No return.			
Dublin	No return.			
Kildare	No return.			
Kilkenny	No return.			
Kings	Reynagh union	19	53	0
	Shinrone and Ballingarry	16	69	50
Longford	Cashel	22	125	0
	Clongish	17	77	55
	Colmcille East and Scrabby	56	117	14
	Templemichael and Ballymacormick (excl workhouse)	30, aged 12+; 10 aged <12	60, aged 12+; 25 aged <12	*c.* 20
Louth	No return.			
Meath	Navan	71	284	> 200
	Stamullen	No registry	Slight increase	0
Queen's	No return.			
Westmeath	Castlepollard	NA	66	0
	Caulry	31	49	NA
	Clonmellon, Killallon	43	102	NA
	Moate	28	71	NA
	St Mary's, Athlone	56	122	25
Wexford	No return.			
Wicklow	No return.			

King's County

Reynagh Union, Ardagh Diocese

Commentary

The union of Reynagh is in King's County, bordering County Galway to the west; it was coterminous with the civil parishes of Gallen and Reynagh. Its return was compiled by Revd Joseph Smyth, curate of the parish. Revd John Kenny, who died in 1844, had been parish priest of Reynagh Union from 1799, and, in 1839, when he resigned his duties a meeting of the Protestant and Roman Catholic inhabitants of the Union presented him with 'a handsome chased silver salver and claret jug'.[408] Kenny was succeeded by Revd Kieran Egan, 'the patriotic and revered parish priest of Gallan

408. *Dublin Evening Post*, 10 January 1839; *Freeman's Journal*, 4 March 1844.

and Reynagh, who [in 1845] has most kindly undertaken to act as Inspector of Repeal Wardens for the district'.[409] Egan was an active supporter of the Repeal Association in the union, so it is perhaps surprising to find Smyth as author of Reynagh's return, although the latter was an Association supporter too.[410]

The 1831 census reported a population of 9,741 in the Union, and the population had risen to 10,415 by the time of the subsequent census. In 1841, 29 per cent of the housing was classified as fourth class and the female illiteracy rate was 55 per cent. The Public Instruction Commissioners apportioned the 1831 population as 659 Protestants and 9,072 Catholics. We estimate that the Catholic population was about 10,100 by mid-1845, and perhaps about 8,900 two years later. A population of about 10,000 would typically experience between 115 and 173 deaths in a normal October to March period, so Revd Smyth's figure of 19 deaths for the pre-Famine period period is no more than a partial return. Notwithstanding the deficient mortality figures, the Union had evidently been severely affected by famine by May 1847. His figure for deaths in the period October 1846 to March 1847 was nearly triple the (albeit deficient) number he had reported for the earlier half-year. Typhus was rampant in Banagher Town and dysentery was prevalent, although many were being saved through the provision of soup, and he was untypically upbeat in his predictions for the future.

Return of Revd Joseph Smyth, curate of Reynagh (Rynagh):

Total number of deaths from 1st of October 1846 to 1st of April, 1847? 53. Out of that number 36 died of dysentery during the months of March and April in the lanes of this town, generally very old persons.
Number of deaths known to be caused by famine? I cannot say that any person actually died of famine in this parish, as we had a soup kitchen during the winter here, well supported by local and other subscriptions, and has been the means of saving many poor creatures from untimely deaths.
Number of deaths during the same period last year? The corresponding period last year, total number of deaths was 19 in the parish of Rynagh.

I regret to state that typhus fever of a most malignant character is spreading to a frightful extent in this town. We have seven cases in the main street. Dysentery, brought on (I am sure) by cold and insufficiency of bad food, is most prevalent among the poor classes of people.

The act for the temporary relief of destitute persons [Soup Kitchen] is in full operation at present. Nearly ten tons of Indian meal are distributed every fortnight, without which the people would inevitably perish.

At our meetings of [the] relief committee I am getting the greatest opposition from the ratepayers who are members of it, as they wish to strike off some persons who are in the greatest misery upon the slightest pretext.

409. *Freeman's Journal*, 26 August 1845.

410. *Dublin Weekly Nation*, 1 June 1844; *Dublin Weekly Register*, 15 March 1845; *Freeman's Journal*, 19 October 1847.

There never was a finer or more extensive crop of wheat and oats than there is at present, and a very good prospect for the next season. Very few emigrants from this parish to America, except some boys and girls whose passage was paid by their friends resident there.

Source: *The Pilot*, 12 May 1847, 4.

Shinrone and Ballingarry, Killaloe Diocese

Commentary

Shinrone parish is located in south-west County Offaly, in Clonlisk barony, on the border with County Tipperary. Ballingarry parish is in Lower Ormond barony, in north Tipperary. The two parishes are contiguous. In 1841, 34 per cent of the housing was classified as fourth class and the female illiteracy rate was 49 per cent. The return for the area was compiled by Revd Edward [not C.] O'Leary, curate of Shinrone since at least April 1845, when he is listed as a patron of a rail construction project connecting the ports of Galway and Waterford.[411] O'Leary was, along with many priests in the area, a supporter of Repeal and a member of O'Connell's Association.[412]

O'Leary's mortality figures show that the number of deaths had increased sharply in the parish, from 16, in the October 1845 to March 1846 period, to 69 for the same period a year later. These figures almost certainly omit children. Nonetheless, the tone of the report is fairly positive. Notably, he comments on the important part that local Public Works had played in keeping people alive. Six months previously a 'very numerous meeting of the magistrates and gentry' of the area, which O'Leary had attended, had found much public support for the Works, which, it was claimed, had provided relief to 6,000 inhabitants. Subscriptions of £137 15*s*. were collected at the meeting. A further meeting at Shinrone on Thursday 2 October 1846 attracted magistrates, gentry, and clergy. A Mr Hammersly, 'requested to know if the public works last season gained the approbation of the people (cries of yes)'. It was also stated that Sir Robert Peel's plans were excellent: and that 1,193 families, amounting to 5,965 persons, were relieved.'[413]

Return of Revd C. O'Leary, curate of Shinrone:

Number of deaths from 1st October 1846 to 1st April 1847? 69.
Number of same known to be caused by famine? 50.
Number of deaths during same period last year? 16.

About one half of the lands usually cultivated as yet lies idle. The prospects for the coming season are by no means consoling. The land in very many cases has been prepared for seed, but the landlords, for the most part, have not only

411. *Freeman's Journal*, 28 August 1846; *Waterford News-Letter*, 22 April 1845.
412. *Freeman's Journal*, 28 August 1846.
413. *The Pilot*, 26 October 1846. Referring to Peel's introduction of maize imports.

not assisted the poor farmers to plant seed, but are retarding the progress of planting by threats of ejectment. But for the drainage of the River Brosna we would have a sadder season about the town (Shinrone). Many are emigrating, but they are the hardy, hard working men, who would prove a blessing to any country if rightly ruled. They bear with them much of the capital of the country. May their hatred for Whiggery be as lasting as their love for Old Ireland.

Source: *The Pilot*, 21 April 1847, 4.

County Longford

Cashel, Ardagh Diocese

Commentary

Cashel parish is located in south County Longford, on the eastern shore of Lough Ree. The Catholic parish, also known as Newtowncashel, was coterminous with the civil parish of Cashel. The report for the parish was compiled by Revd Edward McCann, parish priest of Cashel since at least 1834/5.[414] McCann, an 'indefatigable friend', was a supporter of O'Connell, collecting the Justice Rent for him in 1837 and joining the Repeal Association and collecting its Rent throughout the 1840s.[415] Following the conviction of John Mitchel for treason felony in 1848, McCann sent a petition signed by 800 of his parishioners to the Repeal Association, which was read at the weekly meeting in early June. 'The persecution inflicted on the patriot Mitchel has excited the indignation of all good men, and it is our intention, one of those days, to send in our subscription for his bereaved widow and helpless orphans'.[416]

In 1843, supposedly the 'Repeal Year', the Association acknowledged the receipt of £20 from 'that small parish' of Cashel.[417] In fact, the parish was not particularly small. It had 5,087 inhabitants according to the census of 1831, and 5,559 a decade later. In 1841, 27 per cent of the housing was classified as fourth class and the female illiteracy rate was 68 per cent. The Protestant population was tiny: the Public Instruction Commissioners counted a mere 129 Protestants (2.5 per cent) in 1831. We estimate the Catholic population at about 5,650 by mid-1845, and about 4,800 two years later. A pre-Famine population of that order would lead us to expect between 64 and 96 deaths in the October 1845 to March 1846 period, well above the 22 deaths reported by McCann. By his own admission, children were not included in his totals, but even the inclusion of children would not boost his pre-Famine figure to a more plausible level. Nonetheless, McCann reported 125 deaths in the parish between October 1846 and March 1847, well above the figure that would be expected in normal times. Nobody had died of starvation, according to McCann, although a lack of sufficiently nutritious food was the ultimate cause of the elevated death rate.

414. *First report of the Commissioners of public instruction*, appendix II, 40.
415. *Dublin Morning Register*, 1 March 1837; *Freeman's Journal*, 5 July 1843; *Dublin Weekly Nation*, 12 August 1843.
416. *Freeman's Journal*, 6 June 1848.
417. *Dublin Weekly Register*, 12 August 1843.

Return of Revd Edward M'Cann, P.P. of Cashel:

Number of deaths from 1st October, 1846, to 1st April, 1847? 125.
None died from actual starvation, but almost all from want of sufficient and nutritious food. No means have been taken to stay the progress of fever and dysentery, which are making frightful ravages.
Number of deaths during the same period last year? 22.

I did not include in this return the children; they died in the same proportion.

Source: *The Pilot*, 19 May 1847, 2.

Clongish, Ardagh Diocese

Commentary

Clongish parish is located in west County Longford, in the barony of Longford. The Catholic parish was coextensive with the civil parish of Clongesh. The return for the parish was compiled by the parish priest, Revd S. T. Dease, a recent arrival in the parish.[418] During the Famine, Dease was a member of the Newtownforbes Relief Committee.[419] The population of Clongish was fairly stable in the immediate pre-Famine period. The statutory censuses reported 6,736 inhabitants in 1831, drifting downwards to 6,504 in 1841. In 1841, 16 per cent of the housing was classified as fourth class and the female illiteracy rate was 55 per cent. Clongish had a large Catholic majority, but it had a significant Protestant community too; the Public Instruction Commissioners identified 1,240 Protestants (18.4 per cent) for 1831. Dease's counts of deaths did not include all deaths occurring in his parish. We estimate the Catholic population by mid-1845 at about 5,500, and at about 4,800 two years later. A population of about 5,500 would typically have experienced between 63 and 94 deaths between October 1845 and March 1846, well above the 17 deaths that he reported. The 77 deaths reported for the Famine period, which lie within the expected death range for normal times, was also probably a partial count.

Return of Revd S. T. Dease, P.P. of Clongish:

Number of deaths from 1st October 1846 to 1st April 1847? 77.
Number of same known to be caused by famine? 55.
Number of deaths during the same period last year? 17.

Many all but perished by the wayside. Present state of the parish awfully destitute – prospects by outdoor relief miserably inadequate – some emigration, but there would be more if means were forthcoming.

418. Revd Michael O'Beirne was parish priest until late 1843, when he was succeeded by Revd Richard O'Ferrall. Likely, Dease succeeded O'Ferrall as P.P. *Limerick Chronicle*, 18 November 1843.

419. *Dublin Evening Post*, 2 October 1847.

A great number of the landed proprietors never contributed, particularly one, who, though he owns one-third of this parish, not only has not come forward to alleviate the miseries of the people, but has sent law papers (as it is said) to 120 of his tenants.

Source: *The Pilot*, 12 May 1847, 4.

Colmcille East and Scrabby, Ardagh Diocese

Commentary

The Union of Colmcille East and Scrabby lies partly in County Cavan, but is mainly in County Longford. In 1841, 24 per cent of the housing in the *civil* parish of Columbkille (not coterminous with the Catholic parish of Colmcille East and Scrabby) was classified as fourth class and the female illiteracy rate was 68 per cent. The report for the parish was compiled by Revd Thomas McGavar, parish priest, since at least 1834/5.[420] McGavar supported O'Connell and the Repeal Movement, organising the collection locally of £40 10s for the O'Connell Annuity, and contributing to the Association's Repeal Rent.[421]

The union was not coextensive with any combination of civil parishes, so we are unable to reconstruct pre-Famine population estimates for the area, but McGavar notes that the 'population amounts to 3,000' in his submission. That figure is likely an underestimate, as the 1841 census reported the population of Scrabby civil parish alone at 2,836. McGavar's figure for deaths in the period October 1846–March 1847 is about double that of the same period for the year before. While the Famine was clearly taking its toll on his parishioners, this is a lower increase than was reported for many other parishes, although he notes the names or relationships of eight parishioners who died 'of actual starvation'.

Return of Revd Thomas M'Gavar, P.P. of Colmcille East and Scrabby:

Number of deaths from the 1st of October, 1846 to 1st April 1847? 117.
Number of same known to be caused by famine? 14 from actual want, and 21 of fever.
Number of deaths in the same period during the past year? 56.

Two of the cases in fever were attended with drink off a shovel, reached into their huts, lest the person who administered the drink should inhale the contagion. On the public works I have only 234, the population amounts to 3,000, and the nine-tenths of them require public employment. The government rations will commence on a small scale on to-morrow. The occupants of small farms have not prepared their lands for crops – some of them are about yielding up the ground to their landlords – this shows a bad omen for the coming year. From

420. *First report of the Commissioners of public instruction,* Ireland, appendix II, 40.
421. *The Pilot*, 7 September 1835; *Freeman's Journal*, 11 February 1843; *Dublin Weekly Register*, 1 March 1845.

the awful state of my parishioners, I am not able to spare one hour from attending to their wants, both in spiritual and temporal exigencies.

Stephen Dermody and daughter, Peter Brady and wife, Peter Reilly, Pat Reilly, John Sheridan, William Cooke, all died of actual starvation.

Source: *The Pilot*, 7 May 1847, 1.

Templemichael and Ballymacormick, Ardagh Diocese

Commentary

Templemichael and Ballymacormick parishes are located in mid-County Longford in the Poor Law Union of Longford. The union workhouse was located in Glack townland in Templemichael civil parish, south-east of Longford town. In 1841, 21 per cent of the housing was classified as fourth class and the female illiteracy rate was 50 per cent. Two returns were submitted from the union, both prepared by Revd Gregory Yorke, curate of the parish since at least 1843.[422] Yorke was a supporter of the Repeal Movement, and a member of the Association, who collected the Repeal Rent for his parish.[423] At a 'large and influential meeting' in Longford Town in June 1844, organised to support the 'Repeal Martyrs', Yorke 'at much length impressed on the people the necessity of peace and perseverance, and in scathing language denounced the baseness of the Catholic who could remain neuter [neutral] while the man who struck the fetters from his limbs [O'Connell] remained the inmate of a prison'.[424] In September that year Yorke sent £3 10*s* collected from his parishioners to the Association, 'making since the incarceration £85' from the Union, and in November Yorke, 'an earnest and effective supporter', contributed £1 to the O'Connell Tribute.[425]

As noted, Yorke prepared two submissions for the Association, the second one providing clarifications and corrections to the 'hurried report furnished on last week'. In his first report Yorke noted 60 deaths in the period from October 1846 to March 1847, compared with 30 during the same period a year earlier. In addition, he reported that workhouse deaths had increased considerably, from 56 in the earlier six-month period to 423 in the Famine period. His second report clarified that the deaths recorded in the first report had dealt with adults only, and in addition to the 423 workhouse deaths given in the first report were 160 deaths of children under the age of 12, boosting deaths in the institution to 583 between 1 October 1846 and 1 April 1847. He also noted that 25 children under 12 years of age had died outside the workhouse during this period. This compared with 10 child-deaths a year previously. Yorke explained his omissions by saying he was overworked, from the trials of the Famine. He also used the opportunity to correct an error in his first report regarding the provision of relief.

422. *Weekly Freeman's Journal*, 6 May 1843.

423. *Weekly Freeman's Journal*, 13 May 1843; *Freeman's Journal*, 1 September 1843; *Dublin Weekly Nation*, 2 September 1843.

424. *Weekly Freeman's Journal*, 15 June 1844.

425. *Dublin Weekly Register*, 28 September 1844; *Dublin Weekly Register*, 23 November 1844; *Dublin Weekly Register*, 22 March 1845.

Return of Revd G. Yorke (first report), curate of Templemichael and Ballymacormick:

Number of deaths from 1st October 1846 to 1st April 1847? 60, and 423 in the poorhouse; total 483.
Number of same known to be caused by famine? About 20.
Number of deaths during the same period last year? 30, and 56 in the poorhouse; total 86.

Were it not that the poorhouse is in this town, we would have many melancholy cases to report; some poor persons were so wasted with want, that they often died in the probationary ward [of the workhouse]; many lived only a few days after admission. We accuse the bungling and heartlessness of the government for not giving permission to employ a sufficient number of each family [on public works].

We are inundated by the poor, who are all dismissed off the works – left to starve or steal if they can; although we are doing the best we can in committee to give relief under the new [Soup Kitchens] arrangement, still the poor may starve, as a fortnight must elapse before any relief can be given to them. Very great exertions have been made by the people in business; very large contributions were raised to enable the poor to have cheap meat [corrected in Yorke's second report to read 'meal'], to give soup and clothing, and for cleansing the cabins of the poor. Seed has been given to a great many of the poor for their fields and gardens from private charity. The lands are cropped for the most part. There are fair prospects for the next year. The ladies have dissolved their [private] soup committee since the new relief scheme has been introduced, and are buying seeds for the poor.

Emigration is double what it was last year, but owing to the exorbant [sic] prices charged by shipowners, it is greatly on the decrease.

One of our priests here is only recovering from a very bad typhus fever, caught in the discharge of his ministry.

Source: *The Pilot*, 12 May 1847, 4.

Return of Revd Gregory Yorke (second report):

In the hurried report furnished on last week of the deaths in these parishes, the 423 stated to have died in the poor house, I have omitted 160 who died in the same period, and all under 12 years of age; nor have I given you the number of those from infancy up to 12 who died in other parts of the parishes, the tot of whom for the last six months is 25, whilst the corresponding six months of last year they were not more than 10. When I wrote to you before I was surrounded by several persons, some of whom were soliciting to be put on the relief lists, others calling on me to go to attend the sick, whilst more of them requested orders to get seeds to sow their gardens, so that I could not get a quiet moment to give your queries the proper replies.

In the published report of the information I gave you I perceive one letter wrong, which makes the word cheap MEAT instead of cheap MEAL, which it should be

Source: *The Pilot*, 19 May 1847, 2.

County Meath

Navan, Meath Diocese

Commentary

The Catholic County Westmeath parish of Navan, in central County Meath, was coextensive with the three civil parishes of Ardsallagh, Donaghmore and Navan. The return for Navan was compiled by Revd Eugene O'Reilly, who had been ordained in April 1793, and was appointed curate of Navan in 1797 and parish priest in 1827. He later became vicar-general, and archdeacon, and Notary Apostolic of Meath, and he built the large Catholic chapel in the town. 'In the long roll of priests who edified and ornamented the Church of Ireland, not one can be pointed to who was more distinguished for piety, patriotism, and every ecclesiastical virtue, than the late lamented Father Eugene'.[426]

O'Reilly was steeped in the social and cultural life of the town. In 1802 St Finian's, the Roman Catholic Boys School of Meath, was opened in Navan, under the patronage of the Bishop, with O'Reilly as its first president. This gave him a high profile in the town, throughout the diocese and beyond. He retained the presidency until 1827.[427] He was a long-standing supporter of O'Connell. 'He was a sterling patriot, a friend and follower of the great O'Connell, always on the people's side, and ever ready to subscribe liberally to whatever was calculated to promote the welfare of Ireland'.[428] He contributed to O'Connell's Catholic Rent, to support the 40-shilling freeholders during the campaign for emancipation, advising that all contributions for support should be channelled through the Association: 'I observe by the public prints, that it is in the contemplation of some Counties to confine their subscriptions to the relief of those only who have suffered in such Counties. From this intention I beg respectfully to dissent. The Old Catholic Association has been the medium through which a spirit of union and co-operation of all the Catholics of Ireland has arisen. The New Association is acting in the same spirit'.[429]

O'Reilly was unequivocally in favour of Repeal, to be achieved 'respectfully', by peaceful, constitutional action, and he joined the Association in 1834, along with his coadjutors, Revd McEvoy and Ennis.[430] He acknowledged that Repeal would not prove the panacea for all grievances, but problems could be resolved, he favoured, by appeals to parliament. Thus, his name regularly appears in the contemporary press, calling for meetings of the electors of Meath to petition parliament on measures of importance, and he was a stalwart at high profile political dinners in the county.[431] For example, although I warmly advocate a repeal of the Union as a measure likely to render incalculable advantages to unhappy Ireland, yet, I fear, in the all absorbing interest which its discussion

426. A. Cogan, *The diocese of Meath, Ancient and Modern*, Dublin: W. B. Kelly, 1874, i, 238–9; 245, 246; *Freeman's Journal*, 3 April 1840.
427. Cogan, *Diocese of Meath*, i, 240; *Dublin Evening Post*, 28 December 1816.
428. Cogan, *Diocese of Meath*, i, 247.
429. *Dublin Evening Mail*, 21 August 1826.
430. *Dublin Morning Register*, 27 December 1834.
431. See *Dublin Morning* Register, 22 September 1828; The *Pilot*, 7 April 1834; *The Pilot*, 14 July 1834, for examples. Also, *Belfast Commercial Chronicle*, 5 April 1837.

has excited, the public attention is diverted from the many severe grievances which still continue to press on Roman Catholics', and he listed examples such as

> [t]he Vestry Bill, the Subletting Act, the intolerable burthen of tithes, the penal code which exists against the Catholic clergy for marrying Protestants and Catholics, absenteeism, corporations, Kildare-place society, rearing foundlings in the Protestant church, for which Catholics are bound to pay, the Irish pension list, the building of Catholic houses of worship, without any legislative aid [...].[432]

The population of the parish was rising steadily in the pre-Famine decades; the statutory censuses reported 7,713 persons in 1831 and 8,699 in 1841, implying a yearly growth rate of 1.2 per cent during the 1830s. In 1841, 51 per cent of the housing was classified as fourth class and the female illiteracy rate was 56 per cent. The Protestant community was small; the Public Instruction Commissioners identified only 272 Protestants (3.5 per cent) for 1831. O'Reilly organised a census to be conducted in his own parish in 1834, presumably with the intention of submitting it to the Public Instruction Commission, which undertaking prompted a stern attack from the local Conservatives. As O'Reilly wrote:

> Sir, I have been informed, merely by accident, that in the *Evening Mail* newspaper Mr. Lambart, of Beauparc, is reported to have stated, at a Conservative meeting in Tims's [Trim?], that the census of the parish of Navan has been lately increased by sending the Catholics of one house, after enumeration, into another for the purpose of numbering them a second time. This census was taken under my direction, and I wish, through the medium of your independent and liberal paper, to give this report the most direct contradiction. Nothing of the kind was ever done or even thought of by me, or those employed by me. Such a trick could only be practiced. by such a one as Mr. Lambert's informant; and I now challenge him, or any other person, for the accuracy of that statement.[433]

O'Reilly's census was not used by the Public Instruction Commissioners. We estimate the Catholic population of the Union to have been about 8,750 by mid-1845, and at about 8,000 by mid-1847. A pre-Famine population of that order would typically have experienced between 99 and 149 deaths in the six-month period from October 1845 to March 1846. O'Reilly's figure for deaths for this period falls a little short of what might be expected, which likely points to the omission of children from his total. According to his figures, mortality had advanced by a factor of four a year later.

Return of Revd Eugene O'Reilly, P.P. of Navan:

Number of deaths from 1st October, 1846 to 1st April 1847? 284.
Number of same known to be caused by famine? Over 200.
Number of deaths during the same period last year, 71.

The land is generally tilled. Prospects of coming crops so far favourable – the poor, however, unable, for want of seed, &c., to plant potatoes. There exist just grounds

432. *The Pilot*, 2 February 1831.
433. *Dublin Morning Register*, 16 October 1834.

for apprehension that food will continue scarce and dear. All possessing the means either have emigrated or are about to go, so that destitution and debility are sure to be the prominent characteristic of our future population. Were Mr. Putland's admirable suggestion embodied in legislation, the most salutary results could not fail to be realised in an improved system of tillage, augmented employment to the labourer, increased and cheapened supplies of food. But what prospect of legislation on this subject from the apathy and incompetence of an alien Parliament.

Source: *The Pilot*, 28 May 1847, 4.

Stamullen, Meath Diocese

Commentary

Stamullen is located on the Meath coast, bordering County Dublin. It is a large parish, encompassing the civil parishes of Ballygarth, Julianstown, Moorechurch and Stamullin. In 1841, 57 per cent of the housing was classified as fourth class and the female illiteracy rate was 56 per cent. The return was prepared by Revd Patrick Nowlan, parish priest of Stamullen since October 1826.[434] Nowlan was a supporter of O'Connell, and a regular contributor to O'Connell's fundraising campaigns, but he appears to have been ambiguous on the detail of Repeal.[435] In April 1843 he wrote to the Association, exploring the possibility of membership, while outlining that he was less interested in Repeal than in the creation of a devolved parliament in Dublin to look after Irish affairs. O'Connell accepted his membership application, while rebuking Nowlan for his naivety. Nowlan had written:

> No reflecting Irishman who has attentively heard or read your speeches, and particularly the late discussion in the Dublin Corporation on the baneful effects of the Union with England, can for a moment hesitate to admit that its Repeal would be most conducive to the interests of Ireland; yet, when I reflect upon the sacrifices – it is necessary to state them – made by England for its accomplishment, I tremble at the consequences which might result from disappointed expectations on the one side, and determined resistance on the other. But agitation and exertions for the obtainment of a local or a domestic legislature to watch over the peculiar concerns of Ireland, would be neither so difficult or so dangerous, and might be equally advantageous. I am, therefore, in favour of the latter experiment. Conscientiously holding those opinions, I feel that I should be doing wrong if I did not give expression to them. Should you, after this explanation, and with this limitation, do me the honour of proposing me a member of the Repeal Association, I shall feel very much gratified, and beg leave to enclose my subscription of one pound for that purpose.

O'Connell:

> [...] accepted the terms on which the reverend gentleman joined them, knowing as he did that there was not in the community a more respectable clergyman, and he had much pleasure in moving that he be admitted a member of the Association. The rev. gentleman

434. Cogan, *Diocese of Meath*, ii, 257.
435. *Dublin Weekly Register*, 31 December 1836, 7, c; *Dublin Weekly Register*, 8 January 1842.

> was somewhat mistaken in thinking that England had made any sacrifice in effecting the Act of Union. She made no sacrifice, unless, indeed, the sacrifice which she made of the total violation of every principle of honour and justice.[436]

Nowlan's return is untypical in that it is one of a small number commenting positively on the state of the parish. Although he acknowledges that deaths were elevated during the six-month period after 1 October 1846, particularly among the aged and the very young, none of those deaths were linked directly to the Famine. 'Not a single individual has suffered in this union from famine' he stated boldly, and 'all who needed relief from destitution of any kind [...] have received relief since the 10th of December last, and still continue to receive it'. Relief was funded by subscription and from government funds. Nowlan was confident that the parish was amply positioned to provide relief for all requiring it. Nowlan's return should be compared with the handful of other positive commentaries, such as those for Rossglass, County Down, and Faughanvale, County Londonderry.

Return of Revd Patrick Nowland, P.P. of Stamullen:

No registry of deaths is kept.
Not a single individual has suffered in this union from famine.

The deaths from Oct., 1845 [sic. should be October 1846], to 1st April, 1847, have been somewhat more than for the same period of the previous year among the aged and the very young children, arising, in my opinion, from the change of diet – from the substitution of Indian meal, imperfectly cooked, for the potato and the oatmeal stirabout.

All who needed relief from destitution of any kind – from temporary want of employment, or, if employed, from the inadequacy of wages, to support large families at the high price of provisions, have received relief since the 10th of December last, and still continue to receive it. The source from whence procured is subscriptions from landlords and occupiers, together with an equal amount from the government as a donation. Only three or four Liberal Irish non-resident proprietors have declined, although their rents are most punctually paid. Their names will be found in the subscription list published in the Evening Post of 22d, and Mail of 23rd April.

Only one public work has been commenced in this district, on which (before its suspension on 30th April) not more than 100l. has been expended. If left to our exertions, without subjecting us to the cumbersome machinery and expense of the temporary relief act, we will be quite equal to the burden of relieving all who need relief until the middle or end of next September.

Land is cultivated to a greater extent than last year. Emigration has been this year on the increase, as many in this parish of the labouring class have been enabled to pay their passage, &c., from their savings, and from assistance received from relations already settled in America. No landholder – not one – has been disturbed.

Source: *The Pilot*, 19 May 1847, 2.

436. *Waterford Chronicle*, 8 April 1843.

County Westmeath

Castlepollard, Meath Diocese

Commentary

The return for Castlepollard was prepared by Revd Walter Murtagh. Murtagh, from neighbouring Moylagh, County Meath, was ordained in 1824 and became parish priest of Eglish parish, King's County, in 1837. He was translated from Eglish to Castlepollard in May 1846, so one of his earliest administrative undertakings in his parish would have involved preparing his census for the Repeal Association.[437] Murtagh was a supporter of Repeal, a member of the Association and a Repeal Volunteer.[438] As a member of the King's County Independence Club he supported the call for the 'uncompromising adoption of a broad national and regenerative policy, stopping short at nothing less than full and complete justice to Ireland, by placing her upon a perfect equality with Great Britain'.[439] In 1840 he was one of hundreds to sign a petition calling for 'a meeting of the inhabitants of the Province of Leinster, to be held at Croker's Hill, City of Kilkenny [...] for the purpose of considering the propriety of adopting a petition to Parliament praying for a Repeal of the Legislative Union between Great Britain and Ireland'.[440] The 'great popular demonstration' took place the following week.[441]

The Catholic parish of Castlepollard in north Westmeath covered the three civil parishes of Foyran, Lickbla and Rathgarve. The national censuses reported the population of the parish at 7,573 in 1831, increasing to 8,034 by 1841. In 1841, 45 per cent of the housing was classified as fourth class and the female illiteracy rate was 64 per cent. The parish had a small Protestant community; the Public Instruction Commissioners identified 578 Protestants for 1831. We estimate the Catholic population at perhaps 7,700 in mid-1845, falling to about 6,800 by mid-1847.

Murtagh's account of the condition of Castlepollard parish, in east County Westmeath, is less negative than many of the reports in the Death Census, although his recent arrival in the parish must be borne in mind. Unfortunately, he omitted to give a number for deaths during the period October 1845 to March 1846, making it impossible to examine the scale of increased mortality. In normal times a population of 6,800 would experience between 78 and 116 deaths in the October to March period; thus, the 66 deaths reported by Murtagh for the Famine period, which fell below the minimum number anticipated for a non-crisis period, must have been a considerable underestimate.

437. Cogan, *Diocese of Meath*, ii, 409; *The Pilot*, 12 June 1846.
438. *Weekly Freeman's Journal*, 10 June 1843.
439. *Dublin Evening Post*, 6 October 1838.
440. *Freeman's Journal*, 10 October 1840.
441. *Kilkenny Journal*, 17 October 1840.

Return of Revd Walter Murtagh, P.P. of Castlepollard:

Number of deaths in this parish from 1st October 1846 to 1st April 1847? 66.
Number of deaths known to be caused by famine? The greater number of deaths was occasioned by want of nourishing food. I will not say that any one died from absolute starvation; but certainly the majority died from the effects of want.

As to the present state of the parish, half the people are not half provided for, and the arrangements that are on foot for the purpose of giving relief are but tantalizing the poor people, and increasing their misery and discontent.

All available land for tillage in this parish is tilled, and the crops are, so far, promising the best.

Emigration has not been so extensive in this parish as in other places. The number of individuals who emigrated could not far exceed one hundred.

Source: *The Pilot*, 21 May 1847, 4.

Caulry (Ballyloughloe), Ardagh Diocese

Commentary

Caulry Catholic parish, coterminous with Ballyloughloe civil parish, is located in west County Westmeath, near the towns of Moate and Athlone. The report for the parish was prepared by Revd Farrell Duffy, parish priest of Caulry. Duffy was a Repeal supporter, and a member of the Association, and in November 1843 he was a Repeal Volunteer.[442] Also in November 1843 he contributed £1 to the O'Connell Tribute, as did Gregory Yorke, who compiled the return for Templemichael and Ballymacormick.[443]

The statutory censuses reported the population of Caulry at 4,733 in 1831, rising marginally to 4,793 ten years later. In 1841, 23 per cent of the housing was classified as fourth class and the female illiteracy rate was 64 per cent. The Protestant community of the parish was small, amounting to only 349 in 1831, as reported by the Public Instruction Commissioners. We estimate the Catholic population at about 4,600 in mid-1845, and about 4,050 in mid-1847. From a population of that order, we would expect to observe between about 53 and 79 deaths in the six months between October 1845 and March 1846, so it is probable that the deaths reported by Revd Duffy excluded children. Nonetheless, the increase in mortality during the Famine period appears relatively small.

Return of Revd Farrell Duffy, P.P. of Caulry, and administrator:

Number of deaths from the 1st October 1846 to 1st April 1847? 49.
Number of same known to be caused by famine? I consider that many of them died owing to changes of food, want of clothing, and colds caught upon public works, and also exhaustion from continued running between committees and engineers.
Number of deaths during the same period last year? 31.

442. *Freeman's Journal*, 21 November 1843.
443. *Dublin Weekly Register*, 2 December 1843.

Great distress prevails at present; we are relieving many by giving them a weekly supply of meal, but [to] not more than one half of the applicants.

The land is generally well tilled.

The emigration of this is greater than that of any other year past. Many small farmers have sold their land – some took out all their families – other only part. The passage money was paid for many by friends in America.

Source: *The Pilot*, 11 June 1847, 4.

Clonmellon, Killalon etc., Meath Diocese

Commentary

The union of Clonmellon straddled the Meath/Westmeath border. In 1841, 23 per cent of the housing in the *civil* parish of Killua (not coterminous with the Catholic parish of Clonmellon and Killalon) was classified as fourth class and the female illiteracy rate was 54 per cent. Its return was compiled by Revd James Dowling, who was ordained in 1823 and was appointed parish priest of Multifarnham, in February 1831. He was translated to Clonmellon in February 1844, on the death of Revd James Murray.[444] On his arrival in Clonmellon, Dowling was quickly dragged into a controversy concerning the expulsion of tenants from the lands of Patrick Russell Cruise, at Darvistown [Dervotstown] and Paristown, which necessitated the return of the landlord from America to 'restore the unhappy wanderers to the homes of their fathers'.[445] Dowling sided with the tenantry. A public dinner was held in Russell Cruise's honour, at which Dowling, acting as chairman, referred to John Smyth, Russell Cruise's agent in the matter, as 'an exterminator'. There followed a frosty exchange in the public press, with Smyth defending his actions, while criticising Dowling's involvement in the controversy.[446] Dowling hit back, by means of a forceful letter in defence of the tenants, who were restored. Dowling objected that John Smyth

> introduces my name, and complains that he has been denominated an exterminator by me. I really cannot understand what this gentleman is about. He repudiates the name of exterminator – he shouts out "malice and falsehood," and thunder at the very idea; and then, all of a sudden, he wheels around, and in that bold unblushing spirit that would seem to say, "thinkest thou I wish the shame to be concealed?" he publishes to the world a correspondence that is rampant with extermination in every line.
>
> There is a non-exterminator for you with a vengeance. But it is no new thing with me to call Mr. John Smyth an exterminator. I like Philip of Macedon's plan, to call a stone a stone. I did, therefore, feel it my duty, in conjunction with others, publicly to prefer a charge of extermination against this gentleman so far back as the summer of 1843. Mr. Smyth, of course, denied our charge in all its details. The matter was investigated by a committee

444. Cogan, *Diocese of Meath*, ii, 291–3, 480.
445. *Weekly Freeman's Journal*, 2 November 1844.
446. *Weekly Freeman's Journal*, 2 November 1844; *Freeman's Journal*, 30 November 1844.

of the Repeal Association, and on the 21st of September they produced a report establishing all our allegations against Mr Smyth. On the 3d of October Mr. O'Connell made a speech in the Association on the subject of that report, which is to be found in the *Freeman* of the next morning, and in which the following passages occur:

'I have gone through those general propositions to come to the particular case to which I referred, and I am bound to say that never could a charge be borne out more fully than the statements of the reverend gentlemen who made the complaint. The statements of Mr Balfe and the Rev. Mr Dowling's statement are borne out, and every one of them reported upon by the committee, and the affirmative of the proposition borne out completely. See how the case is, and I will first take Darvistown. There are a number of tenants living there comfortably and occupying farms. The lease of their landlord expires, and though they committed no crime, they are, I may say, sentenced to death. Instead of giving the tenants those lands again, a single individual is chosen, and the entire land given to one individual who never had any thing to say before to their possession or occupation. There could not possibly be a worse case – it violates every sound principle, and exhibits a forgetfulness of every honest and generous emotion of the heart'.

On the same day that this scathing speech was spoken by the Liberator, Mr Mark O'Callaghan gave notice of motion, 'that the name of John Smyth, attorney-at-law, be erased from the roll of the members of the Loyal National Repeal Association'. That motion passed the Association on the 30 October, and the report of the proceedings in the *Freeman* of the following day informs us that 'The announcement was followed by loud cheers'. Now, with these damming facts upon record surely Mr. Smyth has no right to complain of being denominated an exterminator, nor to expect that I or any one else should take the trouble to prove the charge over again. However, he is now in a position to sport with the embarrassments of others, and to treat with scorn all who sympathize with the exterminated tenantry of the country. But he ought not to forget that the place he fills was won by the sacrifices and exertions of the people of Ireland. I therefore submit, in sober sadness that, circumstanced as he is, he would be much more becomingly employed in restoring the honest and solvent men that he exterminated from my parish, than in writing frothy and frantic epistles in the newspapers.[447]

Unsurprisingly, Dowling was a supporter of O'Connell and a disciple for Repeal, and his involvement with the Russell Cruise case cannot have done his standing any harm with his parishioners.[448] His return is bitter and hard-hitting, referring to Cromwell and comparing the Famine to the scorched-earth policies pursued in earlier times. His return is one of only two which provides a breakdown of the number of deaths occurring per month (the other return containing this detailed information is Donohill and Kilpatrick, County Tipperary). The mortality numbers that he cited, which counted adults only, highlighted the dramatic increase in deaths that occurred from December 1846 onwards, with about as many deaths occurring during April 1847

447. *Freeman's Journal*, 5 December 1841, for full details of the speech and comments.
448. *The Pilot*, 28 November 1845.

than had occurred in the first four months of 1846. If the deaths of children were included – 'of whom we keep no entry', he foresaw more than 700 dying in a single year – 'about the fifth of our entire population'. He believed, almost certainly with some exaggeration, that the mortality rate was about 200 per 1,000 people, about eight times the rate that would be observed in normal circumstances.

Return of Revd James Dowling, P.P. of Clonmellon:

Number of deaths from 1st October 1846 to 1st April 1847? 1846 – October, 6 deaths; November, 5 deaths; December, 10 deaths; 1847 – January, 11; February, 19; March, 20; April, 31 – [total] 102.
Number of deaths during the same period last year? 1845 – October, 0; November, 3; December, 8; 1847 – January, 9; February, 6; March, 7; April 10 – [total] 43.

I send the returns in detail. I do not think we have had any case of direct starvation; but the increased mortality we attribute entirely to disease originating in insufficiency of food. I fear greatly that we have not yet seen the worst of it, for numbers of the people here or elsewhere appear to be withered beyond all hope of renovation. As it is, the number of deaths in the last month, if doubled, to take in the children, of whom we keep no entry, would be at the rate of over seven hundred a year, which is about the fifth of our entire population.

In Elizabeth's reign her ministers 'pacified' Ireland by sending her soldiers to cut down the standing corn with their swords; and so successful was the starving policy that they were able to boast that 'little was left in Ireland for her Majesty to reign over but carcasses and ashes'. If Irish carcasses be still an object of ambition to statesmen and political economists, our present rulers must be immortalised. And yet, I dare say that, in the excess of their modesty, they may endeavour, like Cromwell after breaking faith with the Garrison of Drogheda, and slaughtering them in cold blood for five days, to give the whole merit to Divine Providence, 'to whom, indeed, the praise of this belongs'.

Source: *The Pilot*, 21 May 1847, 4.

Moate, Ardagh Diocese

Commentary

Listed as 'Kilcleagh or Moate', this Catholic parish was coextensive with Kilcleagh civil parish. Its report was compiled by Revd Peter Murray, Roman Catholic Administrator. A supporter of O'Connell, and Repeal, Murray collected the Repeal Rent in his parish, and proposed names of individuals to the Association for the position of Repeal Warden.[449] He attended the banquet in O'Connell's honour, following the 'Great King's County Repeal Demonstration' at Tullamore in July 1843, which 'was got up on strict

449. *Dublin Weekly* Register, 1 July 1843; 23 March 1844; 28 September 1844; *Weekly Freeman's Journal*, 6 July 1844.

teetotal principles',[450] and in 1844 he was chairman of the local meeting held at Moate, to oppose the 'insult and wrong to the Catholics of Ireland' following the 'striking from the Jury List, balloted for the State Trials [in 1844], *every* Roman Catholic' and to denounce the wrongs 'so multitudinous as to render their publication in detail utterly impractical'.[451] The 'active patriots of this locality' were recognised for 'presenting the creditable sum of £16 15*s*., through the public spirited and respected administrator, Rev Peter Murray'. Around 20 individuals contributed from 2s. 6d to £1 each.[452]

This contribution came from a parish whose statutory censuses had reported populations of 6,152 in 1831 and 6,444 in 1841. In 1841, 20 per cent of the housing in the *civil* parish of Kilcleagh (not coterminous with the Catholic parish of Moate) was classified as fourth class and the female illiteracy rate was 61 per cent. The Public Instruction Commissioners reported the denominational breakdown in 1831 as 658 Protestants and 5,502 Catholics, and based on this breakdown, we estimate the Catholic population at about 6,000 by mid-1845, and about 5,300 two years later. A typical population of 6,000 would experience somewhere between 68 and 102 deaths in a normal October to March six-month period, well above the 28 deaths that Murray had reported for the October 1845 to March 1846 period. It seems likely that only adult deaths were being reported by him for both six-month periods.

Burial registers are available for Moate, and these confirm the mortality figures returned by Murray: 28 burials were recorded in the period October 1845–March 1846, and 71 twelve months later. The average number of burials per year in the period from 1830 to 1845 was 43, but burials soared during 1847, reaching 158 before falling back to more typical levels.

Return of Revd Peter Murray, Roman Catholic Administrator:

Number of deaths from 1st October 1846, to 1st April 1847? 71.
Number of deaths known to be caused by famine? I think the third part of those died from the effects of bad food, and from not having proper nutriment when they became sick.
Number of deaths during the same period last year? 28.

At present there are a great number sick, and the numbers are increasing. A soup shop has been established in Moate, which relieves a great number. There are two relief committees in the parish, but very slow in their operations.

I should think that at least thirty families have emigrated, and many others intend to depart as soon as possible. The cultivation of land has been well attended to in this neighbourhood; I think as well as in any part of Ireland.

Source: *The Pilot*, 5 May 1847, 4.

450. *Dublin Weekly Register*, 22 July 1843.
451. *Dublin Evening Post*, 23 January 1844.
452. *Weekly Freeman's Journal*, 23 March 1844.

St Mary's, Athlone; Ardagh Diocese

Commentary

St Mary's parish, Athlone, was largely coterminous with the civil parish of the same name. Its parish priest at the time of the Death Census was Revd Kieran Kilroe, who had been located in the parish since at least 1838, when he was curate.[453] A supporter of O'Connell, Kilroe was a member of the Repeal Association, and a supporter of the Liberal interest in the town.[454] Following John Collett's narrow election victory in the 1843 by-election in Athlone borough, and his subsequent admission as member of the Association, Kilroe, and Revd Martin O'Reilly in the neighbouring parish of St Peter's and Drum, who also submitted a report to the Death Census, addressed the Association by way of the following letter.

> Athlone, 1st May, 1846.
> Dear Sir, You will be kindly pleased, after acknowledging the splendid subscription of our excellent member, John Collett, to do us the honour of having our humble subscriptions, and those of a few of our parishioners, added to the Repeal Fund in connection with his. [Collett had contributed 20 guineas to the fund.]
>
> From the well known benevolent disposition of Mr Collett, and from his true and refined ideas of rational liberty, we fondly anticipated that such would be the result to which his abhorrence of the misrule of our country, and the deprivations of the poor of this unhappy land would lead him.
>
> We hitherto postponed to send our annual subscription to the Conciliation Hall, in order that we might have the glory and the honour of exhibiting to our countrymen and honest Englishman more faithful than many of the Irish themselves.
>
> Any compliment paid by the members of Conciliation Hall to our worthy representative we shall feel paid to ourselves, and we hereby take occasion to publish before the world that he enjoys our unbounded confidence.
>
> We are, dear Sir, yours very faithfully,
> Martin O'Reilly, St Peter's
> K. Kilroe, P.P. St Mary's
> [There followed a list of subscribers to the Fund, which included O'Reilly and Kilroe, and Revds Edward Wallace, St Peter's, Patrick Dardis, St Mary's, John J. O'Donovan, Patrick Healy and Thomas Philips, all paying £1.][455]

Kilroe was immersed in the life of the town. He was elected to the Commission for Paving and Lighting in Athlone in 1846, and was on the Athlone Relief Committee during the Famine, contributing £5 to the fund at the close of 1846, and contributed £1 (O'Reilly contributed £5 and Vicar Moffatt £2) to the fund for victims of a destructive fire in the town in March 1847.[456] Some months later, when the Regiment which had

453. *Dublin Weekly* Nation, 17 December 1842; *Catholic directory and annual register for 1838* (London, 1838), 100.
454. *Dublin Weekly Register*, 2 December 1843.
455. *The Pilot*, 6 May 1846.
456. *Westmeath Independent*, 11 July 1846; 12 December 1846; *Athlone Sentinel*, 26 March 1847; *Dublin Evening Post*, 16 March 1847.

fought the fire was being withdrawn, Kilroe added his name to the expression of appreciation issued to them.[457] He could work with his Church of Ireland counterpart, Revd James Moffatt, when the occasion arose, such as when they both wrote to their M.P., Collett, seeking a relief contribution. Collett sent ten guineas, 'in addition to one of the same amount sent 13th May, 1846'.[458]

The population of the civil parish of St Mary's declined slightly during the 1830s, from 7,396 in 1831 to 7,264 in 1841. In 1841, 14 per cent of the housing in the *civil* parish of St Mary's (not coterminous with the Catholic parish of St Mary's, Athlone) was classified as fourth class and the female illiteracy rate was 51 per cent. The parish was predominantly Catholic, although it also contained a large, and influential, Protestant community. The Public Instruction Commissioners reported 1,088 Protestants (14.7 per cent) and 6,304 Catholics (85.3 per cent) in the parish in 1831. Kilroe's figures for deaths seem to be deficient. Based on the above population numbers we estimate the parish's Catholic population in 1845 at about 6,500. In normal circumstances we would expect between 73 and 110 deaths in a six-month period from October to March, somewhat above the 56 that Kilroe reported for October 1845 to March 1846 and only slightly lower than the number he reported for the Famine period. Kilroe's return probably excluded children, although the presence of a workhouse in the parish further complicates matters as he himself mentions.

Return of Revd K. Kilroe, P.P. of St Mary's:

Number of deaths from 1st October 1846 to 1st April 1847? 122.
Number of same known to be caused by famine? 25.
Number of deaths during the same period last year? 56.

From the circumstance of the workhouse being in this parish, the number of deaths recorded is considerably less than we should otherwise have to report. Many from this parish, when in the lowest state of exhaustion from famine and disease, were admitted and there died in a few days. The number that died in that establishment, which at no time contained more than 800, amounts to 405 from 1st October, 1846, to 1st April, 1847.

It frequently occurred that persons dropped down dead on the streets, or on the roads returning from the public works, as the people emphatically express it, 'dropped from their standing or stanning.' Fever and diarhoea are making frightful ravages; labourers employed on the public works have been nearly all dismissed; they are in a starving state. We try to relieve them from the remnant of our former contributions. There is no hope of the relief act [i.e. the Soup Kitchen Act] (so complex is its machinery) coming into operation for three weeks to come. The land is generally tilled and cropped – the exceptions are but few. Several have emigrated, viz, small farmers, and the sons and daughters of persons in middling circumstances.

Source: *The Pilot*, 28 April 1847, 4.

457. *Westmeath Independent*, 17 July 1847.
458. *Westmeath Independent*, 12 December 1846.

BIBLIOGRAPHY

Parliamentary Debates and Papers

Hansard's Parliamentary Debates, third series.

1824 (577) *Abstract of Answers and Returns, Pursuant to Act 55 Geo. 3, for Taking an Account of the Population of Ireland in 1821*, BPP, House of Commons Papers, vol. 22, xxii.411.

1833 (634) *Abstract of Population Returns for Ireland, 1831*, BPP, House of Commons Papers, vol. 39, xxxix.59.

1834 (356) *Commission for Inquiring into the State of Religious and Other Instruction in Ireland*, BPP, House of Commons Papers, vol. 43, xliii.399.

1835 (369) *First Report from His Majesty's Commissioners for Inquiring into the Condition of the Poorer Classes in Ireland*, BPP, House of Commons Papers, xxx.

1835 (45, 46, 47) *First Report of the Commissioners of Public Instruction*, vol. 33, 829, 34, 829.

1836 (43) *Third Report of the Commissioners for Inquiring into the Conditions of the Poorer Classes in Ireland*, BPP, House of Commons Papers, vol.30, xxx.1.

Poor Laws – Ireland: Three Reports by George Nicholls Esq. London, 1838.

1843 (504) *Report of the Commissioners Appointed to Take the Census of Ireland, for the Year 1841*, BPP, Command papers, vol.24, xxiv.1.

Accounts and Papers, House of Commons (28 vols), xiii (session: 22 January–28 August 1846).

1846 (735) *Correspondence Explanatory of the Measures Adopted by Her Majesty's Government for the Relief of Distress Arising from the Failure of the Potato Crop in Ireland*, BPP, Command Papers, vol. 37, xxxvii.41.

1847 (834, 860) *Public works – Ireland. Report of the Board of Public Works in Ireland, Relating to Measures Adopted for the Relief of Distress in June, 1847*, BPP, Command Papers, vol. 17, 603, xvii.

1847 (836), *Distress (Ireland). Third Report of the Relief Commissioners, BPP, Command Papers*, vol. 17.

1847 (859) *Distress (Ireland). Fourth Report of the Relief Commissioners*, BPP, Command Papers, vol. 17, xvii.143.

1847–48 (876) *Distress (Ireland). Fifth, Sixth and Seventh Reports of the Relief Commissioners, and Correspondence Connected Therewith*, BPP, Command Papers, vol. 29, xxix.27.

1847 (797) *Correspondence, January to March 1847 Relating to Measures Adopted for Relief of Distress in Ireland. Board of Works Series.* BPP, Command Papers, vol.52, lii.1.

1847 (764) *Correspondence from July 1846 to January 1847 Relating to the Measures Adopted for the Relief of Distress in Ireland. Board of Works Series*, BPP, Command Papers, vol. 50, L.1.

1847 (816) *Thirteenth Annual Report of Poor Law Commissioners, with Appendices*, BPP, Command Papers, vol. 28, xxviii.1.

1847–48 (963) *First Annual Report of the Commissioners for Administering the Laws for Relief of the Poor in Ireland, with Appendices*, BPP, Command Papers, vol. 33, xxxiii.377.

Temporary Relief Commissioners, Seventh Report, Supplementary Appendix. London, 1848.

1849 (1047) *Public Works, Ireland. Final Report from the Board of Public Works, Ireland, Relating to Measures Adopted for the Relief of Distress in July and August, 1847, with Appendices*, BPP, Command Papers, vol.23, xxiii.725.

1849 (1118) *Second Annual Report of the Commissioners for Administering the Laws for Relief of the Poor in Ireland*, BPP, Command Papers, vol. 25, xxv.87

1850 (1243) *Third Annual Report of the Commissioners for Administering the Laws for Relief of the Poor in Ireland*, BPP, Command Papers, vol. 27, xxvii.449.

1851 (1381) *Fourth Annual Report of the Commissioners for Administering the Laws for Relief of the Poor in Ireland*, BPP, Command Papers, vol. 26, xxvi.547.

1852 (1530) *Fifth Annual Report of the Commissioners for Administering the Laws for Relief of the Poor in Ireland*, BPP, Command Papers, vol. 23, xxiii.155.

1852–53 (1542) *Census of Ireland 1851: Part I, Area, Population and Number of Houses, by Townlands and Electoral Divisions, County of Mayo*, BPP, Command Papers, vol. 92, xcii.453.

1856 (2134) *Census of Ireland 1851: Part I, Area, Population and Number of Houses, by Townlands and Electoral Divisions, Part VI, General Report*, BPP, Command Papers, vol. 31, xxxi.1.

Temporary Relief of Destitute Persons in Ireland, BPP, Bills and Acts, I, I.243.

Seventeenth Detailed Annual Report of the Registrar-General of Marriages, Births, and Deaths in Ireland, 1880. Dublin, 1881.

Eighteenth Detailed Annual Report of the Registrar-General of Marriages, Births, and Deaths in Ireland, 1881. Dublin, 1882.

Nineteenth Detailed Annual Report of the Registrar-General of Marriages, Births, and Deaths in Ireland, 1882. Dublin, 1883.

Twentieth Detailed Annual Report of the Registrar-General of Marriages, Births, and Deaths in Ireland, 1883. Dublin, 1884.

Twenty-first Detailed Annual Report of the Registrar-General of Marriages, Births, and Deaths in Ireland, 1884. Dublin, 1885.

Twenty-Second Detailed Annual Report of the Registrar-General of Marriages, Births, and Deaths in Ireland, 1885. Dublin, 1886.

Newspapers and Periodicals

Athlone Sentinel
Atlas (London)
Banner of Ulster
Belfast Commercial Chronicle
Belfast Protestant Journal
Clare Journal and Ennis Advertiser
Cork Constitution
Cork Examiner
Dublin Correspondent
Dublin Evening Mail
Dublin Evening Packet and Correspondent
Dublin Evening Post
Dublin Monitor
Dublin Morning Register
Dublin Observer
Dublin Weekly Herald
Dublin Weekly Nation
Dublin Weekly Register
Evening Mail
Freeman's Journal
Galway Mercury and Connaught Weekly Advertiser
Globe and Traveller
Irish Times

Kerry Evening Post
Kerry Examiner and Munster General Observer
Kilkenny Journal
King's County Chronicle
Limerick Chronicle
Limerick Evening Post
Limerick Reporter
London Evening Standard
Londonderry Journal
Londonderry Standard
Mayo Constitution
Morning Post
Nation
Newcastle Courant
Newry Examiner and Louth Advertiser
Newry Telegraph
North Munster Antiquarian Journal
Pilot
Public Ledger and Daily Advertiser
Saunders' News-Letter
Sligo Champion
Southern Reporter and Cork Commercial Courier
Sun (London)
Tipperary Free Press
Tipperary Vindicator
Tralee Chronicle
Vindicator
Waterford Chronicle
Waterford News-Letter
Weekly Freeman's Journal
Weekly Vindicator
Westmeath Independent

Contemporary Books

The Catholic Directory and Annual Register for the Year 1838. London: Dolman, 1838.
The Catholic Directory and Annual Register for the Year 1839. London: Dolman, 1839.
Thom's Irish Almanac and Official Directory, 1850. Dublin: Thom's, 1850.
Battersby's Registry for the Whole World, or the Complete Catholic Directory. Almanac, and Registry, for 1848, Dublin: Battersby 1848.
Duffy, Charles Gavan. *Four Years of Irish History, 1845–49*. London: Cassell, Petter, Galpin & Co., 1883.
Doyle, Bishop James. *The Life of the Rt. Rev. Dr Doyle, Compiled from Authentic Documents: By the Author of 'The priesthood Vindicated'*. Dublin: Coldwell, 1835.
Lewis, Samuel. *Topographical Dictionary of Ireland*. London: Lewis & Co., 1847.

Mitchel, John. *The Last Conquest of Ireland (Perhaps)*. New York: Lynch, Cole and Meehan, 1873.

Newenham, Thomas. *A Statistical and Historical Inquiry into the Progress and Magnitude of the Population of Ireland*. London: C. and R. Baldwin, 1805.

———. *A View of the Natural, Political, and Commercial Circumstances of Ireland*. London: T. Cadell and W. Davies, 1809.

O'Connell, John. *Recollections and Experiences during a Parliamentary Career from 1833 to 1848*. London: R. Bentley, 1849.

O'Rourke, Rev. J. *The History of the Great Irish Famine of 1847, with Notices of Earlier Irish Famines*. Dublin: James Duffy and Co., 1875.

O'Laverty, James. *Historical Account of Diocese of Down and Connor*. Dublin: Duffy, 1878–87.

Wyse, Thomas. *Historical Sketch of the late Catholic Association of Ireland*, 2 vols. London: Henry Colburn, 1829.

Secondary Sources

Alfani, Guido, Luca Mocarelli and Donatella Strangio. 'Italy'. In *Famine in European History*, edited by Guido Alfani and Cormac Ó Gráda. Cambridge: Cambridge University Press, 2017: 25–47.

Andrews, Ann. *Newspaper and Newsmakers: The Dublin Nationalist Press and the Mid-Nineteenth Century*. Liverpool: Liverpool University Press, 2004.

Arnold, David. *Famine: Social Crisis and Historical Change*. Oxford: Blackwell. 1988.

Bourke, P. M. A. 'The Use of the Potato Crop in Pre-Famine Ireland'. *Journal of the Statistical and Social Inquiry Society of Ireland* 21, Part 6 (1967–68): 72–96.

Bourke, P. M. A. 'The Irish Grain Trade, 1839–48'. *Irish Historical Studies* 20, no. 78 (September 1976): 156–169.

———. *'The Visitation of God': The Potato and the Great Irish Famine*. Dublin: Lilliput Press, 1993.

Boyce, George. *Nationalism in Ireland*. London: Routledge, 1995.

Burke, Edmund. *Thoughts and Details on Scarcity*. London: F & C. Rivingston, 1800.

Buttimer, Neil. 'The Great Famine in Gaelic Manuscripts'. In *Atlas of the Great Irish Famine*, edited by John Crowley, William J. Smyth and Mike Murphy. Cork: Cork University Press, 2012, 460–72.

Clarkson, L. A. and Margaret Crawford. *Feast and Famine: A History of Food in Ireland, 1500–1920*. Oxford: Oxford University Press, 2001.

Cogan, A. *The Diocese of Meath, Ancient and Modern*. Dublin: W. B. Kelly, 1874.

Connell, K. H. *The Population of Ireland, 1750–1845*. Oxford: Clarendon Press, 1950.

———. *Irish Peasant Society: Four Historical Essays*. Oxford: Clarendon Press, 1968.

Connolly, S. J. *Priests and People in Pre-Famine Ireland, 1780–1845*. Dublin: Gill & Macmillan, 1982.

Coogan, Tim Pat. *The Famine Plot: England's Role in Ireland's Greatest Tragedy*. New York: St Martin's Press 2012.

Cooper, M. O. and W. J. Spillman, 'Human Food from an Acre of Staple Farm Products'. *Farmers' Farmers' Bulletin*, Washington DC: US Department of Agriculture, Office of the Secretary, 1917: 1–11.

Corporaal, Marguérite and Peter Gray eds., *The Great Irish Famine and Social Class: Conflicts, Responsibilities, Representations*. Oxford: Peter Lang, 2019.

Crawford, E. Margaret, 'Subsistence Crises and Famines in Ireland: A Nutritionist's View'. In *Famine: The Irish Experience, 900–1900*, edited by E. Margaret Crawford. Edinburgh: John Donald, 1989: 198–219.

Crawford, W. A. 'Ulster as a Mirror of the Two Societies'. In *Ireland and Scotland, 1600–1850: Parallels and Contrasts in Economic and Social Development*, edited by T. M. Devine and D. Dickson, 60–69. Edinburgh: John Donald, 1983.

Crooks, D. W. ed. *Clergy of Killaloe, Kilfenora, Clonfert and Kilmacduagh, Biographical Succession Lists Compiled by Canon J. B. Leslie.* Belfast: Ulster Historical Foundation, 2010.

Cullen, L. M. *An Economic History of Ireland since 1660.* London: Batsford, 1972.

Curran, Declan, Lumomyr Luciuk and Andrew G. Newby eds., *Famines in European Economic History: The Last Great European Famines Reconsidered.* London: Routledge, 2015.

Daly, Mary E. *The Famine in Ireland.* Dundalk: Dundalgan Press, 1994.

Darwen, Lewis, Donald MacRaild, Brian Gurrin and Liam Kennedy, '"Unhappy and Wretched Creatures": Charity, Poor Relief and Pauper Removal in Britain and Ireland during the Great Famine'. *English Historical Review* 134, no. 568 (June 2019): 589–619.

———. '"Irish fever" in Britain during the Great Famine: Immigration, Disease and the Legacy of Black '47'. *Irish Historical Studies,* 44, no. 166 (2020): 270–94.

Davis, Richard. *The Young Ireland Movement.* Dublin: Gill & Macmillan, 1987.

Delaney, Enda. *The Curse of Reason: The Great Irish Famine.* Dublin: Gill & Macmillan, 2012.

———. 'There but for the Grace of God Go I: Middle-Class Catholic Responses to Ireland's Great Famine'." *English Historical Review* 135, no. 577 (December 2020): 1433–60.

Devine, T. M. *The Great Highland Famine: Hunger, Emigration and the Scottish Highlands in the Nineteenth Century.* Edinburgh: John Donald, 1988.

———. *The Scottish Clearances: A History of the Dispossessed, 1600–1900.* London: Penguin, 2018.

Devereux, Stephen. *Theories of Famine.* New York: Harvester Wheatsheaf, 1993.

Dickson, David, Cormac Ó Gráda and Stuart Daultrey, 'Hearth tax, Household Size and Irish Population Change, 1672–1821'. *Proceedings of Royal Irish Academy* 82 C (1982): 125–81.

Donnelly jr., James S. 'The Soup Kitchens'. In *New History of Ireland, V: Ireland under the Union, 1801–70,* edited by W. E. Vaughan, 272–331. Oxford: Oxford University Press, 1989.

———. *The Great Irish Potato Famine.* Stroud: Sutton, 2010.

Driver, Felix. *Power and Pauperism: The Workhouse System, 1834–1884.* Cambridge: Cambridge University Press, 1993.

Dyson Tim and Cormac Ó Gráda, eds., *Famine Demography: Perspectives from Past and Present.* Oxford: Oxford University Press, 2002.

Edsall, Nicholas C. *The Anti-Poor Law Movement, 1834–44.* Manchester: Manchester University Press, 1971.

Eriksson, Andrés. 'Food Supply and Food Riots'. In *Famine 150,* edited by Cormac Ó Gráda, 67–93. Dublin: Teagasc, 1997.

Froggatt, Peter. 'The Response of the Medical Profession to the Great Famine'. In *Famine: The Irish Experience 900–1900,* edited by E. Margaret Crawford, 134–56. Edinburgh: John Donald, 1989.

Gillespie, Raymond and Gerard Moran eds., *'A Various Country': Essays in Mayo History, 1500–1900.* Westport: Foilseacháin Náisiúnta Teoranta, 1987.

Gray, Peter. 'The Triumph of Ideology and Famine Relief'. *History Ireland* 3, no. 2 (1995): 26–35.

———. *Famine, Land and Politics: British Government and Irish Society 1843–50.* Dublin: Gill and MacMillan, 1999.

Gribben, Arthur, ed., *The Great Famine and the Irish Diaspora in America.* Amherst: University of Massachusetts Press, 1999.

Gurrin, Brian, K. A. Miller and Liam Kennedy. *Irish Religious Censuses of the 1760s: Catholics and Protestants in Eighteenth-Century* Ireland. Dublin: Irish Manuscripts Commission, 2022.

Gwynn, Denis, 'William Smith O'Brien'. *Studies: An Irish Quarterly Review* 35, no. 140 (1946): 448–58.

———. 'Smith O'Brien and the "Secession"'. *Studies: An Irish Quarterly Review* 36, no. 142 (1947): 129–40.

Haines, Robin. *Charles Trevelyan and the Great Irish Famine.* Dublin: Four Courts Press, 2004.

Hakkinen, Antti and Henrik Forsberg. 'Finland's Famine Years of the 1860s'. In *Famines in European Economic History: The Last Great European Famines Reconsidered,* edited by Declan Curran, Lumomyr Luciuk and Andrew G. Newby. London: Routledge, 2015.

Hatton, Helen E. *The Largest Amount of Good: Quaker Relief in Ireland, 1654–1921.* Kingston and Montreal: Queen's-McGill Press, 1993.

Hay, Edward. *History of Insurrection of the County of Wexford.* Dublin: John Stockdale, 1803.

———. *History of the Irish Insurrection of 1798.* New York: John Kennedy, 1847.

Healey, Jonathan, 'Famine and the Female Mortality Advantage: Sex, Gender and Mortality in Northwest England, c. 1590–1630'. *Continuity and Change* 30, no. 2 (2015): 153–92.

Hoppen, K. T. *Ireland Since 1800: Conflict and Conformity.* London: Routledge, 1989.

Hughes, Kyle and Donald M. MacRaild. *Ribbon Societies in Nineteenth-Century Ireland and its Diaspora: The Persistence of Tradition.* Liverpool: Liverpool University Press, 2018.

Jackson, Alvin. *The Oxford Handbook of Modern History.* Oxford: Oxford University Press, 2014.

Keane, John B. *The Field.* Cork: Mercier Press, 1991.

Kelleher, Margaret. *The Feminization of Famine: Expressions of the Inexpressible.* Cork: Cork University Press, 1997.

Kennedy, Liam et al. *Mapping the Great Irish Famine.* Dublin: Four Courts Press, 1999.

Kennedy, Liam and Peter M. Solar. *Irish Agriculture: A Price History.* Dublin: Royal Irish Academy, 2007.

———. 'The Famine That Wasn't: 1799–1801 in Ireland'. QUCEH Working Paper, No. 19–06 (October 2019): 1–33.

Kennedy, Liam and Clare Murphy eds. *Account books of the Franciscan House Broad Lane, Cork, 1764–1921.* Dublin: Irish Manuscripts Commission, 2012.

Kennedy, Liam. *Unhappy the Land: The Most Oppressed People Ever, The Irish?* Dublin: Merrion Press, 2016.

———. 'The Irish Population Explosion in Long-Run Perspective'. Unpublished paper, Queen's University, Belfast, 2018.

———. 'Afterlives: Testimonies of Irish Catholic Mothers on Infant Death and the Fate of the Unbaptised'. *Journal of Family History* 46, no. 2 (2021): 236–55.

———. 'Famine as Genocide? Ukraine and Ireland'. In *Ireland, Ukraine and Empire,* edited by Stephen Velychenko, Joe Ruane and Ludmilla Hrynevych. New York: Ibidem Press, 2022.

Keogh, Daire. *'The French Disease': The Catholic Church and Irish Radicalism, 1790–1800.* Dublin: Four Courts Press, 1993.

Kerr, Donal A. *'A Nation of Beggars'? Priests, People and Politics in Famine Ireland, 1846–1852.* Oxford: Oxford University Press, 1994.

———. Kerr, Donal A. *The Catholic Church and the Famine.* Dublin: Columba Press, 1996.

Killick, John, "Transatlantic Steerage Fares, British and Irish Migration, and Return Migration, 1815–60." *Economic History Review* 67, no.1 (2014): 170–91.

Kinealy, Christine. *This Great Calamity: The Irish Famine, 1845–52.* Dublin: Gill and Macmillan, 1994.

———. *A Death-Dealing Famine: The Great Hunger in Ireland.* London: Pluto, 1997.

———. *The Great Irish Famine: Impact, Ideology and Rebellion.* Basingstoke: Palgrave, 2001.

———. *Repeal and Revolution: 1848 in Ireland.* Manchester: Manchester University Press, 2009.

———. *Charity and the Great Hunger in Ireland: The Kindness of Strangers.* London: Bloomsbury, 2013.

Kinealy, Christine, Jason King, and Gerard Moran eds., *Children and the Great Hunger in Ireland.* Hamden, CT, 2018.

Lee, J. 'On the accuracy of pre-Famine Irish censuses'. In *Irish Population, Economy, and Society,* edited by J. M. Goldstrom and L. A. Clarkson, 37–56. Oxford: Oxford University Press, 1981.

MacDonagh, Oliver. 'Ideas and institutions, 1830–45'. In *New History of Ireland, V,* edited by W. E. Vaughan, Oxford: Oxford University Press, 1989: 193–217.

MacMahon, Bryan. *The Great Famine in Tralee and North Kerry.* Cork: Mercier Press, 2017.

Mason, William Shaw. *A Statistical Account or Parochial Survey of Ireland.* Dublin: J. Cummings and N. Mahon, 1814–19.

McCaffrey, L. J. *Daniel O'Connell and the Repeal Year.* Lexington, KY: Kentucky University Press, 1966.

McGowan, Mark. 'Famine, Facts and Fabrication: An Examination of Diaries from the Irish Famine Migration to Canada'. *Canadian Journal of Irish Studies* 33, no. 2 (2007): 48–55.

MacKiernan, Francis. *Diocese of Kilmore, Bishops and Priests, 1136–1988.* Cavan: Breifne Historical Society, 1989.

Miller, David W., 'Irish Catholicism and the Great Famine'. *Journal of Social History* 9, no. 1 (1975): 81–98.

Miller, K. A. *Emigrants and Exiles: Ireland and the Irish Exodus to North America*. New York: Oxford University Press, 1988.

Mitchell, Brian. *A New Genealogical Atlas of Ireland*. Baltimore, MD: Genealogical Publishing Company, 2002.

Mokyr, Joel. *Why Ireland Starved: A Quantitative and Analytical History of the Irish Economy, 1800–1850*. London: Routledge, 1985.

Mokyr, Joel, and Cormac Ó Gráda, 'New Developments in Irish Population History, 1700–1850'. *Economic History Review* 37, no. 4 (1984): 473–88.

Moody, T. W., et al. eds. *A History of Ireland: Ireland under the Union, I, 1801–70*. Oxford: Oxford University Press, 1989.

Neal, Frank. *Black '47: Britain and the Irish Famine*. Basingstoke: Macmillan, 1997.

Newby, Andrew, and Timo Myllyntaus, ' "The Terrible Visitation": Famine in Finland and Ireland 1845 to 1868: towards an agenda for comparative Irish-Finnish Famine Studies'. In *Famines in European Economic History: The Last Great European Famines Reconsidered*, edited by Declan Curran, Lumomyr Luciuk and Andrew G. Newby, 145–66. London: Routledge, 2015.

Noack, Christian, Lindsay Janssen and Vincent Comerford eds. *Holodomor and Gorta Mór*. Cambridge: Cambridge University Press, 2012.

Nowlan, Kevin. *The Politics of Repeal: A study in the Relations between Great Britain and Ireland, 1841–50*. Toronto: Toronto University Press, 1965.

O'Brien, Helen. *The Famine Clearance in Toomevara, County Tipperary*. Maynooth: Maynooth Studies in Local History, 2010.

Ó Ciosáin, Niall. *Ireland in Official Print Culture, 1800–1850: A New Reading of the Poor Inquiry*. Oxford: Oxford University Press, 2014.

O'Connell, Maurice R., 'John O'Connell and the Great Famine'. *Irish Historical Studies* 25, no. 98 (1986): 138–43.

———. *Daniel O'Connell: The Man and His Politics*. Dublin: Irish Academic Press, 1990.

O'Connor, Thomas, "Murray, Daniel." In *Dictionary of Irish Biography*, edited by James McGuire and James Quinn. Cambridge, 2009. http://dib.cambridge.org/viewReadPage.do?articleId=a6110 [accessed 3 July 2019].

Ó Gráda, Cormac. *The Great Irish Famine*. London: Macmillan, 1989.

———. *Black '47 and Beyond: The Great Irish Famine in History, Economy, and Memory*. Princeton: Princeton University Press, 1999.

———. *Eating People is Wrong, and Other Essays on Famine, Its Past, and Its Future*. Princeton: Princeton University Press, 2015.

Ó Gráda, Cormac and Kevin H. O'Rourke, 'Migration as Disaster Relief: Lessons from the Great Irish Famine'. *European Review of Economic History* 1 (1997): 3–25.

O'Mahony, Michelle. *Famine in Cork City: Famine Life at Cork Union Workhouse*. Cork: Mercier Press, 2005.

Ó Murchadha, Ciarán. *The Great Famine: Ireland's Agony, 1845–52*. London: Continuum, 2011.

O'Neill, Kevin. *Family and Farm in Pre-Famine Ireland: The Parish of Killashandra*. Madison: Madison University Press, 1984.

O'Shea, James. *Priest, Politics and Society in Post-Famine Ireland: A Study of County Tipperary, 1850–1891*. Dublin: Prometheus Books, 1983.

O'Sullivan, Niamh. *In the Lion's Den: Daniel McDonald, Ireland and Empire*. Hamden, CT: Quinnipiac University Press, 2016.

Phoenix, Eamon. *Two Acres of Irish History: A Study through Time of Friar's Bush and Belfast, 1570–1918*. Belfast: Ulster Historical Foundation, 1988.

Póirtéir, Cathal. *The Great Irish Famine*. Dublin: Mercier Press, 1995.

———. "Folk Memory and the Famine." In *The Irish Famine*, edited by Cathal Póirtéir, 219–31. Dublin: Mercier Press, 1995.

Power, Patrick. *Waterford and Lismore, A Compendious History of the United Dioceses.* Cork, 1937.
Quigley, Kathleen, 'Daniel O'Connell and the Repeal Crisis within the Irish Repeal Party, 1843–1845'. *Albion: A Journal Concerned with British Studies* 2, no. 2 (1970): 99–107.
Rafferty, Oliver, ed. *Irish Catholic Identities.* Manchester: Manchester University Press, 2013.
Read, Charles, 'Laissez-Faire, the Irish Famine, and British Financial Crisis'. *Economic History Review* 69, no. 2 (2016): 425–29.
———. *The Great Famine in Ireland and Britain's Financial Crisis.* Woodbridge: Boydell and Brewer, 2022.
Rudnytskyi, Omelian, Nataliia Levchuk, Oleh Wolowyna, Pavlo Shevchuk and Alla Kovbasiuk. 'Demography of a Man-Made Human Catastrophe: The Case of Massive Famine in Ukraine 1932–1933'. *Canadian Studies in Population* 42, no. 1–2 (2015): 53–80.
Sen, Amartya K. *Poverty and Famine: An Essay on Entitlement and Deprivation.* Oxford: Oxford University Press, 1981.
Smyth, William J. 'Classify, Confine, Discipline and Punish – the Roscrea Union: A Microgeography of the Workhouse System during the Famine'. In *Atlas of the Great Irish Famine, 1845–52*, edited by John Crowley, William J. Smyth and Mike Murphy, 135–39. Cork: Cork University Press, 2012.
Solar, Peter M. "The Potato Famine in Europe." In *Famine 150*, edited by Cormac Ó Gráda, 113–27. Dublin: Teagasc, 1997.
Vaughan, W. E., and A. J. Fitzpatrick. *Irish Historical Statistics, Population, 1821–1971.* Dublin: Royal Irish Academy, 1978.
Walker, B. M. *Parliamentary Elections in Ireland, 1801–1922.* Dublin: Royal Irish Academy, 1978.
———. 'Politicians, Elections and Catastrophe: The General Election of 1847'. *Irish Political Studies* 42, no. 1 (2007): 1–34.
———. 'Villain, Victim or Prophet: William Gregory and the Great Famine'. *Irish Historical Studies* 38, no. 152 (2013): 579–99.
Whelan, Kevin, 'The Catholic Church in County Tipperary, 1700–1900'. In *Tipperary: History and Society*, edited by William Nolan, 244–45. Dublin: Geography Publications, 1985.
Wilson, David A. *Thomas D'Arcy McGee: Volume 1: Passion, Reason, and Politics, 1825–1857.* Kingston and Montreal: McGill-Queen's University Press, 2008.
Wrigley, E. A., and R. S. Schofield. *The Population History of England, 1541–1871.* Cambridge: Cambridge University Press, 1997.
Wylie, Paul R. *The Irish General: Thomas Francis Meagher.* Oklahoma: Oklahoma University Press, 2012.
Zadoks, J. C. 'The Potato Murrain on the European Continent and the Revolutions of 1848'. *Potato Research* 51, no. 1 (2008): 5–45.

Theses and Digital Resources

Penelope J. Corfield. 'Does The Study of History "Progress"? And How Does Plurilogue Help?' 2016. https://www.penelopejcorfield.com/PDFs/6.2.3-PJC-2016-01-No61MonthlyBlog.pdf [accessed 25 January, 2022].
Darwen, Lewis. 'Implementing and Administering the New Poor Law in the Industrial North: A Case Study of Preston Union in Regional Context, 1837–1861'. PhD dissertation, Nottingham Trent University, 2016.
Irish Famine Archive. 'The Grey Nuns'. http://faminearchive.nuigalway.ie/eyewitness-accounts/grey-nuns.
National Library of Ireland: Online Catholic Parish Registers (https://registers.nli.ie/).
O'Neill, Timothy P. 'The Famine of 1822'. MA dissertation, University College Dublin, 1965.
———. "The State, Poverty and Distress in Ireland, 1815–45." PhD dissertation, University College Dublin, 1971. http://titheapplotmentbooks.nationalarchives.ie/reels/tab//004587433/004587433_00014.pdf. [accessed 15 June 2022].

INDEX

N

Q

R

Y

Z

www.ingramcontent.com/pod-product-compliance
Lightning Source LLC
LaVergne TN
LVHW040316150826
845500LV00063B/90
9781801360548